USING SOCIAL THOUGHT

The Nuclear Issue and Other Concerns

D0022444

Using Social Thought
The Nuclear Issue and Other Concerns

R. P. Cuzzort

UNIVERSITY OF COLORADO, BOULDER

Mayfield Publishing Company
Mountain View, California

Copyright © 1989 by Mayfield Publishing Company

All rights reserved. No portion of this book may be
reproduced in any form or by any means without written
permission of the publisher.

Library of Congress Cataloging-in-Publication Data

Cuzzort, Raymond Paul
    Using social thought: the nuclear issue and other
concerns/Ray Cuzzort.
        p.   cm.
    Includes index.
    ISBN 0-87484-800-8
    1. Nuclear warfare.   2. Arms race — History — 20th
century. 3. Nuclear disarmament. 4. Sociology — Methodology.
5. Sociology — Philosophy.   I. Title.
U263.C89   1989
355′.0217 — dc19   88-34581
                                                          CIP

Manufactured in the United States of America

10 9 8 7 6 5 4 3 2

Mayfield Publishing Company
1240 Villa Street
Mountain View, California 94041

Sponsoring editor, Franklin C. Graham; production editor,
Linda Toy; manuscript editor, Joan Pendleton; cover
designer, Ingbritt Christensen. The text was set in 10/12
Meridien Light by Digitype and printed by Maple Vail.

Contents

U
263
.C89
1989

CHAPTER 9
The Quest for Dramatic Realization:
War as Drama   233

CHAPTER 10
Symbols and Sacrifice: The Place of
Language in Human Conflicts   261

CHAPTER 11
The Uses of Social and Political
Imagination: "Solutions" to the Nuclear
Arms Crisis   289

Preface

A COMMENT ON THE RELEVANCE OF SOCIAL THEORIES

Many of the social theories we study and embrace in sociology were developed by writers who were not especially concerned with practical matters. They were interested more in working out a coherent system of ideas than in applying those ideas to everyday life. Ordinary people, however, tend to be more pragmatic. They want to know about the relevance of an idea or a theory before they spend a lot of time thinking about it. They want to know how it can be applied to their lives. This book attempts to answer the question that underlies their concern: Why study social theory?

For most of us, relevance does not need to be profound. People are customarily satisfied to know that a particular idea, theory, or piece of research will give them pleasure, enhance their lives, make them look better, assist them in bringing up their children, get them better jobs, or help them win friends and influence people. The problem I elected to examine in this book, however, is not so superficial, although it is intensely personal. The issue considered here is the nuclear arms race, with its attendant threat of human extinction. Nothing else in our time deserves so much of our serious thought and study.

In this book, I show how social theories can be applied to the nuclear issue to deepen and broaden our grasp of this problem. But I also go further. In the course of writing the book, I sometimes found that a theory had obvious connections to other problems. When this happened, I let the theory have its way. Consequently, this book is about social theory and its applications. The nuclear impasse is a basic theme that illustrates the applicability of theory.

This book draws on the ideas and works of nine different modern social analysts and critics. Several died before the first atomic explosion in 1945. Each sought to develop a general "theory," or interpretation, of human social actions. Social theorists seek *general* understandings that can be applied to *specific* social issues. The works of Durkheim, for example, can be used to bring new understanding to a great variety of human events — religion, war, educational systems, suicide, cultural change, modern sports, eating habits, and so forth. The same is true of the other writers. Each analyst's work can be used to shed light on nearly any human problem that might be of interest to us.

It is easy to look on the works of social philosophers and theorists as somehow intellectually separate from the affairs of the world. Like higher mathematics, social theory is commonly viewed as speculative and detached from practical concerns; it is irrelevant to our lives. However, nothing could be further from the truth. Social theory, whether it comes from folklore or from the pens of scholars and specialists, is remarkably practical stuff. It is the basis of how we guide our lives and how we react to other people. It is nothing less than how we view the world itself.

THE NUCLEAR ISSUE

This book was completed just as the Reagan-Gorbachev meetings ended in Moscow in June of 1988. These negotiations, at best, will reduce current world nuclear forces—approximately 48,000 nuclear weapons—by no more than 7 percent; other estimates are as low as 4 percent. With the present treaty in place, we could still destroy the population of the earth hundreds of times over. As few as 30 of these devices could kill, instantaneously, more men, women, and children than were killed in all the wars fought in the entire 20th century. Obviously, we still have a long way to go.

Meanwhile, even as the great powers are signing treaties and talking about arms reduction, they continue to pour their wealth and energies into ever more destructive techno-military systems. They use nuclear weapons to promote national policy in much the same way as they did at the beginning of the nuclear era. The people of the world are revolted, frightened, and puzzled by the truly horrific problem these weapons pose. Clearly, no problem is more relevant to our times—or more difficult to solve. With no real solution in sight, can we turn to social theories to help us understand this issue?

HOW SOCIAL THEORIES GENERATE CREATIVE SOLUTIONS

The premise of this book is that social theories can indeed help us grasp and solve serious problems. Because they arise in profoundly creative minds, these theories stimulate our imaginations and give us a new vision of the possible. We use the term *creative* loosely these days, applying it to everything from kindergarten art to the latest hairstyle. Although there is a form of casual creativity that is within the reach of all of us—indeed the whole point of this book is to promote the creative use of social theory—we should not lose sight of the fact that *profound* creativity is something quite different. It is something difficult, demanding, and rare.

In any field there is a small core of creative genius at the heart of the discipline. Extending out from that small core is a community of intellectuals, teachers, writers, researchers, students, and active workers who form the greater totality. In the social sciences, we think of such intellectual giants as Weber, Durkheim, Marx, Hegel, Simmel, Schutz, Mead, and Burke. This leads us back to earlier thinkers — Kant, Locke, Smith, Machiavelli — and beyond them to the still earlier geniuses from whose work they, in turn, drew their inspiration. This book reveals how genius can inspire people of ordinary talent and interests. The creative power of true genius generates layer upon layer of creativity and understanding at all levels of life.

In an earlier book, *Humanity and Modern Social Thought*, I tried to show that social theory — the work of great thinkers in the social sciences — is deeply engaging. In this book, I go further. My goal here is to show that social theory is not only stimulating but also something to be used. The originality and ingenuity of great works in the social sciences grant us new vision, whether we apply them to personal situations or global topics. The usefulness of social theory is limited only by our ability to be imaginative in applying it.

Social theorists and analysts do not build machines, fly rockets to the moon, cure the world of deadly ailments, or "do things" that are immediately visible. But their accomplishments are no less profound than any of these others. They provide us with the ideas we need to address our social problems. It is for us to put the ideas to work. If we fail to use the ideas, it is not the theorists but ourselves who must be blamed for the lack of accomplishment.

THE PROPER ROLE OF METHODS

Theory can in no way be replaced by methods. Since the beginning of the twentieth century, there has been a disturbing tendency to give methods the prominence that rightfully belongs to theory. Methods, of course, are a necessity in any discipline — whether it is science, where experiment rules, or the arts, where aesthetic methods are crucial, or even religion, where ritual and ceremony are a form of "method."

But when method takes up more time and energy than theory, something is amiss. And this is what has happened in sociology. From classical antiquity down to the end of the nineteenth century, theory always dominated social philosophy. Now theory has been displaced by statistical methods and quasi-experimental studies. The priorities are wrong; theory should always be behind the steering wheel.

Because methods are not the source of creativity in any field, the consequence, for the social sciences, has been a kind of "drying up" of the sociological imagination. Methods are a "brake" operating against the tendency of theory to run away with its fantastic notions. Such brakes are needed to control the excesses of theorists; but when the brakes are applied too severely, everything comes to a stop. A truly rigorous scientific epistemology, if applied to the problems social philosophers think about, would produce complete mental paralysis. There must be a proper balance of method and theory.

A central theme in this work is that sociology is not defined by its methods — which are basically the same throughout the intellectual realm — but rather by its theories. Physicists, biologists, and social scientists might use the same basic forms of statistical reasoning as their method of study, but the three fields differ considerably in their theoretical concerns. Sociological work is distinctive insofar as it draws upon and is inspired by theories developed within the field of sociology. To ignore theory, to be unaware of its potential and its uses, is, quite literally, to be ignorant of the field itself.

SINGLE THEORY APPROACHES VERSUS MULTIPLE THEORY APPROACHES

Sociology, then, is defined by its theories, and social theories are meant to be integrated into life. They are meant to be used. Furthermore, the greater the variety of theories we understand and appreciate, the greater the variety of uses to which we can put them. Social issues are commonly approached in terms of a particular point of view — Marxism, exchange theory, interactionist theory, or some other specific perspective that appeals to a particular author. There is, however, an awkwardness in this because no sociological theory has managed to establish itself as superior to any other, and, I am convinced, none ever will. Certainly no sociological theory has ever managed to dominate or eliminate other theories in the manner we see happening in the natural sciences.

That is why this book endorses no particular point of view. Instead it draws on many perspectives, all quite different in nature. I have come to prefer the broadest possible approach to social issues, one that draws on the thoughts of *numerous* social theorists. In this book I attempt to discover and apply what sociology *as a set of theories* offers to our understanding of human concerns. The quest is toward a more wholistic sociology.

When we draw on various perspectives simultaneously to address a specific concern we begin to see just how practical and rich modern social philosophy and theory are. I am not referring here to the common practice of considering several positions and then endorsing and defending one in an adversarial fashion. I am referring to an approach in which we address an issue by seriously considering multiple points of view. This approach, admittedly, creates problems. It calls for extensive training in social philosophy and an open-mindedness to the possibilities suggested by diverse theories. It means our intellectual support group shifts from a particular theoretical community to the social sciences more generally. It has obvious drawbacks and dangers in a time of ever-increasing specialization. Yet, there is much to be gained from taking an inter-theoretical approach to human problems.

INCORPORATING THEORY INTO A TOPIC

Here, I used this approach to deal with the issue of nuclear arms. But readers who are concerned about other issues, such as pollution, population growth, crime, mental illness, or any other current social "problem" should try, at least once in a while, to consider the matter from multiple points of view. How would Goffman, Weber, Durkheim, Merton, or any other thinker interpret the same issue? To incorporate the ideas of many thinkers in this fashion is truly to experience an "expansion" of consciousness.

A NOTE ABOUT THE PERSPECTIVES DISCUSSED IN THE BOOK

This is not a sourcebook in theory. It is, instead, a book intended to stimulate discussion and to demonstrate through the presentation of a small set of selected examples how social theory can be applied. There is no attempt to outline all of the social theories now taught and discussed in social science courses in Western culture. The discussions that follow draw on a small, but nonetheless diverse, set of ideas. The theories I have included here are ones with which I am especially familiar. They are points of view I happen to find exciting, challenging, and fruitful in their applied forms. I did not include theories with which I was completely unfamiliar or that I found especially difficult to use in an applied sense.

For example, any social scientist should be generally familiar with exchange theory as it is used in sociology. However my own attempts to apply exchange theory to social issues resulted in efforts that seemed difficult and forced. Similarly, I found it difficult to apply the theories of writers who take a "thematic" approach to human cultures and societies, such as Pitirim Sorokin. There is nothing wrong with such theories; they can be innovative and insightful. For example, David Riesman's notion of the "inner-directed" versus the "other-directed" person is an engaging idea, as is Ruth Benedict's use of "Apollonian" versus "Dionysian" culture patterns. But when applied across a range of topics, these ideas do not generate new understandings. They seem to be self-contained perspectives.

Thoughts of this nature have led me to believe that there is a way of evaluating social theories that has not been examined in the literature as carefully as it should be. Theories are currently evaluated in terms of scientific reputability — their "testability," their logical coherence, or their ability to generate pseudo-experimental studies. But there are other ways of evaluating theories. One criterion is the extent to which a theory generates alternative ways of viewing social issues — whether it opens, rather than closes, our awareness of the complexity of a problem. There are plenty of theories that lead us to the edge of an issue; the best theories take us deeply into the same concern.

For example, Marxism, in its commonplace, original form, remains a powerful intellectual tool for the examination of human social affairs. Dramaturgic theories are also surprisingly powerful — as are modern phenomenological and structural-functional theories. Other theories, such as the cyclical or thematic works of writers such as Sorokin, Riesman, and Benedict — though remarkably interesting and worthwhile in and of themselves — do not seem to be creatively productive in the same fashion.

Several reviewers of this work in its early manuscript form commented on my limited use of so-called "conflict theories" in sociology. I must repeat the remark I made above — this is not a sourcebook for social theory. However I do want to point out one feature of this discussion. Theories that are generally not considered conflict theories — for example, structural-functionalism and much of symbolic interactionism — turn out to have innumerable applications and implications when the topic itself is conflict. This becomes evident in the course of this book.

FOOTNOTING

Footnotes have not been included in the main text of this work in order to maintain readability. However, a footnote appendix is included where references can be found. The serious reader should review the appendix to find out more about the sources used in the book. Also included in the footnote appendix are the various reservations, qualifications, and other asides that would have been distracting had they been placed anywhere else.

AN EXPRESSION OF GRATITUDE

I would like to express my appreciation to the various people who supported this effort. I must mention, first, Boyce Nute and Franklin Graham of Mayfield Publishing Company who committed themselves to publishing a work that threatened to be controversial. My hope is that the reception of the book will affirm their faith. I also appreciate the work of Joan Pendleton and Linda Toy, whose editorial assistance was exceptional.

I would also like to express my deepest appreciation to my colleague Dr. Edith W. King of Denver University. Without her encouragement and assistance, this and other projects of mine would still be lying around my study in various stages of disorganization.

Numerous people supplied both honest appraisals and steadfast support of my early attempts at formulating this work. Among this group of dedicated friends and colleagues I would like to single out Professors Gary Kiger, Utah State University; C. Dale Johnson, San Diego State University; William Perdue, Eastern Washington University; Thomas Sullivan, Northern Michigan University; and John McCartney, Mercy College at Detroit. Their reviews were lengthy, critical, and encouraging. They spared me more potential embarrassment than I care to think about.

Professor Stanley Lieberson at the University of California at Berkeley has been an inspiration. I am grateful to him for his penetrating accounts of the limits of quasi-experimental procedures. Professor Florence Karlstrom of Northern Arizona University, exhibiting great patience, strength, and sensitivity, gave me many valuable insights with her lengthy commentary.

Others who helped this book along the uncertain road to publication are Donald Sterling, Rolf Kjolseth, James Vrettos, Michael Blain, Daryl Evans, Katherine Giele, Nancy Hewitt, Joseph Hopper, Robert Hunter, Harry Miles Muheim, and Jane Muheim. All gave much appreciated support and valuable suggestions. What is good in the following pages is to be credited to them. Errors, of course, are the sole responsibility of the author.

Finally, I would like to dedicate this book to the wonderful people who comprise the faculty of the Sociology Department at the University of Northern Arizona in Flagstaff. During an exciting semester spent there in the spring of 1986, I found that a truly intellectual, inquisitive, and argumentative spirit is alive on some American campuses. Long and lively sessions of debate and argument took place three or four times a week and commonly extended into the wee hours of the morning. It was a privileged time in a privileged place. Let me close this preface by giving special mention to friends and colleagues whose ideas appear more often in this book than they might suspect — Professors Michael Kanaan, Richard Skeen, Florence Karlstrom, and Bryan Short of the English Department, and all of the stimulating and hardworking members of the Department of Sociology and the College of Behavioral and Social Sciences at Northern Arizona University.

USING SOCIAL THOUGHT
The Nuclear Issue and Other Concerns

Chapter 1

Using Modern Social Theory

THE EXTENDED VISION

This work has its beginnings in an incident that took place during a spring semester in 1981 or 1982 when I was teaching a small class in social theory at the University of Colorado. On the day the story begins, I called for questions about several issues that had been raised. Hands went up. "Is the examination going to be objective or essay?" "How many questions will there be?" "Will it be a long examination?—I need to catch a plane."

It was the usual thing. I wanted my students to comprehend vast powers and global forces; they were not willing to look beyond the textbook. I wanted the world; they wanted to know what the final examination would look like. Trying to control an urge to pick up my notes and walk away from it all, I said, "We'll talk about the examination when we meet next week. But right now I want you to think things through better than you're doing. Social theory is not something you study for the sake of taking examinations. Social theory was not designed by old people to plague the young. Social theory was not created as a special torment to test your character—though it can be a test of character. The important thing about social theory is that it enables you to see. It is an unusual form of vision.

"Social theory is something you *do*. You must *do* it if it's to have any value at all. You wouldn't take lessons in golf just to take a final examination, get a grade, and go on to something else. You learn golf because you want to *do* it. You learn social theory because you want to *do* it. You want to *do* it because it allows you to see what you otherwise would not see."

Someone asked, "What do you mean by 'doing' social theory?" It was a good question. Just what in the hell had I meant?

"That's a reasonable question," I said. "We can begin by suggesting that social theory is about people and their social lives. It's intended to inform us about social forces we otherwise wouldn't know about. Social theory is the product of superb academic minds coping with religious, philosophical, economic, and political issues. These people devote their lives, their thoughts, and their spirits to such study and, in so doing, acquire understandings the rest of us find neither the time nor the patience to attain.

1

"However, we can learn from them. We can take these understandings as they were passed on to us and use them to enhance *our* understanding of *our own* community and *our own* lives. Not until we do this is the study of social theory worth even a second of our time. Social theory is for the people, to be used by the people, to deal with problems that people have uniquely created for themselves. It isn't just for old professors like me. It isn't for examinations and quizzes. It's for everyone. It's for you and me — everybody. It can be applied to any situation, any topic, nearly anywhere and at any time. If it doesn't find itself being used by us, it is surely sterile stuff. Most certainly it's wasted if it's not used. It should be part of our day-to-day lives.

"Theory is used in all fields — from mathematics to literature. What's important is that it *is used*. Social theory is different, possibly, from theory in other fields insofar as it has the potential to be used by all of us to deal with nearly any circumstance we might encounter. For example, Max Weber's ideas on bureaucracy are useful to everybody in this day and age of global bureaucracies. You, for example, are low-status bureaucrats this very moment and probably do not have any real understanding of the fuller implications of your own bureaucratic lives. Could you, if I asked for it, give me a thorough and inclusive definition of what a bureaucracy is? What does the word mean? How has bureaucracy revolutionized human life? What does bureaucracy mean with respect to your day-to-day existences?

"In order to use a social theory you must do something with it. A theory is a tool. When you use a tool you do something with it. That's all I mean. You apply it. You create with it. You build new ideas by bringing the theory into contact with different issues and concerns. A social theory is not meant to be an academic museum display piece — though there are intellectual purists who treat social theory as though it were. It's not intended to be looked at, dusted off once in a while, and then put back on the shelf until the next group of scholarly tourists come for their guided tour through the museum. It's not sacred literature. It's not precious dogma. It *is* rough and ready stuff.

"I'll try to demonstrate my contention. Give me *any* topic, any topic at all — assuming I'm generally familiar with it — and then give me any one of the theories we talked about this semester. I'll come to class on Monday and present a formal essay on the topic from the perspectives of whatever theory you choose. Now, somebody give me a topic — any topic will do. Anything. Someone come up with a topic."

Possibly because everyone was getting hungry, a student mentioned food as a possible topic. I accepted the topic. Another person suggested Durkheim as a theoretical approach. I told the students I would come back with a formal lecture on food from a Durkheimian point of view. I walked out of the classroom feeling I had been rather sharp. I had made my point. Or had I? I still had to show them.

It is time to bring this tale to a close. I worked hard on a little informal lecture on how the production and consumption of food is influenced by varying forms of social structure — a Durkheimian notion. Regrettably, it would be too distracting here to go into a full discussion of how the demonstration went. The important thing is that I, along with the class, gained new understandings about food, how people think about it, how it is produced and consumed in America, and how it is socially influenced. More significantly, I began to see more clearly how knowledge of a social theory is a broad form of knowledge.

At least this little affair was a modest demonstration of what could be done with theory. The students seemed to like the whole thing well enough. The rest of the semester was spent looking at four or five other topics through the "lenses" of different theories. We considered such diverse matters as the American pet seen through the perspectives of modern phenomenology, I.Q. tests as Marx might have thought about them, and the subject of romantic love as a structural-functionalist would approach it. The class became more lively.

Several years passed. Finally, in a further attempt to show how theory can extend our vision, I decided to put together a series of works in which various social theories are applied to the topic of nuclear war and nuclear arms. This book is the consequence.

The following chapters attempt to show how social theories can be used to shed new light on a variety of concerns. They are intended to reveal what you can *do* with social theory. In preparing this material, I invariably found, as I moved from one theoretical perspective to another, that there was always a surprise waiting. In applying theory we uncover novel understandings. That is the great value of theory. When applied to matters of interest to us, no matter how grand or how small they might be, theory generates significant understandings.

The intent of this book, then, is to show, through examples, how sociological theory can inform the imagination and guide it in ways that enhance, rather than constrain, human social vision. This book is *not* intended to offer its readers a false sense of security by suggesting that social theorists have discovered truth where others failed. Rather, they seek to induce questions and extend our vision beyond its current scope. It is important that this be understood at the outset. Theory, as I present it here, is not a quest for truth. It is, instead, a quest to open up imagination. The diverse theories of modern social science provide us with the means for expanding our vision. Figuring out the extent to which that vision is true or false is left for the reader to determine through discussion, argument, experience, and further involvement with the issues considered in the pages that follow.

THE FORM OF THE CHAPTERS

Each chapter in this book moves through a roughly similar general form or progression.

Outline of Theory

A particular theory or idea or sociological theme based on the works of an academically established writer or group of writers is broadly outlined. The outlines are broad and general because this book is not meant to be used as a sourcebook on theory—other books are far superior in that regard.[1]

Such outlining is required for several reasons. First of all, most readers of this book will have either no experience or limited experience with the literature I draw on for theoretical inspiration. The outlining of a theory and a broad indication of its nature helps less experienced readers see the connection between the theory and its applications.

Second, all of the theories dealt with here represent, in one way or another, major intellectual movements in and of themselves. Structural-functionalism, for example, is now covered by whole libraries of scholarship. No single writer can come close to treating this literature fairly. However, my intent is not to review functionalism, but to show how it can be used to deal with a particular issue. It is necessary, then, to show what specifically was taken from functionalism in interpreting the nuclear arms issue. It is the same with the other perspectives covered in the book.

These "outlines" of theory are not refined. My primary intent was not to provide a carefully polished and perfected summary of scholarly theories, but rather to display how even a rough grasp of a theory, a working outline of its general ideas, is sufficient to generate deeper insights into a given topic. People, it seems, all too readily become paralyzed by the thought that they will make a mistake or that possibly they overlooked something. With social analysis it is impossible not to make a mistake, and it is just about as impossible not to overlook something that another analyst would consider crucial. In this book the idea is to take a rough-and-ready approach. Social theory does not break easily if you drop it or stumble and step on it.

Let me hasten to add that I do not want to encourage a purely cavalier attitude toward social theory. It is difficult to learn—even in its rougher forms. It is not easy to learn, in large part, because we all resist studying what we think we already know. Learning social theory requires an admission of ignorance. Few people, if any, believe they are ignorant of social affairs. On the other hand, we should never be afraid to improvise a bit. The real test of the worth of social theory is not how well it can be known, but how fruitful and novel our understandings and observations are when we apply the theory to the world of human affairs.

Three Major Concepts

Each of the following chapters draws on three major concepts from a given theory. This mechanical device does several things. First, it warns you that I was forced to be selective in outlining the theory—Goffman's works, for example, include perhaps several hundred novel concepts. A brief review obviously cannot deal with all of them.

Second, this device reveals the extent to which you can begin to enliven your imagination with only a few concepts. You do not need to wait until you understand a theory in its entirety to begin using it. A good grasp of a concept is the *first* step in the development of a lively and creative sociological imagination. In music, for example, you discover right away that you can play thousands of popular songs with just three chords. It is not, of course, necessarily good music; however, even professional musicians commonly rely on just a few fundamental patterns to achieve diverse effects. It is the same with social theory; a few concepts, well applied, can lead to new understandings.

Nuclear Arms Issue

Each chapter, in a discursive fashion, brings a particular theoretical perspective, along with selected concepts, to bear on various features of the nuclear arms issue: atomic weapons, peace talks, international hostilities, political leadership, the military, peace movements, etc. I did not try to fit the topic of the "nuclear genie" into a rigid format. As a theoretical idea took over, it usually seemed reasonable just to let the idea go its way, so to speak. The consequence is a set of arguments and interpretations in which things happen much as they do in the real world—by happenstance and the inspiration of the moment.

I also did not hesitate to introduce other concerns where I thought the discussion would enhance the reader's appreciation of the extent to which social philosophy is applicable to our day-to-day lives. My goal is to draw the reader into "doing" theory on his or her own. Where a digression seemed to advance this aim, I left it in the discussion.

Above all, this book is *not* intended as a statement of the "truth" or as an endeavor to close off all further argument and thought about human social quandaries. All too often social science is presented as an organized body of answers—and I like to think modern social science does answer many of our concerns. However, this book is not intended to offer answers, neatly packaged and ordered. It is, instead, directed toward helping you develop better answers for yourself. To come back to the music analogy, don't read this book as though *listening* to a piece of music. Instead, I hope you'll move toward the greater pleasure of *composing* and *playing*. In sum, we should take an active rather than a passive role in the study of social theory.

SOCIAL THEORY

By "doing theory," I mean seeing how a theory or a particular concept can lead to a unique kind of insight or concern regarding nuclear issues or anything else we might happen to be interested in. Anyone who seeks to use a given theory to promote understanding will use it in terms of his or her experience. There is no fixed way. The following chapters provide only one kind of example—illustrations based on my experience, reading, training, and understandings. I hope you will discover the pleasure that comes not just from knowing, but knowing how to apply what is known.

Theory and Fact

Social theory should not be viewed as something that can be mechanically applied to a problem, as though it were an intellectual computing machine —toss in the facts and answers will spew forth. It calls for the creative application of imagination combined with broad knowledge. As with improvisational music, one should have a solid sense of the musical score plus the imagination to know when to improvise from the score.

One of the purposes of theory is to help us comprehend facts we find puzzling. Another purpose is to guide us toward new and previously unsuspected facts relevant to our concerns. If we approach a topic from, let us say, a phenomenological perspective, we will look at a different set of facts than if we were to approach the same topic from the perspective of Marxist theories or structural-functionalism.

Facts are incomprehensible unless they are contained, somehow, within a theoretical point of view. The reason is obvious when you think about it for a moment—facts are infinite in variety. We cannot possibly look at all of them. Curiously enough, then, theories enable us to see by preventing us from being blinded by the infinitude of experience. This is particularly true of human social experience. Even the simplest social moment is virtually infinite in its potential complexity. As creatures with finite limits we cannot, by definition, deal with infinite complexity. We must rely on selective perception, and here theory always intrudes in human affairs. How we select what we consider important in any social encounter is determined by the ideas or "theories" we bring to the encounter.

In sum, social theory is useful in dealing with *any* kind of human situation or topic—including our immediate personal lives. Those who see more clearly the social forces working on them have a better chance of dealing effectively with social policies, traditions, and humanly generated forms of madness that have a potential for harm. Social theory can be used imaginatively by professional writers and analysts. It can also be used imaginatively to enhance one's personal life. However, there is a price—it takes time and a great deal of thought.

Folk Theory and Modern Social Theory

It is a common impression that Americans are mistrustful of theory. I encounter no small number of college students who openly admit they are not particularly inclined toward theory. Americans are pragmatic. They want to get things done. They want facts. Theory is suspect. In the realm of human social affairs, this attitude is shockingly shortsighted. The reason is simple: Social life among human beings is, by its nature, a matter of those various "theories" we bring to our encounters with other people. You cannot interact with other people, even in ordinary, day-to-day ways without bringing "theory" into the relationship.

A fine example of a social theorist — albeit a simpleminded and wrong-headed one — is a bigoted racist. Racism is a theory. It is a mean-spirited and injurious theory; but, nonetheless, it is a theory. It is a bad theory. It is bad because it is far too simpleminded — social reality, it happens, is not racial or biological reality. For example, languages are not a matter of race. A white-, black-, yellow-, or red-skinned person can speak perfect French, English, Swahili, or Chinese. You cannot identify people by race simply by listening to a recording. Language, a social form, has a structure of its own; but this is not dependent on race. There are, of course, ways in which social forms are dependent on biological conditions, but the dependencies are far, far more complicated than common racist beliefs even begin to comprehend.

Indeed, the appeal of racism — as a social theory — rests in its gross simplicity. It is a theory for those who refuse to think or, more unfortunately, are otherwise incapable of thinking. It is bad for the more important reason that it simply does not fit any kind of *carefully established* fact. It is also bad because it leads its adherents to engage in actions that hurt large numbers of innocent people. Its being a bad theory does not, of course, deter those who so strongly endorse their belief in its arguments that they are willing to kill anyone who might have the temerity to disagree with them.

There are hundreds of other examples. We all rely on theories of what constitutes the masculine or feminine ideal. We have theories of what makes people good or bad, successful or failures. We have folk theories, and rather complex ones, of how various actions should be carried out — how a president should act, what a bus driver should do, why women rather than men should keep house.

Anyone who bumps up against these "theories" discovers how substantial they can be and, paradoxically enough, how insubstantial they are. We comprehend on occasion how "theoretical" our own lives are when a theory to which we subscribe is challenged by someone who endorses a contrary theory. I recall, for example, an occasion during the Vietnam War period when a group of young students thought they would torment an extremely hawkish pro-war spokesman who visited the campus. He devastated the group with his arguments. After the experience was over one student said, "We broke our teeth on that guy. What happened? We go to college for four years and he made us look like idiots. What good were all those classes?"

The students had just discovered something — their deeply held convictions were not God-granted facts but simply opinions. Unfortunately, for them, they did not know how to sustain their theories when they were being attacked. They thought their theories were self-evidently true. They found out otherwise. Our typical reaction in such instances, however, is not to look on the situation as one in which two theories stand in opposition. Our usual reaction is to conclude that the other person is "crazy," "perverted," or "all screwed up." In this fashion we mask our own theoretical formulations about people as reality rather than theory.

In the social realm, even more than in the physical realm, the observations or experiences that incline us to accept a particular theory are complicated and deceptive. We can return to racism as an example. When racists point to higher crime rates within racial ghettos as proof of racial inferiority, they are deceived by a complex set of events. A more careful review of the facts suggests that race has little to do with the quality of social actions. People, regardless of racial identity, can and do carry out the same acts — good or bad. Any ghetto population is unique, regardless of race. The arguments are much more convincing that poverty rather than race is associated with specific forms of crime.

Physical observations are also deceptive. The triumph of modern physical theory was to clear away some of the deception. Consider, for example, the implications of a story told, as I recall, about the famous philosopher Wittgenstein. A friend was expounding on the stupidity of ancient people who believed the sun went around the earth. Wittgenstein is reputed to have said, "What would they observe if the sun actually were going around the earth?" The point, of course, is that the same observed condition can reasonably be explained by two perfectly contrary theories. In this case, reality was "deceptive." It took people thousands of years to figure out that the older "simple" truth about the sun was, in fact, not as reasonable as the idea that the earth goes around the sun.

Nowhere is this problem of deception more evident than in the social realm. Social theories are closely related to the societies they serve. Because the same event can have contradictory rationales, human communities and cultures tend to select explanations that suit their purposes. For example, it is obvious the United States and the Soviet Union control huge nuclear arsenals. The reason — that is, the "theory" — for our arsenal is that we need it to defend ourselves from their aggression. Their theory is, curiously enough, precisely the converse; they are not aggressive, they say, and argue in turn that it is we who are the aggressors. So it goes with simple social theories.

Social theory is not only academically significant. In its various minor and major forms it is also the very stuff of human social existence. We rely on it to get through every ordinary day we live. Generally, we do not worry about it. Just as ancient people got along well enough by thinking the sun goes around the earth, we get along pretty well by thinking all kinds of peculiar things about ourselves and other people. It is when we run into problems that we are forced to think more carefully about what we are doing. Academic social theory calls on us to examine our thinking about people — and how they might be thinking about us. If, in various ways, folk theory becomes seriously harmful or has great potential for harm, then it is time to re-examine it.

The Nature of Theory

A theory can be defined in various ways. Certainly it is an argument of some kind that leads us to anticipate particular consequences from a given situation. In electronics, for example, there is a theory (Ohm's law) that tells us what to anticipate with respect to the voltage at one place in a circuit when resistance is changed at another point. The theory of gravity tells us what to expect with regard to the attraction between heavenly bodies when mass and distance are known.

Social theories also lead us to expect certain consequences from a given situation. If we are paranoid in our theories, we expect peace talks to be a prelude to the weakening of our own military position. However, unlike the case with Ohm's law, social theories have the peculiar ability to create the expectation they were designed to anticipate. We call this reflexive feature of social theory the *self-fulfilling prophecy*. This, if nothing else, makes social theory fundamentally different from theories in logic and the natural sciences. *Social theory can create the conditions it is supposed to explain.*

Once more we can return to racism as an example. If racists believe race accounts for a given social condition—let us say, crime—then they will see the actions of the members of a selected racial group as criminal across a wide range of alternatives. The theory leads the racist to expect the racial group to commit crimes. Once the expectation is in place, it creates the conditions for which it was intended as an explanation.

This is a wicked problem. The wisest course with respect to social theory is to be careful with regard to what it leads you to expect. Perhaps the best course of all is never to expect too much from *any* social theory promoted by anybody—including social scientists. On the other hand, do not go overboard by becoming cynical or *totally* skeptical. After all, cynicism and skepticism are also social theories—small theories, perhaps, but theories.

The difference between "folk" theories and "academic" theories is largely one of refinement and awareness. Folk theories are unwitting. They are so much an ingrained part of our thinking that we are intolerant of criticisms of what seems to be solid, rock-hard, good common sense. For example, there was a time in our culture (and vestiges of this thinking are still with us) when people thought insanity was a matter of being possessed by demons. What was once considered reality is now more generally recognized as a theory of insanity. Again, it is a bad theory. It confuses the "demonic" actions of a deranged person, the effect, with the cause of such conduct.

There was a time when people endorsed the belief—and belief is a form of theory—that kings were gods. Modern social theory is more inclined to view leadership as a natural structural problem for any human group. Leaders are needed to deal with critical decisions, and people will be assigned the task—whether they are gods or not. To a surprising degree, leadership can be assigned through random processes and a group can function surprisingly well. In modern America we accept numerous peculiar beliefs about leadership—several of which are a throwback to the idea that the leader is a god. The reality is that leaders are people—fallible, emotional, mortal human beings—hoopla to the contrary notwithstanding.

Physical Theories and Social Theories

We are, one way or another, all theorists. We live in a social world, and we have to reach conclusions about it. In a similar fashion, we all have theories about the physical world in which we live. We all know basic physical truths: If we fall out of the tree, we will strike the ground. If we put a hand in the fire, it will get burned. If we leave water out in the extreme cold, it will turn solid. Everyone, in any culture, has a knowledge of physics and a kind of "theory" about how the physical world is made up. They are usually bad theories.

The difference between folk science and modern physics is obvious. For the well-trained social scientist, the difference between folk forms of social theory and more refined academic theory is equally obvious. A person who studies modern anthropology, sociology, social psychology, political science, economics, and history comes away with a sense of the social world that is different from an untrained person's. It is also superior in the same way a physicist's knowledge of the physical world is superior to the untrained person's knowledge. There would be little point in the training were there not a difference.

At the same time, we should not forget that all modern science— indeed, all modern knowledge—has the same humble point of origin: folk knowledge. Modern science is a refinement of crude folk observations that were compiled over thousands of years. Modern social science, in a similar way, is the refinement and the elaboration of ideas that have already made their way into folk awareness. A nice example, perhaps, is the present popularity of so-called dramaturgic theory in sociology and social psychology. In its modern form, this is a refined and elaborate point of view, but the central idea beneath this theory has long been a part of folk awareness. Shakespeare anticipated modern dramaturgic theories in the 16th century when he observed that all the world is a stage and we are but actors on it.

Every major current social theory of any repute in modern academic circles can be found, usually sloganized in some manner, in ordinary commonsense expressions. Structural-functionalism, for example, is suggested whenever someone talks about a social system as a "machine." Marxism is lightly echoed in the phrase, "Money speaks louder than words." Durkheim's concept of mechanical solidarity is found in the phrase, "Birds of a feather flock together."

The basic point here is that social theory is not especially different from what we do all the time. To study social theory is to discover how "theoretical" we are in our own lives and how "theoretical" everyone else is. It is a serious attempt to correct errors that come from an adherence to simpler forms of thinking—just as modern physics is an attempt to correct errors coming out of commonsense understandings of the world. Remember, common sense tells us matter is solid. When we study physics we learn how "empty" matter, as we know it, really is.

Controlled Fantasy

It is regrettable, if true, that people find academic social theory intimidating. As I indicated, one reason it should not be intimidating is because we are all folk theorists to begin with. Furthermore, here is a realm of thinking where one can engage in fantasies. Theory provides social scientists with the utmost challenge to their creativity. Certainly, the imaginativeness of people throughout history is a testimonial to the extent to which they indulge in amazing fantasies in an effort to find a sensible accounting of their lives.

Social theories that have been popular at one time or another range from the belief that one's clan came from animal ancestors (totemism) to the idea that social success might be a sign one was chosen by God as a candidate for heaven (Calvinism) to the belief that the state is an instrument through which genetic superiority must be established (Nazism). The precedent for fantastic speculation with respect to human communities is all too well established.

Theory is not merely fantasy; nor is fantasy necessarily theory. Yet the two terms are more than kissing cousins. Theory is a kind of controlled fantasy. It is a place where speculation is not only allowed—but where it is also essential!

Fantasy plays two roles in intellectual work—even in the most solid and reputable of the sciences. First of all, fantasy gives birth to the wildest ambitions or dreams of intellectual workers. In physics the fantasy of splitting the atom was eventually realized. In aeronautics the dream of flying to the moon became a matter of historical fact. Other fields have their fantasies. Psychologists dream of training a chimpanzee or a porpoise to use symbols and tell us about life among the members of another species. Biologists fantasize about creating living matter from purely inert stuff. Computer experts dream of creating a machine capable of thinking with the intelligence of a human being. In sum, fantasies can be inspiring. They are, surprisingly enough, often fulfilled. Science, as well as the arts, is enlivened by fantasy.

Fantasy serves another purpose. It engenders wide-ranging exploration of alternatives and possibilities. In natural science, for example, it is not unreasonable to speculate, as a matter of fantasy, about the implications of something traveling faster than light (the hypothetical *tachyon* or swift particle). Einstein, according to several accounts, fantasized as a youth about what the world might look like if he were riding a streetcar at the speed of light. It occurred to him, in his fantasy, that the hands of the clock at his point of departure would be stopped as he looked at them. Therefore, at the speed of light, time slows down to the point where it no longer exists. When we think of Einstein as a genius of *fantastic* creativity, we are using the proper terminology.

Fantasies commonly begin with the question: What if . . . ? What if the world were composed of tiny particles? What if living matter consisted of uniquely arranged compounds? What if intelligence were interactive with environment in such a manner that certain environments might enhance it? What if social actions could be predicted with near-perfect precision by a complicated mathematical formula? (Do mathematical modelists in the social sciences ever closely explore the full implications of this fantasy?) And so on.

It would not be necessary to bother with this aside on fantasy and speculation were it not for the fact that speculation has something of a bad name in modern corporate societies. This is unfair. People are forced to speculate about the world around them. It simply cannot be avoided. Speculation and fantasy are necessary for any kind of intellectual activity. Indeed, the society that cannot generate fantasy, even if capable of otherwise sustaining itself, is like a body being sustained by machines. It is essentially brain dead.

There is, of course, a catch. To be effective and to produce its finest results, fantasy must be somehow contained or controlled. This is true in science; it is true even in literature where fantasy is given considerable license. Fantasy must be grounded in either logic or experience — preferably both. Fantasy that breaks totally with these qualities becomes impossible to understand. It moves into the domain of madness; it is utterly incomprehensible.

Conjecture, speculation, and fantasy are a part of social theory — as they are of any other kind of theory. One should consider fantastic questions. For example, what if people were all social equals — if classes based on privilege were abolished? What if nation-states decided to engage in limited nuclear wars? What if a large social system were composed of individuals who looked exactly alike — that is, were clones with no biological characteristics that could be given racial implications? What if human societies achieved their "reality" in the same way a stage performance achieves its apparent "reality"? Social theory is speculation over such questions. Theory considers what might happen to our lives if certain conditions were changed here and there.

Our theoretical speculations are simultaneously inspired and controlled by the speculations of earlier thinkers. We draw on the theories of older men and women of genius to guide us, *but not to bring our own sense of speculation to an end.* Students of social theory generally come to the subject with the desire to find the final and ultimate answers to human conflicts, trials, and troubles. Yet all theory can offer is the promise of more refined, more elaborate, and more probing forms of speculation. The fantasies go on. This is disturbing to those who seek dogma and finality. For those who embrace creativity, novelty, freshness, and a sense of new possibilities, it is an adventure with few parallels.

Compare studying social theory to trying to create a perpetual motion machine. Some people, knowing how fruitless this is, turn away. Others give it a try. In doing so they do not, of course, succeed in creating a perpetual motion machine. However, they do find out so much about friction, leverage, the physics of motion, and other related matters that they develop new understandings and interests in matters that encompass far more than the original intention to find the perpetual mobile. It is the same with social theory. A reasonable opinion holds that any kind of final and dominant social theory is probably impossible. However, the quest to find one is intellectually gratifying in other ways and also leads to occasional ideas that prove to have value in the realm of practical human affairs.

ON BEING SOCIOLOGICALLY INFORMED

The social sciences are not the same as the physical sciences. They are not the same as literature. What, then, constitutes a sociologically informed piece of work? How does it, for example, differ from good journalism? Certainly one thing to look for in a work that claims to be sociologically informed is the extent to which it draws on established sociological theories. No matter how elaborate its methods, a work claiming to be sociological is not valid in that claim if it ignores those social theories that grant significance to the methods.

This book tries to show how the application of theoretical points of view generates novel perspectives on nuclear and other issues. However, the "flavor" of each chapter is acquired through the strong measure of theory that was added. Theory is essential in defining one's professional legitimacy. Anyone can express opinions about the social world and speculate and fantasize. However, such speculation and opinion is not sociological unless it is sociologically informed. It is not sociologically informed unless it makes explicit the theoretical foundations from which it is derived.

Of course, sociological theories have been applied to social issues in the past. However, this book differs in at least two ways. First of all, it does not attempt to argue that a particular theoretical point of view is *the* single best way of approaching the problem to the exclusion of other points of view. Second, it argues, through example, that when several theoretical views are applied to an issue the breadth of understanding that is generated transcends any individual sociologist's approach to interpreting and comprehending human social experience. It is good to have Marxists, exchange theorists, dramaturgists, symbolic interactionists, and others fighting for their special points of view. Theory can be used in other ways, however, and they should also be attempted. What is sought here, then, is a kind of theoretical ecumenicalism—an attempt to embrace sociology as a whole rather than through any of its more specific theoretical parts.

LIMITS AND POTENTIALS IN MODERN SOCIAL SCIENCE

As science, modern social science is limited. We do not need to dwell on this statement but can sum up the situation by saying probably no one in his or her right mind would want to ride in an airplane designed and built by social scientists. Imagine, for example, an aircraft in which the throttle was only "significantly" related to thrust, rather than perfectly related—and, so on with the rest of the controls, the ailerons, the rudder, the elevators, and the landing gear. Social scientists, including psychologists and economists, deal with probable relationships, not precise ones. A relationship can be probabilistically significant and yet be substantively low. An airplane built by social scientists might result in elevators that were correlated with the controls only 20 percent of the time—this could be a significant degree of relationship, but hardly one sufficient to inspire trust in the controls. However, as a colleague of mine nicely pointed out, it is equally true that no one would want to live in a human community designed by aeronautical engineers.

Social science is science insofar as it seeks to understand human social communities in naturalistic and experiential terms rather than through religious or spiritual ideas. Social science does not reject God or practice antireligious sentiments. It simply seeks naturalistic understandings. Religious thinkers deal with religious matters; social scientists deal with the world as it can be observed.

This is the way natural science is. It is not against God nor does it rely on supernatural forces as an explanation for anything. It remains within the realm of observation and leaves the supernatural to theologians. A physicist once put it this way: In an equation God must appear on both sides because God is always omnipresent. This is *perfectly* logical given the idea that if God exists he must be omnipresent. If God is on both sides of the equation he can be factored out. For example, consider the formula $EG = GMC^2$ in which G stands for God. God has to be on both sides of the equation by virtue of his omnipresent and perfect nature. This is mathematically redundant, however. So, we simply divide both sides of the equation by G and we get $E = MC^2$. It is a simple, precise, and logical *tour de force*.

If, as sociologists, we believe in God, we can be comforted by the thought that the omnipresent and perfected nature of God allows us to go on with our work. We should let God go on with his. Academics would not need to bother with this argument were there not those who look on social science as an antireligious enterprise. It is not.

Good social science, like good natural science, is concerned primarily with observation and theories based on observation. Science sprang out of Protestant religious ideology and, like Protestantism, is inclined to view relationships with God as a matter for the individual to resolve on his or her own. I cannot speak for my colleagues, but religious claims that the social sciences are godless are absurd and dangerous. The position taken in this book is that, if anything, God gave us intelligent minds to be used in the active pursuit of awareness rather than in the passive and blind acceptance of dogma. Any other use of a human mind is, using the term in its richest and truest sense, tragic.

The social sciences are more closely allied with science than literature. However, given the character of our subject — human social relations — we also must recognize that this is a subject dealt with by literary and journalistic writers, religious thinkers, political demagogues, and a host of others who are not necessarily sympathetic to the social scientist's approach to life. Because they share a common subject with fiction writers, social scientists seek to divorce themselves from literature *qua* literature. It is possibly for this reason that social scientists commonly go out of their way to use jargon, mechanical prose, and other writing styles that can hardly be considered esthetic.[2]

The social sciences, as science, are faced with severe problems. Our data are not perfectly reliable; relationships between social variables are generally weak; the problem of deception always exists; and a particular finding may be meaningful in one context and not in another. Even more profound is the possibility that as scientific rigor is introduced into the study of human affairs, there is a tendency to move away from social variables into more physical variables. A purely scientific attitude toward human social actions ignores what it is supposed to be examining.

For example, the most scientific approach I know of in the field of psychology — that of behaviorism — simply ignores essential human issues and questions. It is concerned with behavior, or physical movement, not with unobservable mental states. Behaviorists refuse, as a case in point, to deal with the problem of motives (which are a matter of something "inside" the person and, therefore, unobservable) — despite the fact that until motives are established, human *social* actions cannot take place.

When I say a social action cannot take place without establishing motives, I should indicate why this is so. If you learn that the motive behind someone's pushing you violently was to save your life, your assessment of the action is more likely to be positive. The social nature of the act depends, in part, on your understanding of the motives involved. If behaviorism, in its quest for scientific objectivity, ignores this, then it ignores the factors it should be examining if it is to inform us about human actions.

The problems the social sciences encountered in the quest for scientific rigor are instructive in themselves. We are more aware today than we were even fifty years ago of how resistant social forces are to being studied and understood. This awareness forces us to consider the limits of a purely scientific approach to the world. The frontiers of science are not in outer space — a domain scientists know with much greater certainty than we know even the simplest social interaction between two human beings. The frontiers of science exist within the social sciences.

Somewhere between microbiology and human sociocultural reality science begins to unravel as a method. It is here that science begins to display serious limitations. This is a worrisome matter — a challenge to the entire Western concept of knowledge itself. The issue certainly deserves more thought from those dedicated to science as a method than simply shrugging the problem away by retreating into places where the method works and ignoring everything else as unworthy of consideration. In street language this amounts to nothing less than a "cop-out."

The study of human societies and cultures over the past several hundred years has its achievements. We discovered that cultures vary tremendously from place to place. We discovered that cultures are characterized by internal dynamics which suggest that as cultures grow, they develop a greater capacity for growth. We discovered that the size of an organization powerfully affects its organization and the activities it engages in. Funny things, for example, happen to little religious sects as they become successful and grow into great big churches.

We discovered that qualities once thought to be biological are actually social, either in part or entirely. We also found, though more rarely, that what we thought to be social qualities have a biological base. We discovered that rough common forms appear to be characteristic of social systems at various stages of their development; feudalism, for example, was experienced in many cultures as they moved from early stages of development into modern stages. Let me add, however, that stages of development in cultures and societies are so crudely delineated that few modern scholars accept the notion of stages without qualifying it almost to the point of meaninglessness.

The social sciences are significant in terms of their general findings. They are also significant with respect to the kinds of questioning they arouse. It is the intent of this book to encourage understanding not only through learning what is known but also through questioning established beliefs, ideas, and policies. I am not arguing, of course, that established beliefs, ideas, and policies are to be questioned and then rejected out of hand. Good questioning leads to rejecting whatever is unreasonable and accepting whatever passes the test of thoughtful examination.

Throughout this book, I assume the moral stance that authoritarian dogma, whether of the left or of the right, religious or secular, is just that — authoritarian dogma. I happen to like the idea of freedom — though it poses a lot of problems. Above all, I like having, and believe others should have, the freedom to question. To question, to argue, to discuss, and to probe is worthwhile in its own right. With questioning comes insight and new vision. To be effective, questioning must be informed. It is the task of theory to assist us in giving form to the questions we would like to ask about human social life.

THREE REASONS FOR STUDYING SOCIAL THEORY

There are three major reasons for engaging in serious sociological studies. There are others, but they cannot be developed here. For example, contrary to popular notions, the odds for making a fortune as a social scientist are probably better than they are for making a fortune as an athlete — no small number of social scientists are millionaires. Sociologists also enjoy having TV and newspaper writers ask them for opinions concerning events of the moment. Besides that, sociological research and study can also be deeply engaging and interesting — as is true of any other intellectual activity.

Any Social Action Is Necessarily Theoretical

The first reason for the pursuit of sociological knowledge is that, no matter who you are, you really have no choice about it. One way or another we all must make judgments about the social order. We are forced to develop theories of one kind or another and rely on these theories to deal with the demands of day-to-day social life.

One difficult aspect of learning what modern social thought is about is our inclination to think we already know how human societies work. If sociologists tell us something that does not correspond with our established beliefs, we tend to reject the sociologist's argument — we know better. The sociologist, in this instance, is looked on as a pointy-headed intellectual. If what the sociologist tells us agrees with our beliefs, we then say the sociologist is simply telling us what we knew for a long time. This time the sociologist is an empty-headed intellectual.

Not only do we already have fixed notions about human societies, but these notions also have a sense of "certainty" about them. If we are of a conservative bent, we know poor people are poor because they simply lack the drive and the ability to rise above their circumstances — they choose their miserable fate. ("Why do they insist on living the way they do?") If we are of a liberal bent we know poor people are poor because they are the victims of a ruthless social and economic system. ("What was done to these poor people?") Either view is, of course, too simple. Poverty is an extraordinarily complex issue. No one has any solid understanding of it.

To begin with, then, we already function as social thinkers. We acquire a variety of ideas about social systems from the time we are born. This knowledge is essentially folk knowledge. It is biased. It is simple. However, the world is not simple. We can no longer afford to rely on biased and simplistic knowledge. Or, to put it a little differently, reliance on folk knowledge is not enough.

We need something more comprehensive and carefully thought out. It is the task of the social sciences to think through issues and obtain information derived from the unique times in which we live. Folk knowledge trusts ideas developed at an earlier time under different circumstances. Of course, folk knowledge also radically simplifies the theories and understandings of earlier philosophers, thinkers, and writers.

Prisons of the Mind

Another reason for studying the social sciences is that they are a liberal form of study — liberal in the sense that they free the individual from what, in effect, are "prisons" of the mind. Social knowledge based on folklore and common sense tends to move toward "hard" understandings. Folk knowledge leads us to believe our group, whatever it might be, is good and other groups are certainly suspect and, more generally, downright evil.

Sociologists have a phrase for this: "In-group virtues are out-group vices." That is to say, what *we* do is good. If *they* do the same thing, it is bad. For example, *we* are ambitious; but *they* are pushy. *We* are a proud people; *they* are arrogant. *We* enjoy a high standard of living; *they* are a bunch of greedy pigs. *Our* bombs are for defense; *their* bombs are for world domination.

People have long had a fear of the alien, the stranger, the outsider, the person who is not a member of the "in" group. Now, in fact, such fear is occasionally reasonable; I am not saying it is always unfounded. However, turning against people simply because they are outsiders is not rational. We can do as much damage by fearing what we should not fear as we can by not fearing the truly dangerous.

Fear and simplistic explanations lead people to develop inflexible attitudes and beliefs. Carried to the extreme these attitudes become authoritarian thinking. You do not need to live in a dictatorship to be caught up in authoritarian thinking—it happens to all of us. Authoritarian thinking is characterized by extreme rigidity and a total dedication to the belief that there is one correct way of doing things while all others are wrong. It also is sloganistic thinking. It cuts through the Gordian knot of social complexity but, in so doing, enslaves us and blinds us not only to the complex lives of our presumed enemies but to ourselves as well.

If social science has discovered any general principle with regard to sociocultural systems, it is that people develop innumerable ways of living together that prove workable and effective. No single system is inherently superior to all others. (There might, however, be a generalized system— capable of incorporating diverse specific manifestations—superior to other generalized systems. In this fashion the old relativism versus absolutism issue over which so much time is wasted in argument might be resolved.)[3]

People commonly dislike the idea that social and cultural communities can be radically different from their own and still be acceptable to those who live in them. They accept their own system as best. Sociologists refer to this as ethnocentrism—the inclination of people to think the world, so to speak, is centered on their ethnic group. It is not. Ethnocentrism, carried to the extreme, leads to the belief that our own culture is superior to all other cultures. It is simple enough to move from this notion (that is, theory) to the further notion (theory) that it is then our God-given task to subordinate all other people to our way of thinking.

People seek illusions of certainty about their communities and their moral character. However, hundreds of thousands of ambitious social scientists, working for over a century, have not established, as yet, even a single certain, rigorously indisputable social argument. If they were not successful, after a long and careful effort, then to whom can we turn for the "truth" about society? The lesson the social sciences offer is that *no one* has such knowledge. Sociology, and the social sciences more generally, do not offer the world knowledge in the same sense the natural sciences do. What they offer, among other things, is the *enhancement of critical awareness.*

I do not mean by this that to become a sociologist is to become a carping critic of anything and everything. That does not constitute true critical awareness. Instead, critical awareness is an ability to see various possibilities where, previously, a more limited number were recognized. The social sciences offer people an opportunity to determine for themselves the merits or demerits of whatever they are told about themselves and about others. It is one thing to act blindly and another to act with awareness.

For example, romantic love is considered by the men and women of Western culture to be virtually instinctive. It is more likely the case it is not. It seems to be a socially sustained and socially acquired ideology with a rich and varied history. Historical accounts inform us that at one time only people of noble character could experience such an exquisite and consuming emotion. Until recently in American history blacks were considered biologically incapable of real romantic feelings. To be aware of the greater forces of social and cultural institutions enables us to take a critical look at what, in this instance, was an unwarranted insult and gratuitous denigration of black people.[4]

The social sciences force us to become critical thinkers. They lead us from dogmatic forms of understanding to those that call for fuller awareness and more profound thinking about the human condition. The social sciences are liberating. If a person seeks freedom and liberation, then the study of the social sciences is essential to the discipline of the self that freedom implies. If a person is seeking the comfort of dogma and certainty — an escape from freedom — then the study of the social sciences will, in all likelihood, prove frustrating. The serious study of social theory is not for people who are looking for simplicity and quick answers.

In sum, the task of the social sciences is not so much to provide hard and fast knowledge as it is to keep people constantly aware of the fact that social reality is uncertain stuff. It is the job of the social sciences to prevent people from coming to the conclusion that they know the ultimate truth about human societies — other than the possibly disappointing fact that there is no ultimate truth. Society and culture are not fixed in concrete. They are human creations and, as such, respond to the ways in which we think about them. The social sciences are dedicated to promoting informed and critical social thought.

The modern social sciences are the end product of a long social history that moved Western culture more and more toward democratic values and away from authoritarian programs. Given this thrust in Western history, it is reasonable, then, to view sociology as one of the forces in Western culture promoting freedom of thought — not dogmatic certainty. Its task is not to sustain simple stereotypes and political slogans. Instead, deeper sociological understanding keeps before people the constant awareness that society is never knowable with any perfected certainty—even in its simple and elementary forms.

Social Theory and War

Now we can turn to a third reason for studying human social systems. The rationale behind this appeal is based on the general observation that the only means humankind has established, so far, for the clear resolution of serious social arguments of any kind is violent confrontations—war, terrorism, rebellion, rioting, and destruction. Violent confrontations are our basic means of solving abstracted social conflicts. This is true at the national level; it also applies at more local levels, down to fights and disputes between individuals. It even carries into the single individual—for we typically fight with ourselves. The most serious form of individual conflict, of course, is the peculiar practice of suicide when one part of us elects to destroy another part and, in so doing, destroys the entire individual. When two people or two nations cannot resolve a social argument peacefully, they must either abandon the dispute or resolve it violently.

Although this manner of resolving social disputes is painful, it is evidently the only way in which profound social arguments can be resolved. It is the only way they have ever been resolved. (Lewis F. Richardson used the nice phrase "deadly quarrels."[5]) War and violence are ancient devices. Until the present, they proved to be effective enough procedures for determining who was "right" and who was "wrong" in situations where rational arguments or the amassing of evidence were without effect. These "deadly quarrels" killed countless millions of people. Nonetheless, they did not totally interrupt the progress of human social and cultural development. Things went on despite the toll taken by war. There were even a variety of positive side effects to the killing and the struggle.

Before July 1945 there was no likelihood the world itself would be destroyed by such conflicts. The times, of course, changed. Arguing with fists, spears, arrows, or even machine guns, tanks, and hand grenades is one thing. Arguing with nuclear weapons is something else again. Such weapons are, however, what we now rely on for settling disputes. So far we have not resorted to the actual firing of such weapons since they were dropped on two Japanese cities in 1945. Nevertheless, the threat of their use has been indulged in more than occasionally by the major powers over the past 40 years.

The entire world is now in a precarious situation—nuclear technology includes the making of weapons. Why are these weapons so important? Why must we keep them when, obviously, they are the most dangerous implements of war ever imagined? The answer is that they remain the last resort for the resolution of social disputes. Weapons have a variety of functions, but certainly one is that they determine who is correct in a social or economic argument. Without social argumentation over standards of living, human rights, freedom, territorial or political boundaries, life-styles, and other matters, nuclear weapons would be unnecessary. To possess a nuclear weapon is to be able to impose your argument on those who might otherwise disagree with you. Keep constantly in mind that an argument, by definition, always involves at least two indignantly righteous sides.

One way to lessen the probability such weapons will be used is to work toward the end of lessening social conflict. At the present time, however, there does not seem to be any major effort in this direction. If anything, international hostilities and animosities are as severe as they always have been. I am aware, as I write this, that current peace talks offer hope. However, armed might, such as the world has never known before, ready for use within minutes or even seconds, remains a constant underlying reality. Designs for new weapons are now in place that will be still more efficient and more responsive than those we now rely on. After all, weapons technology is progressive, and that does not mean weapons become less potent in their destructive capacities. It means precisely the opposite.

And so our inability to create an effective social science places us in considerable jeopardy. The most serious threat to life on this planet now comes not from the physical universe nor from biological threats such as disease or lethal illness. The most serious threat to life on this planet comes from our inability to transform our social and political systems in a manner which will assure coming generations that serious social issues will not be resolved by nuclear forms of argument. That we are willing to use the threat of such devices to achieve the ends of social and political arguments is, in itself, a serious problem. For such threats are of value only if they have a real probability of being acted on. And, if they do have a probability of being acted on, then, as time passes, the likelihood of such an event occurring increases.

If for no other reason, then, it is essential that we begin to examine our social, cultural, political, and economic systems in a more rational manner —in a new manner. The ancient forms of social knowledge must be respected, but we are called on to find something even better. For example, the traditional adversarial systems in which the right lines up against the left, the conservative against the liberal, the wealthy against the poor, the "ins" against the "outs," the young against the old, and men against women is dramatic and, in its pathological way, a lot of fun. People get to call each other names and engage in little games that enliven the moment. There is drama in it, but the basis of drama is conflict—and the point is that profound conflict, at this moment in time, threatens the planet itself.

To remain caught up in the old ways of thinking about human social and cultural systems is, to put it simply, dangerous. In this age of nuclear weapons we find ourselves using social principles that were radical and innovative back in a historical period when material technology was concerned with the problem of how to shape metal. These old ways are no longer completely sufficient. In other words, whether it comes from the social sciences or from another source such as our religious institutions or even the mass media, we must create a new sociology. We have no choice. That is, we have no choice if we commit ourselves to the welfare of future generations as totally as we committed ourselves to the welfare of this present generation.

The image that comes to mind is one of two cats with their tails tied together. Cats are not especially heavy thinkers and, when their tails are tied, their approach to the problem is generally to claw each other to death. It looks foolish from a human perspective. If the cats were sensible, they would sit down, think the matter through, come to see that with a little chewing on their bonds they would be free to go on living active and full cat lives—all nine of them. Instead, they do not think. They die. They seem to have little choice because they cannot think. The only hope for choice, given current world conditions, is to think about our circumstances as we have never before thought about them and then display the courage to act out new ideas.

If we do not change our social and cultural systems—and such systems are massively resistant to change—human life, as we know it, has a low probability of surviving past another few centuries. The study of society—institutional systems—is as necessary for the survival of humankind as is the study of technology or the physical sciences. It is more necessary. In a sense we "mastered" the physical world; we can make astonishingly ingenious machines. We achieved a hard-won "mastery" over the biological world. We have not as yet, however, been able to master our own social and cultural systems.

There is more than a suggestion in all of this that the physical and biological worlds in which we live are simpler and, in that respect, more malleable and benign than the sociocultural worlds of our own making. Here, then, in our own societies and cultures, is a reality that poses a serious challenge. It must come to be understood and controlled better than we have done in the past.

This venture is possibly vain and ultimately impossible, but we are forced into it. We must try. To rely totally on the old systems of understanding is, in a serious way, to abandon any hope for the future—for history shows us the old ways were never able to resolve deep issues by any means other than the use of killing force.

NUCLEAR WAR—THE PECULIAR SOCIAL PROBLEM

One obvious limitation of social science comes out of the fact that although it talks about various social problems, none of these problems has ever been resolved. Other fields go about the business of solving their problems. The social sciences merely go on talking about what they refer to as "social problems."

There is a good reason for this. The solution to a social problem commonly, though not necessarily, proves to be another social problem. For example, we can readily control drugs as a social problem, but to do so in any effective fashion means introducing authoritarian procedures that, in a democratic society, are looked on as something to be avoided—such procedures would be considered a problem in themselves. We see how quickly Americans resent even a modestly authoritarian program such as urine tests for drug use.

We can readily end poverty by transforming the manner in which wealth is distributed. We have little difficulty producing wealth. However, the means whereby this redistribution could be achieved would also have to come from an authoritarian system of political control that would violate American beliefs in freedom of the individual and the operation of the free market. For example, one device that promotes the unequal distribution of wealth is inheritance. We could outlaw or severely restrict inherited wealth. But this solution would surely be viewed as morally reprehensible and "unreasonable." To deny inheritance would interfere with the right of the individual to dispose of his or her wealth according to choice.

We could control pollution by seriously cutting back on or enforcing restrictions on material consumption. Over the long run this is probably the only way in which pollution can be effectively controlled. However, Western ideology finds such an alternative stifling, if not downright subversive.

Social problems are not solved. They are *negotiated* through political processes. We accept crime, for example, until it reaches intolerable levels; then we introduce stronger authoritarian controls—until the controls reach intolerable levels. We control pollution when we find ourselves being threatened by it. The control, however, is not total unless the threat is total, immediate, and commonly comprehended. Like everything else, we negotiate pollution rather than solve it. So long as it is tolerable, we tolerate it.

Social problems, then, are not like mathematical equations; that is, problems with specific solutions that can be determined after the matter is carefully reviewed. Social problems are negotiated. One does not negotiate quadratics in algebra. They are solved or not solved. This is the delight of mathematics. You know when you are right. Just as importantly, you know when you are wrong. Social problems, throughout the whole of human history, have never been solved. We have crime today and, in one form or another, people lived with crime two thousand years ago. We still have starvation, poverty, war, madness, and a host of other human troubles. Nothing seems to have changed all that much. Humanity manages to stumble along fairly well without having its social problems solved in any Utopian fashion.

Nuclear technology changed this situation. There now exists a social problem—of an awesomely unique character—that demands nothing less than a perfect solution! Anything less than a perfect solution possibly means the end of the world. At the same time, because people always negotiate social problems—and the issue of nuclear war is a social problem—the old ways are still being employed to forestall nuclear devastation. We are still relying on the negotiation of the problem. There is little incentive to change. Such methods appear to have worked for the past 40 or more years. After all, we have not had a nuclear war so far.

However, the old ways do not actually work because the possibility of nuclear conflict still remains with us. It is the *possibility* that is the problem! So long as there is any probability nuclear conflict can take place, the world is in peril. We continue to play with the possibility. We "negotiate" it. Today the possibility is low; tomorrow, if the enemy does something we do not like, we will enhance the possibility. This does not solve the problem; it only plays with it. So long as the possibility is greater than zero, the problem of nuclear holocaust is with us and the eventual occurrence of nuclear disaster becomes a certainty.

To see the peculiarity of this situation with a little more clarity, it is necessary to consider several ways this "social problem" differs from other social "problems." First of all, other social problems, such as crime, are tangible. We can keep records and determine if crime is increasing or decreasing. Criminal actions are with us in the immediate present. Nuclear conflict is not, however, a tangible social problem. It is a social problem that does not exist in the moment. In an odd way it does not exist at all. It exists, as a problem, only in terms of the probability of its occurrence — not the actuality of its occurrence. So long as there is any probability of occurrence of nuclear conflict, then nuclear conflict must be seen as a social problem. But, again, it is not a problem like crime or poverty or divorce — all of which are of the moment.

What is negotiated, then, with regard to nuclear conflict is its probability. To have nuclear weapons and, at the same time, clearly convey that there is absolutely no probability they would ever be used makes such weapons pointless. This is why "no first strike" policies make little sense. There must be some probability a first strike can be provoked. Otherwise, the weapons have no purpose. Therefore, we find ourselves living in a world in which the probability of the use of nuclear weapons is always a value greater than zero. Unfortunately, we do not know what the real value is.

Much is made of the fact that we have had 40 years of peace although or, worse yet, *because* there are thousands of nuclear weapons in the arsenals of the world. The contention is then set forth that nuclear weapons ushered in an era of true peace among the people of the world. Nothing could be more absurd, silly, and downright dangerous than this assertion. It amounts to saying that because there were no accidents over the past 40 years at a particular airport, the airport is perfectly safe. Our more general knowledge tells us the airport was probably pretty darned lucky.

Weapons have, over the centuries, been the means whereby a local group is assured a degree of security against the weapons of its neighbors. Although a world without weapons is nice to think about, if someone else has a lot of weapons and you do not, you are vulnerable. This is basic military "realism." This realism works, in its lethal fashion, when weapons are limited and their killing capacity is finite. When, as is the case with modern nuclear devices, you have weapons that move beyond that restriction, the old rules no longer apply.

Nuclear weapons do not keep the peace so long as there is any probability they might be used. They do not provide even the smallest degree of security. They threaten everyone, every day, in a total fashion. They are instruments of global terrorism. They stand as the most perplexing paradox ever confronting human imagination and ingenuity. To say they keep the peace is to be totally incognizant of the extent to which their power permeates the daily affairs of nations. It is to be unaware of the abstracted nature of their threat. The simple menace of the use of such weapons is sufficient to make them the most wickedly obscene danger to human life ever known.

Nuclear weapons exist as threat. If they were not threatening, they would not need to exist. The logic is elementary and, as far as I can see, perfectly telling. Even if there were no ill will on the part of those in possession of such weapons, the possibility of an accidental involvement with them remains a threat. When you have both ill will and the possibility of accident, you find yourself living in the worst of circumstances. To say, then, that 40 years of peace were achieved *because* we rely on nuclear devices is not particularly perceptive. It is peace bought at an outrageous potential price—a price that might, of course, be exacted at any moment.

If the probability of nuclear war in any given year were as low as 1 in 200, there would be a better than 50:50 probability we would experience this event within 150 years. This suggests that systems for preventing nuclear conflict must be at least 99.5 percent efficient each year to assure a better than 50 percent chance civilization will last another 150 years.[6] At the same time, the work of social science, if it reveals anything at all, indicates social systems do not come close to being this reliable or predictable.

We have reached the point, then, where we are confronted with a social problem of astonishing magnitude that demands nothing less than a perfect solution. We can continue the quest for technological "fixes." We can also work toward the end of promoting new forms of social awareness. We can work toward attaining a world order in which social conflicts can be handled by less than ultimate forms of threat and counterthreat.

Quite frankly, no serious writer with whom I am familiar is optimistic about either technological or institutional reform solutions. Once again, however, we have no choice in the matter. All of us must work at them or witness the end of civilization as we now know it. Certainly the least we can do is put our minds to the problem.

Let me close this introduction with an anecdote. I was hiking, a number of years ago, with a friend, Ray Alsbury, in an extremely hazardous area in the Colorado Rockies. Ray, a skilled rock climber, moved out on a shelf of angled rock to practice his art. Cautiously he moved upward. Below was a precipitous drop of three or four hundred feet. Then, he began to lose his balance and slide downward. It appeared certain he would fall to his death. However, he managed to recover. He moved back toward the trail, and we continued our walk. I asked if he was afraid as he felt himself slipping.

"Hell yes, I was afraid," he said.

I asked how he managed to deal with such a terrifying moment.

He said, "I kept my eyes open. Never shut your eyes. Even if you fall, keep your eyes open — remain aware — to the very end."

This is a time when we must "keep our eyes open." If we slip, some insane day, and fall into the denouement of a final hydrogen hell, we must not go with our eyes closed.

Chapter 2

Emile Durkheim: The Contemplation of Cultural Suicide

THE MODERN ERA IN SOCIAL PHILOSOPHY

The late 19th century is now viewed as the remote past. For young people of today, born after the Vietnam War and for whom the troubled events of World War II are ancient history, the Victorian period is as distant as biblical times. It is commonly confused with the medieval era — a period extending roughly from the 6th to the 16th centuries. The Victorian period, however, marks the beginning of modern technological-industrial society as we now know it. The reign of Queen Victoria of England extended from 1837 to 1901 — it began only 150 years ago. During that period virtually every modern invention we accept as truly modern had its birth. Everything we enjoy — television, computers, planes, cars, movies, and so on — derives from the astonishing cultural creativity that took place during the second half of the 19th century in Western culture.

Modern social philosophy and social science also had their beginnings in this period. The late 19th century marked a turning point in how people approached social issues. It was a time when new voices were heard. Until the beginning of the 19th century, the most powerful interpreters of the human scene were poets; philosophers who specialized in religious and ethical topics; and people who, through advantages of power and wealth, could publish political pamphlets and books. Not until the middle of the 19th century did a new approach begin to take form. It was a way of thinking that ignored poetics and favored careful analysis and the use of data over arm-chair speculation and reliance on theological dogma. One figure to achieve particular eminence as a representative of this new mode of thinking was the French academician Emile Durkheim.

Emile Durkheim, a French sociologist and intellectual of the early 20th century, was born in 1858 and died in 1917. It is difficult today to comprehend the radical and brilliant quality of his work because we tend to take for granted sociological theories and research practices that were virtually unknown prior to 1900.[1] That these ideas and practices are now general is, to a great extent, attributable to Durkheim's influence.

Durkheim was unique. For example, he was among the first to attempt a systematic analysis of social data by relying on carefully developed empirical information. He carried out one of the first theoretical-empirical-scientific studies of the problem of human suicide.[2] Where the poet dealt with suicide as a dramatic or artistic happening and the student of ethics approached suicide as an ethical problem, Durkheim tried something new. He sifted through all the statistical information on the incidence of suicide he could find. His ambition was to ascertain whether a sociological approach to suicide was reasonable. His work led to dozens of later studies of suicide that do not always agree with Durkheim's conclusions. Nonetheless, they show their respect by trying to be as meticulous in the use of data as Durkheim was in his pioneering effort.

Durkheim's influence on the methods of modern social science was extensive. He moved social philosophy in the direction of a concern with facts. Reasoned speculation had its place, but it could not be trusted by itself. At the same time, Durkheim was influential with regard to a theoretical position he promoted and defended — a point of view known as *social determinism*. The word *determinism* is somewhat misleading although it is commonly used in the literature of Western social science. When applied precisely it means a strict deterministic relationship between several events. For example, lowering the temperature determines the freezing of water.

In social philosophy determinism means, more broadly, that a theorist draws on a general set of conditions to account for social issues. For example, a biological determinist would be drawn to biological factors to account for, let us say, the rise of religious beliefs. An economic determinist would rely on economic factors. A social determinist would argue that social events such as the rise of a new religion are best accounted for by looking for other social events, as opposed to biological or physical conditions, that brought them into being. For example, the traditional celebration of Christmas has been radically altered by changes in other parts of the society such as urbanization, the melding of ethnic cultures, the rise of consumerism, the development of mass communications, and cheap and efficient transportation.

Durkheim based his argument on the notion that whatever we might mean by *social reality*, it is different in character from whatever we might mean by physical, biological, or psychological reality. Groups of individuals have properties different from those of the individuals who make them up. Social happenings, he argued, are determined by social events — not by physical, biological or psychological conditions.

An example can be found in the human practice of war. Psychological theories of war remain popular. In their simpler forms they argue that something in the individual, psychological make-up of human beings inclines them to go to war periodically — aggressive tendencies, innate hostilities, death wishes, an "adventure gene," an inborn necessity to fulfill the evolutionary teleology of the "survival of the fittest," and so on. Durkheim opposed this idea. War, he argued, is a social event and, as such, is explained by other social conditions or events — nationalism, political economics, religious forces, organizational conflicts, and so on.

Human social systems, if they are ever to be understood, must be studied in terms of their own particular social dynamics. We err when we try to comprehend what is social by reducing it to a "lower" or different level of reality. Durkheim spent his life trying to correct the excessive biological and psychological forms of determinism that were popular in the middle of the 19th century in Western culture and that remain popular down to the present time.

This essay, in which Durkheim's ideas will be directed toward the nuclear arms issue, draws on three major concepts found in his work:

1. Collective representations
2. Social normality
3. Anomie

COLLECTIVE REPRESENTATIONS

Like any effectively creative thinker, Durkheim paid close attention to and was puzzled by something we are likely to take for granted — the simple fact that people grant certain objects, places, events, or individuals "special" qualities. These special qualities transform what would otherwise be ordinary objects or events into something extraordinary. More specifically, as Durkheim saw it, the object is transformed from something without social implications into something with social implications. As this happens, the object takes on a special significance and becomes socially valuable. A mundane example of this process can be seen in the sale of a celebrity's T-shirt. In itself the T-shirt is a profane or ordinary object. The fact that it was worn by a famous person changes the object into one with "special" qualities. Note that the physical object retains precisely the same physical form. Its enhanced significance can, therefore, come only from its sociological transformation. So powerful is this kind of transformation that on occasion we are inclined to think we can actually see something different in the T-shirt. It is hallowed. It possesses a "spirit." It has something "special" about it. The something that is hallowed, spiritual, or special, Durkheim would argue, is more likely to be something sociological.

Durkheim argued, then, that these objects or events or persons are given special significance through collective social processes. In turn, they are significant only insofar as they are relevant to collective interests. He called such objects *collective representations*. Collective representations are, to use a crude physical analogy, like social magnets. They attract and hold the sentiments of the entire community. They are the focal point of communal beliefs, feelings, sentiments, concerns, fears, and so forth.

One particularly interesting and especially significant form of collective representation is the sacred person or sacred literature. The sacredness of these things protects them from criticism and grants them special collective powers that, by definition, ordinary people or conditions cannot transcend. It is typical of sacred literature or persons who represent sacred traditions that any kind of criticism — even dispassionate, rational discussion of them — is met with open hostility. A clear illustration is the manner in which virtually any kind of criticism or deviation from sacred prescriptions is dismissed as the work of "Satan" by the members of various Christian communities. Any action that might challenge sacred dogma is seen as the work of the devil. This device is not exclusive to specific religious sects, however. It appears wherever the sense of the sacred is strong. The invective might not involve Satan, but an attempt to mute rational or critical discussion will occur in some form.

Durkheim was a general theorist. His observations with respect to sacred objects were not restricted to any particular religious group. Sacred objects are a part of all societies or cultures, and they serve much the same function wherever they are found and whatever form they might take. Regardless of where they are found and the nature of their form, sacred objects are communally sustained and highly resistant to change.

It is this feature of the sacred object, person, or event that is worth considering later with respect to international conflict in an age of nuclear arms. Because sacred personalities and sacred literature are simultaneously powerful in their impact on large numbers of people and are, at the same time, removed by their sacredness from rational examination, human social systems are vulnerable to intensely irrational responses to a great variety of things — especially anything that threatens or involves the sacred forms. Any threat to sacred objects, by definition, will be met with an intensely emotional *collective* response.

SOCIAL NORMALITY

The modern mentality in Durkheim's thinking reveals itself in his concern with the idea of social normalcy. Before Durkheim's time, people had little basis for even raising the question of what constitutes a normal social system. After all, they had no way to compare themselves with other societies. However, the growth of world trade, global exploration, and the discovery of hundreds of other societies and cultures forced people to reconsider what they had long taken for granted. People began to compare — almost always in a way that made Western civilization seem superior — their European forms of community with these newly discovered cultures.

The richness of comparative possibilities enabled Durkheim to see that societies differ much as individuals do. However, instead of being concerned with problems of cultural and social inferiority and superiority, he tried to set his sights a little lower. Just as we are necessarily concerned with the question of what is normal for the individual person, Durkheim took on the question of what is normal for societies. What is typical of societies?

Possibly the most shocking conclusion he reached, for his times at least, was the claim that crime is not something abnormal within human social systems. It is normal insofar as it is found in all societies. Indeed, crime may be essential to the workings of any society. This was a novel argument to develop during the moralistic period that established itself in Europe at the turn of the century. It has an offbeat quality nearly a hundred years later.

Durkheim put it this way: "There is, then, no phenomenon that presents more indisputably all the symptoms of normality, since it [crime] appears closely connected with the conditions of all collective life. . . . What is normal, simply, is the existence of criminality, provided that it attains and does not exceed, for each social type, a certain level. . . ."[3]

Durkheim looked on crime as a kind of "enemy within." Just as a threat from an external enemy serves to unite a community, so does the threat of crime within a society. Also, just as enemies are often created by political leaders to unite people, societies require crime to maintain their solidarity. What shocked the people of Durkheim's day — and still does — was his observation, in effect, that if crime did not naturally exist, society would somehow create it anyway. Or, as Durkheim put it, even a community of saints would find sinners in its midst.

As we explore the problem of nuclear war and the issue of nuclear arms, we shall touch on the problem of whether it is normal for human societies to engage in violence. Like crime, it is such a common practice that it appears to be the norm rather than the exception. If so, then Durkheim helped make a case for those who argue that war is the natural condition of human cultures and the only realistic attitude is one that promotes readiness for war.

ANOMIE

If there is a single concept likely to be associated with Durkheim's writing, it is *anomie* (also spelled anomy). The word means, basically, to be without a name, to have no sense of social identity, or to be socially "lost" (*a-nom*, or "without name"). It also can be derived from the Greek term for law, *nomos*. In this case it means to be without laws or in a state of lawlessness or normlessness. As is the case with the Marxist notion of *alienation*, it is a term easily tossed about. It is not, however, as simple as it at first appears to be.

Although modern sociologists and social psychologists run into trouble defining what anomie really is, the search has led to new levels of understanding how being human is a matter of being deeply, deeply embedded within a broader collective matrix. Later in this book we shall consider the work of an American sociologist, Harold Garfinkel. Garfinkel found that social definitions — norms — so thoroughly permeate the life of human beings that it is difficult to put people into situations in which they experience anomie.

The concept of anomie is relevant to a discussion of nuclear war when we ask whether war is a breakdown of social norms or, to the contrary, a product of the pathological heightening of the power inherent in social norms. We shall consider such a possibility in the final sections of this chapter.

It helps to understand and appreciate Durkheim if we are aware, at the outset, that Durkheim's primary concern was to get people to see that a psychologistic or individualistic approach to human social systems is a near-sighted point of view. Americans, in particular, have trouble with structural approaches to human societies — preferring to deal with problems on an individual level. For example, we like to think that World War II was a consequence of the individual genius of a single, despicable individual — Adolf Hitler — abetted by a few evil henchmen. A Durkheimian approach suggests that if Hitler had never existed, the structural situation in Europe in 1920 would have led to war in any case.

I will now develop each of these three central concepts in Durkheim's work more broadly and then attempt to show how these concepts enlarge our understanding of specific social issues — with emphasis given to the problem of nuclear warfare.

FURTHER CONSIDERATION OF COLLECTIVE REPRESENTATIONS

Americans not only are inclined toward individualistic explanations of social events, but their use of the term *society* also suggests they rely on a primitive awareness of what they are talking about. The term *society* is a high abstraction, and a good understanding of the nature of social forces calls for more than simple common sense.

Consider, for example, just how easy it is to use the word *society* to refer to nearly anything we want to refer to. We talk about society being strong or weak. We talk about society doing this or that. We feel we should revolt against society or support society or conform to society's demands or otherwise respond to something we vaguely comprehend as society. We know there is something "out there" that we can refer to as society, but just what that might be is difficult, in fact impossible, to pin down. Generally, people come back to individuals as a reference point in their quest to establish an understanding of what is going on in their social lives.

I think, as I write this, of a bit of graffiti scrawled on the sidewalk of a park through which I occasionally stroll in the evening. It reads: "SCREW SOCIETY." It is an instructive little message. Here the word *society* is used in a magical sense to refer to something that is simultaneously abstracted, hated, and yet palpable. It is, of course, completely impossible to do anything physical to a society. You can kill people, but you cannot, in any meaningful way, "kill" a society or "screw" it. Note, in this bit of graffiti, the implicit individualization of society.

Social reality is real — all too real at times — but it is not physical. Or, to put it another way, there are surely those who believe that when Rome fell there must have been a loud crashing noise. Actually, the Roman system, in lively ways, continues to pervade all of modern Western culture. The intriguing thing about social systems is not the ways in which they are like individuals, but the ways in which they are different. For example, they do not "die" the way individuals do. They are, despite the recommendation of the graffiti, beyond being screwed.

The truth of the matter, of course, is that society is something of a peculiarly abstracted nature. None of us has ever observed a society. Moreover, none of us is ever going to. Society is not something we can see, or touch, or hug, or put on a scale and weigh, or somehow deal with in any direct manner. Its nature is forever removed from our immediate and direct sensing. If this is so, then why do we seem to know it so well? Why are we able to discuss it so casually and believe we know what we are talking about when we talk about society?

Not only have we never seen a society, but we also have never actually seen or directly observed anything that is social in character. We might, for example, think we have seen a student or a businessperson or a homemaker or a teacher or a criminal or a politician or a scientist on one occasion or another. Actually, it is impossible to experience any of these social realities in a direct manner.

What we observe in such instances is a physical being who *represents* a social status or social position of some kind. *In order to make a social, as opposed to a physical, observation, we must be told or otherwise informed of what we are seeing.*

This opens up a tremendously messy philosophical and scientific can of worms by raising the question of whether we are properly observing something if the reality of that event is contingent on our being told or otherwise informed that it is what it is. If we must be told, then is the reality in what we are being told, or in the event itself? (Think, again, of the sacred object: Is its sacredness within the object itself, or does it lie in what we were taught to believe about the object? How we answer this question is critical with regard to how we approach social issues.)

Consider an ordinary social moment. You attend a party and you are introduced to a young woman. You are told she is a nuclear physicist. Her social position is established by the information you were given by the host. If you were told something different, you would respond differently. You also quite likely would have "seen" a different person before you. How would you react if you found out, later, that the host had lied to you? The young lady was really a firefighter.

Because social character — as opposed to purely physical qualities — is derived from complex forms of symbolic communications and resides within those communications, then the validity of social reality can be no greater than the validity of the communications upon which it rests. In other words, if you are misinformed as to the true social character of an individual, social action and interaction will be disrupted. This is the basis, of course, for a great deal of comedy and humor in literature and on the stage. We laugh at the disruptions that come out of such social misinformation.

Because it is important that social reality be presented as validly as possible if appropriate social interactions are to take place, modern society depends more and more on the use of credentials. This is distressing to people who argue they do not want to be labeled or defined by a piece of paper. Durkheim might have argued that, at one level, this is true—you are whatever you are. However, *at a social level*, you are what you are socially defined as being. If you want to pass as, let us say, an expert on nuclear affairs, then you must carry credentials that qualify you to act as one. Such credentials can be obtained only from those who are themselves already credentialed.

To gain insight into Durkheim's thinking it is important, at the outset, to comprehend how completely dependent we are on being abstractly informed in order to have a sense or awareness of our social worlds. For example, even if you accept the argument that you have never seen a social status, you might yet remain convinced you have at least seen such things as a church, a university campus, or a historical monument. But the argument is exactly the same. Such physical objects can be perceived directly but their social meanings must always come from "outside" the object. The meanings they have as social entities cannot be directly perceived.

The *social* use to which a physical object is put cannot be established by the object itself. In other words, the same physical object can have innumerable meanings. In ordinary times, for example, a church building might serve as a church building. During a crisis the same building might serve as a hospital, or it might be an arms depot. For this reason social deception is surprisingly easy. In war a church building might wind up being almost anything other than a place of worship.

We now come to the crucial question: If the social world is not directly visible, how do we come to comprehend it or perceive it? How does "society" manage to become so "real"? This is not an easy question to answer and its profound difficulty intrigued Durkheim. How, for example, did primitive people gain a sense of or interpret the social systems in which they lived? As is the case with us, people in simpler societies had no direct access to social reality. As simple communal systems became established at the beginnings of human history, the problem of identifying the community, as a social unit, took on the same kind of abstracted nature we find it taking today.

Durkheim's response to the question of how social reality manifests itself provides us with one of the deeper sociological visions in all of Western social philosophy. In effect, he argued, society is generated through devices that come to represent the society as a whole. These are representations of the collective or *collective representations*. Such "collective representations" are invested with social value through collective processes of various kinds. For example, a ritual instills within people a sense of the social meaning of the items and the literature used in the ritual.

Ritual is defined here simply as any collective process that transforms an individual object into a social object. This process can take place in a variety of ways and across a range of levels, extending from a family's suddenly endowing an infant's burble with special meanings to a national spectacle taking place over months or years of time and involving millions of people. (Think of the recent rejuvenation of the Statue of Liberty.) The more extreme forms of ritual transform an object, event, or person from an ordinary or "profane" condition into one having "sacred" qualities. Durkheim believed all societies must concern themselves with the establishment of devices that represent the community as a whole. Because these devices are social in character, they function to promote integration and solidarity within the community and a consensus with regard to what is important for the community as a whole.

As a quick aside, note that in modern society the mass media take on ritualistic functions. Simply appearing before mass audiences of millions of people produces a collective effect. Modern communications technology makes it possible to create collective representations of great variety and influence almost instantly. These media events have inspired cults capable of lasting over decades of time. The Elvis Presley phenomenon is one example. Professional football teams and players are yet another. Others come and go.

The concept of collective representations brought Durkheim to the conclusion that religious institutions, sacred symbols, and sacred literature are fundamentally social devices. They exist as ways, so to speak, of making the social order "real." They are representations of the social order. Only through such devices can social reality come into being and human communities acquire the solidarity necessary to sustain them through generation after generation. Every society — every organization — distinguishes between its sacred and profane features. This distinction is crucial to sociological understanding, for it is essentially a distinction between what is effectively social and what is not.

Whatever is considered sacred in a society is given its awesome sacred qualities by virtue of its capacity to represent values, sentiments, power, or beliefs that are shared in common — the sacred object comes out of and is supported by the total society. The profane object, on the other hand, is not supported in this manner. It may have considerable utility, but it gains its value primarily from the extent to which it is useful to the individual — it has little or no public relevance. Those who attack a sacred work because it is irrational must keep in mind that they are attacking more than a particular item or person, they are also attacking whatever the sacred event represents.

Durkheim also found it interesting that nearly any conceivable kind of object or event has been used as a sacred device among the various cultures of the world. What might be an awesome sacred icon in one social context might equally well be an object of contempt or humor within another. If this is so, Durkheim argued, the "sacredness" of the object does not come from within itself but must come, instead, from the collective that defines the object as sacred. It is a perfectly logical argument.

Now we need to see how Durkheim's distinction between the profane and the sacred offers us a new way of looking at the problem of nuclear weapons. Possibly the best way to see how Durkheim might alter our thinking is to keep in mind Durkheim's argument that there is a difference between the individual and society. It is one thing to examine psychological factors, and another to examine social factors. Collective representations are necessary to sustain social units, not individuals. The individual, purely as an individual, has no need for a collective representation. This holds true by definition. However, collective representations generate an awed response on the part of individuals, thereby helping to develop a sense of commitment to the community. Collective representations generate mass action and mass sentiments. They heighten emotionality in the name of the collective. In so doing they simultaneously diminish rational evaluations of the moment and promote a sense of separateness.

This process worked well enough for human communities over the long sweep of history—although it also divides people from each other and generates intense conflicts. Now, in an age of nuclear armaments, we must question the extent to which we can continue to indulge in the luxury of devices that inhibit a clear vision of ourselves and those others with whom we must share this crowded planet. Collective representations generate a sense of "we" above "them." They tend to relegate social analysis and understanding to the level of slogans, maxims, and unquestioning acceptance of the policies symbolized by the collective symbol. It is a dangerous state of mind to allow in this age of total armament.

The collective representation nicely delineates the persistent argument by Durkheim that the individual and society, though closely united, nonetheless have separate characteristics. Once again, consider the fact that collective representations are necessary for the functioning of collective units. They have no purpose for the individual purely as an individual. Or, to illustrate the point all too simply, no single individual has any need for a Statue of Liberty. Such a representation comes out of the traditions and lives of millions of people acting in concert. The symbol itself creates the collective processes that, in turn, re-create the symbol.

Society is not simply a massive spreading out of the individual psyche across the landscape. Society is something unique, something with its own qualities and its own demands. Durkheim looked on society as a form of reality *sui generis* (of its own kind, or unique). Moreover, social systems do not relate to each other in the same ways individuals relate. This is an important consideration because psychology dominates American thinking about human issues. We turn to individualistic explanations to account for problems that, in all too many instances, are not the product of pathological individuals but are instead the consequence of social forces.

Durkheim's discussion of social reality argues that there must be a process that transforms our actions from individualistic actions into actions that are incorporated into the broader community or social structure or collective. This process is a matter of creating collective representations, an extreme form of which is the sacred object. It is the task of the collective representation to enhance action by giving the actor a sense of being part of something "bigger" than himself or herself. The collective representation enables social identification to take place. The relevance of this for the nuclear issue lies in the process of social enhancement on the one hand (the feeling of importance we get from knowing our actions have collective significance of some kind) and social differentiation on the other hand.

Social differentiation is a logical consequence of collective representations. If our sacred object is, let us say, a circle, then it cannot, by definition, be a square. To accept both representations would confuse social identity and interfere with the effort of the community to assure the effectiveness of its collective representation. In effect, this is what is asked of us when we are called on to become members of a global community. And yet another problem interferes with attaining a sense of global communal identity or collective representation. There are hierarchies or "levels" of sacred symbols, ranging from those that are specific to immediate groups such as a fraternity or sorority to those that encompass these groups. Today the highest level of collective organization is generally represented by the nation-state and the symbols appropriate to the nation-state. Those who promote a global system that would embrace the nation-state have yet to establish effective collective representations for such an organization.

The social differentiation implied in the process of creating collective representations further implies that the collective representations of other groups—even friendly groups—are threatening. We can, for example, accept the Union Jack of Great Britain as the flag of a friendly nation, but we can pledge allegiance only to the Stars and Stripes. Alliances of any sort are, of course, tenuous and subject to change as relationships between nations, not individuals, change. But the alliance of the individual to the broader community or nation is not subject to change—loyalty to the interests of the group is a central concern of any major organized human collective.

Implicit in Durkheim's view of social differentiation is the idea that if only two communities existed, living next to each other on a hypothetical plain, each would develop its particular collective representations and those representations would be antithetical to each other. Again, there is almost a mathematical logic to the argument. To have two different communities you must have two different sets of collective representations. Because it is the purpose of such representations to differentiate the communities, the function of the representations will be to divide people into two distinct groups.

Moreover, because these representations provide people with a sense of importance, the division will become important and be sustained. The only way to break the division is to break the process of creating collective representations.

I should make clear, at this point, that I have taken Durkheim's ideas and shifted their focus. Durkheim was caught up in the question of how human societies are possible. What holds large numbers of people together in the form of collectives? What keeps, for example, hundreds of millions of "Americans" together as a national unit? We, however, are now considering the possibility that the same thing that holds people together in powerful ways at one level also separates them in equally powerful ways at another.

The implications of this for the nuclear impasse are now more obvious. It is not psychological but social processes that promote the division between the so-called major "powers." One way to ease the tensions between these powers would be to attempt to destroy the process of social differentiation. This would mean getting rid of the flags, the sacred symbols, the icons, and all of the other accoutrements that exist to promote the integrity of the community—in this case the nation-state. Obviously, any politician—Russian, American, or of any other nationality—who even halfway seriously suggested such a policy would be viewed as insane or as a traitor—or, more likely, both. Given the current political and ideological climate that pervades the world at the present time, I seriously worry about even mentioning the removal of collective representations as a purely speculative fantasy in this essay.

The process of social differentiation, operating within its own logic, demands that the collective representations of one nation be sustained while those of threatening nations be impugned. So we constantly ridicule virtually every achievement or failure of the Russians while they, in turn, ridicule virtually every achievement or failure of Western nations. Meanwhile, at a covert level, both sides are paying each other the respect implied by their efforts to steal each other's industrial and technological secrets.

The Transformed Individual

I have been emphasizing the way collective representations enhance social differentiation. Collective representations also endow, as it were, the individual with a sense of the power of the collective. Collective representations identify the individual with the collective and the power of the collective. Through the collective representation—whatever it might be—the individual is transformed from an ordinary person into a representative of a power that transcends ordinary individuality. In other words, we cannot be important as individuals without societies that grant us significance. I shall return to a similar theme later in this book. For the moment I want to point out that there is a paradox, a kind of Durkheimian paradox, in the fact that the only way we can achieve special notoriety as individuals is through a communal or collective system. Or, to put it differently, we cannot be uniquely individual merely as individuals.

One of my favorite examples of what Durkheim is talking about appears in an anecdote told by "Broadway Joe" Namath, a former professional football quarterback of considerable reputation. He said men would come up to him as he was enjoying an evening in a restaurant and ask if they could touch him. Namath, as a celebrated individual, a "hero," represented the interests of millions of people and was, in a sense, a "collective representation." Men, awed by his presence, sought the collective force by touching it. The Durkheimian question here is: Just exactly what do you touch when you touch the shoulder of a celebrity — power, identity, control, contact with someone who represents the awesome power of the community as a whole? Would you get the same awesome sense of touching "something" if Namath came into the bar as a hobo — even though he was precisely the same individual?

Modern football, celebrated through the collective communication of games — the *mass* media are well named — is an obvious illustration of the collective representation. Societies, by their character, especially enhance those who are part of their collective representations. At the very least they worship them; at the fullest, they worship them and endow them with every material advantage. In our culture, then, we not only adore and worship our professional athletes but we confer on them wealth far beyond what we are willing to give those who function as secular public servants — the president of the nation, for example. The president, of course, is also a collective symbol and a relatively well-paid one. But the salary of our president would, of course, not be competitive in any of America's major sports and even several minor ones.

Collective representations do not need to be "rational" in any common-sense meaning of that term. For example, football does not accomplish anything of economic merit in itself. When the game is done, all that has been objectively achieved is the movement of a small, inflated, oblate, spheroid leather ball up and down a small grassy pasture. This, of course, is carried out with great effort, emotionality, a considerable number of broken bones, and an occasional death or two. If nothing of any merit of an objective nature is accomplished, then what is going on? The answer is fairly self-evident. What is accomplished is purely social. People gain a sense of their collective — they win or lose with "it" in football games — and that sense of the collective is worth, at least in America, a lot of money in the open market.

I shall return to this theme — the ability of collective representations to heighten emotionality — in later chapters. Let me note here that people gain their sense of power as individuals through the extent to which they believe they represent collective forces. Once more notice the peculiar apparent contradiction in this. We "find" ourselves in the moment we abandon ourselves to communal or social forces. If nothing else, this little observation forces us to recognize that people are as much, if not more, "sociological" in nature as they are "psychological." What is important in the ability of the collective representation to transcend individual powers or abilities is the fact that such representations acquire the capacity to move beyond criticism. At the highest level they become "sacred" icons or ideas or individuals. Collective representations are essential to any organization and are necessary for the continuation of human communities, but they achieve this end through generating a sense of social differentiation and social enhancement.

One bizarre extreme consequence of this process is the mentality of men who are elated because they machine-gunned worshippers in a synagogue or killed innocent people standing in line at an international airport waiting to buy tickets. Such actions are carried out "in the name" of various collective representations—whatever they might be. We kill our own kind in the name of "holy" motives. Again, to underscore the vision of Durkheim, it is essential to see that this is not a matter of individual psychologies or emotions or anything else—it is a matter of how communities are to be sustained. In the world we live in, it is a matter of how nations are to retain their integrity as nations. It is a matter of the "logic" of collective representations.

To sum up this particular discussion, sacred symbols or collective representations have the ability to constrain critical thought and to promote highly emotionalized perceptions of those who live under different representations. This has been the function of such representations for thousands of years. The question now, in an age of nuclear armaments, is whether we can afford to continue generating social solidarity by means of devices that simultaneously constrain reason and promote antagonisms.

THE PARADOXES OF SOCIAL NORMALITY

We generally have a good notion of what we mean when we say something is "normal." Durkheim relied primarily on a commonsense statistical idea of what is normal. From this perspective, what is normal is what is most common. Statisticians call this the *mode*. For example, the average Nobel Prize winner is an older, educated person who is also male. This is the mode. What is "normal" for this group, then, is older, educated males. Durkheim, thinking like a scientist, asked the question: What is typical of human societies? What are most societies like? This questioning process is much the same as that used by a naturalist trying to establish an idea of a typical buffalo herd or the typical nesting behavior for a particular species of bird.

Durkheim also asked the question: What is the ideal society like? However, he was not interested in the ideal as a Utopian conception of society, but rather as a conception of how a social system must necessarily be put together. An ideal Durkheimian society, for example, would include rather than exclude crime because Durkheim was convinced that crime promotes social solidarity. His interest in the "normal" human social system included both statistical data and the ideal form of society. I shall not dwell on this distinction here. Both approaches led Durkheim to similar conclusions.

Asking what is normal of human societies is too broad a question. We must revise the question and ask specifically: What is normal for any kind of human society *at a particular stage in its development*? Is it, for example, normal for societies organized by clans to have diffused polytheistic religions? Conversely, is it normal for complex nation-state systems to have monotheistic religions? Recent research, interestingly enough, suggests that polytheism is normal for simple societies. Monotheism is typical of more complex societies. If this is so, religious ideology seems to be a function of social organization. This is a nice example of the difference between Durkheimian "social determinism" and popular "psychological determinism," which views religion as a response of the individual to the awesome wonders and horrors of life.

I do not have time to probe Durkheim's interest in religion as a social force in great detail. However, a University of Michigan sociologist named Guy Swanson found that polytheism is normal for one kind of social structure and is not found in other types. He reported his findings in *The Birth of the Gods*, which I recommend for those interested in religious issues and for those interested in finding out more about the possible effects of social structure on our personal beliefs.[4] Swanson found, for example, that witchcraft as a religious belief is associated with particular forms of social structure and not with others. This book is a clever example of the use of Durkheimian theory in social research.

We already saw that Durkheim believed collective representations are characteristic of any human society. They are socially necessary and therefore socially "normal." They are also uniquely human and emotional. The irrational nature of collective representations can make them the butt of ridicule for literary satirists. For example, the Miss America contest is, by almost any standard, a silly ritual. Durkheim might agree, but he would counter by saying that if we did not employ Miss America as a collective representation, we would employ something else — probably also objectively silly, but socially necessary. Collective representations, of varying sorts, are typical of all human societies. They generally provide a nice study in the difference between material pragmatics and social pragmatics.

The most shocking conclusion reached by his questioning was the argument that criminality is "normal." Durkheim argued that criminality is normal, in the first place, because all societies have criminal elements. Second, he believed criminality is normal because it is necessary for the proper functioning of the moral order of any community. He was explicit about this, arguing that "crime is normal because a society exempt from it is utterly impossible."

Here was an argument that raised eyebrows among Western intellectuals who came from a cultural tradition in which crime was and is viewed as something abnormal. We again need to hammer at the distinction between the individual and social systems of which individuals are a part. Individual criminals might be a small portion of the total population of the community and, therefore, abnormal. However, criminality is found in all societies; and, therefore, crime is normal as a social condition, but not as an individual event.

We can gain a deeper insight into the psychologistic orientation of Western mentality by noting that the work of Sigmund Freud, which came a little after Durkheim's, shocked Europe much more than Durkheim had by suggesting that criminality is normal to the individual. According to Freud, we all contain within us a kind of raging asocial element that does not hesitate to dream of criminal actions and, on occasion, carry them out. Even saintly souls, Freud suggested, are not freed from such desires. Christian doctrine had long accepted the notion that people are "sinful" creatures, but accepted also the idea we can be "cleansed" of our sins. Freud argued that no matter how you might try, you cannot purge yourself of desires that are, by their nature, inherently asocial—you can only repress them.

Returning to Durkheim, we are forced to consider the possibility that crime is a structural part of any human society—in one form or other. However, Durkheim conceded that there could be abnormal levels of crime within any society that changed it from being normal to being abnormal. It is not crime *per se* but the incidence or level of crime in a given society at a particular time that might be abnormal. For example, Colin Turnbull describes a primitive mountain community whose members went from being peaceful and gentle to mean-spirited when faced with starvation conditions.[5] Children were much more likely to be left to starve. The new rates of crime were indicative of an abnormal state of affairs for the society.

What determines normalcy is a difficult question. It was not effectively answered by Durkheim and has not been answered well by any modern social researcher. This does not invalidate the question, however. Even if it cannot be given a specific answer, it directs our thinking away from the psychological question of what is normal for the individual (also a question not especially well-answered by modern psychology) to the issue of what is normal for the community at large.

Durkheim was not the only person concerned with the problem of what is normal for large collections of people. In the period just preceding and then following World War II population experts raised the question of an optimum or ideal size of population for a given society. Such a problem should be scientifically easier to solve than the Durkheimian problem of the typicality of violence. However, it was never solved. Because scientists tend to give up on questions they believe cannot, in principle, be answered, the question was essentially dropped. In a way it is too bad because it remains a good question.

When we raise the question of the extent to which criminality is normal for a given class of societies, we can gain some insight into possible social, as opposed to individual, abnormalities by comparing America's crime statistics with those of all other societies having an advanced technological-industrial economy combined with an elaborate bureaucratic-corporate form of social and political organization. We find that the United States has the highest incidence of violent crime per 100,000 people of any nation in the world (Table 2.1).[6]

It is not violent crime in itself that is *socially* abnormal, but the fact that more of it is taking place in the United States than is characteristic of other societies at a similar stage of development. Rather than approach the problem from a psychological point of view, Durkheim argued that the problem is not an individualistic one but is, instead, something that calls for an examination of the sociocultural system as a whole. Americans do not like governments practicing violence and oppression. However, they appear to have a high tolerance for oppression and violence when such actions are carried out as individualized ventures.

We cannot ignore the argument that crime is a sociological as well as a psychological problem. If crime were strictly a problem within the individual — a "bad seed" — and assuming that genetic populations are randomly distributed over the globe, then the rate of crime among social systems would vary in a random fashion. Obviously, this does not happen. At best all that can be suggested is that social units have a bearing on crime; a detailed consideration of whether such units create crime to an inordinate degree or attract individuals who are criminally disposed is beyond the scope of this chapter.

There is, of course, reason to be worried about statistics that tell us that violence is excessive for a social system of our type. We must not be insensitive to the immediate personal grief suffered by those who are the victims of violent crime in this country. More broadly, however, there is the concern that comes from thinking about one of the world's more violent social systems also being one of the world's most heavily armed nuclear powers. Despite the rhetoric of peace that characterizes our political posture before the world, the fact is that the United States is a violent nation. So is the USSR, so is Britain, so is France, so is Japan, so is Brazil and any other modern nation. Durkheim would accept violence, of some kind, as normal to the modern nation-state. Indeed, it is typical of virtually any advanced society. Even so, we should keep in mind the fact that the violence of ancient city-states makes modern international relations sometimes appear restrained and even "civilized."[7] The violence of medieval systems in both Western and Eastern cultures was also remarkable.

T A B L E 2.1
Crime Rates in the United States and the Developed Nations, Average 1970 – 75 (Rates per 100,000 population)

	Total Crime Index	Murder	Rape	Assault
United States	4,400	9.1	23.1	196
Developed nations	1,546	2.7	24.0	115

The question is not whether the USSR is violent and we are not—both systems must rely on violence to some extent. The question, from a Durkheimian perspective, is whether or not the degree of violence is socially normal or abnormal. Although scientists abandoned the hope of finding a way to determine what is a reasonable amount of violence, politicians and demagogues did not. In effect, political rhetoric tries to convince us that the violence that takes place within the enemy's society is abnormal while ours is, somehow, a normal problem being reasonably dealt with in humane ways. The data in Table 2.1 provide food for thought with regard to such rhetoric.

It is worth mentioning the fact that violence is morally repugnant while it is, at the same time, typical, at least to some degree, of any relatively complex society. This situation makes any particular social system vulnerable to social condemnation. So it is, then, that the propaganda mills of international antagonists are granted a steady supply of material to use for damning the violence of those systems they wish to criticize. We can readily take our enemies to task for their inhumanity while they can do the same thing with regard to us. An interesting recent exchange along these lines was the Republic of South Africa's reply to criticism from the United States about apartheid policies. South Africa pointed out that we Americans should keep in mind that we wantonly cheated, starved, killed, routed, and destroyed great numbers of Native Americans when we settled the continent and then, pouring salt into the wounds, braggingly referred to our violent actions as "Manifest Destiny." Although South Africa's attempt to justify its evil actions by pointing out that other people are doing the same thing is not morally sound, there is still bite in the criticism.

The much more difficult question to deal with is not whether, let us say, the USSR is violent—it obviously does not hesitate to use violent means to achieve its ends—but whether the level of violence found within that particular system can be considered normal or typical for its stage of development. There is no good way to answer this question. Even if there were, we would still be faced with the question of whether or not "we" must endure "their" normal inclination for violence. After all, bears and eagles reveal a violent nature on occasion. It is typical of such animals. This does not mean we need to let them strike us when we happen to stroll into their territory.

The problem of crime, violence, inhumanity, immorality, and other repugnant human conditions takes on a more complex coloring when viewed from a Durkheimian perspective. Repugnant actions are repugnant actions—whether we engage in them or someone else does. At the same time, as social elements, such actions are different in meaning than when they are seen as individual acts. Violence engaged in to retain the integrity of the community differs from violence engaged in to satisfy the personal ambitions of, let us say, a petty crook. How do we deal with socially generated violence as opposed to violence with its locus in some pathological condition of the individual?

This is the question now raised by terrorism (and, I must add, nuclear weapons are a higher form of the new global terrorism). Terrorists, regardless of the cause to which they are committed, think of themselves as warriors—that is, they are justified in their violence because it serves the ends of the communities to which they belong. They are "freedom" fighters. Those who are the victims of their violence tend, on the other hand, to see them more simply as individuals and, in doing so, come to the conclusion that they are degenerate thugs.

It is generally conceded that a realistic approach to human communities is one that recognizes violence as a part of the social condition. Durkheim might have suggested that it is "normal" or "typical" of human communities. At the same time, he would have pointed out that violence, in and of itself, is not the issue. The issue that must be addressed is the issue of *excessive* violence. The problem to be dealt with is whether or not the degree of violence being expressed by a given society is greater than might be expected given its state of development.

Obviously, the employment of nuclear weapons in a final confrontation between the great powers would have to be acknowledged by any sane observer of human affairs as the most extremely violent response to international antagonisms that one could imagine. So it is, perhaps, that we can find solace in Durkheim's philosophy. Although it is true that violence is normal to all societies, there might be social constraints placed on the extent to which violence can be carried. There is reason to hope that modern highly integrated societies, to a greater extent than individuals, are less likely to engage in all-out violent responses to situations. The reason for saying this is that it also happens to be "normal" for human societies to sustain themselves over time.

So, Durkheim might respond to this discussion by noting that it is unusual—in fact, it is practically unheard of—for an entire community to destroy itself as a collectively established action. What is typical is for communities or social systems to surrender to frustrating conditions rather than commit collective suicide. Individuals occasionally "run amok." Societies, however, are slower to respond to circumstances and, therefore, are less inclined to rely on "final solutions." This is the position taken by those who believe nuclear war, should it take place, will not come about as a consequence of rationally decided strategies between the major powers. Instead, if it takes place, it will be the result of an accident—the misreading of a radar scope, the accidental firing of a missile, or a misjudgment by a submarine commander whose communications system inexplicably goes dead.

I shall refer a number of times in this book to the current debate over whether nuclear war means nuclear "winter" and the end of the world or a nuclear "autumn." That scientists are even bothering to argue the issue is interesting in its own way. With respect to the nuclear winter issue, what is being argued is whether we can be absolutely certain that engaging in an all-out war in this modern age will be suicidal at a social or total level. What makes the argument especially interesting is the question of what defines social suicide in this instance. Military planners and policy strategists do not hesitate to talk about losing 20 or 30 million of their own people. This, for more than a few strategists, would not be considered "suicide." For others it might come plenty close enough — being a cultural "basket case" might be worse than losing it all.[8]

In any case, there is, for the first time in human history, a serious concern over whether we might collectively destroy ourselves. In other words, societal suicide is now a possibility. If it is, then we might wonder whether the nature of individual suicides might shed any light on such a happening. Durkheim was interested in the suicide of individuals because he thought that through the study of suicide subtle and previously unsuspected aspects of human social interrelations might be uncovered.

ANOMIE AND NUCLEAR ARMS

Nuclear war and suicide are morbid topics, but they are serious aspects of the world in which we live and therefore deserve our serious attention. Durkheim examined individual suicide as a sociological rather than a psychological study. He raised the question of whether it was possible that suicide was, for some forms of social system, a normal pattern. If so, then how might one go about trying to establish the connection between suicide and social forms in such a way as to show that suicide is a sociological (communal) as well as a psychological (individual) event?

The conception of the problem was brilliant. Keep in mind that this work was carried out a century ago. Durkheim argued that what appeared to be an unusually individualistic sort of action was, in fact, tied into the social fabric. The individual person committing suicide might think it was because he or she had suffered a personal indignity or frustration. However, at a different level the suicide took place, Durkheim suggested, because the suicide victim lived in a particular kind of social structure. Durkheim's research was directed toward the general goal of forcing people to become more aware of the subtlety and power of social forces. If he could demonstrate that a dramatically individualistic action, suicide, was associated with forms of communal organization, then he had established the significance of sociological studies. In a day and age that tended to focus almost exclusively on psychologistic approaches to human problems, it was a *tour de force* effort.

Now we can ask the question: If suicide is associated with social forms, what kind of social form is likely to develop a high incidence of suicide as a normal social condition?

We can consider only two of the forms of relationship between the individual and the community that produce unusually high levels of suicide. The first form is one in which the individual is well integrated into the community and responds to its demands without question. If, then, the community calls on the individual to sacrifice himself or herself, the individual does so willingly. Durkheim referred to this as *altruistic suicide*. A commonly used example of this form of suicide is the Japanese practice of *seppuku* — more commonly referred to in Western culture as *hara kiri*. The term *hara kiri* is from the Japanese *hara* for "belly" and *kiri* for "cut." *Hara kiri* is a traditional form of suicide in which death is caused by a self-inflicted cut into the abdomen.

This form of suicide is of great interest to anyone concerned with human issues and the nature of human action. It implies that people can, under proper social conditions, accept communal directives that contradict what might seem to be more "fundamental" biological or physiological imperatives. That is, if we presume the desire to live is both strong and virtually universal among living creatures, then the power of social control is revealed in the extent to which it can interfere with the biological urge to survive.

Altruistic suicide is not limited, of course, to Eastern countries. It can be found in any social community where the individual is heavily inculcated with a sense of loyalty and duty to the group or where the individual's personal identity is closely tied in with his or her social identity. If, for some reason, the community must call on the individual to commit the ultimate sacrifice, the individual does so because there is no distinction between the character of the individual and the social position occupied by the person in the community. A pertinent example appeared in the newspapers recently when a Japanese man committed suicide because his croquet team did not perform as well as he thought it should in a national competition. At least that was the ostensible reason for his suicide.

There is another form of suicide that Durkheim believed took place in communities where the individual is not tightly constrained by the norms of the community. Durkheim found, for example, that the suicide rates for Catholics and Protestants differed considerably in Europe at the turn of the century. His data suggested that Protestant groups generally had a higher rate than Catholics. The greater religious freedom found in Protestant communities, Durkheim argued, placed the individual in more uncertain circumstances. The social bond is a major organizing element in our lives. To lose our position with respect to the community can have an effect on whether we want to continue to live. Durkheim referred to this form of suicide as *anomic suicide*.

As we saw earlier, anomie means to be without a name or without norms or laws. With this term Durkheim introduced a novel concept into modern social philosophy. Basically, he argued that we are social creatures. When our social existence becomes uncertain or ambiguous or remote, we experience profound distress. In its extreme forms, this can lead to a moment when we feel we would rather be dead than continue living in a state of social namelessness. We would expect, then, to find that people whose statuses are ill-defined or confused would be more inclined to end their lives through suicide. A modern example might be the astonishing increase in suicide among American young people over the past decades. If any group in

American society today faces problems with regard to its status or its identity, it is that of young people. They are regarded neither as children nor as adults. They have no well-defined rituals that tell them where they belong within the greater social system. They must manufacture their own cliques and cults if they are to find an identity, and they appear to be doing this with great fervor.

We are speculating here on the topic of suicide, and we are drawing on Durkheim to provide us with a foundation for such speculation. Do Durkheim's musings on individual suicide provide us with a basis for speculating about the nuclear impasse? There is a tremendous difference between suicide at the individual level and suicide at a collective level.

Before moving into this morbid, but nonetheless vital topic, it is necessary to note that cultural suicide might occur in either of two ways. The form we will discuss in detail has to do with cultural suicide that is a consequence of the death of all of the members of a given culture. It is, of course, possible for everyone to remain alive and change from one cultural form to another. In this circumstance cultural suicide would have taken place even though the members of the culture remain alive. It should be self-evident that it is not in the nature of human cultures to "commit suicide" in either form.

The case of the followers of the Reverend Jim Jones a few years ago suggests how exceptional group suicide is. In this case a cult group left the United States to settle in Guyana in South America. According to press reports, their leader called on all of his followers to commit suicide by drinking Kool-Aid laced with cyanide. Although the group effort was not completely successful — a number of people ran into the woods — the fact that a large number of people committed mass suicide at the request of their spiritual leader was shocking news. Even so, by no means was this an event that could be considered the self-destruction of an entire culture.

Individual suicides are relatively common; collective suicide is rare. Leaders of groups may talk about fighting "to the last man, woman, and child," but the fact is that fighting to this extreme rarely takes place. What is much more common is for groups, when confronted with bitter options, to accept the option that offers hope for continuation. In World War II, for example, surrender was a bitter option for the Japanese, but rather than suffer total annihilation, they surrendered. Japan, remember, traditionally accepted personal or individual suicide as an honorable form of atoning for disgrace. Yet Japan could not accept collective suicide as a way of meeting the disgrace of defeat in war. I cannot help adding that, at least insofar as Japan is concerned, it was a wise decision. Japan is now alive and well and, if current trends continue, a much more likely candidate to dominate American industry and commercial interests than is Russia within the next several decades.

Individuals, then, commit suicide while cultural and social systems retain their continuity. This situation has apparently endured throughout the entire history of humanity. However, we live in a unique time. For the first time in history cultural suicide is a subject that demands thought. There is evidence indicating that the major restraint on the nuclear powers at the present time is the possibility of cultural suicide. That is, any kind of nuclear exchange carries with it the strong likelihood that all involved will be destroyed. This is the underlying premise of détente achieved through Mutually Assured Destruction (MAD).

In *The Fate of the Earth*, a popular book of a few years ago dealing with nuclear war, Jonathan Schell offered a brooding passage, taking up a third of the book, on the possibility of the extinction of life on earth.[9] Certainly it is something to think about. In fact, however, we simply do not know whether nuclear arms mean the end of life on earth. Probably they do not. Something will survive. Nonetheless, the meaning of extinction is something we should think about. At a lower level, we need to consider, not the overwhelming question of total extinction but, instead, the possibility of cultural suicide. How people respond to this morbid question determines how they view the feasibility of nuclear war.

Durkheim's concepts of altruistic and anomic suicide have, so far, simply drawn us toward the idea of cultural suicide in general. In keeping with the general character of Durkheim's thinking, we noted that individual and cultural suicide are two distinctly different matters. Anomic suicide, for example, requires that there be a community and that the individual somehow be separated from it. This might happen in the case of a displaced person or it could come about, as is the case with Protestantism, through cultural traditions that emphasize individuality and thereby separate the individual from the greater community. (I simplified matters by ignoring Durkheim's notion of *egoistic suicide*. I can only recommend that anyone interested in pursuing the matter more intensely review Durkheim's approach in its original form.) In either case, there is a community and there are individuals whose lives within that community are affected by the manner in which it is organized.

But entire cultures, by definition, are not parts of greater communities. A culture cannot experience anomie nor can it experience altruism or, for that matter, anything else. A culture cannot experience anything. So, it seems, the concepts offered by Durkheim do not have any special significance in considering the possibility of cultural suicide.

Yet, it remains an interesting question. First, is cultural suicide possible? In this day and age it seems conservative to point out, at the very least, that it is possible. If we are more liberal, we might be inclined to say it is even probable. If it is, then what kind of understanding might social theory bring to this kind of happening? Here the task of theory is to direct our thinking toward an examination of what is not known through what is known. We can presume that cultural suicide would not occur because all of the people of a nation-state suddenly decided it would be a good idea to give up on life. In fact, there would be massive resistance at a popular level to the threat of cultural extermination. Indeed, this is the collective justification for the construction of nuclear weapons. They are intended to protect us against annihilation. The irony in nuclear weapons is that they are capable of doing the very thing they are designed to prevent.

If cultural suicide takes place, it will come about through the actions of a small minority of the total sociocultural system. Whoever acts, in whatever fashion, to make use of nuclear weapons as a defensive or offensive gesture will have to be aware that in such action human civilization, as we now know it, will come to an end. In that more general sense, the act will imply a suicidal consequence. The individual who carries out the act will be aware that it means the end not only of the lives of others but also almost certainly of his or her own life as well.

Cultural suicide, if it is now a possibility, will come out of the fact that those who believe we should fight and die to the last person are now in a position to carry out such a program. In the past, there were leaders who rhetorically spoke of fighting to the last person. However, the logistics of the times would not allow it. As a result, wars did not result in the demise of everyone associated with the losing side. There are occasional historical instances where large numbers of people were destroyed on the losing side, but not as a consequence of a suicidal commitment to continue fighting. Now, the military-political leadership of modern nation-states can put teeth in the rhetoric of "last man" stands.

Coming back to the Durkheimian concepts of altruistic and anomic forms of suicide, we can hardly attribute anomie to the leadership of today's major powers. If anything, they are astonishingly dedicated to the social systems they represent and the work that is assigned them. The decision to launch a nuclear strike, if such a decision is ever made, will come from the dedication and the same motives as those that led samurai warriors of feudal Japan to kill themselves when their leader asked them to.

I am thinking here only of a strategic decision to use nuclear weapons. I am not including in this discussion either an accidental launching of a missile or the launching of a missile by a confused or even possibly insane submarine commander. Although political and military observers are pretty much agreed that the likelihood of nuclear war as the consequence of a decisive or planned action is unlikely, the records inform us that such decisions have been given much serious thought.[10]

From a sociological point of view, the question is: What kind of social circumstances would lead people to think in this manner? What would lead people to conclude that the world had become so dangerous that the only way to cope with the danger is to destroy everything? The only conclusion we can reach, when we review the matter from a Durkheimian stance, is that such action would have to come from a modern warrior-elite caste totally integrated into a declining order. It would have to be someone who seriously believed that it is better for everyone to be dead than to be Red or, in some other fashion, different.

We are in danger not because we are losing our sense of social purpose but because people believe they understand it all too well. If nuclear war comes about as a result of a decisive act, rather than through accident, the decision will be based on the belief that total physical catastrophe and loss is preferred to the loss of what we commonly refer to as "a way of life." The decision will be made by those who are, oddly enough, acting in a totally altruistic manner.

SUMMARY

We began our application of Durkheim's theories to the issue of nuclear war by suggesting in a purely speculative fashion, that what Durkheim named *collective representations* promote uncritical and highly emotional personal involvements with the collectives being represented. At a time when nuclear weapons are being brandished, we might consider it advisable to move toward less emotional and more critical attitudes. However, following Durkheim, we saw that even though this might seem rationally desirable, it could be sociologically dangerous. Collective representations, from a Durkheimian point of view, are essential to any ongoing human collective effort.

Our discussion of the concept of social normalcy led us to make two observations. First, the United States seems to be unusually violent when compared with other social systems at a similar stage of development. This is relevant to a discussion of attitudes toward war and the violent solution of social concerns. Second, we noted that while it is nearly impossible to define what we mean by social normalcy, this does not prevent politicians, journalists, and others whose task it is to shape public opinion from claiming that they know. Here, the lesson we get from the study of Durkheim is that we should be on guard when anyone tells us they know what is "normal" or "proper" with respect to large-scale social structures.

Finally, in a speculative and uncertain fashion, we drew on the ideas that Durkheim brought to his studies of human suicide. We noted that, if nothing else, the idea of "cultural suicide" helps make clear the distinction between cultures and individuals. Individuals commonly commit suicide; whole cultures practically never do. We concluded that if such an event ever occurs, it will be the result of actions taken by men and women who are in unique positions of leadership and who are highly dedicated to their societies. Ironically, then, the least altruistic act one could ever possibly imagine will be generated by the most altruistic and public-spirited members of our culture.

Durkheim's works provide the reader with a Gallic sociological mentality. We discover the ironies and paradox of social life in his writing. Durkheim was clever as well as profound. His ideas lead one quickly away from ordinary understandings of human social life and social affairs into a realm of pervasive and powerful forces.

Above all, Durkheim remains, even today, one of the best correctives I can think of for the kind of thinking that attempts to resolve social issues by turning to psychological characteristics. The central message repeated over and over in Durkheim's work is that social reality is not the same as psychological reality. The demands of a collective system are not the same as those of the individual.

Durkheim wrote a short essay with the title "Who Wanted the War?" In it he blamed Germany for World War I. He also noted that, as individuals, people on the whole do not want war. Why, then, is war so common in the history of humankind? If we are not desirous of war as individuals, then what leads us into these horrifying and ugly killing fields? The answer is more sociological, said Durkheim, than psychological.

Chapter 3

Karl Marx: Weapons, Economic Interests, and Alienation

THE STRUGGLE FOR JUSTICE

Two figures from the Victorian period dominate how we now look at ourselves in this, the latter part of the 20th century — Sigmund Freud and Karl Marx. Both were savagely attacked by representatives of older philosophies. Both enlisted legions of interpreters and revisionists who altered their original works to the point where, in a number of instances, they are hardly recognizable. Both generated concepts and ideas that were powerful enough to become a part of day-to-day understandings of personal and economic affairs — used by ordinary people as well as writers and professional intellectuals.

The fate of their work, in recent times, is peculiar. Both remain popular in academic circles — although Freud is given greater respect in Europe than in the United States. Although Freudian thought is acceptable across a wide range of status and economic levels in the United States, Marx remains threatening. Perhaps this situation tells us something about what can happen to those writers who commit themselves to a serious concern with justice. Those who poke about in the body politic or the economic corpus, attempting to open up and reveal unjust and unfair actions, are not generally treated kindly by vested interests.

As we enter into a discussion of Marx's ideas, I recommend that you set aside prejudices — pro or con — and draw on the powerful and eminently sensible aspects of Marxist reasoning. After all, Marx was a product of the later industrial revolution. He strongly endorsed virtually everything dear to an American's heart — productivity, consumption, material wealth, happiness through industrial riches, peace, labor, love, decency, fairness, justice, progress, and stability.

The approach taken to Marx is the same as that taken toward all the other theorists considered in this book as well as anybody else who seriously writes about human affairs. His work should be read, questioned, and used where it can be used and abandoned where it cannot. It should not be accepted uncritically as dogma.[1] I recall a moment in the early 1970s when a young, vehemently radical college student waved a tiny Marxist tract in front of my face and shouted, "Everything you need to know about economics and sociology is in here." He then called me a bourgeois lackey or something similar and we parted company. Now, 15 years later, I hope the memory of that earlier moment is an embarrassment to him — otherwise, how will he know he ever grew up? There can be little doubt that the entire library of Marxist work that now exists does not tell us all there is to know about human societies. However, Marxism does remain one of the most influential and engaging of all modern political philosophies.

We can find much to like in Marx's work and much that is faulty. So it is with all social philosophy and social theory. Marxism should not be leaned on as gospel nor, certainly, should it be rejected out of fear. There are telling arguments in Marx's writing, and they are worth our consideration. At the same time, there is much that calls for critical reexamination. No one has the last word in explaining why people conduct themselves as they do. Marx is no exception.

There is considerable irony and paradox in the American attitude toward Marxist thinking. Americans accept much of the Marxist argument — materialism, class interests, economic interpretations of social issues, and even a vision of social progress in which people will be freed from economic forms of oppression. Americans are probably less accepting of the notion that the ruling and laboring classes are in conflict. Even though American social thought has strong elements of materialism and economic determinism in it, Marxism is generally viewed with suspicion as a tool of authoritarian socialist governments. It is looked on as inflammatory. Some even look on it as worse than a false theory; for them it is also subversive and corrupting. Marxism seems to evoke extreme responses — on the part of both those who espouse Marxist doctrines and those who reject them.

A more moderate position is taken here. Much of Marxist thinking is worth reviewing. What he had to say about contemporary Western forms of economic practice — and the societies coming out of these practices — offers a powerful format for examining present-day social and moral issues. Nevertheless, those who elevate Marxist thought to the pinnacle of dogmatic truth abandon the agony of remembering how little we really know about ourselves. In this regard, they are no different from any of the other, all-too-numerous, men and women who find comfort in dogma.

Karl Marx was born in 1818 and died in 1883. No other political or social philosopher of recent times inspired so much hope and, simultaneously, generated so much hate. Now, in the final decades of the 20th century — and over one hundred years since Marx passed from the scene — there is considerable truth in the observation that modern nations divide among themselves in terms of whether they are Marxist or not. It is a testimonial to the power of social philosophy in general and Marxism in particular.

No observer of the modern political world can pretend to be informed and at the same time be ignorant of at least the elements of Marxist thought. At the core of Marx's contributions to political writing is an impassioned, driving revulsion over the inhumanity of the early years of the industrial revolution. Marx grounded his analysis in human economic practices, but his primary concern was a quest for justice. Marx saw, in ways that we are not capable of seeing in this more sterile age, the extent to which workers—men, women and children—were brutalized in the mines and industries of Europe. He responded by trying to comprehend, through an act of the intellect, what was happening. Why were people being forced to work in such unnatural ways—sad-eyed children working in factories from dawn to dusk, women working in the mines, men exhausted from long hours and little pay? What was the reason for it? Why had it come about? What had so hardened the human spirit that it no longer seemed to care about the countless poor and impoverished in its midst even as nations were becoming wealthy in ways never previously dreamed of?

Certainly one cannot fault Marx for raising the question. His analysis of the situation, given the limited information available to scholars in his time, was brilliant. More to the point, it was an astonishingly thorough analysis. The elementary theme behind Marxist theory is simple—there is a division between the rich and the poor. Exploitation is a way of life for those in power and, more interestingly, they have little choice in the matter. The rich exploit and take advantage of the poor. They must do this, essentially, to avoid being exploited themselves. Marx's modern economic world is a vicious jungle, bloody red in fang and claw. However, philosophers and ordinary people had already been aware of this situation over the centuries. The division of the world into the rich and the poor was generally conceded. What, then, created the fuss over Marxism?

We can be concerned with only several things here. First, Marx argued that the impoverished classes are the product of economic forces. Poverty is not a moral condition but an economic one. This statement does not sound radical today because the extent to which poverty was viewed as a moral or God-induced condition in earlier times is difficult for us to comprehend in this more secular era. Just as the nobility were ordained to rule by godly intervention, so the poor were also a product of God's divine plan. Marx could not accept this. He was a naturalist and a rationalist. He wanted to know what was happening on the basis of what could be observed and directly experienced. That experience, in turn, had to be subjected to severe rational questioning. Rather than explaining poverty through religious ideas, he concluded that poverty is a direct and natural consequence of the exploitation of labor. Furthermore, those in positions of economic power have little choice but to force wages to as low a level as possible—thereby creating poverty.

Second, Marx thoroughly documented his claim that the interests of those who owned the means of production and the interests of laborers are antagonistic within a competitive economic system—there is a perpetual structural conflict between people in terms of their class interests.

Third, Marx argued that the conflict could be resolved by establishing a state in which the efforts and the interests of labor are justly recognized and accepted.

Finally, he argued that the excesses of exploitation within the modern competitive industrial state would force labor to revolt and bring about a new socialist community in which no person would be permitted to profit at another person's expense. In sum, he offered hope to the oppressed. His work was a work of great idealism and humanistic concern. To ignore this aspect of Marxism is to ignore its strongest element of appeal. He offered a vision of social reform in which the inhumanity of people toward other people would eventually be curbed so that we would all find fulfillment in our productive lives and enjoy the full fruits of our labor. His program was nothing less than a program designed to bring justice back to a world in which injustice so obviously prevails.

What made Marxist theory unique was the thoroughness of the analysis —the richness of the data and historical records that Marx drew upon. Marx also moved outside the realm of religious moralizing. The long historical sweep of human divisions, from a Marxist point of view, was a natural process that came out of humanly created structures. It was not a God-given order; it did not flow from any divine plan. People were the source of their problems and people would, eventually, resolve them.

This made Marx a target of those who turn to God to explain the human condition. His vigorously antireligious arguments still make him anathema to the religious community. The surprising recent radicalization of a small cadre of Latin American Catholic priests provides us with an interesting possible exception. However, this development is unusual. Where poverty is as potent as it is in parts of Latin America, it is difficult not to see the validity of economic interpretations of human travail and misery.

At the same time, the argument that the wealthy and the elite elements of society exploited the poor made Marx the target of the powerful and the entrenched. For centuries the wealthy and the noble had been looked on as the brightest and the best the world had to offer — after all, one of the things wealth can buy is a celebrated reputation. Now Marx was calling them, in effect, a bunch of mean-spirited, tight-fisted, exploitive, inhuman economic machines. The repository of good was in labor. So the battle continues down to the present.

Marx, however, offered more than a rational, scholarly analysis of the historical forces that, as he viewed the world, had brought about the inhuman events of his time. He did more than identify the true nature of the grand historical game and the teams who were playing it. He also offered a vision of social reform — of a new society and economy — that would serve the interests of all people rather than cater to the status pretensions of a restricted few. There was, at least, a way out of the lethal historical conflicts that had tormented humankind over the millennia. The new society would have to come, however, from revolutionary struggle. The road to the new Utopia would be splattered with blood.

At this point, of course, Marxist philosophy becomes fearsome, for it not only calls on the exploited to take up arms, but also calls on them to aim their rifles and cannon against the respected, entrenched, and powerful, but exploitive, leadership of the community—who just happen to control an impressive armory of their own. If nothing else, we might concede that Marx honestly recognized the problems inherent in any serious quest for justice and fairness in the world.

Conflict between the owners of the means of production and the working classes, he argued, is inevitable. At the same time, he believed the final resolution of the conflict would be one that would bring about a socialist state where class interests would give way to the interests of all people. In sum, Marx offered the exploited and the oppressed people of the world a Utopian vision. At last, so it seemed, there was a possible way of breaking the endless generation of human poverty and misery. Much more important than this, however, was the hope that the seemingly eternal cycles of human conflict could be broken. Marxist thought is strikingly visionary. This fact is all the more unusual because it is a secular, materialistic philosophy rather than a mystical approach to life. The combination of hardheaded materialism combined with progressive visionary optimism gives it great appeal. Marxist philosophy is usually included among so-called conflict theories by sociologists. However, it is important to see that Marxism rejects conflict in principle by arguing there is a final form of conflict that will eliminate conflict—a kind of revolution to end all revolutions.

ECONOMIC CONTRADICTIONS

Marx saw modern capitalistic economies forced to deal with internal contradictions of various kinds. Most of us are familiar with the Marxist argument that any economic system—other than the final socialist community—contains within it the seeds of its own destruction. For example, the industrialist operating within a capitalistic economy is placed in a situation where reducing the costs of production calls for minimizing the costs of labor. However, labor constitutes the market for the goods being produced by the industry. The industrialist, then, is faced with the simultaneously contradictory demands of having to reduce wages on the one hand and enriching the market that labor represents on the other. John Maynard Keynes, of course, later suggested this contradiction could be resolved by programs that would simply lop off the inconsistency by enriching the market through deficit spending—a solution that evidently has its own problems.

Another internal contradiction arose out of what Marx saw as an inexorable movement toward ever greater and greater concentration of the ownership of the means of production into the hands of fewer and fewer people. In the competitive struggle for advantage and profit characteristic of capitalistic ventures, less efficient firms would fail and come under the domination of more efficient firms. However, as this occurred, competition would be undercut by the rise of monopolistic structures.

Marx expected the internal contradictions in industrial-capitalistic economies to lead to erratic conflicts represented, on occasion, by periods of boom and bust, stability and instability. Eventually, these fluctuations would lead to such severe disruption and hardship that massive revolution would be the only response. It appears he was wrong in this judgment — at least in the short run.

He grossly underestimated the extent to which modern Western economies would make concessions to labor interests. He also was not able to anticipate technological changes — modern television, for example — that would both ease the burdens of labor and also provide diversions from political concerns. The anticipated socialist revolutions did not take place in Western economies. At the same time, we should not ignore the fact that even anti-Marxist nations such as the United States incorporated reforms that, objectively viewed, are socialist in nature.[2]

Nevertheless, Marxist logic is compelling. And the final verdict is not in. Even though capitalistic countries remain lively and deal effectively with economic problems *within* their boundaries, the problems posed by the contradictions inherent in capitalism were shoved outward, so to speak, onto the shoulders of third-world nations. The slums of major cities in capitalistic nations such as England and the United States testify that serious problems still exist. The slums of third-world nations are a horrifying testimonial to the fact that global economics are still in a primitive stage of development. In sum, within nationally defined capitalistic systems sufficient reforms took place to weaken the Marxist argument; at a global level, the injustices that infuriated Marx in 1850 still continue and appear to worsen.

If nothing else, a reading of Marx forces us to respond to the age-old moral question of the extent to which we are our brother's keeper.

Within national boundaries, then, uncontrolled capitalism has been reined in. Virtually all European economies moved from the unbridled capitalistic practices of the late 19th century toward more collectivist solutions. England, France, Spain, and Italy, to name just a few major powers, adopted socialistic programs. In 1982 France, for example, nationalized six of its largest industrial concerns. Ninety-five percent of France's banking activity is controlled by the state. The United States is virtually alone in its ideological commitment to noncollective solutions to collective problems.

In the following sections of this essay emphasis is given to three Marxist concepts or ideas:

1. Dialectical materialism

2. Surplus wealth

3. Alienation

Before we turn to these ideas, let me mention that Marxist scholarship is tremendously varied and now includes an overwhelmingly broad range of interpretations. I will draw on basic, simple Marxism as it is set forth in

Marx's major work *Capital*. This theory is now commonly referred to as "vulgar" or common Marxism. Vulgar Marxism is as good a place to start as any. It represents Marx before European and American intellectuals had an opportunity to torment his ideas. It is Marx wearing rolled-up sleeves and overalls. It is a rugged piece of work, one that impresses us with its honesty, simplicity, and breadth and the fact that it represents a serious struggle with the problem of human injustice.

DIALECTICAL MATERIALISM

At the heart of Marx's theories is the belief that the material order is more fundamental than the realm of ideas and beliefs. This point of view is referred to as "materialism." Marxist thought uses the human capacity to produce material goods as a basis for the interpretation of social development. Marx stated it as follows:

> The mode of production in material life determines the general character of the social, political and spiritual processes of life. It is not the consciousness of men that determines their existence, but, on the contrary, their social existence [that is, material existence] determines their consciousness.[3]

If we accept the argument that the social processes of life are determined by the mode of production in material life, it follows that consciousness itself is determined by the mode of production that prevails in a society. This notion, certainly, is not at odds with popular American conceptions of what makes life worthwhile and what makes a social system work. Marx is saying, in a sense, that at the bottom of everything — systems of justice, religious practices, sexual morality, leisure activities, family structures, and so forth — is what we might broadly refer to as business and industry. When former Secretary of Defense Charles (Engine Charlie) Wilson suggested that what is good for General Motors is good for the country, he was, albeit unwittingly, sloganizing Marx's fundamental idea — that the economy forms the bedrock of the society.

Marxist materialism is generally referred to as "dialectical" materialism. The word *dialectic* is derived from a Greek term referring to argumentation. In an argument a position is taken, a counterargument is offered, and the argument is then resolved. Marx looked on the history of humankind as a battle between vast forces — a kind of unending argument between those who control wealth and those who do not, between the material realm and the realm of ideas, between those who must sell their time to live and those who buy the time others must sell.

Where European philosophers were arguing that history is a matter of a clash between ideas, Marx argued that it is a clash of material forces — the forces of production and exchange and consumption. Instead of viewing history as, let us say, a confrontation between orthodox and heretical religious movements or Christian and Islamic cultures, Marx viewed history as a confrontation between people in terms of their material interests.

In an argument an idea (a thesis) can imply its opposite (antithesis) and the ensuing debate can lead to a compromise point of view (synthesis). Marx borrowed this observation and applied it to the forces of production, suggesting that any kind of productive system (thesis) contains within it a contrary force (antithesis) and the resultant strains produce a new productive order (synthesis). The new system, as it establishes itself, generates internal contradictions that lead to a continuation of the dialectical process. History, then, is a process of necessary and inexorable change. Struggle is unavoidable. Struggle is not only unavoidable between nations, but it is unavoidable within nations as well—as the laboring classes are forced to struggle against the entrenched interests of those who possess the means of productivity.

As we just noted, there was nothing especially new in the idea that history is a record of struggle and turmoil. What was new was the slant Marx offered. The important struggle is not at the level of ideas but is "deeper." It is embedded in the structure of the economic system itself. Where previous social philosophies, especially religious interpretations of the human condition, viewed struggle as a product of the imperfect nature of human character, Marx located the struggle within natural economic processes. All modern economic doctrine, Marxist or not, accepts the rudimentary idea that human economic conditions are best explained in terms of economic principles without resort to concepts that move outside the economic realm.

The relevance of this for the nuclear crisis is straightforward. Nuclear weapons serve economic interests. They both protect established wealth and also serve the economic interests of those who are able to profit from the construction and maintenance of such weapons. Later we shall consider more subtle possibilities.

SURPLUS WEALTH

We now take surplus wealth as a given, although in simpler societies wealth is generally sparse and life is lived from moment to moment. It is not unusual, for example, for members of a hunting society to return from a successful hunt, apportion the meat and food to various members of the community, feast and eat until nearly everything is consumed, and then go back out for more. Under these conditions, surplus wealth is minimal. Modern economies accumulate vast amounts of surplus wealth—that is, wealth above and beyond the simple necessities of individual members of the society.

Two questions are raised by the fact of surplus wealth. First, why would people be led into producing more than they need as individuals? What provided the "push" that moved earlier simple communal systems from marginal living with minimal surpluses to modern systems with vast surpluses? We cannot explore this interesting question here. That large numbers of simple cultures managed to survive over periods of thousands of years without amassing much surplus wealth or even being interested in the possibility suggests that such wealth is not the product of a natural individual desire for wealth. The answer lies in the historical development of social and economic communities.

The second question, which is of special relevance for the exploration of modern intra- and international relations, has to do with the question of how national economies deal with the problem of surplus wealth. Once you have a big pile of surplus wealth, what do you do with it? What kinds of problems does it pose?

For Marx the question of surplus wealth was especially pertinent. He argued that surplus wealth is created through the ability of the laborer to produce more than is needed for simple sustenance. It is difficult to argue against this. More important than the question of how surplus wealth comes about is the question of what happens to it after it is created. This surplus wealth, Marx believed, is taken from labor by the owners of the means of production in the form of "profit." The creation of the idea of "profit" in economic practice is a complex issue. Here we must be satisfied simply with the fact that, if nothing else, Marx leads us toward a deeper questioning of what profit is and how it comes about.

The elemental moral argument in Marxist ideology can be stated clearly: Labor should receive the full value of that which it produces. The real world, however, is one in which labor is given back only part of what it produces. The producers of wealth are not, in the final analysis, the ones who have much to say about what is done with the wealth they bring into being. The taking of surplus wealth from individuals requires force of some kind. How do you get people to give up what they worked to create? By what devices do the owners of the means of production co-opt the wealth created by labor? Marx summed up the process by drawing on a general term — exploitation.

He went further, arguing that bourgeois economies rely on powerful agents of production such as factories or large mines and farms. Bourgeois economies are defined by the fact that these agents of production are not owned by those who work in them. Moreover, economic pressures lead inexorably to conditions in which owners are forced to give laborers no more than is necessary to sustain them in their work. This process antedates modern capitalism, of course. For example, in feudal economies surplus wealth was taken from the producing classes by the elite or noble classes through military force. Controlling profits was important then as it is now. Consider the fact that in medieval Europe it was illegal on certain estates for peasants to grind flour at home. They were required to bring their flour to the mill controlled by the lord of the manor who then charged for the service. (The economics of criminality are suggested by this anecdote — imagine having a bag of "hot" flour in your pantry; that is, one you ground yourself instead of taking it to the lord's mill.)

Marx predicted a grim future for modern economies — massive poverty, depressions, wealth that would become tremendously concentrated in the hands of a few, and — throughout all of this — the rampant exploitation of labor. At the same time, it is evident that modern economies are not as grim as this picture suggests they should be. The labor forces of western Europe and North America are relatively well paid and comfortable. In part this can be attributed not only to the successes of laissez-faire capitalism but also to the organizational success of labor unions. Though, as Marx anticipated, labor had to fight and fight bitterly for its current position in Western economies, it did not overthrow capitalism. The labor battles of the late 19th and early 20th centuries in the United States were more reformistic than revolutionary. Labor fought for higher wages and better working conditions. It fought, as it were, for more equality with management, but not to over-throw management or industrial ownership. Moreover, there has been a major transformation in modern Western economies. They are not pure capitalistic systems — political and economic rhetoric to the contrary. They are mixed systems.

In modern nation-states the separation of the worker from surplus wealth is not so much the direct work of the owners of industrial systems as it is the work of governments. *However, it must be constantly kept in mind that the government is primarily in the hands of and is strongly influenced by people of wealth.* For example, during his first term of office President Reagan appointed 160 judges. Twenty-three percent of these appointees were millionaires. Million-aires make up less than one-half of one percent of the general population. Only 2 of the 160 appointees were blacks. Blacks make up roughly 12 percent of the total population. Our government represents the people, but it seems to represent some people and their interests much more vigorously than it represents the interests of others.[4]

Whether it is government in the form of modern democratic bureaucra-cies or government in the form of feudal lords, the means for removing surplus wealth from those who produce it remains the same — force. The important thing is that decisions with regard to what will be done with surplus wealth are removed from the control of those who created it and are given to others, whose task is to decide what should be done with it. A Marxist perspective suggests that if surplus wealth comes under the control of industrialists, it will be used to promote the interests of the industrialists. A Marxist attitude toward government is never far removed from a consider-ation of the economic context within which that government operates. The question remains: Whose interests are being served by government?

In terms of the nuclear arms issue, the question becomes: Do such arms protect the people or do they protect industrial, political, and monetary power? We shall consider this question in more detail after briefly examin-ing a third concept to come out of Marxist writing — the concept of alienation.

ALIENATION

Finally, we turn to a Marxist concept that greatly influenced Western social thought with regard to the relationship between the individual and the means of production. Marx argued that modern economic processes lead to the *alienation* of the individual. Alienation refers to estrangement—it is a process whereby what was once familiar is transformed into something no longer familiar, well known, accepted, or commonly acknowledged.

The modern factory, for example, is not concerned with individualized craftsmanship but with specialized productivity at an assembly line. In the process, the worker is alienated from the earlier form of personal work and craftsmanship that gave significance to his or her life. Modern life, in its various productive modes, created a new kind of person—a person alienated not only from older traditions, rituals, crafts, skills, and arts but also from a sense of community and ultimately even from an understanding of self.

The concept of alienation is similar to the notion of anomie in the writings of Emile Durkheim. However, the two concepts are also different. Durkheim attempted to deal with the question of what happens when a person becomes detached from social or communal controls and traditions. Anomie refers to being "nameless." It refers to a breakdown in the structure of norms and laws that hold communities of people together in an organizational whole. When the structure is strong, each individual within the community has a sense of worth or completeness of self. To experience anomie is to experience human existence without meaningful social content.

Alienation is a consequence of economic imperatives. For example, the drive to accumulate profit can alienate a manager from the human qualities and the feelings of those whose work must be managed. In such an instance, the manager is deeply caught up in economic norms that call for driving workers to perform at maximum capacity. Therefore, anomie is not the appropriate term—the manager is all too fully responding to the economic norms encompassing the moment. However, because the manager "loses contact" so to speak with other human beings and, finally, his or her own humanity, the manager becomes alienated.

People—men and women and children—of the modern era, from a Marxist perspective, have lost contact with the products of their efforts and, ultimately, each other. It is an age of alienation. Perhaps nothing in the whole of human history suggests a deeper degree of alienation than the fact that the world's new men of power rationally contemplate the wholesale, instantaneous, technological slaughter of hundreds of millions of people as a purely, coldly calculated, strategic matter. At least in the old days when you undertook the slaughter of large numbers of people you had to look them in the eye and listen to their screams as you pressed your sword into their protesting bodies.

Now, as C. Wright Mills so nicely phrased it, the cold manner has entered the souls of men. One is divorced from the product of one's labor. The cold manner is, at the personal level, the consequence of alienation stemming from economic forms.

THE MATERIAL FOUNDATIONS OF GENOCIDE

Let me preface this section by pointing out that a discussion of genocide is pertinent to a discussion of nuclear war and other human concerns. Nuclear war is, of course, war. Genocide is also a form of war or a consequence of warlike conditions. It is the ultimate expression of the desire to destroy a hated or unwanted population of human beings. In the discussion that follows, a Marxist treatment of genocide and related matters should be associated in your mind with some of the issues that underly nuclear threat and the desire to obliterate, by whatever means, a feared enemy.

The first American permanent colony was founded in Jamestown in 1607. The initial landing party consisted of Captain John Smith and 105 cavaliers. To the west stood the North American continent—an area of almost nine and a half million square miles. Within the short span of 300 years it was carved into separate nations, territories, and states and now contains a total population of approximately 400 million people.

The hunting-tribal economies of the Native Americans could not match, in physical or material power, the growing industrial systems of the settlers who came from Europe. The western migration swept over everyone and everything in its path. There are many ways to react to the western migrations of the pioneers—ranging from the maudlin sentimentality of Hollywood western movies to the jingoistic sloganizing of historians who looked on the westward movement as the fulfillment of what was referred to as a "Manifest Destiny"—a vision with religious overtones.[5]

A Marxist perspective is not so romantic. Essentially it claims that the demands of the new Western industrial economies were such that the expansion and development of markets and territories were inherent characteristics of the economic system itself. The new economy could not possibly survive on the basis of social systems that were effective for smaller hunting nomadic groups. Such systems were not tolerated and were eventually obliterated. Just how incongruent the Native American and the new arrivals from Europe were in their economic systems is suggested in the story of the sale of Manhattan Island by Native Americans to Peter Minuit in 1626 for roughly $24 worth of beads. The story is viewed, even today, as an example of a Western trader striking an ingeniously shrewd bargain for valuable property. More to the point, however, is the fact that the Indians were not of the same *economic* culture. They had little awareness of what the "trade" was about. Their understanding of property rights was by no means the same as the understandings of the new European arrivals for whom land was primarily a matter of property rights.

But there was more to it than simple naivete or "savage" innocence. The

Native Americans were not *economically* compatible. This meant they were, from a Marxist view, of no economic value — either as labor or in any other fashion as active participants in the new economic order. As a result, they were treated like any other object or being that is economically useless — they were, to use a current phrase, "trashed." The important point is that they were eliminated, again in terms of Marxist thought, because they were *economically* without value. They were not useful to the material interests of the new economy.

The westward expansion opened up an entire continent for what would now be called economic "development." The new economic system, brought from Europe, dedicated to competitive productivity and with the resources offered by six or seven million square miles of virgin country, generated wealth more rapidly than had ever before been believed possible. When Americans talk about transforming the wilderness, it seems at times as though the so-called virgin forests were unoccupied. Of course, there were large indigenous populations occupying the land before Captain Smith arrived.

We concede something to the Marxist position when we admit that it is difficult to view these early Native Americans as laborers, entrepreneurs, workers, or economic creatures in the same sense those who followed Captain Smith were. They were looked on as something else and eventually were destroyed or pushed aside because they were economically incompatible with the incoming European economic cultural forms.

WHO GETS TO SPEND THE SURPLUS WEALTH?

From 1607 when the first settlers were barely able to provide for their needs, down to 1985, the gross national product went from a few dollars to over three and a half trillion dollars. Three and a half trillion dollars, as a measure of wealth produced in a single year, is impossible to grasp by an act of the intellect. (The late Senator Everett Dirksen summed it up in a famous quote in which he said, in effect, that as a representative of the American people, he found himself having to spend a billion here and a billion there. He went on to add that pretty soon it adds up to a lot of money.) The "nouveau riche" nations are not simply wealthy, as nation-states, but are wealthy in terms so massive that their economies are beyond the comprehension of any single person or group of individuals. Such wealth can be talked about only in general terms.

It is evident that the tremendous sums of wealth found in modern nations are not distributed evenly among the people who produced it. If wealth were, for example, distributed evenly to each member of the working force in 1985, every employed person in the United States at the time would have been given approximately $30,000. The typical paycheck, *prior to taxation*, was roughly half that sum. It is not necessary to belabor the obvious point that governments or, as Marx might say, the ruling elites appropriate wealth. We are making note of the extent to which wealth is appropriated and, in the course of the appropriation, is removed from the discretion of those who created it.

The government publishes figures on sums of money it appropriates through various means. The figures in Table 3.1 were not corrected for inflation and they are, at best, only crude estimates. Even so, they suggest that the amount of funds appropriated by the government increased radically through the years. From 1960 to 1980 the government per capita appropriations increased sevenfold. During the same interval personal income levels increased about five and a half times. Or, to sum things up, people are getting rich, but the government or ruling elite is getting richer than the population in general—at least in terms of its ability to appropriate wealth.

Governments, once they appropriate funds, are confronted with the problem of the allocation of the wealth under their control. This is true of any modern state. From a Marxist point of view, the fundamental proposition directing these decisions is that such wealth should promote the economy. In a sense, the end of national wealth is to generate more national wealth. Marx did not believe in rhetorical arguments to the effect that such wealth is used to promote liberty, freedom, and democracy throughout the world. The wealth of nations is an instrument of national interests, and national interests are defined primarily in material terms, not lofty rhetoric. From a Marxist point of view, when material interests and loftier ideals clash, material interests prevail. Or, as the folk saying goes, money speaks louder than words. The maxim reduces Marxist thought to its barest bones.

Those who control money or, more properly, the means of production will use it to protect their interests—whatever such interests might be. Forms of protection vary, but the ultimate form of protection comes out of

TABLE 3.1

Appropriations by the Federal Government Compared with Total National Population, United States, 1890 to 1980.

(*Source*: U. S. Treasury Financial Management Service and Statistical Year Book.)

Year	Appropriations (in Millions)	Population (in Millions)	Per Capita Appropriation
1890	395	50	$ 8
1910	1,044	92	11
1925	3,748	115	33
1940	13,349	132	101
1950	52,867	151	350
1955	54,761	160	342
1960	80,170	178	450
1970	222,200	203	1,095
1980	690,391	220	3,138

the right to use force to assure security. One basic maxim of a Marxist perspective is that money is used to protect money. Capital protects capital. Obviously this is simplistic. Nonetheless, it helps clarify otherwise puzzling aspects of the relations between nations. Today we live with the puzzling situation in which our security — individual and collective — is placed in serious jeopardy in the name of attaining security. As we sought to make our lives more secure, we only made them less secure. This mad state of affairs is less puzzling if we begin to see the extent to which the elaboration of forceful devices is designed to protect capital rather than people.

One of the more unusual manifestations of this mentality was the development of a device about which little is written in the current press — the "neutron bomb." This weapon was greeted enthusiastically by Western nations. It was touted, at the time of its appearance, as a "clean" atomic device. (The rhetoric of nuclear weaponry makes an interesting study in its own right.) The major claim to fame of the neutron bomb, it seems, was its ability to destroy people without destroying the buildings, factories, and other forms of fixed capital in which they worked and lived. Less talk has been given to this weapon in recent years. It offers, however, further insights into the notion of alienation.[6] It also offers insights into the priorities of our times.

It is difficult not to offer Marx at least a small acknowledgment when thinking of the enthusiasm that first greeted early announcements of the neutron bomb. Science had come through with the most astonishing kind of accomplishment — a weapon that left buildings and factories standing while destroying thousands of people. The enemy could be destroyed while surrendering capital wealth intact. One wonders if it is possible for science to create an anti-neutron bomb that would destroy every last shred of material wealth while leaving all of the people alive. Your reaction to this tongue-in-cheek suggestion might give you some indication of how your priorities stack up with respect to materialistic versus nonmaterialistic approaches to life and the destruction of capital versus genocide.

So far our discussion of Marxist concepts has focused on the notion of materialism as an approach to interpreting human affairs. This perspective emphasizes economic over other human interests. Drawing on this perspective, several major points were made:

1. When people are not compatible with an economic system, they are harshly dealt with.

2. Economic concerns, at least in Western cultures, take precedence over humane concerns.

3. Recent history has seen the accumulation of vast amounts of surplus wealth.

4. The use of surplus wealth is determined by industrial or governmental elites.

5. Wealth is used to protect wealth.

These are a few of the fundamental conclusions that derive from a materialistic perspective. However, we defined Marxism as being both materialistic and dialectic. We now turn toward a few of the implications of a dialectical interpretation of human history.

THE DIALECTIC

The simplest version of the dialectic is to see it as an argument. Even in ordinary conversations we commonly find ourselves saying the contrary simply to sustain the conversation. A companion might say it is a nice day and we reply maybe it is, but still and all it is rather cloudy and looks like rain. This is a commonplace illustration of the dialectic. One person sets forth a thesis (It is a nice day) and another says something different, the antithesis, by replying it really is not all that nice. In this commonplace example the "tension" created by contrary statements becomes the basis for an extended discussion of the weather.

If history can be looked on as an extended discussion between people, then that discussion, from a Marxist point of view, comes out of a tension that exists between people. Marxism is commonly referred to as a "conflict" theory of history and human relations. The disparities between people in terms of material wealth — and the power such wealth confers on its owners — divide humankind into two fundamentally opposed categories or "classes." The members of one class must sell their labor to anyone willing to buy it. The members of the other class are those who control enough wealth to be able to purchase labor. As is the case with any rational buyer, those who purchase labor seek bargains.

Everything else being equal, the cheapest labor is hired (that is, bought). Marx looked on the relationship between labor and the purchasers of labor as one inherently in conflict. There is a simple economic logic to it: Labor wants to sell itself as dearly as possible, and the buyers want to purchase labor as cheaply as possible. Actually, for a long period, labor was willing to sell itself for something it called, vaguely, a "living wage." Obviously, the buyers of labor found ways to make such wages astonishingly low — after all, one can live at a bare subsistence level, even today, for a surprisingly small amount of money.

Let me note here that even though Marx definitely sided with labor in this conflict, he argued that the buyers of labor (capitalists) have little choice but to conform to market demands. An industrialist who paid more for labor than the going price, Marx observed, would risk losing everything to competitors who were willing to go with what the market established in terms of labor supply and demand. *The economic system itself* had divided people into opposing camps. Again, notice that Marx viewed this as a consequence of the natural progression of the economic order. That labor was pitted against capital was not something ordained by God or by an inherent flaw in human nature. It was the consequence of an economic system in which the quest for profit forced those who owned the means of production to create cheap labor. The only recourse of the working classes was to find some way to resist the cheapening of labor.

And so the Marxist vision views the sweep of history as one of conflict. At one level there is conflict between industrial powers in the quest for markets or, more broadly, the control of wealth. At another level, there is a conflict between the interests of capital and the interests of labor. Because the owners of capital are concerned with protecting wealth, it is in their interest to demean labor.

Thorstein Veblen, a turn-of-the-century American economist, wrote volumes on this subject. His *Theory of the Leisure Class* is an acerbic commentary on the extent to which we are derisive toward those who serve us with their labor.[7] Veblen pushes his case to its limit and can be accused of being overly sentimental or even romantic in his affection for those who do the hard work of the community. However, there is much truth in the observation that we are contemptuous of labor. Even the people of the USSR are not always laudatory toward labor. According to a survey reported by the *Times* of London (July 31, 1985), students in the Ural region are scornful of jobs such as lathe operator, metal worker, bus driver, and, curiously enough, doctors. The medical profession, dominated by women and poorly paid, is held in low esteem in the USSR.

The concept of the dialectic, then, argues that there is an inexorable tension between classes and between nations. The driving force behind this tension is the need to control wealth and deal with problems that have their roots in the material world. The dialectic is broader in its implications, however. The dialectic suggests there is also a kind of "tension" between the material order of a society and the ideas, beliefs, traditions, institutions, and other nonmaterial elements of the society.

For example, we might consider a material order in which scarcity prevails. The nonmaterial order, at the same time, might promote a moral program that advocates generosity. Marxism argues that where there is this sort of dialectic, the nonmaterial order will ultimately be modified in ways that are in keeping with the demands of the material realm. Eventually the norms of generosity will move more toward traditions in which thrift and tightfistedness are extolled as virtues.

From this kind of argument Marxism was led to see religion, the family, education, recreation, and all of the other varied programs of any human community as reflecting the primary interests that come from the way in which a society produces wealth. For example, people are familiar with the Marxist slogan that says religion is the opiate of the masses. Marx believed religious beliefs and practices take a form in keeping with the interests of a society's ruling elites. It is in the interest of such elites to keep labor pacified and willing to accept low wages. Religion serves such interests when it preaches that real rewards come after death rather than in this world. It also serves such interests when it preaches that while one is on earth one should serve without complaint.

As another example, modern psychology, a prominent and influential institutional structure within modern capitalist economies, created I.Q. tests and the idea of time-motion studies. From a Marxist perspective, both of these innovations, along with a variety of others, serve the interests of the owners of the means of production more than they serve the interests of labor. (I.Q. tests, for example, help establish the rationale that people are "losers" because they, as individuals, are mentally deficient, not because the system itself is inhuman.) The social sciences, generally, provide the ruling classes with more information about the poor and the indigent than they provide the poor and indigent with information about the ruling classes. The major point is that there is an interaction between the material and nonmaterial orders of any community. Moreover, from a Marxist standpoint, the material order dominates the nonmaterial order.

At this point we have considered a few of the implications of dialectical materialism. We reviewed the materialistic assumption and then considered that assumption within the context of the argument that human communities are confronted by several dialectical divisions. The fundamental division is one between the material and nonmaterial elements of the community. The second is the division between the working and ownership classes.

The nature of these divisions can be illustrated with a reference to our own society. There is, for example, a division between the material and the nonmaterial elements of the culture. A rather interesting case in point is the prevalence of Christian religious ideology (nonmaterial culture) and the prevalence of a commodity market economy (material system). Christianity preaches asceticism and poverty. The commodity market economy preaches consumption and commodity fetishism. The epitomization of the struggle between these forces is the modern celebration of Christ's birthday. Even an unusually insensitive observer of the American scene is aware of the discrepancy between Christian asceticism and the orgy of consumption that takes place during the final weeks of December. Americans practice a number of "isms"; but few of them, even especially devout Christians, practice any kind of true asceticism. For that matter, they are not inclined to practice any kind of asceticism whatsoever. A possible exception is dieting. However, even modern dieting is not directed toward spiritual discipline of the flesh but is directed toward a contrary end—the acquisition of a physically attractive body.

In addition to the "strain" between material and nonmaterial components of a human community is the strain between the classes. The division between the classes is possibly more disguised in the United States than in Europe. Americans, in general, think of themselves as middle class—whether they are or not. Nonetheless, the history of labor disputes in the United States is a long, bitter, and bloody one. Eventually, we find the dialectic at work among subcommunities within the greater community. As a case in point, within a university the humanities are generally at odds with the science and engineering communities. The conflict is more than an intellectual difference; a Marxist would note that it is also a matter of who gets the best budget and the most substantial material support.

How are all of these conflicting elements to be resolved? It was in response to this question, perhaps, that Marxism generated its greatest appeal. For whatever one's view with regard to Marxist doctrine, it cannot be faulted for cynicism or for lacking hope for the future. Marx believed in the perfectibility of humankind. He, along with virtually all major social philosophers of Western culture, from the late 18th into the early 20th centuries, believed in progress. The world, Marx was certain, would get better and better. A just and peaceful world was possible — Utopia could be attained. However, the price for Utopia is heavy — requiring revolutionary struggle and the eventual overthrow of established ruling classes. Only when labor overthrows capitalism can humankind hope to resolve the curse of class conflict and live in peace.

Marx was in favor of a less revolutionary solution and even speculated that it might be possible for some modern nations — the United States, for example — to attain a perfected socialist economy without a bloody revolution. The traditions and the interests of the owners of capital are such, however, that it would be unreasonable to assume labor can win its rights without violence. The class with the most to gain from a class system is the upper class. It will not graciously give way to a classless society. So, materialism, the dialectic, class-struggle, revolution, the subordinance of institutions and beliefs to material forms of production, exploitation, surplus wealth, labor, and capital are a part of the Marxist perspective. How does this perspective shape our awareness of life in the nuclear age?

We turn first to the dialectic as it appears in the interplay between the material order and the ideological order of a community. A Marxist perspective argues that the various features or aspects of a community are shaped primarily by the material order. Military systems are part of any modern and nearly all ancient societies. The question then becomes: To what extent is the military order, as a social institution, influenced or shaped by economic processes? Military systems serve economic as well as other national interests. A radical Marxist point of view would argue that they exist exclusively to serve economic interests. The economy and the military system interact. The military protects economic interests while the economy serves the interests of the military system.

Throughout the late 18th and into the early 20th centuries the use of the military to create markets and exploit resources in nations incapable of defending themselves was an openly accepted practice. This was an era of unembarrassed imperialism — a time when powerful nations used their armies and navies to create empires. We should keep in mind this was also the age into which Marx was born. The existence of what former president Eisenhower referred to as the military-industrial complex was not only obvious but also a matter of great national pride. The open use of force and military intervention was the measure of a nation's strength and its capacity to gain wealth. Indeed, what is interesting about modern times is not so much that the military-industrial complex no longer exists — it exists as obviously today as it did during the heyday of British, German, and French imperialism. What is interesting is that it is now somehow considered bad taste to use the term.

A Marxist point of view, as a consequence, sees the military as an extension of economic practices and interests. But the phrase "economic practices and interests" is abstract. What, more specifically, is meant by this? For Marx economic practices involved how goods are produced and distributed — with emphasis on production. Those who control — through ownership or tradition — the means of production in any society are those who, in effect, control all other facets of the society. The military, then, serves not the interests of the society as a whole but rather the interests of those who control the means of production. The interests of this group are not in the broader communal good but in continuing and maintaining their control over the means of production. Civilian labor is assigned the task of creating wealth. The military is assigned the task of protecting it. The owners enjoy and amass it and use it to consolidate their further ownership of land, factories, and other means of production. In sum, when the argument is made that the military is necessary to protect national interests, the Marxist questions whether it is the interest of the nation as a whole that is being referred to or the interests of a much smaller group that is primarily concerned with the problem of amassing capital.

From a Marxist view of the world we can gain some insight into a few of the ironies of war. One of these ironies can be seen in the involvement of the United States in the Vietnam civil war during the 1960s. American troops comprised a disproportionately large number of blacks and lower-class men and a disproportionately small upper-class or middle-class representation. The fighting troops of the war were of the working class. These working-class soldiers in Vietnam found themselves fighting people who were, basically, peasant or working-class people. The irony, again from a Marxist view, lies in the observation that American working-class combat units were fighting a group whose interests were much closer to their own than the interests of the industrial-commercial leaders for whom the soldiers were fighting.

Early proponents of Marxism argued that when workers became enlightened they would see it was to their interests not to fight other workers. They would turn, instead, to revolutionary struggle and destroy the existing class system. When this took place, the causes of war would cease to exist and war would become a historical relic. To the chagrin of socialist leaders such as Nikolai Lenin, when war threatened throughout Europe prior to World War I, workers did not identify with their own class interests but, instead, with national interests. However, as was suggested earlier, what passes as "national interest" is commonly the interest of the industrial elites. The military, then, is something of a paradox from a Marxist point of view. It consists generally of various elements of the working class who sell themselves as fighters to protect the interests of those who, again from a Marxist perspective, impoverished them in the first place.

Another possible irony of war is that it typically is most vicious and destructive when it takes place between nations relatively similar in character. This appears to be the case, in particular, with similarity in economic development. World War II was fought between nations that were all major industrial economic powers. Germany, England, and France were more alike than different in their cultural interests and their economic structures. At the present time, the United States and the Soviet Union, despite differences in ideology, are major industrial economic powers; and each places a strong emphasis on secular control in politics and the growth of material science and technology as a progressive movement.

Finally, we can turn to a common observation — often posed as a puzzle or an irony. The animosity that exists between nations is generally not an animosity of the people — so to speak. That is to say, Americans might hate Russia but feel at the same time that its people need to be "saved" or "liberated" or somehow rescued from the circumstances in which they find themselves. There is evidence that the people of the Soviet Union possess an affection for the American people and would like to see us spared the cruelties that capitalism imposes on its people. People do not hate people, but nations hate nations.

The Marxist point of view attempts to account for this hostility between nations by turning to the economic threats that the various nations pose for each other. Nations that are economically similar are also particularly threatening to each other. A few years ago the nations with economies most similar to our own were Germany and Japan. Their military competitiveness was, of course, neutralized by Allied victories in World War II. Despite the fact they are no longer a military threat, they remain a powerful economic one. This perspective transforms our understanding of military institutions and war insofar as it attempts to move beneath the rhetoric of war and lay bare the material foundations of conflict. The Marxist interpretation of war makes it, basically, a violent extension of economic conflicts. Peace does not end the conflict; it continues in its more subdued form. (The Japanese practice of training businessmen in schools that operate like military boot camps lends further credence to the Marxist contention that war is basically an economic conflict and the economic process is basically a war.)

There is, of course, a great deal of rhetoric, much of it of a sentimental and "romantic" nature, surrounding the military — providing the military with a kind of mystique. Until late in American history what is now circumspectly and rather self-righteously called the Department of Defense was once called, with innocent candor and openness, the War Department. Marx tries to cut through such rhetoric into the deeper, more substantial realities across which art and rhetoric drift like foggy clouds. In so doing, he reflects a major trend in modern social philosophy, one represented by the desire to get "beneath things" and find out what is really going on. What is "really going on," he concluded, is determined by who controls real wealth. Military rhetoric disguises the primary character of military operations — to suppress through force any threat to the economic integrity of vested interests and real wealth.

Incidentally, the power of real wealth is difficult to comprehend. I like to point out to students that several of America's wealthiest families currently control assets of more than $5 billion. Suppose we were in a kind of marathon race for a precious prize — let us say, immortal life. The race is 1,000 miles long. Only one person can win the prize. The rules of the race permit any person to purchase a head start in the race at the cost of $1,000 a foot from the starting line. Most of us would have trouble getting a 30- or 40-foot head start. A person with $5 billion could purchase a 946-mile head start. What chance does anyone else have? Marxist theory, perhaps more clearly than American ideology permits, sees wealth as raw power and privilege. The inequities implied by those who can gain astonishing head starts in the race for status, fame, or wealth cannot be rationalized, so far as Marx is concerned, in any way that implies justice or fairness. When it is further argued that such wealth was created by the efforts of men and women who were cheated out of their fair share, the injustice becomes all the more bitter.

The dialectic process can be viewed here in terms of two different levels of communal activity — the material and the nonmaterial. The demands of the material economic structure generate a world of ideas, beliefs, and attitudes that are congenial to the operation of that economic structure — providing for the maintenance and the protection of that structure. There is, however, a strain between the material structure and the nonmaterial structure. As a general example, modern Americans are called on to function as "consumers." The term is, when you think even halfway seriously about it, a barbaric label. We do not think of ourselves in any serious manner as "producers" but, instead, as simple-minded "consumers." A highly productive, automated material economy must have its products consumed if it is to continue — and consumed they are. It needs people who, with a sense of pride, refer to themselves casually and thoughtlessly as consumers; and, more significantly, it needs people who are compelled to act, at all times, like consumers. The modern shopping mall now exists, for large numbers of Americans, as a place where they are able to fulfill themselves — a place where they go for therapeutic reasons as much as to shop. The shopping mall, in a sense, cures the neuroses it creates.

At the same time, the productive process generates pollution that is obviously approaching dangerous levels. The structurally enforced motivation to consume, however that consumption can be sustained, is nonetheless in conflict with the new materially grounded demand for a reduction in pollution. Advertising, the institutional arm of capitalism that promotes rampant consumption, is not about to do a turnabout and advocate a reduction in consumption and a return to truly conservative economic practices. Nor, so far as I can tell, is institutional academic economics inclined to promote any realistic theory of true economics. Instead, it continues to rationalize consumptive economics in the name of rational economic practice. All of this is taking place while material conditions change in such a manner that the advocacy of rampant consumption — as an idealized state of life — is beginning to take on pathological features.

The dialectic pertains especially to the even more fundamental conflict between the working and owner classes. The ideology promoted by the owners effectively gains the loyalty of the workers so long as labor has no reason for being disloyal. When the life of the worker becomes unbearably wretched, the potential for revolution exists; and the dynamics of simple capitalism call for reducing the life of the worker to its lowest survival level. Marx, given the wretched lives of the laboring classes in 19th-century Europe, considered it reasonable to conclude that this misery contained within it the hope of revolution. However, the laboring classes cannot overthrow the exploitive control of the owners without organizing. They cannot be organized without the assistance of intellectuals and those whose interests are directed toward the concerns of the community as a whole.

It is worth mentioning that Marx was not alone in his revulsion. Further intellectual support came from literary figures of the time who were appalled by what was going on. Some of the greatest writers of the 19th century devoted their talents to describing the miseries of labor. In England one can point to Charles Dickens and H. G. Wells. In *The Time Machine*, Wells creates a future in which the workers go underground and labor like moles beneath the earth to support in luxury the indolent who live above. The workers extract only one price — they conduct raids every so often and bring back a number of people from the surface to be cannibalized. In America, though a bit later in time, powerful documents of working life were written by Theodore Dreiser and Upton Sinclair among others.

Through the efforts of intellectuals and radical organizers, in the Marxist view, the workers come to see their common interests. They can then be joined together and organized against the inequities of the class structure. After this successful dissolution of the class system, there will no longer be any need to protect wealth on the basis of special interest. Instead, because wealth belongs to the people as a whole, police and military institutions will be transformed. Where before they served the interests of the owners, they will now serve the interest of the entire community. After the workers of the world unite into one community — affiliated through labor and dedication to moral progress — the institution of war can serve no purpose.

We have been concerned with highlighting the dynamics of the dialectic as it pertains to international and class struggles. We shall close the discussion by making note of two major observations with regard to the dialectic.

First, labor did, indeed, organize during the 19th and 20th centuries. The history of labor organization is the history of one of the major social movements of our time. Labor did not, however, eventually organize toward the end of overthrowing private ownership completely. Most European nations moved toward greater collectivism and socialism in their response to the dialectic — there was a major transformation in the economic structure.

However, the class structure remained relatively intact. In the United States also, labor never effectively organized in terms of overthrowing the class structure. It accepted the argument that the American standard of living is the highest in the world. That is to say, working for what an American considers a "living wage" is not a bad deal.

It is necessary to add that with regard to the relative distribution of wealth, America has a surprisingly large indigent population living on marginal incomes and/or supported by the state. Determining who has the highest standard of living in the world is a debate we do not need to enter here. If you consider natal infant mortality, for example, the United States is certainly not the best country for having a child. At the same time, it is hard to disagree with the assertion that those who live well in America, and they are not an insignificant proportion of the total population, live extremely well—at least in a purely materialistic sense.

The dialectic should have brought about a major transformation of the class structure—one leading to its abolition. It appears to have worked more slowly than Marx thought it might—in a day and age when other facets of life are changing with overwhelming rapidity. With regard to the dissolution of class structure in the United States, social science finds itself in a position similar to that of modern cosmology, which concludes that the universe is either going to expand, contract, or remain pretty much the same—which is not an especially definitive conclusion.[8] Social scientists are still debating whether the United States is more rigid, less rigid, or pretty much the same with regard to class structure.

Second, an especially significant element of the working classes in all modern major powers—the scientific community—shows no signs of organizing as a class. The scientific community is organized in terms of professional interests but not class interests. Certainly there is no indication of a "revolt" by the scientific community. Scientists now exist as a new power group—having a voice in purely scientific issues and a voice that also has policy and institutional implications. Why, then, don't scientists seem to show any inclination toward organizing as a power bloc? After all, one way in which the current thrust toward nuclear holocaust might be checked would be for scientists, worldwide, to recognize such work as an ultimate form of immoral action. That such work is not granted an immoral status but is instead extolled suggests that scientists subordinate their interests to the more transcendent claims of national interests and what C. Wright Mills would have called the "power elites," for whom the scientist functions as a technocratic laborer.

For scientists as an organized group to threaten any kind of strike or organized confrontation would be devastating for the greater social order. There can be little doubt about the potential power of the scientific community as an agency within the larger society. Why are scientists no more capable of forming a world alliance against those who would abuse their creations than any other laboring class? Even a preliminary contemplation of the matter reveals the same problems alluded to earlier when I mentioned that Marxist theorists were astounded by how quickly and totally the working classes of Europe aligned themselves under national banners in the days before World War I.

Scientists, like workers in general, are broadly divided in their social affiliations. A unitary scientific bloc willing to pit its weight against other interests cannot be readily attained. A Marxist organizer might be inclined to argue that scientists seem to be more willing to engage in scab labor than other working groups. There is, in effect, always a significant body of scientists who are willing to act contrary to the moral considerations of other scientists. The Union of Concerned Scientists, for example, has not had any profound impact on curtailing the efforts of scientists who are willing to do research that is, at best, ethically suspect — for example, nerve gas research or research designed to further enhance nuclear destructiveness. Marx might have put it bluntly: Scientists are readily bought.

Still more broadly, scientists view themselves as serving national policy, not making it. As long as this eminently powerful branch of American and world intellectual leadership sees its role as a passive one, the possibility of any kind of major transformation in current forms of social organization seems unlikely. As has been the case with the American labor movement generally, high incomes and improved levels of living appear to have tempered thoughts with regard to revolution. Instead of being a liberal and radical element within the mighty nations of the world, scientists all too often withdraw to their laboratories. Whether American or Russian, scientists do not show any serious inclination toward crossing national boundaries and forming a socially concerned labor bloc. They are, instead, inclined to sneer at the nearly impossible problems that ethical, moral, and social conflicts pose. This is not the sort of population one would expect to find caught up in revolutionary fervor. On the contrary, it removes itself from such messy concerns.

Of course, there are a number of scientific associations profoundly concerned with the ethical and political consequences of modern technological developments. The Union of Concerned Scientists was just mentioned and a group known as International Physicians for the Prevention of Nuclear War also comes to mind. None of these associations is, however, a radically revolutionary organization having as its end the overthrow of established economies. They do not even come close. The question of why a group as powerful as the scientific community has surrendered its power to national interests parallels the problem of why labor in general has never effectively organized on a global basis.

We conclude this discussion of the dialectic by suggesting that although it identifies various elements within human communities that are in a state of tension, it is possibly overly optimistic with respect to the quick resolution of those tensions. The economic interests of labor in general and the power possessed by specific professional groups within labor — the scientific community is a case in point — are subordinated to national interests. Nevertheless, even if Marxist thinking is much too optimistic with respect to how social conflict can be resolved, it is still capable of offering deep insights into the nature of our social lives by the very questions it poses. Furthermore, it is tempting to suggest that if national interests are capable of dominating the material interests of labor, Durkheimian theory might help us understand this anomaly. That is to say, people are more profoundly influenced by the power of collective representations than by purely material economic concerns.

FURTHER NOTES ON ALIENATION

We shall bring this discussion of Marx to a conclusion with a brief sketch of the idea of alienation. Alienation has a broader appeal than many of Marx's other ideas. People who disavow a Marxist perspective are still likely to use the term *alienation* in much the same sense Marx used it. The word, of course, refers to the process of transforming things into foreign or "alien" events. Those aspects of life that were once familiar and fulfilling become estranged and unfulfilling. What was once "close" becomes "distant."

The worker becomes alienated, first of all, from the means of production. Peasants are forced from the land and driven to cities where they labor in factories owned by others. Where once peasants toiled over the land and saw and lived with the consequences of their labor, they are now separated from the final products of their labor. What once was "close" is now "distant." Labor, like everything else, must be sold in a "labor market." The worker is forced to surrender a profoundly significant aspect of self and put it up for sale. It is a severe analogy, but the Marxist view suggests the worker is forced into a kind of "prostitution." Like the prostitute who becomes cynical toward those who purchase her or his body, workers become alienated from those who purchase their labor.[9] Work is transformed from an act with profound meaning to trivial movements and actions — dismembered and removed from the end product.

Remember that this concept was introduced into Victorian Europe at a time when there were strong currents of optimism with regard to technology and progress. Indeed, the well-to-do had reason to be optimistic. The new technology was creating wealth more rapidly than had previously been thought possible. The promise for the future — again, for those in comfortable circumstances — seemed limitless. It was a time when writers began to envision new Utopias. Into this current of progressive optimism Marx threw the notion of alienation. Of what good was technological progress, he argued, if it meant the loss of one's self? The power of Marx's rhetoric is possibly at its most persuasive level when he writes of alienation. Consider the following paragraph where he talks about labor selling itself in bits and pieces:

It is the same in religion. The more man puts into God, the less he retains in himself. The worker puts his life into the object, but now his life no longer belongs to him but to the object. . . . The alienation of the worker in his product means not only that his labor becomes an object, an external existence, but that it exists outside him, and that it becomes a power on its own confronting him. (1844)[10]

Workers are now seen as people who are forced to deny themselves. They are unhappy, discontented, undeveloped mentally and physically. Workers are people who are at home when they are not working and not working when they are at home. This observation sounds ordinary in today's world. But it should be understood within a broader human context. There was a time when home, work, and life were inseparable elements—each blending into the other in a continuous whole. Within the modern industrial community work becomes not a fulfillment of life but, to the contrary, something to be avoided, to be run away from. Work, as a character says in one of Sam Shepard's plays, is a place where you don't have no fun.

Some forms of work are highly gratifying, but they are generally the exception. Any index of alienation from work in modern society would have to make use of the extent to which modern men and women find their happier moments in their hobbies or in mind-deadening forms of entertainment. We have come in recent years to look on entertainment as "escape" and we spend a lot of time "escaping." Marx might argue that the eagerness with which we turn to sports, television, film, hobbies, and other "recreations" offers an insight into the effects of work, as it is now defined, on those who must conform to its demands.

A small illustration of Marx's concept of alienation can be found in American universities. Throughout the United States, in the buildings of hundreds of campuses, boxes filled with student papers stand in front of thousands of offices of various professors. There the papers sit, carefully graded, waiting for students to come and pick them up. A month later the boxes are still there and nearly all of the papers are still in them. The students never bother to pick up their own papers. Their work did not sufficiently involve them to merit even the small gesture of coming back to get it. One can go further, for evidently academic alienation is even stronger than this example suggests. It is not unusual to hear students talking about how happy they are, at the end of their college careers, to throw away their notes, their books, their papers—everything and anything associated with their intellectual and mental work. It was not always that way.

This is a banal example of labor stripped of its meaning, but it is not an insignificant one. It offers a personal sense of what Marx means by alienation. Work is done, but work with no personal significance for the worker. It is not fulfilling. Students have a name for it—"Mickey Mouse" work. In this instance the worker is not only alienated from work—which generates the primary sense of alienation—but also from teachers who oversee the work. The modern university transforms the excitement and adventure of learning into a routine where the student learns how to endure a world in which "Mickey Mouse" assignments are a way of life for people who must sell their labor; that is, they are forced to sell themselves. Once college students master this fundamental lesson—how to work while in a state of alienation—they are ready for the adult world of totally alienated work. They are now ready to give themselves over completely to "Mickey Mouse."

I might add, lest the above comments appear to point only to the students (a much-abused group in modern social criticism), that professors as well are not always especially enthusiastic about their work. Large numbers find escape through reliance on objective tests, "dummy-down" texts, predigested summaries, and other devices designed to skirt the demanding, but rewarding, efforts that come from real involvement with teaching. Demoralization in academe is a fascinating subject in its own right. It is mentioned here as a way of bringing Marx's ideas a little closer to home.

When they lack fulfillment through meaningful work, alienation transforms people into empty shells—competing against each other for scarce jobs and better pay. They become caught up in what C. Wright Mills referred to as the "status panic."[11] We no longer react to others as people but rather as competitors. We abandon sympathy and empathy in favor of analysis and manipulation. People become objects. Numerous examples are revealed in the ways we come to refer to ourselves. For example, economists refer to "surplus labor." David Riesman, a number of years ago, pointed out that what they are really saying is "surplus people." This avoidance of human terms in favor of "objective" or "dispassionate" terms seems to be a modern way of talking about ourselves and others—a way of expressing the underlying alienation such language represents.

Of course, in the realm of military strategy and national policy formation, the objectification of people is raised to a high level. To the alienation created by industrial working conditions is added the further alienation derived from cultural differences. If, for example, we are alienated from ourselves within our own national boundaries, we are even more intensely alienated from people living outside those boundaries. The enemy is no longer a personal event—few Americans ever personally encounter a living, human, breathing Russian. Few Russians ever meet, face-to-face, a living, human, breathing American. Even if we become locked in a final catastrophic conflict, few of us will ever witness the face of the enemy we kill or who manages to kill us. The enemy is, instead, an objectified but abstracted entity. So it is that both Russian and American strategists can talk calmly and with apparent rationality about recovering losses after suffering 100 million casualties in a nuclear war.

Note that the strategist is as alienated from his or her own people as from the alien enemy. How else could the planners of war even begin to consider 20 or 30 million of their own people being killed by an attack as a "calculated risk" or loss? The psychological or personal experience of the new economic forces, then, is a state of mind in which the individual becomes drained and alienated — alienated from work, from associates, and, at the broadest level, from humanity. War becomes a matter of cold calculation and the movement of remote machines.

When war is not remote, Americans become upset by it. The bringing of the Vietnam War into the living rooms of Americans through television was disruptive to the process of modern warfare because it worked against the process of alienation. It made the participants in the war human once again. It brought what was distant all too close to the American public. President Reagan did not make the same mistake with regard to the invasion of Grenada. That little military episode was not allowed to come into American living rooms. More than any other act of war engaged in by the United States, Grenada was an "invisible" war. Grenada, more than Vietnam, illustrates the true meaning of alienation.

For all of its failings, the concept of alienation enables us to ask powerful questions about ourselves, our modern forms of life, and the issue of our humanity. Marx serves as a foundation for an ongoing critical review of where we are going. We do not have to reject totally or accept dogmatically the writings of Marx — as though they were either the work of the devil or a kind of sacred literature. We get the most from his work when we draw upon it for critical inspiration. As I pointed out at the beginning of this chapter, Marx was an impassioned believer in the perfection of humankind. He offers hope along with a critical temperament.

If alienation is a serious malaise of our time — and it is not unreasonable to believe it is, then we need to think about it. What is it? How can we modify or restructure our culture and our working conditions in the name of more humane practices? How can we reduce international alienation? Is alienation the price we must pay for high productivity and commodity indulgence? Marx sets us on the quest for answers by having a profound insight into the nature of the problems that confront us in these times. Even in ordinary times alienation is not an especially healthy condition. In this new, nuclear age, it appears to be downright lethal.

The forces of specialization that promote alienation by fragmenting people from each other in terms of special interests and knowledge must be countered by programs that encourage broader knowledge, interests, and awareness. In universities, for example, there is still a place for interdisciplinary programs. However, even as I express this thought, I am aware that Marx has the stronger point. Interdisciplinary programs run counter to continuing trends with respect to productivity — which seems to place an ever-increasing reliance on specialization. Specialization, from a Marxist position, is a consequence of how we now produce things. It is not in itself a naturally superior way of thinking about or responding to the world.

One place where alienation, in its older meaning of foreignness, is breaking down is in the international sphere. Global tourism and international trade have gone far to weaken our fear of different cultures. I think, for example, of some American ranchers who toured Russia recently and returned with a new conception of life over there. Russian ranchers, they found out, live with the same problems, basically, that American ranchers live with—cattle dying from blizzards, diseased or lost animals, providing food for livestock, herding animals, and so forth. Exchanges at this level might reduce the sense of alienation fostered by the impersonal forces of the marketplace, separation, and discrimination—for there should be no doubt about it, restraint of travel is a form of discrimination and an alienating force.

SUMMARY

Dialectical materialism implies conflict is central to human affairs. The Marxist approach to conflict directs attention toward the struggle for material control. In this struggle those who control the material means of production dominate those who are involved in other aspects of the life of the community. The protection of property becomes a greater concern than the protection of individuals. Marx viewed the essential struggle as one between labor and the owners of the means of production. It appears to be the case, however, that national interests prevail over class interests. A relevant example of this is the inclination of nuclear scientists to join ranks with national units rather than class units in the creation of war machinery.

Modern states create great wealth and, at the same time, (as in the case of the United States) accumulate potentially catastrophic debts. This peculiar anomaly of modern times makes sense only when we examine the rationale underlying the distribution of surplus wealth. A Marxist point of view suggests that wealth is used to protect wealth. Surplus wealth is consumed in the effort to sustain large protective military systems and deal with the problems of labor "surpluses" that generate extensive dependent populations.

If nothing else, Marxist thinking calls on us to examine the question of who has the right to make decisions as to how national surplus wealth is to be spent. Are the decisions made in any kind of democratic fashion? Are they made by those who created the wealth or by those who preempted it? Such issues cannot be resolved in this brief review, if they can be resolved at all. Raising the questions, I think, is sufficient.

We become alienated from our work, Marx claimed; and more broadly, we become alienated from each other. We no longer deal with people as people but as workers or as entities whose primary significance is derived from the marketplace. Note, in this regard, the American penchant for establishing a person's merit in terms of the amount of money the person controls.

The culmination of the alienated soul is to be found in those men and women who now coldly contemplate the killing of millions of people as though it were an exercise in a college statistics class. The cold manner has entered the hearts of men and, perhaps, the hearts of women as well. Killing has always been an occupation that attracts all-too-willing volunteers. However, only recently did we find ourselves able to kill entire cities in an instant by performing the same casual act that turns on our television sets— pushing a button. That same alienation from life which makes television so appealing has a darker side.

Chapter 4

George Herbert Mead: The Symbolic Nature of Human Conflicts

LIFE IN A SYMBOLIC WORLD

People rely on symbols and language to get things done, but the American mentality evidently has trouble dealing with this fact. As a people, we like to think in solid and substantial terms. For us, reality is grounded in things—good, hard, substantial, and real things. We are impatient with arguments to the contrary. This devotion to substantive, material reality is implied in the shock felt by Western physicists when they found that physical reality itself disappears into nothingness as it is pursued into quantum levels. Massless particles that can zip, without ever stopping, through a hypothetical piece of lead extending across light years of space simply boggle the mind. What is more mind-boggling is that such particles must be accepted as a part of reality—though they defy our understanding of what is real.

Symbols are like massless particles. They are here, and they are at the same time not here. In one sense, they are unimportant. In another sense, they are everything. Symbols, even more so than elementary particles, are vaporous nothings. They have no mass. They have no extension. They occupy little or no space. Symbols are pure creations of the human mind or intellect. They reside within the hidden, subjective domain of symbolic understanding itself. Yet they move about, interact with each other, and create elaborate symbolic worlds with a fury that makes the elementary particles of the physicist seem mundane.

It takes considerable imagination for an American to look at something as solid as the imposing stone and metal skyline of a city—let us say Los Angeles—and understand that without the invisible and active interplay of symbols, such a solid and substantial entity would have never come into being. Modern physicists are not in the least afraid to suggest that all of the known material cosmos had its origins in nothingness. Social philosophy does not go quite so far with human affairs, but one of its branches suggests that the solid reality we think of as our social, cultural, and economic world rests on those fragile and strangely intangible and suspect elements we call "symbols."

Perhaps even more difficult to deal with is the argument — and it is a powerful argument — that our very selves are symbolic constructions. Possibly more than anything else, this is an intolerable idea for most people. Yet the argument, along with the general and specific evidence backing it up, is a persuasive one. The foundation of our experience — our human awareness — is embedded within a symbolic matrix, and we are ultimately symbolic agents.

The branch of modern social theory that turns to the symbol as the basis of human life had its beginning in the lectures, writings, and teachings of George Herbert Mead. Mead was born in 1863 and died in 1931. Like Durkheim and Marx, he was philosophically interested in the question of why people are social to a degree not shown by any of the other creatures on earth. His approach, however, is significantly different.[1] Unlike Durkheim, he concentrated on the individual and how the individual takes on a social character or identity. Unlike Marx, he did not emphasize material acquisitiveness or materialism. Instead, to find the answer to why people are so uniquely social, Mead turned to an especially unique human ability — the capacity to employ language or, more broadly, symbols.

For Mead, symbols are basic to the social nature of human beings. How can this be? How can such an argument be made? How do we determine more precisely the connection between symbols and our social nature? In what way do symbols lead to the intensely close "bonding" of the individual to the community in which he or she comes of age? In what way do symbols unite the individual and the community in such a total fashion that it is difficult to separate one from the other? In what ways are we vulnerable to symbolic manipulations; and, if we are vulnerable, why and to what extent?

Americans are generally suspicious of symbolic explanations of things. Symbols are tools, but they are not commonly accepted as powerful causal agents in their own right. Marxists, for example, try to find a more solid reality in economic forces they view as underlying the symbolic world. Behaviorists turn to physical stimulus and response — the world of meaning is too subjective for the behaviorist to tolerate. We endorse the idea that actions speak louder than words — so does money. Missouri represents middle American pragmatism as the "Show me" state. Americans, to the extent they are materialists, accept that which they can see or deal with directly. We are a "show me" nation.

Given the general suspicion toward and contempt of symbols as causal forces that Americans appear to display, Mead's theorizing is courageous. Although Americans at least give Marx the tribute of generally hating him, they give Mead little recognition of any kind. Save for a relatively small, but nonetheless dedicated, community of academic social theorists, Americans know little of Mead's influence. They show their distaste for Meadian philosophy by the simplest argument of all — by ignoring it. Mead's ideas were never popular in the same sense, let us say, that Freudian or even behavioristic theories became popular. This is too bad because Mead has had a strong influence on modern academic social theory. The arguments developed in this chapter seek to show that Mead's observations and understanding deserve our serious respect and consideration.

In a casual way, it is easy to accept and then slough off the notion that symbols make us social—just as, in a casual way, we believe we understand what physicists are talking about when they say the cosmos is made up of itsy-bitsy particles. However, when, like Mead, we look at the matter more closely, the problems become impressive. Just how are language and social action related? What, specifically, in language, makes people vulnerable to social control? In this quest for an answer, Mead developed one of the major schools of modern social-psychological and sociological theory—symbolic interactionism (commonly abbreviated as SI).

The following discussion focuses on three major concepts associated with Mead's work:

1. Symbolic interactionism
2. The concept of the self
3. The generalized other

SYMBOLIC INTERACTIONISM

The ability of human beings to use and be used by symbols is central to Mead's thinking. We are vulnerable not only to what we, in fact, see and hear but also, and just as significantly, to what we come to believe we see and hear. Because symbols influence our perception of the world around us and, perhaps even more importantly, our perceptions of ourselves, a realistic social philosophy must emphasize symbols. (The terms "language" and "symbols" are used interchangeably throughout this discussion. It should be understood, however, that symbols include more than language. Languages are only one kind of symbol system.)

We not only interact physically with each other but we also interact symbolically. This raises various questions. How do we interact with symbols? Are symbols peripheral or central to human life? Not only do we, as individuals, interact with and by means of symbols but, just as significantly, symbols possess the peculiar ability to interact with each other.

The concept of symbolic interaction forces us to evaluate the extent to which symbols are a part of human affairs. After reviewing Mead's work we come away with a greater sense of how extensively symbols permeate all facets of our social lives. We are never free from them. We are the responsive repository of symbolic realities. A Meadian perspective makes us more critically aware of the extent to which we are, so to speak, suckers for symbols. The language used here is, I admit, singularly unacademic, but it sums up matters fairly well.

THE CONCEPT OF SELF (ME)

We can begin with an elementary assertion. To be consciously aware of something in the world around us, we seem to need a word or symbol for it. To a surprising degree we do not "see" or comprehend what we do not talk about or somehow include in our reservoir of symbols. On the other hand, even though an object might not exist in any physical or real sense, we sometimes "see" it simply because we know it should be there. We know it should be there because our symbolic set tells us it should be there.[2] The basis for these statements, along with a few qualifications, will be set forth later in this chapter.

Meadian philosophy argues that we do not seriously become aware of ourselves until we reach a point where we acquire the capacity to use symbols. Symbols enable us to identify our individual or personal self as something separate from the world around us. In order to comprehend our own existence as social beings, we must be able to refer to ourselves. As we mature, we acquire the extraordinary ability to refer to ourselves and become profoundly concerned with our "selves." We acquire the capacity to look upon ourselves as something "special" within our experiences of the world around us.

It is obvious that the learning of language and the use of symbols begins early in life. Of special significance in this learning process is the acquisition of terms that enable us to refer to ourselves. These are self-referent symbols such as *I, me,* or *myself,* or, of course, our personal names. There are also collective forms of self-referent symbols such as *we, our,* or *ours,* or our collective identities.

Along these lines, let me mention that there are preliterate cultures where one's personal name is so important that it is kept secret and made available only to those who can be trusted. To allow others access to your name would risk giving them a means whereby they might control you. From a Meadian perspective, this extreme concern over personal symbols is not completely unreasonable. Just think, for example, how readily *you* are controlled by virtue of the fact various people know *your name* and know how to use that simple little piece of knowledge to good effect.

Once we acquire a symbol that enables us to identify ourselves to ourselves, we are well on the path to becoming social in a way no other creature on earth is social. Almost invariably, when a statement such as this is made, somebody responds with the argument that there are other creatures as social as people are—perhaps even more so. There then follows a ragtag listing of descriptions of the social life of porpoises, lemmings, ants and bees, the social organization of the South American rain forests, and so on.

In this particular debate we encounter problems with the meaning of the term *social.* Certainly other creatures live social lives of a sort. This must be granted. However, until anyone sees a group of animals or insects putting together an event such as an evening at the theater or weeping because they were not initiated into a sorority or fraternity, it seems reasonable to continue to assert that the most social and, paradoxically, self-aware of all creatures is the hairless primate we call the human being.

Mead placed strong emphasis on this fairly self-evident, singular, and peculiar feature of human life: We are acutely aware of ourselves. Whether we are introverts or extroverts, winners or losers, strolling in a park by ourselves or caught up in a crowd at a party, we remain self-aware. We are the creature that gives much of its thought to itself.

THE GENERALIZED OTHER

We are social beings; we function not simply as individuals but also as beings who are affected in various ways by our interrelationships with others. Even when we are alone, we are still capable of imagining, in creative and elaborate ways, how others might be thinking of us. We are capable of constructing fantasies in which we imagine conversations with others. We imagine whole scenes in which we outwit adversaries and deal with friends (generously) and enemies (vengefully).

Later, in real confrontations, we get an opportunity to play out moments that were earlier exercises of fantasy. Such fantasies come out of stories we are told and that we are capable of retelling over and over to ourselves — even in our deepest solitude. On occasion these stories insist on "telling themselves." When this happens we are forced to listen to the "stories" that will not leave our minds; for example, we relive embarrassing moments, magnifying the embarrassment in our memory, even though we wish the episode would not recur in our thoughts. Such stories depend on symbols for their existence. We can be tortured by the recall of old embarrassments now totally forgotten by those who were part of that long-ago occasion when we blundered.

For Mead what makes human beings the unusually social creatures they are is their ability to relate, at any given moment, not simply to a single individual but also to more elaborate *sets* of individuals. We locate ourselves not simply with respect to one other person at a time but to entire collections of individuals — including those who are before us and those with whom we are related through our imaginative capacities. He referred to this broader relationship with others as a matter of being related to a "generalized other."

Mead illustrated his argument by referring to the astonishing abilities revealed by children playing games. A child playing baseball, for example, must know what is taking place with regard to *all* the other members of the team and members of the opposition's team. It is an action that is unconsciously and naturally carried out. However, it is also an intellectual act of great complexity. It calls for nothing less than the *imaginative* integration of an entire social complex and then the proper placing or locating of one's self within this complex. This is done as an imaginative act. Furthermore, it is an imaginative act that cannot take place without the ability to use symbols as a kind of "mapping" device.

In the following discussion, I will first present several of Mead's elementary arguments and then relate them to various concerns—with some emphasis on the nuclear arms issue. Although symbolic interactionism and nuclear arms might appear to be remote from each other—one is philosophy and the other hard, physical reality—the two conjoin at several interesting points. Nuclear arms are a manifestation of what we are and how we think of ourselves; we cannot understand the nuclear impasse until we come to understand ourselves. To the extent symbolic interactionist thought helps us in this venture, it is worth examining.

INTERACTING WITH SYMBOLS

The debate over whether people are basically genetically directed in their actions or environmentally directed still continues.[3] It is a peculiar debate that probably has greater political than intellectual value. In this day and age of organic chemistry, it should be obvious that people are, on the one hand, biological organisms and therefore restricted by the character of their biological natures. This seems beyond any kind of serious refutation.

On the other hand, it is patently obvious that people also are capable of a tremendous variety of activities even though their genetic characters are relatively fixed. For example, people from different cultures speak radically different languages. Although the capacity to learn a language is definitely a genetic trait, the kind of language we eventually come to know fluently is not. Chinese, Greek, Latin, French, Spanish, Italian, and English all have the common properties of language while differing in significant ways.

Or, to turn to another general illustration, sexuality is physiological. At its lowest, lowest biological level it amounts largely to deoxyribonucleic acid calling out to itself. At the same time, the *form* that sexual expression takes among human beings varies tremendously from culture to culture and from time to time within a given culture. A culture such as ours fosters romantic, highly emotional involvements and jealous concerns between skinny but bosomy, painted women and men who control a symbolic device called "money." This, of course, is a cultural form or ideal. Other cultures have other patterns.[4]

Meadian philosophy accepts the fact people are biological or physiological beings. However, to avoid the infinitely complex ramifications of trying to deal with everything all at once, Mead's thinking concentrates on the problem of what it means to be a symbol-using creature. Meadian philosophy begins with the assumption that we are talking about people who are genetically and physiologically normal. Obviously, people who are not biologically normal can manifest a different approach to symbols—schizophrenics, for example.

Using the computer as an analogy might help us to see what symbolic interactionism is about. Of course, computers and people are not even remotely similar in any serious fashion. The modern penchant for "computerizing" anything and everything is approaching absurd levels. Nothing suggests this more, perhaps, than the quest for artificial intelligence. This is about as reasonable as the quest for an artificial orgasm. Intelligence, after all, is not simply a matter of solving problems and manipulating the world. It is also a matter of subjective experience and emotionality. If you think about it for a moment you will begin to see that highly intelligent people are also highly emotional—stereotypes to the contrary notwithstanding. Indeed, it is the intelligence of humankind—that is, its capacity to play with symbols —that makes people the most highly emotional creatures on the face of this planet.[5]

With this reservation in mind, we can now return to our analogy. It is obvious computers range from elaborately sophisticated mainframe systems down to more limited home computers. Computers differ in their "hardware." However, a computer is more than its hardware alone. It responds in terms of software programs that define what it is to do.

The same computer, given one program, will calculate statistical problems and, given another, will play a game and, given yet another, will take a simple tune and transpose it into the style of Bach or Mozart or Benny Goodman. The software "overlays" the hardware. It takes both the hardware and the software, interacting with each other, to get whatever we are looking for in the way of computations, word-processing, games, and so on. The same hardware becomes something different each time it incorporates different software.

Symbols are much like the software aspect of the computer. They are an element that "overlays" our physiological nature. Without this "overlay" people cannot function properly as social and cultural beings. To ask which is more important, the "hardware" or the "software," is to ask a peculiar question. The answer depends on your interests. If you are interested in how computers are designed, then you spend more time on hardware and de-emphasize the software features. If you are interested in having a computer do word processing or statistical computations, you need to consider software.

To finish the analogy, then, if you are interested purely in the physiological functioning of sex, let us say, then you can reasonably undertake a study of the biology of reproduction, its mechanics, and so forth. If you are interested in how sexuality is defined within the community, then you move from biology into anthropology, social psychology, and sociology. At this point the arguments of the symbolic interactionist are worth listening to. One approach is no more valid than the other. Both are necessary for the total picture.

Like any analogy, the one between being a socialized human being and a computer running an elaborate software program is crude. It is used here merely to underscore the point that symbolic interactionism—though accused of ignoring the biological and idiosyncratic nature of people—has enough on its hands when it takes on the task of examining what it means to be a symbolic creature.[6]

Symbolic interactionism does not argue that we are not biological. It argues, instead, that it is a mistaken notion to believe biology accounts for everything human. Biology no more accounts for everything human beings do than computer chips account for everything computers do. People are both biological and symbolic creatures — talking apes, if you like such images. The symbolic overlay enhances the biological base upon which it is constructed. More importantly, symbolic systems and biological systems are not the same thing. Once symbolic structures come into being they develop a kind of reality of their own. Symbols can accomplish transformations at a speed and with a facility not physically or physiologically possible. For example, consider the difference between *telling* someone how to get to New York from San Francisco and the *actual process* of showing them physically how it is done.

In this section there is time only to indicate in the briefest manner several of the implications contained in the notion of symbolic interaction. On the one hand it refers to the fact that virtually all, if not all, interactions between human beings include symbolic elements. We interact symbolically as well as physiologically. On the other, it implies a kind of interaction between symbols themselves. There is a dynamic that applies to the symbolic realm which generates a host of possibilities for the beings using it — possibilities not available to creatures lacking symbolic systems.

Before we can talk much about symbolic interactionism we need a clearer notion of what is meant by a symbol. There is considerable confusion over this term, and its precise definition remains elusive. For example, any number of people remain convinced that subhuman species can communicate by means of symbols. There is the possibility that a limited use of symbols is possible by lower primates. Even so, there is little likelihood that purely symbolic communication of an extensive and continuous nature occurs anywhere on earth other than among human beings.

We gain a little insight into how vast the gulf is between humans and other creatures with respect to symbols when we consider our desire to "talk" to animals. In a kind of existential loneliness, humans almost universally share the fantasy of being able to communicate with other species of animal at a symbolic level. In simple, primitive cultures it is accepted as a fact that one can talk with the wolf or the rabbit or the muskrat and even the trees and the rocks and the wind. It is a lovely belief to live by, but one that modern rationalism virtually destroyed.

Nonetheless, the fantasy still lives on in Western culture in movie cartoons where mice, cats, canaries, coyotes, ducks, and horses talk and suffer the exultations and agonies of being human. At a more poignant level, it is found in the attempts of people to talk with their pets. In this regard the practice of talking "baby talk" to pet animals is especially interesting. There is something at first amusing and then touching, as you come to understand it, about a grown-up, sophisticated, adult Western man or woman snuggling a dumb, wiggling pet and talking baby talk to it.

Mead distinguished between "signs" and "symbols." Any number of animals communicate by the use of "signs." Even though such communication is limited in nature, it can still be impressive. The best known example of this, perhaps, is the famous honeybee "dance." Bees are able to communicate the location of pollen fields by "dancing" before other worker bees on their return to the hive. A dance of a particular variety is a "sign" telling other bees that pollen can be found at a particular distance and direction from the hive.

The important definitive characteristic of "signs," as opposed to "symbols," is that a sign evokes the same response from the creature observing it. Mead used the example of a dog baring its fangs or a lion roaring in the forest. A lion's roar is a "sign" danger is near. The appropriate response is either flight or preparation for a fight. Signs, then, are relatively unambiguous and fixed in meaning.[7]

Note, in this example, that the lion might be roaring out of pleasure after having a good night's sleep. What the lion might "mean" by the roar and what the other creatures think it "means" are two different things. The major consideration here is that the roar is a sign of danger to those who hear it, and they respond accordingly. Or, to put it another way, little is "arbitrary" about signs. They pretty much mean what they mean.

Many different signs exist among human beings. These are interpreted in much the same fashion throughout the world. If someone shakes a fist at you, your response likely will be to view it as a threat and react accordingly. If someone bows low before you, it is a sign of deference or of submission. A smile is universally reacted to as a sign of acceptance or being pleased. However, such is the symbolic ability of humans that any of these signs can be "reversed" in its meaning. A smile might mean contempt; shaking a fist might mean victory. When, for example, Queen Elizabeth visited New Zealand the Maori greet her with their tongues stuck out. In Maori culture this is a symbol of deference and respect, though we think of it as a universal sign of disrespect.

We have, then, a group of devices or stimulus events or patterns that operate as signs. As I've already said, however, a good deal of confusion exists regarding to the difference between signs and symbols. Part of this confusion arises because signs and symbols essentially do the same thing — they convey information. However, they do so differently. Perhaps the distinction can be made with a brief anecdote.

A few years ago I visited one of the most shockingly impoverished barrios in all of South America — a ghetto in Cartagena, Colombia, known as Chambacu. As I entered the barrio I was surrounded by a group of about ten or twelve young men. The men were hostile; they frowned and shouted words. Several spit at my feet. Their teeth were bared and their fists were clenched. The signs of hostility were unambiguous, and the moment was ominous.

What was interesting, however, was that the *signs* indicated, without much ambiguity, the anger of the men. At the same time the *symbols* of hostility were not in the least obvious to me, because I knew so little Spanish. What was being shouted could have been pretty much anything. Presumably the men were shouting insults. I discovered later that the shouted words were, indeed, insults of a terribly provocative nature—for anyone familiar with the language or the symbols being used. They just as well might have shouted at a deaf man, however, for their meaning was not comprehended by me. The language of signs, in this instance, touched a universal understanding. The language of symbols was particular and, as a consequence, had little effect.

If signs communicate so effectively, then why not rely on them for all communications? The answer is that signs are limited in what they can convey. The dance of the bees can convey only where pollen is located. A clenched fist conveys anger. A smile conveys pleasure. The astonishing accomplishment of the symbol, on the other hand, is its ability to convey anything—including nothing itself![8]

It is not possible, here, to go into the philosophical implications of this observation, but the ability of symbols to refer to nothing is an astonishing accomplishment. No other creature, so far as I know, has any awareness of what nothing is—the world is always "something" for creatures that do not use symbols. People are remarkably aware of the implications of "nothing-ness" in all kinds of contexts. Consider the common reaction, for example, to being told one is "nothing" or the strange response of a child who, when asked what it is doing, replies, "Nothing."

The symbol can refer to anything, everything, and nothing. It does this through a loose, arbitrary arrangement between people as to what a given symbol is going to mean. Symbols achieve their coherence through tradi-tionally established meanings. These meanings, however, are not perfectly delineated (with the possible exception of logical symbols, which are another matter). We discover the arbitrary nature of symbols by noting, simply, that what a symbol means in one context can be entirely different in another.

A facetious but nonetheless clear example of how arbitrary symbols can be is the term "poo-poo." For an American this symbol conveys a sense of baby talk and refers to feces or body wastes—as in "dirty poo-poo under-wear." Imagine, then, going to an oriental restaurant and picking up the menu to find you can order a "poo-poo" platter. In this context the symbol "poo-poo" refers to little *hors d'oeuvres* served along with a small brazier of hot coals or a flame for heating the food. The poo-poo platters I ordered were always delicious, but I never got used to the terminology. I also noticed the term recently disappeared from the menu of my favorite oriental restaurant to be replaced by a "pao-pao" platter.

This example shows that, unlike a sign, an individual symbol is a purely arbitrary convention. A symbol can mean or convey just about anything people are willing to agree it means. (As we shall see in a later chapter dealing with the writings of Kenneth Burke, getting agreement on the meaning of symbols, especially social symbols, can be more difficult than we commonly suspect.)

Particularly astonishing is the capacity of symbols to convey information within sets of symbols and also convey information about other symbols. Where signs tend to function in isolation — a smile, a dance, a fist, a roar — symbols function in relationship to each other. Symbols interact with other symbols in elaborate and complicated ways. Not only do we interact with each other through symbols, but symbols also display the capacity to interact with each other in a purely symbolic fashion. At least it is possible to illustrate what is meant by this.

One can begin with any single symbol drawn at random. Suppose we select the symbol *jazz*. What such a term means is not contained exclusively within the term itself. Its meaning becomes clear only when it is inserted within a set of symbols. For example, compare the differing meanings of *jazz* in the following statements:

> "Blues, a form of jazz, is improvisational music commonly based on the pentatonic scale — the same scale used for Irish music."

> "It was the 'Jazz Age.'"

> "Don't give me no jazz, man."

> "She's got jazz."

Several things become clear with this simple illustration. First of all, just what jazz might mean is in part contextual. Moreover, the same term, in different contexts (the third and fourth statements illustrate this) can convey nearly contradictory meanings. Secondly, the contexts that alter the meaning of the term *jazz* are themselves symbols that, presumably, gain their meaning from contexts. For example, how is the word *give* influenced by its context in the third expression above? Third, because each symbol in a given string of symbols is subject to arbitrary interpretations of considerable flexibility, we begin to see how a symbolic assertion is difficult to pin down in terms of any kind of specific meaning. Different individuals will interpret a given set of symbols in different ways.

The problems that are lightly outlined in the preceding paragraphs have serious implications. They show up wherever human issues are being discussed. For example, people dealing with the problem of artificial intelligence are beginning to discover that the central block to making a machine that "understands" language is the complexity of symbolic systems themselves. The profundity of this observation cannot be sufficiently underscored. Language is loose and nearly infinitely complex. At the same time, we look on it as precise and simple, and this failing leads to many a misfortune.

The untutored approach to language is to believe it is a more or less "mechanical" tool for conveying thoughts. It is virtually anything but mechanical. That symbols work at all (and it is patently obvious that, one way or another, they work all too well) becomes more impressive as one moves into a deeper investigation of the nature of language and symbolic systems.

This argument might be summed up by suggesting that the modern trend is to promote mechanistic thinking—well-ordered, rational, and "cool." However, language simply does not permit this. Although symbolic structures are ordered and display an apparent rationality in the way they are put together and function, the complexity of such systems moves them beyond simple mechanical models. As limited creatures we want simplicity. Nonetheless, the languages we create deny us any real hope of finding such comfort. The moment we acquire language our lives become complicated.

We are not mechanical creatures—either biologically or symbolically. In the *jazz* example we saw how a single symbol is influenced by different symbolic contexts and its meaning, as a consequence, is "fluid" rather than mechanical. Mead was interested in a particular concept that has special relevance for the human condition—the notion of *self*. We can begin by noting that *whatever "self" is, it is at one level a pure symbol*. The term exists. It is a kind of fact.

To make the point, it is now presented in full capital letters—SELF. There it is, right in front of you, on paper, a simple word. It does exist. It is a fact. You might reply that it exists only as a word. As a good American you are suspicious of words. You are correct when you suggest this is a "funny" fact because it exists only as a word. Just because something is a word does not make it a fact—by American standards, at least.

At the same time, the symbolic interactionists point out that words do exist and they do create effects. They might exist as a unique kind of fact, but it is not reasonable to discount their influence because they are not facts in the same sense a stick of dynamite is a fact. Symbols are facts; and among the most powerful of symbols, for sociological purposes, is the concept of self, for it is through the self we become social.

Now, if the term *self* is a word or symbol, it can be manipulated by other symbols just as the term *jazz* was influenced by its symbolic contexts. To gain a mild sense of how symbols can manipulate one's self-concept, put your personal name—which is a self-referent term—in the blank spaces below and see how subject it is, even in this nonserious and casual demonstration, to being defined by symbolic contexts.

Congratulations, _____, you were just selected as a possible winner of $10,000,000 in the Publishers' Resale of Old Magazines Sweepstakes.

_____, as dean of the college, I regret it is my duty to inform you that you are a failure in just about every respect.

Hey, _____, you got a phone call from *Time* magazine this morning. They want you to write an editorial comment on what's wrong with the world.

According to these recent tests, _____, it appears you have occasional problems with homosexual fantasies at an unconscious level.

This general discussion of symbols sets the stage for a consideration of the social significance of symbolic systems. We can now return to the concept of symbolic interactionism and consider the fact that people interact in terms of symbols and that, moreover, symbols interact among themselves.

Mead wondered how people become so intensely social in character. This question is especially significant because in its answers might be clues as to why we fight with such intense bitterness and for such extensive periods of time in the name of our social identities. He resolved the problem by suggesting our social natures are a kind of paradox. The paradox arises out of the contradiction implicit in the fact that our connection with society is through the self. The thing that sets us apart as individuals is also the thing that sets us up to become willing participants in whatever the community designates as important work.

INDIVIDUALISM RECONSIDERED[9]

Mead noted simply that we acquire language and a sense of symbol systems as we come of age. During the process of growing up we acquire several notably important symbols. These symbols identify us to ourselves. They are self-referent symbols. We gradually come to learn that a finger pointed in our direction along with the statement "Don't *you* go near the stove" has something to do with us. (In this instance "you" becomes a self-referent term.) We also discover, after a surprisingly long period of training, perhaps a year or two, that we can identify ourselves to others by using self-referent terms. It is also interesting to note that at just about this time we begin to become aware of ourselves to ourselves. We can begin to point our self out to our self. Before that time we are essentially unaware of our own existence.

Self-referent terms such as the singular *me, my, mine, I,* and personal names or nicknames and the plural *our, ours, us, we,* and collective self-identities must first be understood for what they are: symbols. And, as symbols, such terms can be easily manipulated like any other symbol. The "handles" we use to define ourselves for ourselves are also the same "handles" used by the community to define us. Here, then, from a Meadian perspective, is the thin, thin thread that binds us like steel to the greater community.

The locus of self is to be found within the human capacity to create symbols of self-reference. But symbols can be manipulated, as it were, by other symbols. Once we have symbols for the self, we can incorporate such symbols within a body of symbols. This body of symbols provides a context for the definition of self. Also, as was suggested earlier, because symbols can refer to anything and to nothing, it is possible to embed self-referent symbols within symbolic systems of tremendous variety — opening up the possibility for a virtually infinite variety of socially defined selves.

One difficulty with this philosophy is that it turns away from the materialistic "hardness" of such "toughminded" philosophies as Marxism and behaviorism and concentrates on something as "soft" as symbols. It is difficult to get people to accept the fact symbols should be granted the significance Meadian philosophy grants them. There is a kind of "sticks and stones might break my bones but words will never hurt me" attitude. Americans subscribe to the slogan that "Actions speak louder than words." Only in the most limited sense is this the case. After all, words cannot break our bones — though at the moment you might find it difficult to make such an argument with Palestinians whose hands were broken because certain symbols were barked at young Israeli soldiers.

In my experience it is difficult to demonstrate that symbols are a form of action and that actions are a form of symbol. How do you convince people that social actions cannot take place outside of a symbolic context and that it is rather absurd to believe actions speak louder than words. Let me try to illustrate. When a president, for example, vetoes a popular bill, he has acted. But the action is purely symbolic. The veto is a symbol that is also an action. Or, when the heroine in the musical *My Fair Lady* tells her lover in song to show her, through actions rather than words, that he loves her, the actions are expected to parallel the symbolic commitment.

When a young man tells a lady he loves her he does nothing more than utter a few words. But the utterance is an action — a symbolic act. Or, at another level, a person who is stripped of his or her symbolic significance is as vulnerable as one who is stripped of physical strength or wealth. Wealth, after all, is primarily significant because it is powerfully symbolic. The belief that actions speak louder than words clouds the fact that ideas and actions are inseparable for human beings.

The power of symbols, with respect to human actions, lies in their ability to influence perception. Symbols, whether they can break our bones or not, have serious implications for how we perceive the world around us. This has been demonstrated in study after study after study in the field of social psychology and can be safely regarded as something fairly close to a general empirical principle in contemporary social psychology and sociology.

In a series of major demonstrations in the 1930s, the American social psychologist Muzafer Sherif revealed that in unstructured contexts symbols become, in a sense, the reality we perceive. Let me hasten to add that I am pushing the implications of this study to its extreme limits in an attempt to make a major point in a short space. The interested reader is advised to see the original Sherif report — its implications are impressive.[10]

Sherif conclusively demonstrated that when people observe a stationary pinpoint of light in a totally darkened room and are told it is moving horizontally, they see it moving horizontally. If they are told it is moving across a large distance, they see it move a large distance. If they are told it is moving a small distance, they see it moving a small distance. Later it was found that if they are told it is moving in a circle, they see it moving in a circle. If they are not told anything, they see the dot of light moving in an erratic random pattern. The important thing to comprehend here is that people literally "see" what they are told. Their "reality" is conjoined with their symbolic experience. Symbol and reality become blurred, as it were.

Keep in mind that this power of the symbol to create perceptions is especially effective when the setting lacks a structure or context that might define things differently. For example, if the stationary light is shown in a room not totally darkened, the structure of the room provides points of reference that enable the audience to recognize that the light is not moving.

Now, to develop the significance of this we need only determine how frequently we encounter events that reveal little or no inherent structure; then we can begin to assess how extensively symbols influence our perceptions. You can see how profoundly symbols influence our perceptions by referring to the earlier chapter on Durkheim where it was argued that social events, by their nature, do not display an inherent structure. That is to say, when we encounter someone, we cannot assess from the person's physical being what he or she is socially. We can see what a person is only when we are told what to see. At this point symbols literally create the reality we are informed we are seeing.

More importantly, from a Meadian perspective, just as we cannot tell what someone else is until we are told, we cannot assess ourselves without being told what we are. Moreover, external definitions of self tend to be accepted uncritically. Because there is no inherent, genetically determined social self, *by definition*, we tend to accept the self others ascribe to us. In other words, how we perceive ourselves is subject to symbolic manipulation. This makes the individual virtually helpless before socially imposed definitions of his or her significance to the community.

Sometimes people get upset with Mead because they are aware there is more to being human than is implied in symbolic interactionist thinking. This certainly cannot be denied. The self, in its totality, is a profoundly mysterious entity and Meadian philosophy by no means tells us all there is to know about it.[11]

Mead was well aware of this. In his discussion of the self he allowed for a form of self that is not social but that is embedded within our physical being — the imaginative self, the self that gets things done, the self that corresponds, in several ways, to what Freud meant by the "id." Mead was well aware of other aspects of the self. However, in concentrating on the question of how we become social, the symbolically defined self is of primary concern.

Psychology tends to concentrate on the individual as an individual; Meadian philosophy concentrates on the individual as a social agent. The deeper question remains: Why are people as social as they are — how do they get so totally "hooked into" the social game? Keep in mind Mead is talking about people as *social* creatures and is concerned with the social nature of our definitions of ourselves. For Mead the concept of self is important because it marks the point where the individual and the community are conjoined. In this more restricted sense, Mead's ideas force us to consider the extent to which at least a major part of what we call our "self" is a socially defined symbolic creation.

Mead accepted a position that is basically Lockean. Locke, of course, argued that people at birth are a kind of clean slate (*tabula rasa*) on which experience writes its lessons. (This contention has been effectively challenged in recent years, particularly in the works of Noam Chomsky.) Mead argued, more conservatively, that at birth we are unable to establish what we are as social beings on our own. We must be told what we are. This takes place first when we are provided with a self-referent term that enables us to identify ourselves as entities apart from others. The next step is the manner in which qualifiers are attached to the self-referent. Qualifiers that others attach to the self-referent will at first be uncritically accepted by the young child—it has no basis for rejection. Later, as contradictory qualifiers appear, a simple symbolic determinism breaks down.

During the early stages of growth, then, the child comes into the world with no inherent sense of his or her social position. In such circumstances the individual is perfectly vulnerable to symbolic definitions of the self. If we are told we are lower-class or upper-class, important or unimportant, pretty or ugly, bright or stupid, we believe what we are told. So it is that society, as it were, enters into the individual and becomes the individual in a sense. The individual and the social unit become different sides of the same coin.

The individual remains vulnerable to social definitions of the self throughout life. We are what we are socially defined as being. The self and society become joined through the fact that the self is a symbolic referent subject to highly varied forms of symbolic definitions. A sad example of the symbolic interactionist argument can be found in the eagerness with which disturbed men or women commit crimes in order to get their *names* into the newspapers—that is, to "make a name" for themselves. At a broader level, we are all socially driven by the same impulse that provides pleasure to common criminals when they find they made the front page of the *New York Times*.

Without examining all of the implications of this, we can bring to a close this discussion on the nature of the self by suggesting that when we consciously define ourselves we tend to do so in socially established ways. When asked what we are, we commonly reply in terms of our social statuses: Catholic, teacher, lawyer, student, Protestant, American, baseball player, cook, executive, feminist leader, Republican, etc. Commonplace as this illustration is, it underscores the argument being made by the symbolic interactionists. We tend to recognize ourselves through our social identities. If so, then the individual is a creation of the social order and is inseparable from it. Individualism in any strict meaning of the term is a Western myth.

I must hasten to add that the term *myth* is badly abused in modern English usage. Modern people commonly regard a myth as some kind of error or mistake. The typical form of this abuse is found in reports, usually in the newspapers, that science destroyed another "myth." For example, we might read an article to the effect that science disproved the myth that drinking carrot juice cures cancer. However, the belief that drinking carrot juice cures cancer is not a myth but an erroneous notion. Individualism, on the other hand, is a rather fine example of a myth. It is the unquestioned basis for elaborate constructions of heroic character that appear in literature and drama. It is pervasive in its influence and is a deeply ingrained ideological component of our culture. It is much, much more than simply an erroneous notion—it is a collective comprehension of the idealized self.

I am not interested here in demolishing or destroying individualism as a myth. Myths are an integral and important part of all cultures. The myth of individualism is an important part of ours—as are numerous other myths such as romance, progress, and success. A good grasp of Mead's argument produces a greater awareness of the extent to which our sense of self is grounded in myth. It is in the fusion of myth and self that myth becomes reality.

SOCIETY AS FANTASY: THE GENERALIZED OTHER

As a social entity, the self cannot exist within a vacuum. It requires others who are necessary for the process of defining it. We do not even become self-aware of the aging process—we are not aware of our own aging—until we are told by others that we are old. Consider, for example, the case of a man a few years ago who told a journalist about the moment he discovered he was old. It all happened when he bumped into the back of a car in front of him at an intersection. The other driver leaped from his car, ready for a fight. When he saw who bumped him, he said in disgust, "Hell, I'm not going to fight with an antique old duffer." What is of interest here is that, for the senior citizen, finding out he was "an old duffer" came as a shock! The old duffer had not thought of himself as old until he was told, emphatically, by someone else that he was no longer fit for a fight.

Of course, the mirror offers hints we are getting old but we really do not believe what we see. Our friends and associates force us to accept our new role in life by telling us what we are. In addition, we are told each year that we are aging by a social ritual known as celebrating one's birthday. Many of us who live in the Western world give up on birthday celebrations as the numbing effect of numbers (nicely named) takes its toll.

The social self is yet more complex. We do not form our images of ourselves from what we are told by a single person or even a few close relatives or friends. We form our images of ourselves through contacts with many individuals over extended periods of time. Somehow, our concept of self becomes related not simply to a few other people but to a complex of other people.

The point is developed by Mead's suggestion that we go through three general stages of development in the acquisition of a social self. First, the child simply imitates the actions of those around it. It might see someone reading a newspaper, pick one up itself, and pretend to be reading it—even though the paper is upside down. At this stage the child does not possess a developed sense of self. We will call this the "preparatory" stage—a period of simple imitation.

At the second stage the child "plays" with various roles and actions. For example, even in isolation, children commonly play at being a doctor, soldier, teacher, or some other role. In order to do this the child must "put on," as it were, the role and then enact it. Consider a situation where a child is playing that it is its own mother or father. The child will pretend it is the mother and then scold itself for being bad and send itself over to the corner. Later, as adults, we carry out such reflexive actions constantly.

In order to carry out reflexive actions, the child must be capable of referring to itself from the perspective of someone else! When, as its mother, it sends itself to the corner, it is carrying out an action that is possibly unique among all of the creatures of the earth. I know of no exceptions. Perhaps, to a limited degree, humanly trained chimpanzees acquire such self-reflexive empathetic qualities. However, not even trained chimpanzees have the ability to take on the role of another to the extent found among human children. We will call this period when the child "tries out" various social roles the "play" stage.

The third stage reveals the complexity of the relationship between the individual and the greater community. Mead referred to this as the "game" stage. At this stage of a child's development it acquires the capacity to see itself not only from the vantage point of another person but also from the vantage point of an organized collection of other people.

The illustration used to make this point is a straightforward one. Consider a young boy who decides to play on a Little League baseball team. In this instance the individual must relate not merely to one or two others but to a still-more-complex "other." The "other" now consists of everyone associated with the game. The boy must "see himself" as it were, from the perspective of the coach, the umpires, the members of the opposing team, the players on his own team, the fans in the stands, his friends who are watching, and so forth. He now has the capacity to relate his own actions to the rest of the players. This is an extraordinary accomplishment—even though it is carried out thousands of times by thousands of young men throughout the world during an average summer afternoon.

In playing games the child comes into the world of organized others and finds his or her place being defined accordingly. Now, with the game stage, the other is generalized. It includes many people rather than a few. Mead called this broader, more elaborate group the "generalized other." The community enters into us in the form of others who define what we are. At first we can relate only to specific others. As mature adults we find ourselves fitting into a broader network of relationships.

With the incorporation of the generalized other, the individual becomes a kind of one-man band. We are no longer exclusive, solitary beings but oddly melded creatures—fused, as it were, into the social body. Again, the paradox in all of this is that the fusion takes place through our ability to identify our individuality and then relate that individuality to a complex and imaginary (though, at the same time, real) organized set of others. It is, when you think about it at all, quite an accomplishment! What makes it all the more impressive is that it is done naturally, casually, and in such a total fashion that we take it for granted.

Implicit in this discussion is the suggestion that the self varies with its social context and that this social context is powerfully coercive. For example, in one context a young woman might be concerned with herself as a student at college. In this context the generalized other consists of other students, teachers and administrators, relatives, and perhaps her employers. In another context the young woman might find herself waiting tables at a local restaurant. Her concept of herself is now relative to the generalized other of the restaurant — the diners, busboys, cooks, other waitresses and waiters, health inspectors, and anyone else relevant to the operation of the restaurant.

Our concept of self is flexible and relative to the social contexts within which we find ourselves. The self is relative to the generalized other that provides the organized definition of self. In other words, if you find yourself functioning as a member of a highly organized group such as a baseball team, you acquire a well-defined sense of your position and what is expected of you in relation to the others involved in the playing of the game. Conversely, Meadian theory suggests that if we are caught up in a disorganized group, our own conceptualization of self is likely to reflect such disorganization. In this instance, Mead appears to provide more specificity to Durkheim's arguments with respect to anomie. Durkheim argued that where social norms are lacking (the anomic condition), people become prone to suicide. Suicide, in this instance, is the total abandonment of self. Mead, through a discussion of the symbolic nature of self, offers further insight into Durkheim's speculations.

Possibly this suggestion offers us a little better understanding of the paradox observed by Jean-Paul Sartre, who noticed that young men, in the quest to find themselves, generally do so by joining authoritarian groups. Sartre was commenting on the inclination of young men to find themselves as individuals when they become members of rigidly authoritarian, tightly organized groups — gangs, military units, football teams, fighter squadrons, corporations, etc. It seems so contradictory. Why would anyone join an authoritarian group in order to find one's self?

From a Meadian perspective, it makes sense. If our self-concept is derived from our social memberships, then the most heightened and organized sense of self would come from within highly organized groups. So it is, then, that in the quest for individuality, young men accept the group coercions that come from playing organized sports or going off to war.

It is tempting to point out, further, that young women, at least until recently, were inclined to find themselves in marriage. In this instance, the woman's self-concept is given its integrity through identification with the family as her primary "generalized other." Whether this is so or not, the general position taken by symbolic interactionists is that self and society are related in such a fashion that we "find ourselves" through the social units to which we belong. The paradox lies in the argument that our heightened sense of ourselves as individuals occurs in moments when we are contained within highly organized group activities. Curiously enough, then, we are most individualized when we are most social.

The matter has still further complications insofar as the relationship between an individual and his or her particular generalized other of the moment is not a mechanical one. It is impossible to relate directly to an organization as a real entity. This is true in part because the "reality" of an organization is not directly ascertainable. It is also true because social organizations generally extend beyond an individual's immediate domain of action.

On the one hand, the generalized other is definitely real. It is "there." It exists. It is coercive. There are, after all, such things as baseball teams and schools and other organized groups. On the other hand, in a day-to-day working sense, the only way we can deal with our community is on the basis of how we *imagine* we are defined by the generalized other.

From a Meadian perspective, then, we acquire an imagined sense of self from others. This self-awareness becomes structured in terms of the way we fantasize ourselves fitting into various groups. As we move from one group to another, the nature of the socially defined self shifts. In one group we might define ourselves as a baseball player and in another as a waiter and in another as a loving parent. The significant point is that something as central to our being as our awareness of our self is, to a considerable degree, socially defined. The significance, then, that social factors have in individual lives is augmented by the fact that what is social and what is the self are simply different manifestations of the same process.

SYMBOLIC INTERACTIONISM AND THE REAL WORLD

The theories of George Herbert Mead have the charming quality of being openly philosophical. Mead taught as a philosopher, not as a social scientist. Other academic social observers of Mead's era sought, desperately at times, to disguise their work as science and to disengage themselves from anything as suspect as philosophy. They erred in doing so because social science, like physical science, remains a specialized branch of philosophy and should never attempt to remove itself too far from its philosophical roots. In any case, Mead had his feet firmly planted in the tradition of Western philosophical argument. This was both an advantage and a disadvantage.

It was an advantage insofar as it enabled Mead to avoid the pitfalls of a narrowly defined empiricism that skirted important issues in favor of more solid, though trivial, facts. It allowed Mead, for example, to concentrate on problems that are possibly beyond any rigorous empirical proof —such as the imagined nature of the generalized other and its bearing on self-conceptualization.

At the same time, the abstracted and philosophical nature of symbolic interactionist thinking led, in a general way, to its rejection by mainstream American social science and psychology. American social science is dominated by economics. At the same time, American psychology is dominated by behaviorism and experimental psychology. These schools of thought share one common cultural perspective—they give symbols secondary importance in human affairs. They are driven by a reductionist persuasion that keeps hoping to find more substantial ground on which to base an understanding of human affairs.

Any kind of application of symbolic interactionist thinking to the affairs of the real world requires, at the outset, a recognition of the fact that symbols are not just so much "gas." They are an integral part of the strange reality that embraces us as our social and cultural worlds. Symbols have the ability, the astonishing power, to create reality. Conversely, they can destroy it.

The question we now need to consider is: What can we do with symbolic interactionism in trying to understand the world around us? As an illustrative case, we shall apply Mead's thought to the nuclear arms issue with emphasis on three things: (1) the role played by symbols in human social interrelations, (2) the tight bond between the individual (self) and the community (other), and (3) the concept of national identity.

Symbols and Reality

In Western culture we seem to delineate between what is "real" and what is "symbolic." We consider the real world to be the solid world of substance, things, and actions. On the other hand, we are inclined to think that anything that is not of the real world belongs to the realm of fantasy, fiction, rhetoric, and imagination. As with any simple dichotomy, whatever we gain through simplification hardly makes up for what we lose.

There is a close connection between symbols and reality; and the distinction between the two, upon closer examination, is not in the least a clear one. Consider, for example, the following question: If you go to see a popular film at your local movie house, what was the reality you experienced? If the symbolic content of the film is ignored, then all you experienced was a play of dancing colored shadows. But the reality of the film was not dancing colored shadows. The reality of the film was the drama, the meanings, the involvements, and the resolution of crises that were all symbolic in nature. Or, for a simple little demonstration of what is removed from reality when the symbolic element is reduced, watch a televised program with the sound turned off. Remember, when you do this, that you eliminate only a small portion of what might be generally defined as the symbolic content of the program.

If the reality of something as simple as an ordinary popular movie depends heavily on symbols, then we might generalize from this to the rest of our social experiences. Social reality, as distinct from physical or material reality, is *primarily* symbolic in nature. Meadian philosophy moved modern social thought toward an examination of the problem of reality from a new angle—not what reality *is*, in fact, but how it is *perceived as* fact.

Turning now to the nuclear arms issue, we can consider such weapons from two broad perspectives. On the one hand, we can deal with them as pure physical entities — they cost so much to produce, they can be delivered to their targets within a particular time period, and they can level and radiate an area of known dimensions.

On the other hand, we can deal with them as symbolic objects. What do they mean — security or danger? What circumstances justify their use? What status do they convey to those who build and work with them? How do they affect the manner in which we perceive our selves? Who has the right — that is, the symbolically established authority — to use them? How did they get that right? Are our weapons offensive or defensive devices? This, incidentally, is a proper question to ask of the Strategic Defense Initiative, which is perhaps the most symbolically manipulated weapons system in the history of humankind. Do weapons symbolize strength or weakness? Who gets to tell us what they are and what they are supposed to do? What are the primary symbolic agencies that inform us about such weapons? What symbols do they draw on?

It is not possible even to begin to answer, in any complete fashion, all of the questions raised here. The questions, however, have the purpose of shifting attention from the weapon as physical object to the weapon as symbolic object. For the symbolic interactionist the particularly interesting and possibly the most significant thing about the weapon is its symbolic significance.

Indeed, when it comes to nuclear weapons we find ourselves, for the first time in the history of human warfare, with a weapon that is almost entirely symbolically significant. That is to say, everyone is agreed that the use of such "bombs" for any kind of sustained nuclear war would be tantamount to collective suicide — if not possibly the end of life on earth. The weapons must not be used. Yet, no government that controls them is ready to get rid of all of them, along with the knowledge required for building them again.

Why, then, do they exist? Not only do they exist, but the major powers also insist on producing absurd numbers of them. The only reasonable answer would seem to be that they exist as symbols of power. But they are, paradoxically, potent and — at the same time — sterile collective symbols. They are swords that make a most impressive rattle, but it is understood that they are also swords that must never, ever be drawn from their scabbards.

All of this begins to imply, rather strongly, that a symbolic interactionist approach to nuclear weapons is at least reasonable. To ignore the symbolic nature of such weapons would be a gross oversight. They are, admittedly, the most dangerous symbolic agents ever created by human hands, but they do display symbolic functions; and we cannot comprehend our present circumstances without understanding that general fact.

The primary symbolic function of any kind of weapon — or any sort of life-threatening capacity — is to evoke a sense of seriousness. The police officer's pistol in its holster makes us aware, even during moments of informal encounter, that we are in the presence of someone to be taken seriously. National governments, to be effective, must be taken seriously. A national power in possession of nuclear weapons must display them and must make their presence known if they are to be useful in the serious implementation of foreign policy.

The central pragmatic concern with nuclear weapons is not their actual employment in war as a total weapon—this is generally conceded to be a matter so dangerous as to threaten all of modern civilization. The pragmatic utilization of nuclear weapons must, therefore, lie in their symbolic power. The major powers are faced, then, with the problem of how best to enhance the symbolic significance of such weapons. The issue at this point becomes how to sustain the communication of power—how to reveal the extent to which our side is to be taken seriously. Seen from this perspective, nuclear weapons become an interesting and disturbing exercise in symbolic interaction.

The older phrase for what is being discussed here is *saber rattling*. Saber rattling refers to the practice of opposed sides rattling their arms in an attempt to convince the enemy that concessions would be better than war. Prior to 1945 saber rattling was generally followed by wars that confirmed the claims of one side or the other. After 1945 saber rattling among the major powers became an exercise in planetary symbolic terrorism. Our term for it, since 1945, has been *brinksmanship*. It is a chilling symbol.

This point of view helps make sense out of the continuing arms race. (Given the sanguine serenity that has come with current arms talks, it is necessary to point out that the development of a trillion-dollar ultramodern weapons system, SDI, which is now in progress, must be viewed as a continuation of the arms race.) When a few nuclear weapons can kill, blind, and maim hundreds of millions of people, why continue the insane enhancement of nuclear stockpiles? Obviously the world's existing nuclear arms are more than sufficient to wreak the utmost havoc across the surface of the planet. Why the excess?

If we consider the various ways in which nuclear weapons must be used as symbols, then the arms race acquires a peculiar rationality. The arms race, from a symbolic interactionist point of view, is little different from the age-old question of why wealthy people act as though they need more money than they already control. After all, somebody who controls a million bucks should possess enough to satisfy virtually any kind of material desire.

The question is readily resolved when you begin to comprehend that wealth, among wealthy people, is primarily a device necessary for maintaining a symbolic position—it is relevant to the symbolic definition of self, not the gratification of physiological desire. A person with a billion dollars might own all the money anyone could possibly need for the satisfaction of material needs. However, if another person exists with two billion dollars, then that other person has, as it were, twice as much communicative or symbolic power—a greater symbolic self. In a confrontation, the person with the greater symbolic force will prevail. To be lower on the scale is to be vulnerable. Note that this becomes an open-ended process. There is no upper limit that will stabilize symbolically defined relationships.

A nation with 5,000 nuclear weapons, sitting across the conference table from one with 6,000 nuclear weapons, is at a symbolic disadvantage. It is difficult to see how they are at a tactical disadvantage because 5,000 such weapons can play about as much hell with the world as 6,000 — after all, overkill is overkill. It is a realm where numbers of weapons begin to lose any kind of tactical or logistical significance and become instead like the numbers on a scoreboard in a game of power communications. We find symbolic security in having a larger number of weapons than they control — even if the numbers do not make any tactical sense. We can imagine ourselves to be more or less secure, by simply contrasting numbers of weapons. The numbers have a rhetorical function as well as a purely military function.

What, then, is the rhetoric of such numbers? What do such numbers say? They say that we control the industrial power and the wealth necessary to produce weapons and to continue producing them on and on and on without letting up. They say that we are willing to sacrifice the general welfare of broad segments of our general population for the production of such weapons. They say that we are willing to match the production of each and every weapon produced by any other nation and then raise the ante. They symbolize our willingness to commit ourselves to the production of such weapons to the fullest of our capabilities. They symbolize, in a straightforward manner, that we are willing to die for our beliefs. They say, among other things, that if we are crazy enough to produce such an overabundance of killing force, we are undoubtedly crazy enough to use it — so, look out!

To the extent that we lag behind in the production of nuclear weapons we convey or symbolize that we do not really mean it when we say that it is better to be dead than red. To withdraw from the race is to concede openly before the nations of the world that we accept vulnerability. In this sense, the symbolic nature of nuclear weapons continues the same traditional forms of symbolic values that weapons have always had.

To put it another way, though considerably oversimplified, hydrogen weapons convey much the same symbolic value as a club. When someone approaches you carrying a club over one shoulder, the problem is to determine whether it is a sign or a symbol. Certainly, the meaning of a club or a nuclear weapon is relatively clear and apparently unambiguous — more sign than symbol. Yet this is the modern problem. Is a nuclear weapon unambiguous in its implications? I bring up this point only to underscore the fact that determining whether an event or object is a sign or symbol is not always something that can be achieved with any precision.

Virtually all tactical or strategic designs for the employment of nuclear weapons that make any sense at all are designs that augment the symbolic power of such weapons. For example, the firing of a warning shot in which a single weapon might be detonated over a selected target is meant to frighten the enemy into withdrawing from further hostilities. It is not designed to bring about an intensification of fighting. However, anyone familiar at all with the vagaries of communication is aware that the symbolic use of weapons is as subject to erroneous interpretations as is the case with any other symbolic act. The enemy might misinterpret the meaning of the warning shot, for example, and respond with a few of its own instead of withdrawing. Such strategies are "loose" in their assessments of the risks involved.

Symbolic interactionism, then, offers another perspective for dealing with the nuclear issue. When we look at hydrogen weapons as symbols, we begin to comprehend them differently. Incidentally, to see them as symbols does not give us any special reason to feel optimistic about the future. For one thing, symbolic control, as I mentioned a moment ago, is an open-ended problem; that is to say, there is no definitive way in which symbolic control can be closed or cut off. The wealth of nations can be poured, and is being poured, endlessly into the open pit of symbolic dominance. The only way out, so it appears, is to withdraw from symbolic exchange — and this, of course, is a completely unrealistic option.

It is an unreasonable option for the most demanding of reasons, for to withdraw from symbolic exchange implies nothing less than withdrawing from language itself. To be involved with symbols is to be involved with symbolic exchanges. There is no way out.

Self and Society

The significance of Meadian thought for explorations into the nuclear impasse is similar to what we obtained from a consideration of Durkheim's thinking. The danger of nuclear weapons is enhanced to the extent we remove ourselves from a critical and rational examination of the options before us. Weapons are idle objects until the rationale for their use is confirmed by emotionally heightened hatreds between human collectivities. Because we acquire our self-concept uncritically as we mature, we simultaneously lose whatever ability we might have had to deal objectively and rationally with the social milieu that defined us as social beings.

This is the basic point of Mead's philosophy — the social unit and the self are similar. They are different forms of the same thing. I am reminded, as I write this, of a recent news film that showed a young child of eleven or so years dressed in the garb of a Ku Klux Klansman, standing next to his father and his father's associates, as a cross was being burned. The child's concept of self was being formed by a generalized other. The matrix of symbols within which the child was maturing was one that would define his sense of self in racial terms.

The element of irrationality here springs from the argument that because the self derives from the ways in which it is defined by some "other," it loses its capacity to evaluate the other that defined it. The example of the little Klansperson is a specific instance of a more general process that goes on all of the time. The general point is that the close bond between self and society (the generalized other) makes it difficult for us to see our own cultural and social traditions in any objective manner.

In this illustration we see why it is pointless to tell people who come from a radically different culture or social group that they are "nuts," "crazy," "immoral," or "insane." They are conforming to a different sense of self—marching to the beat of a different drummer. It is difficult, if not impossible, to establish on our own, from inner sources, the outlines of any socially acquired madness that might happen to contain us. No matter how "mad" our community might be, it always manages, somehow, to seem perfectly "reasonable" to us.

And so outsiders usually provide us with much better critical interpretations of our culture than we are able to provide. For this reason we can look back on historical moments with greater objectivity than we have about our own times. It is also the reason we must draw on others to inform us of how we appear to others. Just as we cannot really know our individual selves without asking someone to tell us how we "look," we cannot really comprehend our collective selves until an outsider gives us some insight into how we "look."

I just suggested that Mead's thought has implications that parallel those of Durkheim's ideas. Recall now that a reading of Durkheim suggests that profound rational evaluation of our communities is difficult because collective representations function to constrain objectivity. Collective representations generate an uncritical and sentimental attachment to the group—that is their nature.

Mead's thinking leads to a similar conclusion—that is, people cannot be rational with respect to social action—but it arrives at this conclusion by a different route. Mead suggests that rational approaches to our communities are difficult because we are, in our individual natures, so thoroughly identified with the community that we cannot separate ourselves from it. To challenge our communities in any profound fashion is to undermine our own identities. Note, for example, that virtually all radicals who critically attack the community in severe ways do so in the name of "higher" community principles and, in so doing, affirm the substance of the moral order they only appear to oppose. Such opposition generally attacks what it sees as "corruption" of what otherwise would be a good community.

In the chapter on Durkheim, we saw that one way to diminish international hostilities would be to enhance a broader sense of community—to move from a nationalistic ideology toward a global ideology. To achieve this, people would need to find a way to create collective representations of a global nature that could be as effective as those of a nationalistic nature. The discussion concluded by observing that, in this century at least, there is little indication of global collective representations having any significant influence when contrasted with nationalistic representations.

Mead's work sheds further light on this. The individual social self, as we suggested earlier, is flexible and changes in character as the social setting changes. An example was the young woman who, in one context, is acting as a student and, in another, as a waitress. In Mead's view, as the social unit is organized and well defined, the social concept of self tends also to be organized and well defined. We gave the example of boys playing baseball.

To a surprising degree, as an individual moves across various social units, the self-concept appropriate to each unit becomes salient. It is this ability of the individual to take on various selves that provides a human social system with much greater flexibility than is found in the hives and hills of social insects such as bees and ants. Worker ants and soldier ants remain workers and soldiers throughout their lives. A human being can be a worker in one context, a soldier in another, and a doting parent in still another. With each role or social activity there is an attendant self-concept.

The extent to which the self varies with context is exemplified in Hannah Arendt's account of Adolf Eichmann. Eichmann, in one context, was a loving and sentimental family man—a perfect father according to those who studied his life. When he left his family to "go to work," as it were, he shifted into the character of a hardened SS officer who enjoyed watching women and children being gassed to death. Although Eichmann's case is extreme, there is truth in the observation that we each have a bit of Dr. Jekyll and Mr. Hyde within us. Differing social contexts bring out different aspects of the self.

Mead would suggest, perhaps, in the case of Eichmann that it is a case where the individual moves from a concept of self drawn from one "generalized other" to a concept of self obtained from another. The domestic self is contained within the family unit. The SS self was contained within the military unit and within Eichmann's sense of duty to his country. His defense in his trial—he was eventually hanged—was that he was only doing his duty.

A striking example of the same thing is found in the famous Zimbardo "prison" study in which an American social-psychologist demonstrated that apparently nonpathological, ordinary, day-to-day college students are all too readily changed into sadistic prison guards and whimpering prisoners merely by providing the appropriate setting. Zimbardo selected a small group of young men to be "guards" and another to be "prisoners" in a fake prison located in the basement of the Psychology Building at Stanford University. Though the setting was artificial and the men were engaged in a psychological study, the guards became authoritarian in nature and the prisoners became rebellious and despairing. This study, along with numerous others, suggests that within different parts of the communal organization, virtual selves exist that people act out as they are moved into the appropriate social contexts.

Within all of this we observe a kind of hierarchy of contexts. At the lower level of the hierarchy we are family members; a little further up the scale we belong to our local softball team; still higher up we are members of our community; then we are members of the state and then members of the nation.

Studies of how people react in crises such as floods or earthquakes show that people move quickly down the hierarchy, as it were, to deal first with the immediate family and then the community.[12] Higher social organizational interests are dropped. The self moves toward the most specific generalized other it knows. There are, of course, exceptions to this principle. A civil war, for example, can tear families apart as members side one way or the other with the policies and ideologies of the greater social units. The rending of the family is more an exception than the rule, however.

If this is true, if the self moves toward the most specific generalized other it knows, then any kind of attempt to promote a generalized other at the level of global commitment can only result in weak and highly tenuous ties between the individual and this highly abstracted communal unit. (Later, in a discussion of structural-functionalism, we shall see that there are more realistic routes to a global community than one that attempts to locate it in psychological units such as the self.)

Symbolic interactionism, then, inclines us toward a pessimistic evaluation of the future. It suggests purely open-ended struggles for symbolic dominance. It suggests that we find ourselves most completely within highly organized and localized authoritarian groups. We gain a higher sense of self as the group is extended. At the same time, this higher self must be carefully cultivated to resist the more immediate influence of local groups. It suggests that we cannot achieve any kind of realistic critical sense of our communities because we are, in a sense, the community itself.

If these speculative conclusions are reasonable, then the world appears headed for a continuation of the arms race, in one form or other, until the race is stopped by external pressures — economic collapse or a catastrophic involvement in a total war.

National Identity

It is time to close this discussion of symbolic interactionism as it applies to the nuclear arms issue. In these last paragraphs we will consider the issue of national identity. Nuclear weapons are designed to promote and protect the national interests of the countries that possess them. When it comes to fighting, people fight in terms of national identities. (Although this is true, the individual basically tends to fight because his or her buddies are fighting. The power of the local self-defining unit must not be overlooked.)

There are any number of instances of the nearly eerie irrationality of the individual in such cases. For example, during the Israeli-Egyptian war the two sides would communicate across the lines during lulls and exchange gossip and talk about human concerns. There was a camaraderie about it all. Then they would return to fighting and try to kill each other. Or, in *All's Quiet on the Western Front*, there is a touching scene when a soldier in World War I has a chance to shoot an enemy infantryman who has just taken off his boots and is soaking his feet in a little stream. The soldier puts his sights on the enemy and then sees, clearly, that his gun is pointed at a human being who is experiencing the delightful momentary pleasure of relief from overwhelming fatigue and human misery. He cannot pull the trigger and returns to his unit. For a second the overwhelming humanity of the moment dominates and the rifleman's nationalistic self is subordinated.[13]

National identity and war are closely related. In order to have wars between nations large numbers of people must be united with the national collective. From a Meadian point of view this is done by establishing a self-concept or, as we might say today, an identity that is nationalistic in nature. There appear to be two basic philosophies with respect to national identity. On the one hand there are those who espouse a return to earlier forms of identity between self and nation such that the individual endorses whatever the national leadership prescribes. Moreover, proponents say, national values should prevail over local values. There is something to be said for this point of view because, without national identities, large systems such as nation-states cannot function. I shall refer to this form of national identity as *naive patriotism.*

A nice example of the endorsement of naive patriotism appeared in the newspapers in 1987 in the form of a recommendation by General Paul Kelley of the United States Marine Corps that the nation establish an institute for patriotic values. (We can, I think, safely presume few people would be in favor of establishing an institute for unpatriotic values.) Patriotism, however, in its general, unexamined form, can be volatile stuff. It is something that is rarely handled with the great care it deserves. Certainly it is too important to be left in the hands of generals, militarists, jingoists, and others who find little difficulty buying the argument that excess and irrationality are always to be excused if one's cause is, on the surface at least, just.

There is nothing wrong with patriotism except it has a tendency to move toward excess; and in its excessive forms it becomes vicious and, ultimately, lethal. For example, I can think of no group of people more energetic and dedicated in their patriotic fervor than were the German people in the period preceding World War I and continuing through the years of the next world conflict. We can fault Hitler and other autocratic leaders for a variety of reasons, but rarely can we fault them for the intensity of their patriotic fervor. It was a virtue with which they were filled to the brim.

Patriotism in itself is not a solution to either domestic or world problems for the reasons outlined. Passionate patriotic commitment can be emotionally satisfying to the troubled mind. Unfortunately, it also has a tendency to blind us to our weaknesses and our excesses. In its worst manifestations patriotism amounts to little more than a gigantic, massive, nationalistic ego trip. The excessively moral and patriotic people of the world are as dangerous, in their way, as the excessively immoral and unpatriotic.

Another and, I think, more reasonable approach to national identity is to recognize that we are Americans, or Japanese, or Italian or whatever we might happen to be and that national identities are not going to be uprooted nor should they be uprooted. As this discussion of symbolic-interactionist theory tried to make clear, the national community necessarily is part of our concept of self. We cannot easily remove a part of ourselves from ourselves.

(Expatriates, people who migrate away from their home communities because of dissatisfactions of one kind or another, commonly discover just how difficult this proves to be.)

If what I called "naive patriotism" is dangerous — and I quite seriously think it is — and yet people cannot disavow their national identities, then what is to be done? I would like to propose that people move toward a possibility that is permitted by Meadian philosophy while, at the same time, avoiding the irrationalities of blind patriotic fervor. This possibility exists in what I like to think of as *enlightened patriotism*.

The best example I can think of to clarify what I mean by enlightened patriotism is to consider regional or state identities within the United States. We commonly recognize ourselves as Coloradans, Texans, Hoosiers, Sooners, and so on. However, we also recognize the bonds that unite us as a larger collective. This nation fought a war to prevent regional patriotism from dominating nationalistic interests.

We who had the good fortune to grow up in this nation made the astonishing and radical discovery that to love America is another way of expressing our love for our state. Conversely, our love for our particular state is also an expression of our love for all of the states. It is a love that many of us find little difficulty transferring as we move from state to state. How quickly, for example, we find ourselves rooting for our new teams after we move to a new state while, at the same time, still having a place in our hearts for the old hometown team.

In a global system where travel times are now measured in minutes rather than months and years, we can no longer afford to indulge in the luxury of naive patriotism. We must concede a new world in the making. That world is not here yet. The globe is still sliced into individual nationalistic fiefdoms.

We cannot, as was argued earlier, simply ask people to take on global self-identities. The organization that could create such identities does not yet exist in any fully expressive fashion. At the same time, it is apparent that nation-states do not function with the same autonomy that characterized earlier times.

All we can look forward to, then, is a growing awareness that some kind of enlightened patriotism is a better notion than more naive and simplistic conceptions of patriotism. We must come to see our national boundaries as we see state boundaries. As we travel from nation to nation and familiarize ourselves with others, we broaden our sense of self. We also enhance our changes of reducing the emotional antagonisms that lead to war.

SUMMARY

Symbolic interactionism, developed in the philosophy courses of George Herbert Mead at the University of Chicago, argues that symbols are central to human social existence. Particularly significant is the manner in which our concept of self is vulnerable to symbolic definitions. It is through its capacity to define the self-concepts of members that the community bonds the individual to communal interests.

The relevance of this to nuclear arms and the arms race is that the individual, as a communally defined being, is not able to "see" the community in any rationally critical manner. The reaction to criticism or contrary ways of viewing social policies tends to become one in which opposition is viewed as weird or strange or, in the extreme case, as mad. We are unable to see our own insanities. The symbolic-interactionist point of view shows us how nuclear weapons have become symbols of our military might — how we have gone beyond overkill in an unending process of saber rattling. Nuclear weapons, unlike the weapons of earlier periods, are unique in their symbolic meaning. Patriotism is a matter of defining how closely the individual and the state should be bonded. Drawing upon symbolic interactionist thinking we dared consider this emotionally charged notion and the suggestion that patriotism, like any other symbol, is subject to varied meanings. I suggested that naive patriotism be replaced with a concern for enlightened patriotism, which is by no means an idealistic notion — the American experience is, at its best, an exercise in enlightened patriotism.

Chapter 5

Max Weber: The Age of Rationalism

THE AGE OF REASON

As the immense power of reason (in its newer scientific guise) became apparent in the 18th and 19th centuries, modern philosophers and writers began singing hymns of praise to rationality. This, they declaimed, is now an age of reason; we shall step into a new era of promise. Traditional ways of doing things, it was argued, must be replaced by science, logic, and reason. Moral and economic philosophies grounded in the dreams and fantasies of technological and material advances replaced philosophies grounded in religious sentiments. Progress was sloganized and became "our most important product." Whatever progress might be, the way to achieve it, the new intellectuals argued, was through reason.

All in all, this rationalistic euphoria turned into heady stuff and so it remains down to the present day — though there are signs the euphoria is wearing off. We can see that philosophy, like champagne, is an intoxicating beverage. Both are capable, when *over*indulged in, of producing erratic vision and, eventually, rather severe headaches. We may have approached such a point in the 20th century. However, I raise this point more as a question than as a demonstrable fact. Have we overindulged in rationalism? Is the age of reason beginning to stagger and stumble from its own excesses?

There is no certain answer. However, we can examine the question through the works of one of the greatest geniuses in all of Western social philosophy — Max Weber.[1] Weber took on no smaller task than an examination of the implications of living in the new age — the age of rational decision making. His examination of rationality was dispassionate. It was thorough. It remains, down to the present time, one of the best foundations from which to launch an investigation into the nature of modern, rational social systems.

Max Weber was born in 1864 and died shortly after the end of World War I in 1920. He was a contemporary of Emile Durkheim, and he stands among the foremost social philosophers and observers of the late 19th and early 20th centuries. He held professorships in such major European schools as the Universities of Berlin, Heidelberg, and Munich. He remains famous for his studies of the structure and character of modern bureaucracies.

He is best known for his thesis that modern capitalism is a moral as well as an economic system. As such, he argued, capitalistic economic practices have their origins in moral doctrines developed by leaders of the Protestant religious movement in Europe — especially Luther and Calvin. Weber based his argument on the belief that ideas are significant factors in economic systems. This made him a major opponent of those who argue, along with Marx, that economic systems are the product of purely material or physical transformations in human communities.

The discussion that follows concentrates on three central concepts or issues that are central themes in Weber's thought:

1. Rationality
2. Bureaucracy
3. Religion and economic systems

RATIONALITY

Weber argued that the distinguishing feature of modern social systems is the emphasis given to rational forms of social organization rather than to tradition. Modern societies are organized in ways designed to create efficiency and maximize productivity. Rationality is located in logic and precision. Rational knowledge is considered superior to other forms of knowledge — forms of knowledge that are viewed as myth, fiction, metaphysics, or supernaturalism.

Rationality is dominant over older traditionalistic systems which emphasized tradition or custom as the criterion by which the worth of an action should be considered. One of the questions Weber pursued in great depth was the question of what happens when human societies move from traditionalism to rationalism as a basis of social and communal organization.

BUREAUCRACY

The question of what happens when we become dedicated to rationality in favor of tradition leads naturally to a consideration of modern bureaucracies. From Weber's point of view, the finest example of the efficiently organized modern social unit is the bureaucratic system. Although bureaucracies are commonly stereotyped as bumbling jumbles of red tape, Weber recognized them for what they really are — social systems created to deal with the overwhelming complexity of modern large-scale social structures. The clan and the tribe are sufficient for dealing with relatively small-scale social systems. But when we come to social systems involving hundreds of millions of people working in closely interrelated ways, more elaborate modes of organization are called for.

Modern mass societies provide both the necessity for the development of bureaucratic structures and the means for their development. Bureaucracy is generally associated, in popular thought, with governmental agencies, education systems, and the military. Business enterprises are also bureaucratically ordered. However, as they munch on a Big Mac at McDonald's, people rarely are cognizant of the fact they are dealing with one of the larger bureaucratic systems in American industry. Along with many other things in this modern age, the lowly hamburger has become, so to speak, bureaucratized.[2]

The scale of production of the McDonald's chain staggers the imagination. Indeed, it is beyond imagination. No one can really comprehend what it means when we say a galaxy contains billions of stars, and we really cannot comprehend what it means when McDonald's tells us they sold (by the end of 1987) 60 billion hamburgers — the number changes with astonishing rapidity. In any case, 60 billion hamburgers is a lot of hamburgers. If you ate a hamburger every minute it would take you more than 114,000 years to eat that many.

There would be no need for an organization of this type in a small tribal society. Furthermore, the society would not offer the means for the development of an elaborate system dedicated to the singular purpose of providing huge quantities of food as quickly, cheaply, abundantly, and efficiently as possible. These new forms of organization, these new-style bureaucratic corporate systems, promote the ideal of efficiency as a primary moral ideal. They are, despite stereotypes of the bureaucracy as pretty much an inefficient mess, the most efficient forms of social organization yet achieved. In fact, there are times when they carry the ideal of efficiency to absurd extremes.

The strangest example I can think of to illustrate this argument is the extent to which German bureaucracy, in this century, struggled with the problems of efficient mass extermination. However, we should not be too quick to mention Germany in this regard. Modern bureaucracies in all the major nations of the world today are still putting their quickest and finest minds to this task — whether we like to accept the fact or not. It is grotesque to put it this way, but it makes the point indelibly: Efficient mass extermination is concerned with solving the problem of turning people into hamburger with the same efficiency and in terms of the same rational imperatives that McDonald's relies on to get hamburgers into people.

An issue related to rationality and efficient social systems is that of leadership. Weber was concerned with how transformations in social organization influence the way leaders are selected and how they deal with the problems of leadership after being selected. Once again, Weber relied on the theme of rationality to examine leadership in modern societies. For example, what happens when leadership is "rationalized"? How are leaders selected most efficiently and their leadership qualities best determined? How is leadership effectively manifested? How does a leader achieve "efficient" leadership?

RELIGION AND ECONOMIC SYSTEMS

The third feature of Weber's thinking that we will discuss is his analysis of capitalism. Weber argued, in *The Protestant Ethic and the Spirit of Capitalism,* that modern capitalism was not simply an economic system but a moral system as well. As a moral system it radically transformed older moral codes. For example, though this states the case with great oversimplification, where earlier Western morality condemned greed as sinful, modern capitalistic systems promote greed as a *moral* imperative. One cannot resist noting that early church figures such as St. Augustine would surely never have condoned the modern practice of referring to ourselves by the barbaric, though casually accepted, title of "consumers."

The whole point of present-day capitalistic economies is to promote extensive and expensive consumption. Advertising permeates Western economic practice, and the end of advertising is to create need and promote consumption rather than conservation and economy in its deeper sense. We are not passing judgment on capitalism when we suggest, following Weber, that it establishes greed as a *moral* quality. We *should*, indeed we must, be greedy to make the system work. However, I need to emphasize that the moral character of modern capitalism is different from the moral systems (such as the Christian asceticism of the 12th century) it now overlays.

The progression from a Christian morality in which the individual was enjoined to constrain desire to one in which we are now enjoined to consume as much as possible poses an interesting problem. How did the change take place? Weber argued that several unique developments in Protestant religious thought paved the way for a new moral order—one that proved to be a fertile ground for the development of a capitalistic moral and economic system.

A RETURN TO THE CONCEPT OF RATIONALITY

Max Weber carried out his work in roughly the 40-year period extending from 1880 to 1920. During this period modern bureaucracies, operating within relatively autonomous nation-states, acquired enormous power. They impressed Weber as the most effectively and efficiently organized social systems ever developed within human cultures.

By the turn of the century it was fairly obvious that all phases of human communal experience were being transformed by bureaucratization—education, literature, science, the arts, the military, business, medicine, religion, and even ancillary activities such as entertainment, play, and leisure. Modern professional football, for example, represents the extreme bureaucratization of a leisure activity, though we probably rarely include professional football in casual listings of our favorite bureaucratic structures. What was once a matter of country boys trying to push a large ball into the village of another group of boys has now become massively organized. In few other sectors of American life is so much attention paid to getting the last wretched gram of efficiency out of a collective effort.

Weber devoted much of his effort to the study of modern bureaucracies. His interpretations of this form of organization were based on the concept of rationality. That is to say, modern bureaucracies and corporations are guided by the criterion of rational efficiency. Tradition should not interfere with maximum efficiency in pursuing the organization's goals.

Though people living in industrial-technological cultures find rationality virtually beyond challenge, older or "traditional" social systems operate on a different basis. For example, it strikes a modern person as peculiar that so-called primitive cultures engage in warfare where the entire war stops the moment a single individual is injured. The side suffering the injury returns home to grieve over the insult.[3] The side inflicting the injury engages in a celebration of its victory. After a period of a few months, the battle is once again joined and then brought to a conclusion after another fighter is injured or, perhaps, killed. This form of fighting, in which men engage in what we would see as more of a game than a real battle, is highly constrained by tradition. The amount of maiming or killing is limited. Moreover, the individuals vulnerable to injury during the fighting are restricted to the able-bodied males who form the fighting units.

Modern warfare, of course, moved beyond the tradition that war involves only the military. In the quest to accomplish the ends of war, it is now considered rational to destroy not only the enemy's military system but also the broader industrial-service complex that supports the military system. It became rational to attack all members of the enemy nation — men, women, children, and livestock. Rational considerations of the enemy make the enemy a total complex rather than a partial one. The consequence is that the scale of killing is extended.

At the same time, I don't want you to think that primitive or traditionally regulated war is always relatively gentle and constrained while modern war is unique in its viciousness. The chivalric code of the medieval period would have to be viewed as a fine example of warfare conducted under traditional constraints, At the same time, medieval warfare often devastated innocent civilian populations. A case in point is the Catharist heresy, which led to the slaughter of large numbers of innocent people in the 12th century.

My point, however, is that modern society, from a Weberian point of view, endorses rational assessments of situations and is guided by the ideal of rational efficiency. If tradition or custom interferes in any way with the ideal of rationality, then it is tradition and custom that must give way rather than the ideal of rationality.

The Disenchantment of the World

So pervasive is the idea of rational conduct today that it is difficult for those of us living in Western culture to conceive of any other way to respond to the world around us. We have, in a sense, rationalized the entire world. Everything we touch or deal with becomes an object for rational evaluation. We accept the "disenchantment" of the world. The ideal of rational accomplishment is now a transcendent norm cutting across all nations and all modern social groups. The very term *modern* implies an acceptance of rational programs over traditional or customary programs.

When Weber referred to the "rationalization of the world" he implied two things. First, all societies are now forced to accept the norm or rationality. Second, within any society virtually all aspects of life are subjected to rational evaluations. One of the more unique features of modern times is that just about anything one can imagine has been subjected to the test of rationally maximized effectiveness.

Possibly the best index of how deeply rationality became completely ingrained within Western mentality is the fact that Western philosophy ignores problems that cannot be dealt with in rational terms. This is basically the position taken by a school of thinking known as *logical positivism*. Essentially, logical positivism only accepts knowledge for which positive or observational proof can be given. (Professor Kenneth Boulding once pointed out that logical positivism has been a powerful influence in modern academic thinking because nobody wants to be thought of as an illogical negativist.) To take such a philosophy seriously would mean that by far the most engaging problems and issues confronting humankind today would have to be bypassed in favor of dealing only with those simple enough to respond to rational treatment.

The example generally used by proponents of positivism is the waste of time that resulted when philosophers tried to figure out how many angels could dance on the head of a pin. This question obviously cannot be resolved in any rational or empirical or positive fashion and, rightly, should be dismissed as a meaningless question. The examination of such foolish questions, however, is not without lessons — if nothing else, it provides another illustration of the ways in which people become confused by language. After all, if language leads us to think there are angels and pins, then it is not entirely unreasonable to find people puzzling over how these two things might relate to each other. The positivists, nonetheless, were generally correct in their concern over what they looked on as metaphysical madness.

Regardless of how we feel about angels hopping around on the heads of pins, there is a whole realm of questioning that cannot be abandoned simply because positive knowledge cannot provide answers. For example, when does uniquely human life begin? At conception? A few weeks or months after conception? At birth? A few months or years after birth? No one can answer this question though, of course, people are still trying.

The fact that such questions cannot be answered by positive means does not mean they are to be ignored. However, so compelling is the norm of rationalism in modern society that unanswerable questions of this type are not supposed to be given serious consideration. Unfortunately, the simple solution of positivism to the vexing questions of life is to ignore them. This is neither a courageous nor, ultimately, a wise position to take. Or, to draw on an old cliche, it is a solution that tosses out the baby with the bath.

The discouraging moral consequence of this philosophical stance is the withdrawal of large numbers of men and women, the cream of our intellectual community, into the sterile confines of the laboratory, the computer rooms, and other places where problems generate positive and unambiguous answers. So it is that our scientists and technicians, in all too many instances, take pride in the fact they acquired their expertise and never soiled their minds with the dirty problems of human failure. They can get through an entire college program and never take a single course in social science or ethical philosophy or religion or any other such frustrating effort. There is no display of courage in this; and positivism, all too often, becomes an exalted excuse for moral failure.

Any social or moral issue is not amenable to simple empirical demonstrations. As a consequence, positivism, in its stricter forms, abandoned consideration of such issues. In other words, positivism withdraws at the point where resolution of arguments becomes a serious matter. The consequence is that social and moral issues are still being resolved essentially by fighting or by the imposition of political or economic power. Nonetheless, modern social science owes much of its existence to the idea that even human issues can eventually be handled in purely rational ways. But few among the "real" rationalists, the higher scientists and technologists, lend their support to this dream. Natural science prides itself on its insular intellectual provincialism. The social sciences are, in effect, on their own as they explore the promise of better ways of resolving human controversy.

The Rationalization of Sex and Other Elements of Modern Life

We are concerned, then, with Weber's observation that one of the striking characteristics of modern social systems is that they were taken over, so to speak, by the ideal of rationality. All aspects of our lives now come under the norm of rational questioning. One example, perhaps, is sufficient to suggest —but only suggest— the extent to which the rational approach to the world has become dominant in our time. I refer now to the studies of human sexuality carried out by Masters and Johnson.[4]

What is pertinent about the Masters and Johnson study is that it is certainly difficult to imagine men and women of the late Renaissance or possibly even the early 19th century finding such a work acceptable. However, by the middle of the 20th century, the idea of having scientists examine particularly specific and personally intimate, detailed, and squishy aspects of human sexuality was not only tolerated but also applauded as necessary and proper.

Sex, along with about any other aspect of our lives, is now something to be dealt with rationally. While the traditional mentality of, let us say, the 12th and 13th centuries incorporated sexual conduct into the holy sacraments, modern rational mentality seeks to make sexuality another "problem" that can and should be investigated analytically. Sexuality is incorporated into the rational mentality. Behind the research and empirical investigations of modern sexologists is the guiding norm of the rational attainment of a better sex life or, perhaps more curiously, a more efficient sex life.

Sex, however, is only one indication of the extent to which the rational norm became dominant in modern life. There are others. In fact, it is difficult to think of anything in modern life that has not, one way or another, been profoundly touched by the norm of rationality.

Item: We are told certain foods are superior to other foods with respect to maintaining health. We are, moreover, told *how* we should eat and *when* we should eat to gain maximum benefits from food. What we should eat and when we should eat is determined by dietary experts, not tradition. Our eating practices are rationalized.

Item: We are told that certain ways of bringing up our children are better than others. These child-rearing policies are developed and approved by psychologists and social scientists or other child-rearing experts. Child rearing is rationalized.

Item: We attend movies and are entertained by programs whose popularity is constantly subjected to market analysis. Our entertainment is rationalized.

Item: Our music is orchestrated, organized, and mechanized by synthesizers and electronic augmentation. It is written down and mathematically interpreted. Music is rationalized.

Item: Modern churches turn more and more to computers to keep track of members, promote events, and establish mailing lists. There is "Bible Study" software available. Religion is rationalized.

Item: Political candidates rely on careful, scientifically conducted polls and surveys to establish appropriate images. Politics is rationalized.

Item: The American university is being called on by several state legislatures, as a matter of law, to establish its "product" and show evidence this "product" is being efficiently distributed—truly, an astonishing but nonetheless seriously enacted bit of legislation. So we discover that education is rationalized.

With regard to the last item, the Colorado Legislature, following the lead of several other states, enacted a bill that nicely reveals the press of rationality in modern times. This bill requires universities within the state system to identify the "product" they produce and distribute. They are further required to present cost analyses that show how efficiently the product is being produced and distributed. This reduces knowledge to the status of electric toasters, bicycles, or anything else that can be evaluated in terms of cost efficiency. It is education as commodity — a strange metaphor if ever there was one. This is rationalism being pushed to its breaking point.

One of Weber's major concerns was the extent to which modern societies are organized in terms of what he referred to as rational-bureaucratic systems. Such systems are dedicated to the efficient achievement of whatever goals the system is concerned with achieving. A state university, for example, is concerned with educating large numbers of people or, at least, certifying large numbers of people as being educated — there is, of course, a difference. Note that those who oversee the operations of the university are concerned with doing this as economically as possible. Anyone who is an "insider" at such institutions is aware of how much emphasis is given to productive efficiency measured in *strictly economic terms*. The university may be a center of learning, but it is a center that pays close attention to how efficiently (that is, how cheaply) such learning is taking place.

Efficiency is the major concern of the rational-bureaucratic organization. We modern men and women of the 20th century are so used to the ideal of efficiency and rationality in our institutions that we perhaps lose sight of the extent to which earlier systems were grounded in tradition and custom as ways of getting things done.

The Rationalization of War

War and its practice obviously responded to the modern movement toward rationality. Ironically, the rational quest for ever-more-effective destructive devices produced weapons so overwhelming that major military powers are, at least for the moment, afraid to use them. Nuclear weapons are the ultimate product of the rational quest for destructive efficiency. There still remains the possibility of developing a weapon that could destroy not merely cities but an entire planet with a single blast.

However, until we are confronted with interplanetary enemies, the current 30-megaton nuclear weapon is powerful enough that we can justify referring to it as an "ultimate" solution to the age-old problem of developing an efficient means of killing, maiming, and blinding large numbers of people quickly and very, very cheaply on a per capita basis.

To think about nuclear war is, as Herman Kahn so nicely phrased it, to think about the unthinkable.[5] We must constantly keep in mind that science is a two-edged sword. It produces marvelous machines and devices and ways of thinking about the world. On the other hand, it does not balk at any problem that has an underlying rationally solvable form. The ethical consequences of the problem do not especially bother the scientist—disclaimers to the contrary.

If a problem poses an intriguing challenge for scientists, its appeal is essentially irresistible. The scientific attitude is that science must move forward. If technology burdens people with transitions, shifts, and lethal consequences of varied sorts, then the people will just have to solve that aspect of the situation for themselves. Science is not concerned with potentially unsolvable problems.

So it came about, for example, that the 20th century saw the most rationally developed countries in the world work on the problem of how to destroy large populations efficiently and quickly. At the turn of the century we discovered the amazing powers of the Gatling gun. By the middle of the century Germany was struggling with trainloads of prisoners who were gassed in huge rooms in an effort to deal with the logistics of mass killing. Shortly thereafter we discovered that entire cities could be killed in a matter of a moment or two.

Once again, we should be careful about pointing our righteous finger at the Germans who resorted to the "final solution" in dealing with their enemies. The final solution, of course, consisted basically of finding the most efficient ways possible, given existing logistical constraints, to destroy unwanted people. The Nazi regime was not the only one interested in final solutions of one kind or another—it is an idea that has an eternal and unfortunately, I think, wide appeal.

So compelling is the desire to destroy an enemy or anyone we deem inferior, however such groups might be defined, that we all tend to become enchanted with the dream of an efficient solution to the problem the enemy poses for us. With nuclear weapons the problem is that the dream can be all too readily fulfilled. There were times in recent American history when, had we been certain the destruction would have been complete and we would not suffer serious retaliatory consequences, we would have likely unleashed the same ultimate solution that other nations, in the past, turned to as a way out of their all-too-human problems.

These new weapons, these ultimate products of the rational mind, paradoxically enough, brought us to the most irrational impasse ever encountered by modern nation-states. Nuclear weapons, themselves ultrarational devices in terms of their capacity for efficient destruction, have created a situation in which there is no reasonable way of responding to the problems they generate.

We have, at the moment, no rational way of responding to the threat posed by hydrogen weapons and the extremely efficient systems for delivering such weapons—that is, cruise missiles; ICBMs; sneaky, silent submarines; and the like—that also now exist. We find ourselves, then, with no ancient and well-established traditions, rituals, or customs that provide rules or means for dealing with these new problems. At the same time, we have no rational programs either. We are in a situation where we have neither rational nor traditional systems for responding to the greatest threat ever to face the people of this diminishing planet.

As a consequence, the various solutions that are set forth have a peculiar quality. They must conform to the norm of rationality if they are to be accepted by the people and the leadership of modern nation-states. Yet the fundamental idea of a super weapon is to create a device that makes destruction so efficient and so simple it cannot be countered by any means — *including rational ones*. The development of an ultrarationalized weapons system led to an impasse with regard to solving the problems it created.

No program for controlling nuclear weapons set forth during the years since 1945, when "the bomb" made its appearance, makes much sense. Nuclear weapons represent the supreme achievement of the rational norm. The greatest problem ever facing humankind — the attainment of a super weapon with which to fight one's enemies — was finally solved. As it turned out, there is only one drawback to the solution — the weapon itself cannot be monopolized.

World peace could be autocratically and unilaterally established by a dominant world power if, and only if, it were capable of maintaining exclusive control of *the* weapon. We might not like such a situation if the controlling power were someone other than ourselves. However, if we were the dominant power, then (we like to think) the world could be ordered in terms of good, basic democratic values and the people of the globe would finally be forced to shape up. This dream was quickly shattered when the Soviet Union acquired the knowledge necessary to build the bomb. It did so with such speed that Americans were, at first, convinced that national security had been breached by traitorous individuals in government, education, science, and elsewhere. The 1950s were a time of massive security panic — and the panic remains.

How can we solve the problem posed by a device that was designed by the rational mentality to have no solution? How can we deal with the fact it is now a pervasive part of the modern world? Three basic approaches have been taken: nuclear freezes, mutually assured destruction (MAD), and the Strategic Defense Initiative.

Nuclear freeze A popular approach to the nuclear crisis is to argue for a "freeze" on nuclear weapons. This makes little sense in a world where the United States has 20,000 devices in place and the Soviet Union a similar number. Estimates on the number and variety of nuclear weapons vary tremendously. These figures are considered conservative. Other figures claim the number of nuclear weapons in America's arsenal alone is as high as 34,000. Here statistical enumeration becomes mad after a certain point. Certainly 10,000 weapons of this variety should be enough to make anyone wonder why they exist and what they might accomplish if they ever served the primary purpose for which they were constructed.

To "freeze" nuclear weapons at their current level of development still leaves enough explosive power to destroy virtually every country in the world. So, it is argued, we should reduce the number of weapons. However, this approach runs into trouble. Even if we reduce the number to zero, we cannot forget how to make the weapons. In effect, we must come to live with the hydrogen bomb. The use of only a few, perhaps only 2 percent of what we now have, would suffice to make life intolerable for vast numbers of people.

A strange debate has taken place over the last several years with regard to whether an all-out nuclear war between the great powers would result in a nuclear "winter." There are those who argue it would destroy all life on the planet. On the other hand there are those who argue the aftermath would not be all that bad—there would be a few survivors, perhaps even quite a few. We would experience a nuclear "autumn."[6]

What is interesting is how the debate takes the form of an oddly "cool" rational discussion with each side claiming to be the rational side. This debate, as much as anything, suggests that the rational norm has reached the point of absurdity. The issue should be beyond debate. That there could even be such a debate over the degree of evil of an all-out nuclear exchange suggests that rationalism has moved beyond the proper limits of its usefulness as a social norm. If so, we are left with the problem of trying to find a better way to think about the problems that confront us.

The debate is absurd because even a small nuclear exchange, of just 50 or so heavy nuclear devices, could kill possibly as many as 60 or 70 million people in a few minutes' time. Perhaps the sun might be shining that day; the air could be warm; the birds, in other places, singing. The little smoke that might swirl up from 50 burning cities would probably not compare with the volcanic ash from Mount Saint Helens, and the world would not be plunged into an ominous dark winter.

But it would be dark winter—dark winter, indeed, in the souls of people if they survived that worst moment in human history. There is, after all, a literal and a figurative meaning to words. Scientists seem capable of accepting seriously only what is literal, but what is figurative is what moves us. When we hear about the idea of a nuclear autumn, it is almost appealing—we think perhaps there would still be college football games, Thanksgiving turkeys, frost-tinted leaves, pumpkin pies, and all the other joys of fall. Let there be no doubt about it; nuclear autumn, like nuclear winter, would be pure and total hell.

Nothing suggests more profoundly the final drying up of the human soul, the perversion of imagination, and the selling out of the ethical to the demands of rational positivism than this inane debate. Nothing more clearly reveals the rational mind at work with a problem and solving it regardless of whether it makes figurative sense to solve it or not.

To return to the idea of a nuclear freeze as a solution, we can only conclude that it has not had any noticeable practical success. World leaders give lip service to the idea, but the arms race continues. The idea of a nuclear freeze was even amusingly punned as a kind of sherbet by one American leader—whose ethics must be somewhere around the level of a lemming's —who asked, "What's a nuclear freeze, a frozen dessert?" Even if the nuclear freeze idea were successful, it would be difficult to see how the situation would be any less serious. To freeze in place thousands of nuclear weapons does not seem especially rational.

Mutually Assured Destruction   If nuclear freeze is ineffective, the present policy of "mutually assured destruction," commonly called MAD, seems equally irrational. This supposedly more realistic approach emphasizes the idea of deterrent forces to be kept on the alert at all times so that an attack launched by any country will bring about not only the probable destruction of its enemy but its own destruction as well. This is the policy now followed by the major powers. If the Soviet Union attacks the United States, its destruction is assured. Similarly, if the United States attacks the Soviet Union, its destruction is also assured. There is a rationality of sorts in MAD; but, as the acronym suggests, it is a wild and crazy policy. It is obviously paranoid and it is obviously dangerous—but what else is there to do?

My point is that, from a Weberian stance, modern societies face a major profound crisis—perhaps not too far removed from the crises that faced the Catholic Church in Europe at the time of the Reformation. There is not only the physical threat posed by nuclear weapons but a kind of underlying "normative" threat as well. Rationality itself, as a transcendental norm—a norm above criticism—is weakening. At the very moment it displayed its massive powers, it began to show its wrinkles and infirmities.

Keep in mind that Weber emphasized the significance of the ideal of rationality as a basis for modern social organization and what might loosely be called social "progress." If the ideal of rationality is under attack, no matter how indirectly, then the basis of modern social organization is in itself under attack. Modern governments are faced with the task not only of protecting themselves from nuclear destruction but also with the task of preserving the belief that major problems can best be solved not by tradition or custom but by rational analysis.

Superrationalistic solutions: SDI   We now come to the third approach to the problem of nuclear weapons, that of setting up an invincible and eternal defensive shield against any kind of nuclear threat. This is the idea behind the Strategic Defense Initiative (SDI) or so-called Star Wars program now being researched in the United States and, assuredly, in the Soviet Union. (When it comes to military matters, purely military matters, the two nations are more alike than different.)

In broad outlines the SDI calls for as many as 600 nuclear armed space satellites circling the earth. Each would be capable of directing laser energy at any point on the surface of the earth or above it. The firepower of these satellites could, as one scientist working with the SDI program put it, turn any city on the globe into hamburger. The idea is to be able to destroy the enemy's rockets as they are fired from either their silos or from submarines. That, anyway, is the idea. With a little imagination, of course, one might think of some other things that could be done with a deep-space artillery of such fantastic magnitude and power.

If science and the rational norm need shoring up, then the new proposals set forth by advisers to American presidents with regard to the development of a Strategic Defense Initiative can be seen as having a special appeal. Nothing, in modern society, represents the perfection of rational thought more than its technology. Machines are the epitomization of reason. The efficiency of machines can be determined by mathematical models. Machines can be tested. Machines have a "track record" of accomplishment. Machines are capable of constant refinement and improvement. So it must be, then, that a rational solution to the irrational predicament posed by nuclear weapons must come from technology itself.

At least, this is what a cultural mentality dominated by the dream of rational accomplishment would be inclined to believe. If technology, in the form of hydrogen weapons, led us to our current reliance on policies such as MAD, then technology will get us out of the mess it created.

In a number of ways this commitment to technology does not make much sense. After all, technology got us into this mess in the first place, and now technology is being called on to get us out. (If you were to say enhancing technology will diminish the effects of technology, you would be engaging in an oxymoron—a well-known literary device that is rhetorically effective, even though it is obviously logically irrational. The SDI argues that the hyperrationalized weapons systems of today can be overcome by working to make our systems more hyperrationalized.)

Is the problem a rational-technological problem? Or is it a problem with deeper roots—roots that rest in less rational issues? Possibly it is not our technology but our institutions that are the problem. But social and political systems are not rational in the same way technology is rational. They are a subject the rational mentality does not really know how to deal with. Institutions are rationally "messy." Machines are rationally "clean."

Therefore, from the viewpoint of the rational mentality, it appears to make better sense to avoid the problems of social and political reform—relying instead on the assumption that our institutions are fixed and incapable of reform—and turn to our machines as those devices with the greatest hope of progress with respect to solving the nuclear impasses.

Review

At this point we should review how Weber instructs us with regard to what is taking place in the late 20th century. Following Weber, we noted that the rational ideal prevails. We rationalize virtually every feature of our lives; even human sexuality is now rationalized to an extent that Weber himself would probably have found shocking. The criterion of rationally evaluated efficiency of accomplishment prevails over other criteria.

Certainly ritual and custom, if they cannot demonstrate efficiency of accomplishment, are discarded without much regret. It is interesting to note, in this regard, the general amusement and lack of seriousness that college students of today — along with a fair portion of the faculty — give to commencement ceremonies. These academic rituals are communal celebrations, once deeply moving, of the achievements of the students. However, as rituals, they are now seen as archaic irrational events and, possibly, an interference with the efficient pursuit of either work activities or leisure activities of the individual's choice.

Within a context of rational ideology, each problem is approached in terms of rational available solutions. Apparently irrational solutions, even if they might — oddly enough — be more effective solutions, will be rejected without serious consideration. No screen has been more powerful in modern culture than the screen of rationality. I cannot overemphasize the extent to which it has permeated virtually every aspect of our lives — working and personal.

Weber, then, provides one clue to the appeal that the Strategic Defense Initiative has for large numbers of people. It promises to deal with the threat of nuclear annihilation by finding a defense against it. This, in itself, is a rational argument. If such a defense for all of the people of the world could be found, then certainly it should be put in place — even though the cost might strain our economy to the breaking point. To argue to the contrary would be foolish. The rational appeal of SDI is strong.

Moreover, this so-called defense program will take the form of the most sophisticated and refined machinery ever created by the imagination and draw on the rational intelligence of our finest scientists and technicians. After all, they worked wonders before, they can do it again. Once more, the rational appeal is a powerful one. Not only is the reason for the Strategic Defense Initiative a rational one, but the people involved with its development are also the most rational members of our society. In a sense, they virtually have a monopoly on rationality.

Here, then, is a program that fits nicely into Weber's vision of modern social systems as rational-bureaucratic structures. Its appeal comes out of its apparent rationality. Its critics can claim that a defense against nuclear weapons is impossible. Since the criticism itself commonly comes from other scientists and members of the rational-bureaucratic community, we can ask why such criticism has not brought about a halt to spending any more money on the Strategic Defense Initiative. Implicit in Weber's thinking is a suggested reply.

Drawing on Weber's view, we might suggest that technology is so powerful in its rational appeal that it remains virtually impervious to criticism. After all, rational effort defeated practically all of its critics in the past — from those who said people would never be able to fly to those who argued that the atom could not be split. Who is to say the critics are correct this time? If enough money is put into a defensive system — if the machines are made big enough, sophisticated and powerful enough, and numerous enough, we will at last be safe. The madness of MAD will be put behind us and become a part of an earlier time when society was more Neanderthal in its conduct of its affairs.

To avoid possible misunderstanding, I would like to state I am not, in this chapter, concerned with supporting or condemning the Strategic Defense Initiative — though I think it deserves more serious condemnation than it has received. It is discussed in this context because it represents, better than anything else in current affairs, the influence of the rational mentality on policy making among the major powers.

It also raises questions about what a rational-bureaucratic system implies. Is modern society as rational as it, perhaps, likes to think? Are there irreducible irrationalities in human conduct? Does rationality itself lead to extremes that reveal weaknesses in the rational model? One cannot help believing that if Weber were alive today, he would continue to devote his genius and his scholarship to questions such as these. Certainly the concept of rationality deserves further examination. Rationality is too important to be left solely in the hands of scientists.

BUREAUCRACY AND NUCLEAR CRISIS

Closely associated with the norm of rationality is the idea of rationally established social organizations. These take form in the modern corporate bureaucracy. There are several ways in which the concept of bureaucracy adds to our understanding of the nuclear crisis.

Weber found the large-scale modern bureaucratic system interesting because it moves toward the norm of rational efficiency. Where older social systems were based on tradition or custom, the new corporate bureaucracies are grounded on making things work as effectively as possible. Weber identified a number of major features of modern bureaucracies. Here, primarily because of space restrictions, we will be interested in only three: (1) the determination of competence through *formal* testing, (2) the communalization of property, and (3) bureaucratic leadership.

Formal Testing

First, and possibly the most significant feature of true bureaucracies for our purposes, is the reliance on tests of competency to determine who will occupy various offices within the organization. In older systems a common way of passing on a social position was to bequeath it to an heir. In a modern bureaucracy this would be somewhat like suggesting that when your professor of chemistry retires, his son should assume his post — whether he knows much about chemistry or not. Today, a corporate structure relies on tests.

Nothing illustrates this better than the nearly endless program of testing that is part of life in a modern university. Student, faculty, or staff member, you move through the system according to your performances on evaluation forms and tests — lots and lots and lots and lots and lots of tests. In the ideal bureaucracy nothing else should count — your personal sexual preferences, your race, your religion, your political leanings, your age, or whether you are a man or a woman. Much of modern liberalism received its impetus from this characteristic of the modern bureaucracy, but this interesting possibility cannot be explored here.

This means, then, that your position within a bureaucracy is established by your known ability to carry out the duties associated with the position. In one fashion or other, your ability must be *formally* demonstrated. You cannot rely on your family, your good looks, your charm, your connections, your wealth, or any other extraneous source of influence to obtain a position or a promotion. Keep in mind the reference here is to an ideal form of bureaucracy. In real-life situations bureaucracies fall considerably short of this ideal. Violations of the ideal occur when the boss's son is given the presidency of the corporation over more talented junior executives who work for the firm or when a wealthy woman is able to "buy" an influential post in a college or university.

The ideal type of bureaucracy, then, is concerned with demonstrated efficiency at all levels of organization. People are placed in positions on the basis of their ability to pass tests that qualify them. In the ideal bureaucratic organization no qualification other than efficiency of performance is relied on as a way of determining the merit of the individual. Formal testing procedures are validated through the process of accrediting or "credentialing" a person. (The term *credit* is derived from the Latin *credere* — to believe —and is found in terms such as credibility, credo, incredible, credentials, and discredit.) A person becomes believable because he or she passed the tests set forth by bureaucracy. So it is that college students working their way through the lower rungs of academic bureaucracy acquire credits or believability as they progress from freshman to senior status.

The believability of the individual is, then, a function of the organization upon which the person must rely for "credibility." Weber was interested in this process because it has profound sociological implications. It suggests that leadership moved from the charismatic leader who relies on personal qualities to leaders whose power comes from their acceptability to bureaucratically defined standards of leadership. Believability becomes less a matter of knowing a person as a person and more a matter of knowing a person's credentials.

This process led to what might be termed the "age of the expert." (The phrase is mine, not Weber's.) Experts are granted their credibility by other experts, not by the community in general. We are so used to this process that we can hardly think of alternatives. However, in simpler societies, credibility was commonly based on one's relationship to the community as a whole. Today expertise is a matter of credentials. It is characterized by a high degree of specialization, by demonstrated acceptability to an established bureaucratic hierarchy, by a problem-solving approach to situations, and by the general bureaucratic ideal of rational efficiency in all things.

We noted earlier that it is difficult to think, in Western society, of any approach to the world other than a rational one. We also might comment on how difficult it is to think of relying, at this time in world history, on the judgment of anyone, in any circumstance, other than an expert.

At the same time, you should recognize that the age of the expert is a recent one. Until the recent past, possibly as late as the early 19th century, people we now think of as experts were referred to as craftsmen. They were granted modest status. In past times it was not the craftsman but the "wise" men and poets who had a strong voice in communal affairs. Their time is past. Now the voice of the expert carries the day. No one seeks wisdom any more; instead, if you wish to have influence, you must become an expert. The expert is the product of the modern bureaucratic organization. As we noted, bureaucracies are concerned with performance. This means, among other things, that while the crafts and the wisdom of earlier times were dominated by men, expertise is not sex specific.

Before we discuss other features of bureaucracy and then relate them to the nuclear weapons issue, we should at least consider how expertise influences social and military policy in our time. First and foremost, expertise is — virtually by definition — a quality removed from democratic argument or debate. The judgment of the expert is paramount. If there is a dispute and the arguments of an expert are in question, the resolution of the dispute cannot be dealt with by means of democratic processes but only through the contentions of other experts.

Because nuclear physics and other matters associated with nuclear warfare are technical and matters for expert judgment, the common people are increasingly removed from any kind of democratic judgment in nuclear matters. Military, economic, and political policy also relies, to an increasing extent, on the judgment of experts. The consequence is a growing sense of frustration with respect to democratic processes and a feeling that one's particular understandings of the situation count for damned little.

One consequence, then, of the age of expertise is a frustration of the liberal democratic process. Another consequence is the development of what Thorstein Veblen referred to as a "trained incapacity" to see beyond the purely mechanical limits of any problem brought before the expert. A nice example of this once again is the debate over the possible consequences of a so-called nuclear winter. There are scientists (that is, "experts") who claim that the consequences of a major nuclear exchange would be sufficiently catastrophic to end all life on earth. Others argue it would not do any such thing. The problem becomes defined in terms of extremely narrow mechanical limits congenial to the mentality of the specialist viewing the problem.

If the age of metaphysical theology had its moments of madness while philosophers debated dancing angels and pinheads, modern rationalism is beginning to show its madness, and in several ways it makes the older form look benign. Consider, for example, the astonishingly peculiar nature of the information contained in the following newspaper clipping. (If you cannot figure out why this news item is strange, then you probably are truly a hyperrational child of your time.)

December 4, 1986, Associated Press, San Dimas, California.
A long awaited experimental brush fire to study whether smoke from an atomic war would trigger a "nuclear winter" was scrubbed Wednesday after a helicopter crashed while igniting a test burn.
. . . "It's very disappointing," said Joel Levine, atmospheric chemist for the National Aeronautics and Space Administration. "No other experiment will answer the question we were planning to address."
The chopper was dumping thickened gasoline to start a preliminary burn when the cable suspending the torch from the bottom of the aircraft snagged on telephone lines, causing the crash, county fire Capt. Garry Oversby said.
. . . The controlled fire, which was to have consumed 320 to 480 acres, had been expected to create a 10,000 foot tall smoke plume for study, said Philip Riggan, the Forest Service's scientist-in-charge.

There is no little degree of absurdity in the fact we now witness a group of experts conducting tests by burning a few acres of forest land and setting brush fires to see which of the other experts might be correct. This is every bit as nutty as the debates that came out of an impassioned love for metaphysics by the thinkers of the medieval era.

This intense focus on precision and the establishment of expert credibility, while ignoring the patently obvious moral character of the situation, has a macabre quality to it — it is another manifestation of the banality of evil, as Hannah Arendt so aptly phrased it. The point, however, is that this is the nature of rational mentality.

Virtually any citizen above the age of ten in nearly any educated country in the world will tell you that as few as six or seven hydrogen weapons, if exploded over major population centers, would create a catastrophe greater than any known natural or humanly created famine or plague or disaster in recorded history. We are, for example, already well able to see that American battle deaths, in *all* of the wars the United States ever engaged in, beginning with the Revolutionary War — a period of two hundred years — amounted to a little over 500,000 individuals. Compare this simple statistic with the fact that the two low-yield weapons dropped over Hiroshima and Nagasaki killed perhaps 300,000 people and generated other, longer-term deaths. Two nuclear weapons killed in a matter of moments as many people as America lost in seven or eight major wars. Somehow, in the quest for pure rationality, these commonplace, but horrifying, figures are not enough. Our world demands a grander rational debate to determine the matter of what a nuclear war means in terms of experimentally validated findings.

It is a new world, but not necessarily a brave new world. Nor is it a world of the heart. The heart was shoved away from the halls of wisdom, where wisdom itself is now demeaned. If it is found anywhere, it is in the music halls where rock and roll musicians try, with great and loving labor, to bring it back. It is the age of the expert, of experimental findings, of debates over nuclear winters, and it is an age in which the voice of the general citizen counts for relatively little.

Meanwhile, the experts continue to deal with nuclear winter not as a dramatic issue, a literary issue, a moral issue, or a communal issue — these are nonrational domains. Instead, they deal with it as a potentially resolvable problem — much like trying to see who is correct with regard to whether or not proton decay is taking place. It is this, in part, that led one writer of the early seventies to characterize modern societies as being made up of "one-dimensional" people.[7] It also led another writer, C. Wright Mills, to observe that the "cold manner" had entered people's souls. Mills put it this way:

> In the expanded world of mechanically vivified communication the individual becomes the spectator of everything but the human witness of nothing. Having no plain targets of revolt, men feel no moral springs of revolt. The cold manner enters their souls and they are made private and blasé. . . . Within the unopposed supremacy of impersonal calculated technique, there is no human place to draw the line and give the emphatic no.[8]

We have considered one aspect of bureaucracy — the use of tests to determine the extent to which an individual is qualified to hold an office within the bureaucracy. This rationalization of ability created a society of experts, persons who are, by definition, set apart from the rest of the community. This process has affected democratic processes and removed nuclear expertise into positions where it cannot be challenged by anyone other than someone who is a part of the nuclear community to begin with.

I examined, too lightly perhaps, the strangely rationalized approach to human issues that came out of all of this. At the same time, to challenge rationalism calls for suggesting something better to take its place. Rationality, as a norm, stands above criticism, and this makes it difficult to deal with in social criticism. Therefore, the arguments concerning rationality introduced in the preceding paragraphs must be tempered. It is not rationality in itself that is the problem but the excesses to which it is carried. A more synoptic vision is called for.

The commonsense solution to almost any kind of excess is simple; *if you have the nerve for it,* just put the bottle down. Of course, as it turns out, we somehow never have the nerve for it. Not until rationalism reveals its excesses in terms of impasses such as the one posed by nuclear weapons, will a deeper consideration of the problem be addressed.

The Bureaucratization of Property

A second feature of modern bureaucracies is the fact that property, within the bureaucracy, is not privately owned. Teachers and students, for example, do not own the classrooms, museums, lecture halls, desks, blackboards, offices, and other property they rely on for conducting their academic routines. Bureaucracies are surprisingly communistic in their approach to property.

When we turn to the military, it is apparent the entire system is based not on any sense of private property but rather on common property that belongs not to any individual but to the organization as a whole. Soldiers do not own the guns they carry into battle; Air Force pilots do not own the expensive planes they fly; Navy captains do not own their ships, and so forth. The property of the military bureaucracy is the property of the military bureaucracy and not that of any individual within the bureaucracy. There is a strict delineation between personal property and property that is held within the corporate system as a whole — no matter what the corporate structure might be.

Within such corporate contexts property takes on a uniquely functional quality. Property is of interest in terms of what it is capable of doing, rather than in terms of a personal relationship between the owner and what is owned — the powerful and, at times, overwhelming mystique of ownership. For example, the meager but personally owned home of a peasant can have a rich individual significance because of the status it bestows on the owner, the social significance of passing the home on to the eldest son, the "tradition" of having a home that has remained within the family for the past five or six generations — and so forth.

A military barracks is granted little more social or personal significance for those who spend time there than is a motel. Property, for bureaucracies, is a transient rather than a stable element. This loss of what I call the "mystique of ownership" is among the reasons why Americans find bureaucracy worrisome. While not being able to put their finger on it, they sense that bureaucracies have something wrong with them. Indeed, from an American perspective, they certainly do; so far as property is concerned, a corporate bureaucratic system is, to put it simply, communistic.

What significance such property has for the community is not associated with traditional or ritualistic qualities ascribed to the property but, instead, to rigidly utilitarian qualities. A bureaucracy, especially a military bureaucracy, is not expected to squander the community's resources on frivolous items. Property, whatever it might be (weapons, housing, shoelaces, cars, and so on) is functional, drab, tough, durable, and cheap. At least it is supposed to be as cheap as possible, which is why the cost overrides of military contractors become the stuff of national scandals.

The same holds true for any other bureaucracy. Indeed, when bureaucracies begin to move into the realm of the frivolous and irrational with status pretensions and "putting on the dog," they begin to encounter problems that bring them hard against the realities of a competitive economy.

In any event, my primary concern here is to note simply that the amount of communally shared property, even within a capitalistic state, is enormous. Following Weber, it should be worth a little time to "play" with the implications of the distinction between private property, with its "mystique of ownership," and public property, with its emphasis on pragmatic utility. The relevance of this to a discussion of nuclear weapons consists of understanding the extent to which such weapons are not the property of anyone. Along with everything else that sustains them, they are the property of large collective systems. As such, their control and their use is not in the hands of any individual or even group of individuals who own them. No single person can take pride in having one. They consequently take on a peculiar value.

America's nuclear arsenal cost trillions of dollars to produce. At the same time, it is not something that can be sold or bartered or exchanged. It is astoundingly expensive in its own right while, at the same time, having little or no value *per se*, as property. Once nuclear weapons are produced, they become peculiar economic objects.

Here is an object whose value lies in its production and not in its consumption. What is the economic equivalent? A nuclear weapon is economically more like fine jewelry that costs a great deal to create, but whose consumption has little value other than purposes of display. Unlike jewelry, however, nuclear weapons cannot be bartered.

Like works of art, nuclear weapons are intended for display, not for functional use. Yet, this comparison sounds strange because it is perfectly obvious that such weapons are not in the least like works of art, which are essentially physically harmless things.

Here is an especially functional device. It is neither a work of art nor a device that anyone wants to set in motion. It is produced and then it is moved to strategic vantage points for the enemy to see and consider. Its purpose is to reveal strength through display. At this point, Weber forces us to recognize a feature of nuclear weapons that will be more elaborately discussed in later chapters. (I am inclined to think that where different theories lead to similar observations, the strength of the observation is enhanced.)

Because nuclear weapons, as property, have no use other than to be displayed or to be used as catastrophically destructive tools of war, they have no economic value once they exist. They cannot be sold in any kind of market. All other weapons systems are, in one way or another, available for exchange. To say nuclear weapons cannot be sold does not mean there are people who do not want to buy such devices. Obviously, there are and they are willing to pay huge sums for them. Curiously enough, the free market does not operate in the domain of nuclear weapons.

So it is that the modern nuclear device is not only the ultimate in the rationalization of weapons, but it is also an ultimate form of collective property. There is more than a little bit of irony in the fact that the most collectivized device ever created by human beings stands as a mechanism defending the American modern capitalistic state.

Bureaucratic Leadership

The allegiance of people who are organized within bureaucratic systems is not to individuals as such but rather to the bureaucracy itself. Weber put it this way: "Members of a corporate group, insofar as they obey a person in authority, do not owe this obedience to him as an individual but to the impersonal order." The significant term in this brief quote is "impersonal."

Leadership has become impersonal. This impersonalization may be part of the reason the mass media are relied on so intensely by modern political leaders; for through television especially a sense of personalization can be achieved. We are dedicated to Reagan or Kennedy because they appeared before us and were seen and we could "relate" to them as individuals. At the same time, few Americans can list the names of any of the major advisers to the president and other leaders who hold great power but spend little time in front of television cameras.

Even the seemingly personalized figure of the president is remote. Our allegiance to an individual such as Kennedy or Reagan, as the leader of our nation, is not to the person but to the more abstract political system he represents. People today, to an astonishing degree, do not bother any longer with the names of leaders. They know a few — the president, vice-president, and possibly, the secretary of state — but after that the personalization of leadership drops precipitously. Governors, senators, representatives, the president of the college, the dean of the College of Arts and Science are, to a surprising degree, known not as names but as somebody who is minding the store. It is sufficient to know someone is managing the office. Who it might be in particular is a trivial detail.

This attitude might not be as terrible as pedants like to make it. First of all, the solidarity of bureaucratic systems is every bit as secure as any other form of social organization known in the past. We romantically talk about society being held together by the family or some other primal unit, but modern societies are held together by corporate bureaucracies. That is the simple, blunt truth of the matter.

Second, the selection of individuals to offices is such a minutely detailed process — the higher the office, the greater the detail — that it is not too surprising to find that the occupants of various offices have an almost troubling similarity of character and appearance. I am not denying that occasionally the selection process goes awry. It is a human process and subject to error. In general, however, the selection process works well enough. It is a sociological clone manufacturer. (Abraham Lincoln, some observers like to point out, would not make it past the first series of cutoff interviews — his "image" was bad.)

Finally, offices tend to establish functional boundaries around them that make personification almost, but never totally, irrelevant. You go to the dean, for example, to get things done, not to talk about how good Emily Dickinson's poetry makes you feel. One silly notion, perhaps a holdover from more pleasant, less bureaucratized times, that academics have about students and themselves is that their relationships with their charges should be "palsy-walsy." Students become uncomfortable, and with good reason, if this idea is pushed too far.

A leader's performance is evaluated in terms of the extent to which he or she carries out the already-established directives of the bureaucracy. Major transformations in policy are relatively restricted. The effective bureaucratic leader does not engage in probing questions concerning whether the bureaucracy in itself is worth keeping. Unfortunately, a lot of bureaucracies appear to be superfluous. In any event, the consequence is a highly conservative leadership, regardless of party affiliation. Any kind of radical program has little chance of success. A wise leader does not consider any serious dismantling of the bureaucracy that sustains him or her in a position of power.

One political analysis, during the Watergate hearings that led to the ousting of President Nixon from office, suggested Nixon was left vulnerable by his own people. That is, Nixon had hoped to dismantle huge sections of the American political bureaucracy by operating under the belief less government is better government. The bureaucracy responded, according to this point of view, by dragging its heels when the moment came where the chief executive officer needed someone to come and pull his burning fat from the fires of impeachment.

The deeper significance of all of this is that within the bureaucratized state, we have a narrower choice of alternatives. The left and the right are more similar than different. The only radically novel forms of social thinking lie outside the bureaucracy; they come, if they come at all, from those who are disaffiliated with things. These are the whistle-blowers or the unwashed —and such people are easily dismissed.

More significantly, individual members of any bureaucracy owe their primary allegiance to the offices they occupy. Any leadership that threatens the integrity or furtherance of the programs that are part of the office will be met with resistance. This feature of bureaucracy generates internal problems interfering with the broader rational interests of the bureaucracy as a whole.

We saw earlier that bureaucracies, as social systems, reject traditionalism, custom, or ritual as ways of getting things done. Instead, the dominant norm of rationality is supposed to prevail. In the quest for rational social programs the bureaucracy encourages specialization and impersonal relationships. This, in turn, leads to complex organizations composed of evermore specialized and compartmentalized divisions. It is perhaps worth noting that this rational development promotes efficiency within the compartmentalized divisions but generates a highly conservative and inflexible greater system.

An ordinary example can be found in any modern college or university. The quest for greater rational efficiency leads to specialization and compartmentalization. The university relies on various disciplinary departments to achieve this end. And so education becomes a matter of acquiring specialized expertise within a particular department or "major."

A university president must have important reasons for tampering with the system as it exists. Professors, and students as well, identify with the departments in which they are tenured. They then seek to promote the interests of those departments rather than the interests of the higher administration or, more seriously, the interests of the general community. Each person presumes, in all of this, that the interests of the department are the interests of the general community. What is good for any part of the whole is, therefore, good for the whole thing.

Under these conditions leadership becomes constrained, and imaginative leadership is unusual. A bureaucratic leader responds to the bureaucracy. As a consequence, modern national leaders are limited in their capacity to respond to broader communal or, for want of a better term, folk needs or concerns. The term *folk needs* sounds quaint in this day and age—but that does not mean they no longer exist. They are with us as much today as they have ever been.

For example, (although the conjecture is hypothetical, it is worth considering), what might be the consequences of a democratic vote within the major powers that resulted in two-thirds of the people of the entire world rejecting the further development of nuclear weapons? In all likelihood, it would be publicized in Western papers as an interesting indication of public sentiment while, at the same time, the major governmental and military bureaucracies would continue the further production and enhancement of nuclear weapons. Although such information might not appear in the press in Soviet-controlled communities, the end result would probably be much the same.

Political leadership in America comes through the electoral process. Political leaders offer the public varying images of leadership and new policies. The more profoundly embedded political reality, however, from a Weberian perspective, is one lying deeply within the complexities of modern bureaucratic systems. To understand modern leadership, we must understand modern bureaucracies.

These systems are conservative in nature. They are directed toward the efficient attainment of their particular ends and they are, most significantly of all, removed from the general control of the public at large. Leadership of such systems, in order to prove effective, must be sensitive to the demands that come from within the bureaucratic system itself. The personal, smiling, folksy image of the leader is displayed to the public while the serious work takes place in rooms where facts, figures, policies, and programs are brooded over by men and women who are, above everything else, bureaucrats.

There is certainly an implication within Weberian thinking that modern democratic leadership is constrained by the huge bureaucracies that have now established themselves as powerful elements within the nation. Where the ends of a powerful bureaucracy might conceivably be construed to be inimical to the interests of the community at large, it is the well-organized, well-capitalized, efficient, and rational bureaucracy that has the cards, so to speak, stacked in its favor in any argument to the contrary.

A fine example of the power, impersonality, and communal irresponsibility of the bureaucratic structure can be found in the much-publicized Pinto car. The Pinto was unsafe because it exploded violently when struck from behind. The Ford Motor Company conducted a study to determine whether it would cost more to repair the Pintos owned by consumers or to pay the lawsuits that would turn up. Ford decided it would cost less to deal with suits from persons injured driving the car than it would to repair a fault in the assembly-line model. The ones who were burned by this decision were not the bureaucrats within the Ford company who were responsible for it.

Dwight Eisenhower, in a famous speech, told the American public what Weber might have said about the present situation. We must, Eisenhower said, be ever careful of the military-industrial complex. This very popular president representing a conservative party was well aware of the extent to which a leader has only limited options with regard to controlling or modifying the ambitions and goals of the military-industrial complex.

A major concern with respect to the influence that bureaucracy has on national leadership is that bureaucratic interests and popular interests can move along divergent paths. The present thrust of socioeconomic forces appears to be in the direction of a dominance of bureaucratic interests over the more general interests of the public at large.

Without belaboring the point, I need only mention the recent simplification of the American tax system. Whatever was meant by "simplification," it was not something apparent to the general public or anybody else. The bureaucracy overseeing the tax system of America has more to gain from complexity than from simplicity. It is a case of bureaucracy abandoning the goal of efficiency in terms of universal or public interests in favor of what is effective in terms of the bureaucracy's specific interests. The bureaucracy rationally pursues its own ends, but whether these ends are always beneficial to the greater community remains an open question. When you apply this understanding to a consideration of those bureaucracies in charge of nuclear affairs, nuclear weapons, military nuclear policy, and related matters, you end up in a serious depression.

Of course, the bureaucratic elite respond to commentaries of this variety by saying they are serving the public interests — serving those interests more efficiently and more effectively than can be done in any other way. The military bureaucracy, for example, defends its actions on the grounds it is serving the defense interests of the nation. However, a bureaucracy, once in motion, comes to define its goals in terms of its own specific history and growth as a bureaucracy. To the extent the historical development of a bureaucracy produces a form of bureaucratic autonomy, the bureaucracy and the general public by definition are no longer similar in their interests.

It is possibly this feature of modern society that makes the present time especially puzzling. To what extent do our bureaucracies serve human interests as opposed to what might be construed as more narrow bureaucratic interests? The question has no ready answer. Nonetheless, it is a question of central significance. In the tensions that develop between corporate interests and those of the people lies the fate of modern democracy.

Review

An appreciation of Weber's work sensitizes us to the nature of modern bureaucracies and the role that bureaucratic forms of organization — independently of any other kind of consideration — might have in shaping world affairs. We examined three features of bureaucracy and raised several questions.

1. To what extent has the rise of the credentialed expert produced a situation in which true democratic rule has been diminished?
2. What are the possible consequences of the fact that within bureaucracies property is under the domain of the bureaucracy itself and is not personal property?
3. To what extent is political democratic leadership constrained by the special interests of bureaucratic systems that can differ from those of the general public?

These are difficult questions and there is no pretense at even beginning to answer them in a brief review of this kind. However, they are relevant and pertinent questions. Their relevance is suggested by noting that by the time a young American enters college the bureaucratic self is already a well-ingrained part of his or her character. Grade school and high school, after all, are the early forms of the bureaucratic life.

Most of us will spend the major part of our lives working as agents for bureaucracies of one kind or another. Everything from the meat and potatoes we put on our table to the entertainment we watch after dinner is regulated by corporate bureaucracies. Bureaucracies make decisions generally on the basis of rational expediency, defined in terms of the interests of the corporate system itself, rather than broader moral or social concerns. It is worth thinking about.

We conclude this discussion of Weber by turning to an argument that gave him his greatest public recognition — the argument that economic practices are closely associated with religious beliefs and practices.

PROTESTANTISM AND CAPITALISM

America is commonly referred to as a materialistic society. American ideology subscribes to the belief that you can motivate people by offering them things. It is a culture in which essential reality is located within objects. The American mind finds comfort in discovering the causes of events in physical substance. It is a society that places great emphasis on economic affairs because economics deals with substantive matters — raw materials, products, labor commodities, profits, money, trade, and supply and demand.

Events or individuals are rated in terms of the amount of money they command. The sports page of the modern American newspaper, for example, is an Alice-in-Wonderland gushing of miraculous monetary sums being paid to men whose primary, if not exclusive, talent lies in their ability to juggle various kinds of balls. When an American gets serious we are apt to hear the phrase, "What's the bottom line?" That is, how do the figures add up? Are we looking at a profit or a loss?

At the same time, American society is one characterized by active church membership. Despite general characterizations of the United States as a secular nation, roughly 60 percent of the entire population belongs to formal religious groups or organizations.[9] Americans belong to churches and, at the same time, are dedicated to finding happiness through acquiring material goods. However, they tend to keep these two activities separated. The moments where attempts are made to fuse the two aspirations have a bizarre quality to them — for example, television preachers who willingly corrupt the basic teachings of Christianity by arguing that Jesus really wants you to own three or four condos and a Rolls-Royce or two.

There is a schizophrenic attitude toward religion and economics in America. That is to say, Americans like to believe economics is one thing and religion is something else. Americans also like to think you can keep religion and politics separated. This issue has been hotly debated in American politics in recent years. Unfortunately, we don't have space to discuss it here.

Although we will grossly oversimplify matters, let us presume for the moment that Americans tend to see religion as something concerned with spiritual matters and economics or business as something concerned with material matters. Religion exists to deal with moral issues while economics or business deals with the production and distribution of goods and services. Weber contended that economic practices are also moral practices and, as such, cannot be fully understood unless they are placed within the religious context out of which they sprang.

Materialism, as a philosophical perspective, had strong adherents and advocates by the middle of the 19th century. Western economic theory acquired a kind of intellectual autonomy — that is to say, economic forces were to be analyzed in terms of purely economic forces. As an autonomous intellectual discipline economics acquired a strong voice through the writings of such worldly philosophers as Adam Smith, Jean Baptiste Say, Thomas Robert Malthus, David Ricardo, and others.[10]

But it was the voice of Karl Marx that gained greatest attention in the later decades of the 19th century. It was Marx who argued that physical or material concerns dominate any human community and, over historical time, shape the institutions and lifeways of its people. Marx argued that religion, for example, is an expression of the way in which a given community develops its economic productivity. Or, more simply, economic systems determine the character of religious systems.

Weber was strongly influenced by Marxist thinking. At the same time, his interest in bureaucratic systems and traditionalistic forms of social organization led him to study in great detail the religious systems of the major cultures of the world. He was especially interested in what appeared to him to be an undeniable statistical observation. He was convinced that those areas of Europe in which Protestantism flourished were also areas that responded vigorously and immediately to the development of modern capitalistic economic practices. Was there, he asked, something about Protestant religious beliefs and practices that brought about the development of a unique set of economic practices? In other words, where Marx thought economics determined religious expression, Weber pursued the idea that religion determined or at least helped shape economic expression.

Weber argued that Protestantism created a new set of beliefs with regard to the spiritual implications of work. Although other world religions respected work and sanctioned labor, Protestantism promoted the belief that work, particularly success in one's calling, was a means whereby one could obtain a possible indication of whether or not one was favored by God. Weber argued that this Protestant "work ethic" made capitalistic regions of Europe especially productive and wealthy. What appears, then, to be a purely materialistic matter is, from a Weberian perspective, more complicated — it is also permeated with religious fervor.

Modern capitalistic economies, from Weber's point of view, are driven not simply by materialistic motives but by religious motives as well. The capitalistic industrialist seeks power not simply for the sake of material power but because it can also imply a greater virtue. To be successful in one's work is a possible sign that one is also graced by God — one is a special child of God. Consider what the converse implications of this assertion might be. This is to say, how would a failure be evaluated from this perspective?

Success in this world, the work ethic went on, will be followed by success after one passes from this material planet; that is, the successful man or woman will be transported to heaven itself. The Protestant work ethic, Weber argued, transformed the nature of work. It was no longer enough simply to work. One was driven to succeed in one's work as totally and as fully as possible because work had now been saturated with new religious meanings. The consequence, Weber believed, was a society in which men and women were driven to excesses of effort.

The strengths and limitations of this argument cannot be considered here. It has evoked considerable scholarly criticism and response. The best way, perhaps, to see Weber's position is to view Protestantism as a religious ideology that inspires people to seek in the material world, as well as in holy writings, evidence of God's will. Weber was especially interested in how the

Protestant mentality tried to determine whether God had ordained heaven or hell as the individual's eventual fate. Success was looked on as a sign the person might possibly be favored by God.

The consequence of all this, Weber argued, is a culture in which people are driven by an unusually intense curiosity to know what the world holds in store for them and a culture in which people are more intensely driven to succeed than had ever been the case in earlier human communities. Although there were certainly occasional individuals in earlier times who felt the drive to succeed because of their unique social status or psychological makeup, Protestantism made success a universal aspiration — anyone who subscribed to Protestant doctrine felt the need to be successful, completely successful, in his or her calling. Nothing less than one's eternity was at stake.

In contrast, during medieval times there was a general understanding that peasants, though they were expected to work and work hard, need not aspire to lives any higher than those their parents and grandparents lived before them. To seek any kind of special success in life would be improper. The newer work ethic, however, made the quest for success a moral quality. Not to aspire to success, ultimate and total success, now became the mark of the sociopath. Eventually, the individual was enjoined to seek success even if it meant denying established kin or friendship ties. One of the vexations of the Protestant mentality is its inability to understand why a poor person would not be willing to abandon his or her friends if it means success is more likely.

Anyone who reviews Weber's *The Protestant Ethic and the Spirit of Capitalism* will find it difficult to retain the idea that economic practices are independent of moral or religious ideas within any human community. Wealth is not amassed simply for the sake of wealth. Wealth is of value only if it has social meaning. Weber sought to find the social meaning of work and the quest for material success in Western culture in the new religious ideas of the Protestant Reformation.

In this feature of his work, Weber possibly enlightens us about the paradox that seems to exist in modern Christian countries with regard to militarism. The pathological extension of this paradox can be found in ultraracist groups such as the Brotherhood, the Ku Klux Klan, or the American Nazi Party. These groups, along with other similar radical groups, generally claim a strong dedication and allegiance to Christian morality.

Christian morality, however, is grounded in the belief one should love people — even one's enemies. One should be forgiving and supportive. Christian racist groups are, on the one hand, Christian in belief and, on the other, promoters of the bitterest kinds of hatred. Here are people who appear to have no trouble in managing what seems to be, at least from outside the group, an overwhelming contradiction. They are capable of preaching universal love and, with practically the same breath, what amounts to nearly universal hate.

From a sociological perspective, extremist groups can be informative with respect to the more conventional community. An extremist group, after all, is one that attempts to purify or carry to their ultimate conclusions ideas prevalent within the general culture.[11] The pathology so obvious in extremist groups can be found in more attenuated forms within the greater society. Despite the veneer of Christian love that Americans take upon themselves, they display little difficulty in expressing hatred and contempt for those who are alien to American culture.

The significance of this in the nuclear era is apparent. To the extent paranoia and hatred are rampant, we further endanger ourselves by responding in fear to circumstances that might possibly be benign. It is in this sense that Weber's essay on the Protestant ethic has deep and subtle ramifications.

For one thing, it suggests we are powerfully motivated to succeed and that we now define success in terms of material progress. Those who fail are not simply individuals who lack talent or drive or ability. They are worse than that. They are losers. They are, from the perspective of the Protestant ethic, something even worse than losers. They are people damned by God. To the fears that come from simple frustrations in this world are added fears having to do with religious concerns — ultimately having their locus in conceptions of one's eternal fate. That this is so is not readily apparent. Although Americans go to church in large numbers, their slogans are directed to the here and now.

America is a pragmatic nation. It is driven to the attainment of excellence and the desire to win because it believes it is simply natural to want to be the best. If we accept competitive economic practices it is because they lead to the most productive economy it is possible to create. Competition inspires effort. That this ideology might be permeated, through and through, with religious overtones and undertones is not self-evident.

An appreciation of Weber does not mean we must reject these common themes in American ideology. It does require, however, that we go further into them. America, after all, is not simply productive; it is overproductive. It is a nation in which having great wealth is never sufficient because greater wealth continues to have an appeal. Moreover, wealth is a badge of goodness. Although one can have sufficient material goods to satisfy all of one's physical needs, one can never have sufficient material goods to satisfy one's spiritual needs — if those goods are defined as a sign of personal worth.

So it is, then, that Americans condemn their enemies not simply because they are authoritarian or dictatorial, but because they are unsuccessful in providing their people with a richness of consumer goods. We fear Russia because it is a place we see as drab. In its drabness and in its problems with the production and distribution of wealth, we see a nation that must also not be in God's favor. We are therefore required to defend ourselves against its godless nature. It is a place that we can refer to and accept as an "empire of evil."

So it is that the rhetoric of religion overlays the economic forces that set the major powers against each other in nuclear confrontation, flexing their nuclear muscles. Weber provides us with a point of view that inclines us to see Western society as driven by an underlying and generally unconscious or unaware acceptance of the work ethic of 18th century Protestantism. Contained within this ethic is a moral doctrine that leads, in its logical extension, to the belief that every individual must strive to distinguish himself or herself from all others by being superior. Also contained within this ethic is the implicit belief that those who can be seen as inferior are religiously suspect.

To the political and economic forces that separate the great powers are added, then, the religious forces that are found particularly in Protestant forms of Christian doctrine. We are a nation that practices efficiency in the attainment of its goals. This is what rationalism implies. The goals themselves are defined in broad outlines by Protestant Christian theology.

More simply and generally put, our primary goal is to display to the world that we are the most successful people in the world. Success, of course, is defined in terms of being best at whatever we are trying to do. We are, then, rationally seeking success. But to the extent success implies differentiating between those who are "winners" and those who are "losers," the national mania is to sustain, as efficiently and totally as possible, international differences.

It is obviously a dangerous atmosphere — technological rationality is combined with deeper, irrational, religious sentiments that promote paranoia and a constant emphasis on social differentiation. Of these two forces, the more difficult to deal with is the underlying religious sentiment that defines social reality in terms that are sacred and, by definition, not subject to secular criticism.

On this note we conclude our consideration of Weber's ideas. Let me remind you once again that my goal here is to show how Weber's theories and writings can be used to enhance one's imagination and modes of interpreting modern social issues. Above all, I have tried to show that Weber's ideas are not museum pieces belonging to an earlier age. They are as relevant to today's problems as they were to the times in which Weber lived.

Chapter 6

Structural-Functionalism: Global Structures and the Legacies of Nationalism

THE WHOLE AND ITS PARTS

No human being and assuredly no human society is perfect in terms of the quest for such higher ideals as justice, wisdom, the attainment of the fulfilling life, and so forth. We engage at one time in actions that are good and at another time in those that are bad. For this reason, as individuals and as collectives, we are vulnerable to just about any kind of interpretation of ourselves that others bring to us. We do clever things; we do stupid things. We are strong; we are weak. We are happy; we are sad. We express ourselves across a broad range of qualities and can then be described *as an individual* in terms of any of these particular qualities. It is similar with societies.

These inherent contradictions make trying to arrive at a solid understanding of ourselves or our societies difficult. Two persuasive writers or lecturers can take diametrically opposed descriptive concepts, apply them to any individual or society, and make a telling case one way or the other. When people of opposed political views get finished discussing the character of a prominent political leader, group, or government, a thoughtful listener comes away wondering how the same subject could simultaneously manage to be such radically different and contradictory things.

The Fallacy of Partial Labeling

As individuals, and to a still greater extent as collectives, we are sufficiently complex that we represent, more or less, nearly any specific quality upon which we might be judged. If we are told we are foolish, for example, we have had enough experience with foolishness to know there is a degree of truth in it. We can also be told we are wise and, having had an occasional moment of wisdom, recognize a degree of truth in that statement. We naively accept a partial account as descriptive of what we are as a complete being. This, in part, is why flattery and insult work as effectively as they do. It is also why individuals who committed a minor crime in their youth can later find themselves being referred to as a criminal. Here is an instance where a partial label becomes a total label—one with real teeth in it.

Fortune tellers and astrologers relied on this human tendency to accept a partial feature as describing the whole to impress their clients for thousands of years. They still do. When an astrologer, for example, says you are a person who loves adventure, seeks security, can withstand adversity, and fears failure, you should find little to disagree with. If you are truly innocent, you might even be amazed by the degree of insight this mental wizard possesses. As a purely logical matter, however, how can such a description miss? In effect you were told you like adventure but you do not like it; you can handle challenges but you find them difficult (after all, that is what a challenge is—something difficult).

The astrologer performs a trick we all use on each other every day. A partial characteristic is used to define a much greater totality. This happens in school, for example, when a particular kid is defined by others as a "brain." This emphasis on a partial characteristic comes to define the individual in his or her total character. Obviously, any individual is more than a brain. Indeed, when we begin to think about the entire structure that makes up an ordinary human being, it is overwhelmingly complex. The kid who is defined as a brain is also a person with a stomach, sex drives, aggressive urges, fears, dreams, a heart, lungs, and so on. The label "brain" closes off our perception of the individual as a complex entity.

In a similar way we close off more complete forms of understanding when we approach human social systems in terms of a particular characteristic of the system. Americans, for example, point to their system proudly as a democratic system—and it is something to be proud of. At the same time, the American system is much, much more than simply a democratic procedure with respect to governmental representation. It is a vast complex of events. It is the same with the USSR or any other social system.

The Importance of Examining the Entire System

Societies, being even more complex than the individuals who live within them, make it possible for the imputation of virtually any partial quality to appear valid as a description of the entire system. For example, to some degree or other, you can assert that the following qualities apply to, let us say, a school you know of and not sound outrageously off base: [This school is] authoritarian, protective, callous, concerned, organized, disorganized, sensate, idealistic, religious, irreligious, intellectual, anti-intellectual, lacking spirit, overly caught up in sports, and so on through a long list of descriptive terms—a list that includes its opposites or implied opposites. The point I am emphasizing is that we all use partial descriptions to account for the whole. Functional-structuralism, which we are about to consider, has tried to move beyond this fallacy and deal with social systems in their entirety. For example, different elements within the school might be quite different in character but, in their interactions, make up the total system. The total system should not be defined in terms of any particular part within the system.

Structural-functionalism turns to societies as complete systems in its quest for a better understanding of how human communities work. Before we move directly into a consideration of structural-functionalism as a modern social theory, we need to consider one further aspect of its character — it leans heavily on the metaphor that human societies are structures with functioning elements, just as machines are structures with interacting parts.

Closing Off Infinitely Complex Issues

What is interesting about academically established theories of human society is not their imaginativeness or variety — though they can be imaginative and varied. Instead, what is interesting is that, given the infinite complexity of social systems, the virtually infinite potential variability and imaginativeness of such theories is somehow cut off. Modern social science and social philosophy, for example, draw on essentially four or five major points of view as a basis for theoretical speculations. Instead of an infinite number of speculations, we have arguments going on between the adherents of less than a dozen theoretical schools.

To be more specific, present-day texts categorize sociological theory under five broad headings: symbolic interactionist theory, structural-functionalism, conflict theory, exchange theories, and dramaturgic theory. Theory texts commonly divide or fit their material so that it falls within one or the other of these schools. Instead of a near infinitude of possible approaches, we find ourselves working with an astonishingly restricted number.

The engaging question becomes: What accounts for the predominance today of these few approaches to society? When we seek an answer, we better understand the power of collective perceptions as they shape and give form to our individual understandings of the world around us. What we find, as we look into the matter, is that social theories tend to cluster around major social interests.

I am now lightly touching on a field known as the "sociology of knowledge." This effort is based on the premise that there is a connection between what is necessary for social systems, as *systems*, and what people come to believe about the world. In other words, knowledge is not simply a matter of investigating the outer world and then reaching conclusions. Instead, the world comes to be seen in terms conducive to collective interests.

If the basic premise of a sociology of knowledge is reasonable, it would suggest that of all knowledge, our social theories should be especially vulnerable to the ways in which we organize our societies. Instead of an infinitude of possibilities, we restrict our interpretations of our societies and ourselves to perspectives that are pertinent to the way our society is organized. Or, to put it another way, as theories move from purely physical concerns to social concerns, the form of the theory is increasingly vulnerable to primary social interests.

When we look at the five categories that now characterize the greater domain of modern social theory, we find they tend to parallel dominant present-day social concerns. We have time here for a quick example. A popular school of theorizing in sociology today is known as *exchange theory*. It essentially draws on the metaphor that social relations are a matter of exchanges. For example, from this perspective an enduring marriage is one in which the partners carry out a series of balanced exchanges of affection, care, sympathy, etc. On the other side of things, a marriage in which exchanges are not balanced is likely to lead to separation.[1]

In Western culture economic concerns dominate our social lives. It is not too surprising to find, then, that the metaphor of social life as an economic venture is carried into the realm of social interpretation. The dominance of economic affairs in modern life generates a kind of "metaphorical" dominance generally. Ultimately, our finest social philosophers draw on what might be referred to as "master metaphors" for their interpretations of social order.

Structural-Functionalism and Life as a Machine

This prelude to a discussion of structural-functionalism is necessary because structural-functionalism has dominated the thinking of social scientists from the end of the 19th century down to the present time. Like all social theory, it rests on a metaphorical foundation. I shall distinguish metaphor from analogy with a simple illustration. An analogy would claim society is *like* a structure. A metaphor drops the "like" and becomes: Society *is* a structure. (Social theorists generally eschew the word *metaphor*. Sweeping metaphors under the rug, however, does not mean they cease to exist. They remain as lumps under the rug.)

The metaphor out of which structural-functionalism became elaborated is primarily the metaphor of the machine. Technology is a powerful force in our culture. Our reliance on machines has become a neurotic dependency. The way we talk about, praise, idolize, and worship our machines goes beyond the neurotic into the lower realms of cultural psychosis. (The adulation given the machine by modern people is embarrassing to anyone who likes to believe this is an age of true enlightenment.) The power of technology is underscored by the fact we turn to the machine as a metaphor for understanding our collective natures and our individual natures. It helps advance this argument to notice there are psychologists who like to think people are a form of machine.

Structural-functionalism is popular in sociology, but sociology is not alone in finding the machine attractive as a metaphorical device. Structural-functional analysis is also popular in the biological sciences. To the extent 19th century social philosophy was influenced by biology — and it was strongly influenced — the intrusion of a structural-functional perspective into sociology, anthropology, and political science is to be expected.

The metaphor of the machine is popular, as was just intimated, in psychology. A psychologist devoted to behaviorism once told a reporter he believed people *are* simply complex machines. It was something he had to believe, he went on to say, or he could not function as a behavioral psychologist. The psychologist, in this instance, went overboard. People are not machines; and machines, no matter how clever, are not people. At the same time, there is great power in this image. It serves science well; it is a dominant motif in our culture; it is understood and accepted across the various levels of our society without great criticism; and, like any other metaphor, it manages to bring apparent order out of the chaos of human social experience.

The machine serves, then, as one of the "master metaphors" for our time.[2] We judge ourselves, our communities, our institutions, and our futures in terms of qualities best exemplified in the machine. We speak of accelerating, gaining power, having inputs and outputs, braking, pressure, dynamics, taking off, getting things in gear, oiling the wheels, pushing our buttons, and so forth. Although the machine as metaphor is casual in everyday speech, its use in academic philosophy and theory is more careful. Still, to have a better awareness of a structural-functional philosophy, it is good to have a sense of its root metaphor and the massive uncritical collective acceptance of the machine metaphor that characterizes these times.

The following arguments draw heavily on the work of Robert K. Merton and Talcott Parsons.[3] Both theorists had a strong influence on American social science from 1940 down to the present time. Merton was born in 1910 and received his Ph.D. from Harvard in 1936. He accepted an appointment at Columbia University in 1941 and became Giddings Professor of Sociology at Columbia in 1963. Talcott Parsons began teaching sociology (his first appointment was in economics) at Harvard in 1931 and retired in 1973. He was born in 1902 and died in 1979.

Structural-functional theories probably represent the last serious effort on the part of academic thinkers to capture, somehow, the idea of a society in its totality.[4] Parsons, for example, sought nothing less than to define the entire workings of what we think of as social systems. Though the effort never really succeeded, the struggle opened up further insights into the distinctions and the similarities between people as collectives and people as individuals. Structural-functionalism is worth reviewing not because it is the final word on what human societies are and how they work, but because it provides us with yet another powerful way of approaching human concerns.

What approach does structural-functionalism take? We noted that it relies on the idea of the machine as a kind of metaphor. When we are concerned with studying machines we ask two major questions: First, we want to know what the machine does. Second, to understand it fully, we need to know how it is made. The first question asks about the function of the machine; the second seeks to know its structure. Moreover, when we go inside the machine and look at its various parts we can ask the same questions of the parts. What do they do? How are they made? How do they function together to sustain the complete system?

The basic idea of structure, then, is that there is something made up of interrelated elemental parts in such a manner that each part influences the entire structure. A gasoline engine, for example, has pistons, spark plugs, fuel lines, a crankshaft, rods, valves, cooling system, fans, oil filter, pumps, etc. These separate elements function together enabling the engine to function as a whole. If any part — even an apparently insignificant part — fails, the functioning of the engine is impaired.

Structural-Functionalism and the Rational Norm

Without undertaking a major analysis, let me mention here that structural-functionalism, with its ties to the machine as a metaphor, fits nicely into a cultural tradition permeated by a belief in rationalism. Social philosophers of the stature of Max Weber argue that rationalism stands among the most powerful concepts of modern ideology, and social theories that parallel dominant culture ideologies are likely to prevail over those that do not.

The machine, after all, is the epitome of rational action. The machine represents the ideal manifestation of rational thinking. If society is like a machine, then like any other mechanical device, it can become the object of simple rational examination. More pointedly, the concept that one obtains of society through this metaphor is one that sustains a major cultural theme.

The rationality of machines appears in several forms. We can, first of all, define what we want of a machine — be it crunching numbers, sewing shirts, shooting projectiles, or moving us quickly along the ground. Second, we can evaluate with considerable reliability and accuracy the efficiency of various machines. Machines move us from the realm of messy human ambiguities into a place where problems are definable and solvable. Third, we can identify the various parts of machines and determine how they relate to each other. We can gain a full sense of how the machine is put together. So appealing is the machine and, more broadly, the idea of the machine, that Western philosophers at one point did not hesitate to look on the expanse of the entire universe itself as a huge "clockwork."

We shall examine three concepts central to the structural-functional approach to the social world of human beings:

1. The concept of function
2. The concept of "latent" function
3. The idea of society as a structure or system

THE CONCEPT OF FUNCTION

Any human community, even the most elemental, reveals a division of labor or a partitioning of individuals into subgroups within the community. These subgroups carry out various *functions*. A function is simply what a group does. Unfortunately, what a group might be doing is open to a great deal of confusion. For example, it is important to distinguish between what a group or element is actually doing as opposed to its purposes or goals. An educational institution might, for example, define its goal as educating young people. What it is, in fact, doing might be something different.

Now that I have introduced the idea of the functions of educational systems, let me add that the structural-functionalists were not the first to notice the discrepancies that take place between what people think they are doing and what they are actually doing. Mark Twain, I believe it was, once said that school is a place where you must be careful about letting your education interfere with your education.

He had a point. As an example, consider the fact that present-day textbook publishers engage in what some editors refer to as "dummying down" texts so that they will be popular for big university classes. Like television, the style and content of such books are designed to appeal to the lowest common denominator of classroom intellect. Anything else might cater to that modern educational *bête noir* called "elitism."

On the one hand, students are told that they are being educated; on the other hand, they are being given "dummy" texts. While students aspire to be educationally superior, they simultaneously endorse books that promote intellectual banality. The selection of texts is increasingly a matter of democratic processes in which the students vote — a kind of academic Nielsen rating — for what is good. This situation is mentioned only to illustrate the problems we encounter when we attempt to define the functions of an institution or other social agency. It is worth noting that the functional specificity of the elements of machines is nowhere near as uncertain.

The concept of function makes two basic distinctions. The first notes that communities divide into identifiable elements. For example, as human societies become more elaborate, special systems come into being to educate people. Other systems come into being to provide health care. Still other systems come into being to provide defense needs and so forth. The second distinction notes that these elements have consequences for the community as a whole and for each other in terms of what they are *doing*.

Though this is a basic notion, it deepens our thinking about our communities and ourselves. We are inclined simply to think that an institution or agency does what it is designed to do or whatever it says it does. In commonsense thinking, we generally look on agencies in terms of their stated goals or purposes. For example, educational systems have education as their goal, and we accept them as educational systems. To a greater or lesser extent, educational systems do educate. But it is only one of the things they do. The concept of *function* forces us to think harder. What else is done? To what extent? What are the effects for the community as a whole?

Functionalism looks on the various elements of a society as working in an interdependent fashion. What one element does influences what all the other elements do. The elements function in an interdependent fashion to serve the interests of the entire system. The function of any element cannot be fully understood without comprehending the nature of the system as a whole. Just as we cannot have a good understanding of what a spark plug does unless we see it as part of an engine, we cannot understand a system such as the family or a military institution unless we see how it functions for the entire system (society).

Functionalism is criticized for being an overly conservative social philosophy. There is truth in the criticism. It is conservative because it implies that if an element exists within a community, regardless of what it is, it must be there to serve a function. Merton, for example, argued effectively that what were considered corrupt practices in the machine politics of big city life in America were, given the times, functional to the operation of the greater urban complex. This "cool" interpretation of party politics was a radical departure from earlier moralistic interpretations of corruption.

Functionalism further argues that if the interests of the community as a whole are served by its elements, then those elements are carrying out their proper functions. This suggests that anything goes so long as the community as a whole stays together and maintains its way of life. On the other hand, from at least the perspective of American conservative ideology, it is a liberal form of theorizing insofar as it emphasizes the interplay between collective forces as opposed to a philosophy of individualism. A strong structural-functionalist position gives little credit to the individual as hero or creative agent.

THE CONCEPT OF LATENT FUNCTIONS

Functionalism, then, is concerned with what the various agencies within a community *do*. This amounts to little more than restating the central concern of sociological investigations. However, functionalism adds a twist to the question, and this twist makes its study worth the effort. When we ask what the different agencies within a society are "doing," we can deal with the question in several ways.

We can, first of all, ask what an agency is doing in terms of what it is supposed to be doing. An educational system, for example, is supposed to be educating people — we can examine whether it is accomplishing its goals. This is not, of course, an easy question to answer.

Second, we can ask what a particular system or element is doing relative to other systems or elements within the community as a whole. There are, for example, people in the United States who are convinced that the public educational system is weakening the Judaic-Christian religious system by promoting a purely secular attitude toward the world. The recent ruling of U.S. District Court Judge W. Brevard Hand in Mobile, Alabama, was based on this argument. The judge ruled that social science and history books being used in Alabama public schools preach "secular humanism" and thereby undermine the moral teachings of Christianity. We are not interested here in the correctness of the ruling. What is functionally of interest is that what one system (education) is doing was held to interfere with the functions of another system (religion).

Third, we can ask what a system is doing that no one suspects it is doing.

When we ask this question or ask what a system is doing that moves beyond its legitimate functions, we move into what Robert K. Merton refers to as the *latent* functions of the system. For example, when we say an educational system is educating people we are talking about its *manifest* functions. This function is obvious, apparent, commonly accepted, and usually thought of as a goal of the system.

When, on the other hand, we argue that it is the function of the American educational system to keep millions of young people out of an already overcrowded labor market or to serve as a social-class "sifting" mechanism for determining who will be protected from the hazards of war, as happened in the 1960s, we are talking about a latent function. The concept of latent function is a spur to the sociological imagination.

The concept of latent function should be contrasted with the concept of manifest function. Manifest functions are those commonly recognized or understood as the functions of a particular social unit. They are the legitimate functions of the system. Latent functions are those that are not generally recognized.

Manifest and Latent Functions of the American Family

The following list of manifest and latent functions for the family is intended to illustrate the nature of these concepts. Notice that several of the functions listed here as latent functions are becoming more manifest. For example, the family unit's function as a protection against venereal infection is receiving much greater publicity today than in years past.

A. Manifest

1. To provide stability for child rearing.

2. To regulate the stresses of sexual jealousy and possession.

3. To provide a system that assures dependency rights; to paraphrase Robert Frost, a family is a place where, when you have to go there, they have to take you in.

4. The fulfillment of romantic attraction, or the proper end of romantic attachments.

5. To provide a system for distributing wealth across generations; that is, inheritance.

B. Latent

1. The encapsulation of the child and intensification of the socialization process through more exclusive contact with the biological parents. (This does not happen to the same extent with families in simpler social systems. One of the implications, in our society, is that if the biological parents are pathological, the child is more likely to suffer.)

2. Definition of social status and restriction of social mobility.

3. The sustaining of the legal system in the form of the divorce court, divorce lawyers, etc.

4. Exploitation of labor as in the case of military wives and wives more generally.

5. The control of venereal disease.

THE IDEA OF SOCIETY AS A STRUCTURE

The major thrust of functional thinking is to direct attention toward a social system as a whole. Although we commonly talk about society and its problems, few of us struggle with just how difficult it is to have a vision of society as a whole. Indeed, it now appears impossible to obtain any real grasp of a total social system.

A modern social system contains as many as four or five hundred million individuals divided into hundreds of thousands of different functioning groups and agencies. It is far, far beyond the grasp of any individual. At the same time, it is difficult to deny that such systems exist. Trying to comprehend the nature of an entire social system is much like a cell within a body trying to comprehend what it is a part of. If cells ever became thinking beings, they likely would create images of the whole organism depending on where they were in the total system and what their function was within the body.

A Structural Approach to the Drug Problem

Nonetheless, structural-functionalism asks us to take the entire society into account when dealing with any particular social issue. Consider, as a way of making the point, the publicity given to the popularity of drugs in America. Depending on the source, various aspects of American society come under fire as the cause of the problem. Incidentally, rarely does an agency blame itself. It invariably points the finger somewhere else.

Educational systems are blamed. The breakdown in the modern family is blamed. The mass media are blamed. The courts are blamed, and so on. As we saw in the opening of this discussion, any particular agency is vulnerable to criticism to the extent it is not perfect—and no human agency is perfect. It is this kind of singular approach to social issues that structuralism tries to avoid. Instead of focusing on a single institution or agency as the cause of a condition, structuralism alters the problem radically. Structuralism does not ask the question: Which group is to blame? Rather, it asks the question: How does the drug culture fit into the total system as an element of the system?

Or we can ask the structural question in a little different way: What kind of social structure would contain a drug culture as an element within itself? Drugs are so pervasive in Western culture we sometimes forget there are human social structures in which drugs are virtually unknown—at least in the sense they are known in this culture. Structural-functionalism argues that the entire community must be taken into account rather than trying to place blame on a specific group.

Above all, it is important to point out that structuralism moves our thinking away from simple psychologistic moralizing. Americans like to lean on such notions as the idea that the existing drug culture in America is a product of low self-esteem. Or it is viewed as the consequence of individual character deficiencies. For example, the current "Just Say No" campaign is based on this kind of moralistic simplicity.

The novelty of functionalist thinking can also be seen by contrasting it with a popular social ideology such as Marxism. Marxist thinking is structural—with the structural elements being broad in the form of class divisions. The important distinction here, however, is that Marxists are not in the least disinclined to lay the blame for the world's ills specifically at the feet of the owners of the means of production. We can understand better why functionalism is viewed as a conservative social philosophy when we discover it resists blaming any single group for anything. Marxism focuses its programs for reform and is willing to attack specific elements it considers opposed to those reforms; structural-functionalism does not.

With its unique form of questioning, functionalism accomplishes two things: First, it moves attention away from single elements as the focus of blame in favor of considering the entire system—all elements. Second, it tempers moralizing in favor of analyzing. The functionalist argues that if the drug culture exists, there is a reason for it. Moreover, the reason lies within the total complex of social institutions and agencies rather than within any particular institution. Drugs are a systemic problem, grounded in the way the entire social structure is ordered, rather than an individualistic problem or something caused by a particular element in the system.

Staying with the drug culture problem, structural thinking calls for an examination of such things as:

1. The interplay between economic institutions, medical systems, advertising, and the promotion of drug usage as a consumer item. We are told over and over to believe in drugs as a road to comfort and happiness. Drugs are money, and money is highly valued.

2. American political systems and their emphasis on individualism; political ethics based on letting the person "do his or her thing"; and the pursuit of happiness.

3. Educational systems and their abandonment of responsibility for the moral character of the young and their increasing seclusiveness and remoteness from the family and other agencies in the community.

4. Groups and agencies that profit from victims of drug abuse—such as psychologists and psychiatrists, alcoholism treatment centers, lawyers, the police, saloons, cigarette vendors, etc.

5. The vested interests of major drug producers—pharmaceutical

houses, breweries, distilleries, tobacco manufacturers, over-the-counter drug producers, etc.

6. The nature of the entertainment industries, with their emphasis on novelty, kicks, abdication of responsibility, and vicarious thrills.

7. Science, with its emphasis on experimentation and material or physical solutions to any kind of problem, personal or social.

8. Marriage and the family and romantic ideology with its emphasis on the quest for ecstasy and its acceptance of transcendent forms of emotionality.

9. The development of private spheres of life and the importance of privacy in the American system.

10. Class structure, where drugs represent privilege or where drugs provide a means of attaining "insider" status.

11. The lack of *rites de passage* that enable the young to understand when they become adults. Drugs as an alternative expression of adulthood.

Obviously, this list is limited only by the imagination of the person trying to develop it. Not only can the list become indefinitely long, but functionalism also complicates matters further by arguing that each element within the list interacts with all of the other elements. For the functionalist, an issue such as drugs is a structural issue. To deal with drugs effectively you need to deal with an entire structure.

As I have been writing this material, there has been recent publicity given to declines in drug use among high school students. At the same time, the newspapers also reported record drug busts in various cities and the popularity of new synthetic drugs on college campuses. The basic fact is that the American culture is a drug culture. Drugs are popular and, legal or illegal, are consumed in astonishing quantities by people ranging from grade-school children to senile adults.

There are, of course, sociocultural systems where drugs are not popular. Within the United States the Mormon culture comes to mind. According to popular reports, China is surprisingly drug free, for such a major culture and one wracked by problems with opium earlier in this century (brought in from outside to weaken China). Structural-functionalism asks the question: What is it about these systems as a whole that makes drug use less prominent with the culture? The problem is a structural problem.

It should be fairly evident that dealing with entire social structures is neither simple nor, ultimately, practical. For this reason, among others, functionalism is sometimes criticized for being conservative. In effect, it argues that we have a drug culture because it is functional within the total social structure. If you want to change the problem, change the structure. Because structures do not change very easily, there is probably not much that can be done about the problem.

Put so bluntly, functionalism, with its emphasis on social systems as structures, *seems* to be completely defeatist when it comes to the problem of social reform. Social systems exist as structured units, and they have the kinds of structures they have because such structures are functional. This sounds much like an apology for things as they are.

We can grant this criticism of functionalism and still find value in its approach to human societies. If nothing else, it is a cautionary philosophy. It stands as an antidote to the naive moralizing that is inclined to single out a specific or particular agent as the cause of a problem. It calls for the fullest awareness of communities as a whole in making social decisions. Although we can never approximate knowledge of an entire social system, we should nonetheless work in this direction. In sum, functionalism argues that social policies made without a deep awareness of the implications for the total system are apt to have consequences other than those that were intended.

STRUCTURAL-FUNCTIONAL PHILOSOPHY AND THE NUCLEAR CRISIS

The present nuclear arms impasse reveals, on the one hand, the reality of a structural view. Nothing else in modern times seems to force upon us as severely as nuclear weapons the impression that we are caught in the grip of vast collective forces. Nothing else gives us, as individuals, a greater sense of helplessness. Although virtually everyone considers nuclear weapons the greatest danger ever to confront humankind, no one has as yet created an effective program for the elimination of the threat they pose. Such weapons serve collective interests and can be altered only by modifications in social structures so vast they now gird the entire planet.

On the other hand, a functional approach to the nuclear arms impasse can move us toward a greater awareness of possible differences between what official propaganda tells us and what is actually going on. For example, the manifest function of the Strategic Defense Initiative (SDI), according to governmental descriptions, is to create a purely protective and exclusively defensive "umbrella" that will make the United States forever safe from the threat of nuclear attack. An examination of the possible latent functions of the Strategic Defense Initiative offers another, broader perspective. We shall return to the SDI and a consideration of its latent functions later in this discussion.

A Structural-Functional View of the Military

To begin the discussion, let us first consider military systems from a functionalist point of view. One of the major elements of nearly any human community is a defense or war-making system of some kind. Even though such systems are referred to as "military systems" in this book, it should be understood that simple societies do not have military professionals in the same sense that they exist in modern complex social systems.

What are the "manifest functions" of the military in modern society? Here are a few that are commonly accepted as the "official" notions of what the military does:

1. Provide for national security.

2. Defend against external attacks.

3. Secure national boundaries.

4. Be informed of possible hostile or aggressive actions against the community.

5. Assure the effectiveness of the military organization through loyalty to its objectives.

6. Exercise legitimate control over the means of violence.

7. Enforce the law and quell insurrections.

8. Provide, at higher levels of office, a personnel of unquestionable and unquestioning loyalty.

9. Advise civilian authority of potential external and internal enemies.

10. Maintain a state of readiness at all times, monitoring relevant military movements around the world.

11. Oversee the current state of weapons to assure a posture of strength in terms of number and quality of such weapons.

12. Keep in place a system, voluntary or forceful, of procuring and retaining manpower to achieve the ends of the military unit.

Again, this list can be extended, but it covers a number of the major functions of military units. So far, I only listed the manifest functions. The next question is: What are the latent functions of such systems? Here is a list of a dozen possible "latent functions" of military systems — at least as we know such systems in Western culture:

1. Provide work and security for those not able to find it in civilian life.

2. Professionalize people who cannot afford other training.

3. Provide a cadre of civilian teachers, industrial advisers, and other civilian professionals from the ranks of retired military personnel.

4. Promote and sustain an adversarial perception of anyone outside of the "system." (A good example was the hostility American military officers displayed toward British officers in World War II. At one point, General Eisenhower had to issue formal orders to the effect any officer who could not relate to British colleagues would be shipped back to the states in disgrace.)

5. Discourage sympathetic attitudes toward any group defined as a possible or potential enemy.

6. Provide a substitute for penal constraint for individuals deemed marginally delinquent or criminal.

7. Promote the transition from rural to urban life-styles for draftees or enlistees from agrarian backgrounds. (This function was implied in the old World War I song lyrics about American farm boys turned soldier in Europe: "How're ya goin' keep 'em down on the farm after they've seen Paree?")

8. Promotion of cultural diffusion through contact with alien or enemy cultures.

9. *Rite-de-passage* for males in which the break with parental authority is legitimized through military service.

10. Maintenance of social class boundaries within the general social system through rigid hierarchy.

11. Military "pork barrels" and the promotion of conflicts with regard to establishing domestic political policies.

12. The definition of languages.

I tossed this last function into the list to show the extent to which it is necessary to draw on the imagination to uncover possible latent functions. This "latent function" was suggested by Rolf Kjolseth, a sociolinguist. On one occasion Kjolseth gave a lecture in which he presented evidence showing that different languages are considered the same language (as is the case with different Chinese dialects). On the other hand, similar languages might be listed as different (Dutch and German might serve as an example here). This puzzled the class and eventually a student asked, "What is it then which determines whether languages are defined as similar or different?" Kjolseth thought for a moment and then laconically replied, "An army."

This list of latent functions suggests that many of these functions are a kind of spill-over into the affairs of other institutions. For example, the American military certainly serves the function of providing an occupational outlet for people who otherwise would encounter difficulty finding employment in the civilian world. One cannot even be certain whether this should be listed as a latent or manifest function. However, it appears more on the latent side insofar as it is not generally considered to be a specific task of the military to provide jobs for the jobless.

Providing jobs for the jobless is usually considered to be either the task of welfare systems or government economic policies directed toward welfare. However, this latent function is a powerful one. To some extent it accounts for the power that the military gained in Germany after the Versailles Treaty. The German army, at that time, was a place where one could find both work and a sense of duty and of dignity. After Germany's defeat in World War I, neither work nor dignity were readily available in a country totally disrupted and devastated by its losses. Hitler found the militarization of Germany a solution to the weakening of other central institutions after the war.

The military not only employs people who might otherwise experience trouble in the civilian labor market but also, of course, employs a large share of the technical labor force. Federal military and space obligations for research and development amount to about two-thirds of all expenditures for research.[5] The presence of the military in virtually all branches of research and technical development makes it a major market for the labor skills of technically qualified persons.

Huge military technical programs such as the Strategic Defense Initiative serve not only as possible defense systems but also as massive economic programs. In a real sense the Strategic Defense Initiative functions as a welfare program for scientists and technicians who might otherwise find themselves in the ranks of the unemployed.

The military is a major educational system within the United States. Military technical schools train thousands of individuals each year in activities ranging from flying advanced aircraft to constructing bridges and repairing complex radar systems. In a sense, any military base is also a training center. Although the United States maintains roughly 60 major training centers as part of its military system, primary statistical sources tend to exclude the military from the category of educational statistics.[6] The very absence of the military from educational data is an example of what the structuralist means by a "latent" function. The military does function as an educational system, but this is rarely listed among its manifest functions *as a military system*.

Again, the point being made is that one common form of latent function is where a functionally distinct or different institution preempts, to a degree, the manifest functions of another institution or agency. In this instance, we considered the case where the military, a noneducational institution, takes on several of the functions of educational systems. Other examples would be where religion preempts political or business functions; education preempts religious or military functions; business preempts religious functions and so forth.

Some of the other latent functions listed imply that the military system is not a separate system but has functions that overlap the functions of other elements within the society. The military carries out both police and penal functions. It engages in educational and training functions. It provides the political system with people who serve politically after retiring from the military. It provides civilian political authority with advisers who make political as well as military decisions.

A Functional Consideration of the Strategic Defense Initiative

One of the most expensive weapons programs ever undertaken by any nation in modern times is the so-called Strategic Defense Initiative (SDI). This program, by means of elaborate weapons circling the globe at orbiting altitudes, has as its manifest function the establishment of a protective umbrella over the entire North American continent. In one form it would call for as many as 600 military satellites in space, each capable of destroying enemy missiles through either nuclear-powered lasers or projectiles fired from powerful rail guns. Regardless of form and technology, we are curious here only about the functions of this system. After all, this most unique weapons system achieves its appeal primarily through what its functions are considered to be.

In the first place, the function of this system is touted over and over and over, through official statements and by means of propaganda and advertising, as a singular function — the defense and complete security of the nation against any form of nuclear threat. So completely is this singular function emphasized that the program itself can be stalemated if it can be shown this is certainly not its only function and that, indeed, several other functions may be more significant. However, as things stand, this can only be suggested and not proved.

What can be stated with considerable certainty is that the SDI is not a singular functional program — it is too vast and too complicated to allow for only a singular function. With this in mind, we will consider several other possibilities. Before we do so, let me mention that because SDI is so overwhelmingly presented as nothing but a defensive system, any other functions the program might serve are, implicitly, latent functions.

Diversionary functions   Because it is touted as "the" solution to the nuclear crisis, SDI diverts attention from the institutional, political, and economic forces underlying international tensions and conflict. It also diverts funds and efforts away from institutional solutions into technological solutions.

Subsidy functions   The great wealth being poured into the SDI program provides jobs and security for scientists, technologists, and other workers who find themselves otherwise unemployed.

Ideological functions   A culture that strongly endorses rational solutions to any and all problems finds the machine more attractive as a solution than social reform approaches. The general acceptance and support of SDI, its triumph over its opponents, provide a measure of the strength of science and technology as an element within the greater social system. SDI functions to let us know how powerful the rational norm remains. It functions as a political symbol.

Propaganda functions   Whatever SDI is, it is a new weapons system. As it is currently being planned, it is the most total, complete, powerful, and ubiquitous weapons system ever dreamed up in the schemes of military planners. Now, it should be self-evident that a weapons system is a weapons system. To be planning a new and much more powerful system than we ever knew in the past is, of course, to continue the historical race toward ever more devastating weapons. Yet, the SDI is presented as purely defensive. It therefore serves the function of continuing the arms race while, at the same time, calming the fears of a general populace that has become alarmed over where arms races have already led us.

Political functions   The vast sums of money going into this program, regardless of its viability, provide power to those who are part of the project — scientists, militarists, engineers, and war strategists. Money is power — political power. The political power, then, of those whose interests and knowledge are nearly exclusively technological becomes enhanced by such enormous funding while that of diplomats, political scientists and political theorists, medical organizations, and job training and educational systems is diminished. Federal funding is, after all, a zero-sum game. What is taken in taxation and then given to armament programs cannot be used for other purposes.

Externality functions   By being presented exclusively as a defensive system, the SDI turns attention toward the consequences of nuclear attack and mutes the possible consequences of the damage that could result simply from the defensive system itself. The fallout from several hundred nuclear lasers in space is not something to ignore — the cure might be every bit as dangerous as the disease it is designed to protect us against. The external threat of attack receives our attention, although the threats posed by the defensive system itself are ignored. (Only a few scientists have commented, publicly, on the problems raised by the fallout into the upper atmosphere of large quantities of radioactive materials from the detonation of SDI satellite devices.)

More interestingly, perhaps, the SDI concentrates attention on just one form of attack — massive nuclear strikes from an enemy nation — while diverting attention away from various other forms of attack by which national interests might be imperiled. As we build our defenses against a nuclear strike, we weaken the nation's monetary base necessary for waging international economic battles, which some analysts now look on as significant forms of struggle for power on a worldwide basis. We are much more vulnerable to eventual economic domination than military domination. At the present moment, at least, it almost seems as though we want to be economically dominated. Certainly this possibility receives much less publicity and concern in the media than does the threat of military confrontation.

Social class functions   The SDI is a military program likely to receive the solid support of the middle class, for it is fueled and sustained by an essentially middle-class cadre of technicians and experts. Unlike the Vietnam War, in which the lower classes were disproportionately represented while middle-class young men were protected by college deferments, the SDI provides the middle classes with a military program designed for their talents and sentiments. Indeed, everything about the SDI, the way it works and the manner in which it is rationalized, is strongly overlaid with American middle-class sentiments.

Let us stop at this point, although the list of possible latent functions of the SDI program could be continued for at least several dozen more pages.

You are encouraged to think the matter through and come up with a few I have not mentioned.

LATENT FUNCTIONS AND INSTITUTIONAL OVERLAPPING

I pointed out that institutions and social programs commonly have "overlapping" functions. A defensive system can have offensive functions. A military operation can also serve as a welfare operation. An educational system can have religious functions, and religious systems educational functions and so on. For a theory such as structural-functionalism that wants to see society as a functioning machine, this is a troublesome matter. The mechanical analogy, for instance, would be a machine in which the spark plug also worked somewhat as a carburetor and the pistons worked somewhat like the coolant system and the brakes occasionally worked somewhat like the accelerator. It would be a messy machine to try to understand.

This tendency for institutions to overlap is a recurrent problem in social organization and democratic political ideology. The best known version of the problem is the issue of keeping the interests of the state and the interests of religious organizations separate — the doctrine of the separation of church and state that is central to American democratic ideology. The military, like religion, is supposed to be a system separate from civilian governing authority. However, the separation is always an uneasy one. The recent Iran-Contra episode revealed that military officers of relatively low rank can obtain an inordinate amount of influence in what is presumably the domain of civilian political leadership.

So far we have taken the structural-functionalist concept of latent function and applied it to the military. In doing so, we find the concept basically refers to what might be termed functional anomalies. That is to say, a latent function commonly proves to be a function belonging primarily to another system. The function of the military, for example, is to defend national boundaries and wage war. When we find it engaging in welfare activities — which are the primary concern of religious and charitable agencies — it is performing an ancillary function not properly its concern.

Just as individuals are capable of serving a variety of functions within a social system (student one minute, shop assistant the next, and then Sunday School teacher the next, etc.), institutions seem to vary considerably in their functional versatility. Virtually any institution can establish a dominant position within a given society by extending its functional characteristics. When, for example, the religious system of a community prevails across economic, political, military, educational, and family matters, it dominates by virtue of extending its functions within the society. A case in point might be the current situation in Iran and Iraq where religious leadership is strong within political, military, educational, and family systems. In the United States business appears to be a dominant system.

If there is a lesson to be learned from the functional approach to social systems, it might be that a democratic state must struggle to maintain separation between major institutional systems. In terms of rigorous democratic ideals, religion should be kept out of the affairs of state. Likewise, it should follow that the state must be kept out of the affairs of the family. Education must be kept separate from economic practices. Economic practices must be separate from military concerns. The military must be separate from religion. The family must not intrude in education.

This is implicit in a democratic balancing of institutions. (This might also account, in a sense, for the popularity of structural-functionalism in American social science.) It is the institutional equivalent of freedom of expression. So it is that educators get upset when the family intrudes too heavily into educational matters. The functional strains with respect to these two institutional systems have reached the point in the United States where families are willing to defy state authority by insisting on teaching their children at home. Educational systems, on the other hand, have sought to draw the child away from the family as a center of training. In America this is commonly done as a stepwise procedure culminating in the child's leaving home to go to college.

Yet, just as too much freedom at the individual level creates anarchy and chaos, the same thing happens at the institutional level. The modern university can now properly be criticized for having abandoned its duties *in loco parentis*. The consequence is a youth culture that has less sense of direction and a higher suicide rate than any in the past. Yet, at the same time, given the powerful sweep of modern social organizational forms, who — other than old mossback educators — really thinks there is any hope for a return to *in loco parentis*?

In other words, in a clockwork system in which institutions perform their specialized functions within themselves but in close interdependence with each other, each institution would tend to its affairs and leave problems that are not properly within its sphere of understanding to other systems. This would be the ultimate in hyperrationalized social policy. Politics would be politics; religion would be religion; education would be education and so forth. Would this system be any better than the older systems from which it evolved where every social function was performed by everybody as the occasion warranted?

Obviously, we are nowhere near such an idealistic, mechanically pure, impossible, and probably unwanted separation of the powers of institutional systems as an idealized application of structural-functionalism inclines us toward. The separate systems meld into each other and vie for functional dominance over one another. This is not only the case *between* institutions, such as religion and the state, but *within* functional systems as well. For example, within the American military system the Navy, Air Force, Marines, and Army often fight each other as bitterly as they fight their avowed enemies. The fight is for functional dominance.

The concept of latent function directs us toward an awareness that social institutions are not mechanical systems. And with this recognition, the limitations of a structural approach begin to reveal themselves. The underlying metaphor of a functional approach is that a society is a kind of clockwork, and yet the notion of latent function admits that the social machine is not like other clockworks. After all, the latent functions of, let us say, a spark plug or connecting rod in an automobile engine are rather difficult to imagine. Certainly they cannot be as easily listed as those of a human institution.

The fact that institutions reveal both manifest and latent functions means that defining the functions of any institutional structure is not a simple matter. Among the numerous profound implications of this awareness is that we are forced to reconsider the extent to which the American ideal of separation of powers should be pressed. Is it reasonable to expect the church and the state to be entirely separate entities? If not, then how much overlap should be permitted? If so, then should other institutions — such as the school and the family — also be forced into separate spheres of influence?

The same questions apply to the military. Within Western cultures generally and within the United States and the USSR more specifically, the military has acquired a relatively broad set of functions. Although it is extreme to refer to these nations as military states, it is nonetheless worth asking whether the military has achieved a functional base so broad it threatens to dominate, or at least rival, all other systems.

Civilian political authority still makes civilian political decisions in both the United States and in the Soviet Union — the two major military powers of the world today. However, the trend over the years is for military concerns to take precedence over civilian concerns. More disturbing is the extent to which the American political system now welcomes military authority as an element of the political decision-making process.

Structural-functional philosophy argues that good intentions on the part of individuals are not as powerful as established structural systems. Virtually the entire world would like to see the end of the threat of nuclear arms. At the individual level the intentions are good. At the structural level the situation appears radically different. Nuclear weapons are a structural necessity, not an individual one. So, where individual intentions clash with structural objectives, the structural objectives are more likely to prevail. At least, this is the general understanding offered by structural-functionalism. Perhaps the simplest way to put it is to point out that structural-functionalists believe you can't fight City Hall.

Structural-functionalism argues that the demands of communal systems are beyond the will or the intentions of the individuals who make up the community as a whole. We cannot will nuclear bombs away. We cannot achieve a new world by trying to change our individual minds or awareness. The structure as a whole must change if the individuals within it are to have any hope of realizing their wills or their personal dreams.

Nonetheless, the American approach to social issues remains rooted primarily in psychologistic rather than systemic palliatives. For example, a nationally renowned figure, whom I happen to admire, gives seminars on "imaging" a world without weapons. This approach suggests social reform can take place by changing the minds of individuals. A structural-functional approach argues against such attempts. The notion of "imaging" a world without weapons is gentle and well-intentioned. However, it is misguided. Indeed, it might do more harm than good insofar as it continues to promote the belief that the individual is the locus of social force, thereby turning attention away from the structural situation.

Americans talk about society a lot. However, in odd ways, revealed in the popularity of psychology, the cult of the individual, and a general reluctance to pay serious attention to what their best social scientists tell them, they really do not want to believe in society. Whether they want to believe in it or not, they are amazingly naive with respect to structural approaches to social issues. Structuralism suggests societies create societies and cultures create cultures — individuals, for the most part, simply go along for the ride. No wonder Americans have trouble with it.

Here, then, is a philosophy that places us at the mercy of forces much greater than our individual selves. Social change and reform, if it takes place at all, takes place at the organizational level. Structural changes are brought about by changes within elements of the structure rather than by good will or desires for reform that spring from the individual heart. Sociologists do recognize a place for the individual in their work; however, they tend to view the individual, as a social being, in terms of organizational memberships.

If there is a movement for reform or change it comes out of what is taking place at the structural level rather than an individual level. Let us assume, for the moment, the correctness of a functional approach. We must then raise the question of whether it implies passivity and resignation or, on the other hand, whether it gives us possibilities to work on with respect to solving the problems of our times.

My own view of functional theory is that, oddly enough, it does offer a bit of hope. Indeed, of the several sociological perspectives touched on in these essays, it offers several arguments that provide us with a sense of optimism about the future. What functionalism directs our attention toward are systemic or structural issues. Rather than dealing with the question of whether people are becoming less aggressive or more aggressive or more warlike or more peaceful, functional thinking wants to know what is happening at a structural-functional level. What is taking place in terms of world systems?

The answer to this question appears to be that there is a growing interdependence between world systems. Gone for the foreseeable future are those times when two tribes of people could live within 50 miles of each other without any awareness of the other's presence. This is a time when events in a small country on the other side of the globe can have significant consequences for people on this side of the globe. Whether we like it or not, the world has turned into a global village. Moreover, from a structuralist perspective, the development of global structures appears to be moving quickly and expansively throughout all of the nations of the world. The rapidity of this development cannot be overemphasized. Within a single lifetime we have moved from extremely narrow and provincial communities to a global system that now involves all people of the earth. There is time for only a brief discussion of the nature of this structural change, but it must be considered for it offers promise with respect to the attainment of world peace.

Nation-states have, since the early 19th century, been moving toward blocs of nation-states. The present collaboration between nation-states with respect to trade agreements and industrial-economic partnerships is elaborate and expansive. For example, the once highly separated nation-states of Europe have joined in various cooperative organizations since World War II. The Organization for Economic Cooperation and Development now involves some 25 nation-states working cooperatively to coordinate national policies with respect to economic growth.

To bring the matter home more dramatically, we are forced to recognize that a nation such as the United States is involved economically with other nations. For example, in 1983 we had investments abroad totaling $887 billion. What happens to this wealth, invested in foreign territories, is, of course, of concern to us. What is possibly less generally noted is that foreigners have a major investment in the United States. In 1983 foreigners held assets worth $781 billion in this country. By now the amount is well over $1 trillion.

These billions of dollars represent corporate investments and, ultimately, the corporations themselves. They are indexes of the extent to which these economic structures move into national systems. What is evidently occurring is a blurring or melding of national economies as multinational systems operate across national boundaries. We find ourselves at a point in history where major structural units are taking on new lines of strain. We have, on the one hand, large multinational corporations seeking markets, either labor or commodity markets, wherever they can find them. These corporations, a number of them controlling budgets larger than those of an average national unit, move where the winds of profit blow them. They are no respecters of national boundaries and they are not particularly nationalistic in their concerns. Nationalistic sentimentality is not a part of a rationalistic, profit-oriented corporate system.

They do not worry about nationalistic confusions—if the consequence of such confusion is to the advantage of the corporation itself. I think, for example, of when I recently talked with a car salesperson about the purchase of a small auto. The car had an old, established, and nostalgic American brand name. I liked the idea of driving an American car and talked further about the machine — only to discover, after a few minutes, that it was manufactured by a Japanese firm. On the other hand, I talked with another car dealer about a Japanese auto only to be told its production involved 70 percent of its parts being made in the United States. How do you buy American anymore?

Corporations appear to be on the way to becoming less and less nationalistically sentimental. However, the primary passionate division between the people of the earth, at this time, is nationalistic. In a sense, there are several types of conflict taking place across two forms of massive *structural* systems. First there is the conflict between nation-states. Second, there is the conflict between corporate systems. Finally, there is a less obvious, but nonetheless serious, conflict between corporate interests and the interests of the nation-state.

Nationalism promotes military conflict. It is still the case that serious nationalistic issues can be resolved only by war. War is an extension of diplomatic struggles between nations. The nation-state grants legitimacy to armies and their exercise of violence as a way of protecting the interests of the nation. Corporations, no matter how massive, do not have armies. Obviously, nationalistic military systems protect the investments and interests of corporations. However, within the past 50 years these corporate interests have become a complex tangle of international arrangements. What is of significance for the threat of nuclear war is that corporate interests and national interests are not the same.

National interests and the interests of international corporations are not perfectly parallel matters. To the extent this is true, it suggests there is hope for the future. If we accept nationalistic rhetoric at its face value, then it would appear the United States should have nothing to do with the Russians who, after all (at least until recently), have represented an empire of evil. At the same time, the USSR represents a market for American corporate interests. The fact that an "iron curtain" separates the USSR, as a market, from American industries that could profit from access to that market, implies a strain between what we shall call here corporatism and nationalism.

As corporate structures move across national boundaries, confusing economic interests with respect to national identities, the question of what is to be won by waging a war becomes more uncertain. There is time for only an example or two to illustrate this observation.

The Pepsi-Cola Company now has 16 bottling plants located in the Soviet Union. In 1985 these 16 plants produced 30 million cases of Pepsi. In 1986 the people of the USSR consumed 1 billion servings of Pepsi-Cola. Donald Kendall, the chairman of the Pepsi-Cola Company, stated that by 1991 the company expects to be distributing 70 to 75 million cases a year in the USSR. This would roughly equal the sale of Pepsi-Cola in the United States market in 1960.

This is a minor, almost trivial, little item. Even so, it suggests the difference between nationalistic interests and corporate interests. Pepsi-Cola not only enjoys serving soft drinks to a people who are defined, by the leaders of the United States, as an enemy, but they look forward to serving lots more in the future. Moreover, consider the fact that although the American military system might find it desirable to neutralize the military system of the USSR, they might also, in the process, neutralize Pepsi-Cola's market; and the significance of this is obvious — dead people don't drink Pepsi-Cola. To be more precise: Dead people don't *buy* anything. In a consumer-oriented structure, you do not want lots of dead people around — they make a rotten market. (On the other hand, for a *consumer-oriented structure* poor people are the economic equivalent, or worse, of dead people — not only do they consume little, but they are also in a position where it is especially difficult to pay off debts.)

Although it is a minor news item, it still remains the case that 1 billion soft drink servings is not an insignificant commercial accomplishment. Pepsi-Cola is about as American as mom, hot dogs, and apple pie. Nonetheless, it is doubtful its commitment to American policies extends to the point where it would accept the obliteration of a market that absorbs 1 billion servings of its product each year.

A Marxist might comment that this is just another illustration of the material-economic order dominating nationalistic rhetoric. Structural-functionalism does not negate a Marxist interpretation of what is taking place with respect to corporate interests in markets. It does, however, force our attention toward a broader concern — the "machinery" or forms of organization involved when there is a conflict of interest. Where Marx would emphasize the owner-worker classes as the primary units of struggle, structural-functionalism provides a different slant by suggesting nationalism and corporatism as a different set of units for investigation.

There are other examples of the tensions that come about as a result of the different attitudes deriving from a nationalistic as opposed to a corporate mentality. The reliance of the USSR on American grain products is generally well known. In 1984 the Soviet Union purchased 15 percent of all U.S. grain exports, about one-third of all the grain it obtains from other countries. The Soviet Union, in 1984, was the second-ranked nation, behind Japan, in the purchase of American farm products.

American farmers are obviously interested in finding markets for their products. At the same time, they are also interested in finding reliable and cheap farm equipment. The USSR currently distributes a cheap and rugged tractor in the United States. Farmers, like auto and stereo buyers, might feel guilty about buying foreign over American-manufactured equipment. The economically significant thing, however, is that they nonetheless buy it.

There are, then, new structures in the making — massive, economically grounded, and rationally organized — that are rapidly coming to vie with nationalism as a mass system. We now have international air transportation regulations that enable pilots to fly into foreign airports anywhere in the world without having to have their procedures translated into a different language or set of rules—English is the established language for air transport. We now have in place a global postal system. Rapidly following these global systems are hundreds of major corporate "invasions." Where it will lead is difficult to tell. However, it seems reasonable to believe that as corporations move across national boundaries, they will provide a structural check on nationalistic antagonisms operating against the interests of the corporations.

If so, then in this structural stalemate there is hope for avoiding nuclear conflict. Small wars might take place here and there as conflicting national interests require resolution through force, but a major nuclear conflict would be impeded by the further constraint of loss of markets for multinational corporations. I cannot resist noting, at this point, that this argument has a strong appeal to business leaders who have, for years, argued that free world markets will inhibit war. However, world trade grew before both World War I and World War II and this forces one to consider the matter further. Remember that I have not said the structural strains between corporatism and nationalism will stop war, but they might operate as a further check on nuclear war.

CONCLUSIONS

I will bring this discussion of a structural-functional approach to a close by briefly outlining several of its strengths and limitations.

A few of the possible weaknesses of structuralism are:

1. The root metaphor of society as a machine inclines us toward a more mechanistic conceptualization of social systems than is warranted.

2. Structuralism implies that if an element exists within a society it is there to serve a function for the collective system and is, in a sense, justified.

3. Structuralism inhibits reformistic zeal by implying, on the one hand, that it is necessary to change the entire structure to produce real reform and, on the other, that the structure is so complex you cannot know what the consequences will be for the system as a whole if a change is made in one part of the system.

4. The clear and precise delineation of institutional or organization functions—either manifest or latent—proves to be more an act of the imagination and understanding of the investigator than anything else. Though the functions of a simple machine are readily determined, the functional nature of social units is not in the least obvious. It is the task of sociology, at least in part, to establish the nature of these functions. Structural-functionalism attributes functions and then comments on them. In this it is accomplishing its

sociological understanding through a kind of *fait accompli* or circularity.

Among the strengths of a structural-functional approach are:

1. It directs thought toward the consequences of our actions, either intended or unintended. What we intend has unintended possibilities that can surprise us.

2. It inhibits the tendency to see things as simply superstition, madness, or idiocy. If, for example, there is a group that endorses the values of the Ku Klux Klan, there are reasons for it. What functions does such a group serve?

3. Latent functional thinking makes moral decisions more complicated. At the manifest level policies or programs can be seen simply in terms of polar oppositions. For example, the prolonging of life is good. The shortening of life is bad. The manifest function of modern medical technology is to prolong life. But, in a nation that worships youth, the growing burden of an elderly population could lead to a repressive future—for the elderly or for the young people.

4. Functional analysis, according to Merton, replaces naive moralizing as a form of social criticism. We can, for example, rail against the military and the nuclear impasse. However, from a functional position, we must ask the question: What system can we put in its place that will serve the same functions in a less dangerous fashion? What system will provide so many jobs? Assure national security? Promote loyalty? Provide competent and inexpensive training? Draw on the services of so many scientists and thereby sustain scientific work?

5. In sum, functional analysis suggests that in dealing with any social issue, such as the nuclear impasse, the entire system must be dealt with. If we are to "imagine a world without weapons," we must also "imagine" the structural transformations such a change would bring about.

Whatever the strengths and limitations of structuralism, it provides us with yet another way of examining our social lives. In this chapter I touched lightly on some of the directions such a perspective turns us toward. Most significant, it appears, is the extent to which it turns our thinking toward the interplay of huge, global structural forces—represented by commercial corporatism and rampant nationalism—taking place in the world today. Especially significant in terms of the nuclear arms issue is the suggestion that large, systemic transformations taking place at a global level might have the consequence of reducing nationalistic aggression.

At the same time, the aggression that takes place between corporate units and the potentials for conflict already existing within massive corporate systems are the stuff of modern social satire. We may, in the future, see corporations becoming powerful enough to establish military systems of their own. It happened in the past. For the moment, however, corporate interdependence appears a more lively prospect as an avenue toward world peace than international divisiveness. Admittedly, this is all highly speculative, but it is a speculation worth thinking about. At least this perspective offers a glimmer of hope with respect to an issue that, at times, makes even hope seem a wasted effort.

Chapter 7

Peter Berger: Constraint and Freedom in the Nuclear Age

THE MYSTIQUE OF FREEDOM

If there is any single idea or concept over which the people of the United States would be most likely to go to war, it would have to be the concept of freedom. In the rhetoric of American politics the word *freedom* is tossed about constantly and casually. Probably no other word is so commonly used and so little examined or understood in American social discourse. It is a difficult concept.

We believe, with great passion, that we are a free people. Yet, at the time of the American Revolution, only propertied white males were free in the sense of being able to vote. By the middle 1800s, only white males were free. By the early 20th century, only white males and females were free. It was not until the 1960s that blacks obtained an unrestrained right to vote. So, we can ask, what does the term *freedom* mean?

Certainly there is much freedom in America, and the freedoms we enjoy are unique. However, there is also a great deal of constraint. In no society is anyone perfectly free at any time. Even when we are alone, hiking through the woods, experiencing the free expression of the moment, we are still bound by the constraints of our socially acquired language. If we are never perfectly free, it is also true that in no society are all people, at all times, under complete control. Freedom and constraint in human societies are relative and not absolute qualities.

It should be self-evident that we live in a society that is neither all free, nor all constraining. The question then becomes: How much freedom do we experience compared with constraint or control? What is freedom? How much more of it do we possess than other nations? How much freedom can a society tolerate before disintegration sets in? How is freedom used to shape our opinions and beliefs about ourselves? How is it used to sustain control?

These questions have a metaphysical ring to them, and your first inclination might be to dismiss them because they are unscientific in character. It is true enough that we cannot rely on science, either natural science or social science, for any final, definitive answers. Worse yet, students of literature,

175

philosophy, and religion have discussed such problems for thousands of years and are still locked in argument and controversy. Not much gets settled when we stroll down this argumentative path. It should be obvious, then, that these heavy matters will not be resolved in a discussion as brief as this. However, such questions should not be tossed aside merely because they cannot be answered in any final fashion. We must continue to discuss them because these are questions that — all too often — people believe they know the answers to.

These questions are worth pursuing because in searching for answers we discover new ways of thinking about freedom and constraint. They are worth pursuing because they deal with matters that enliven human political and moral philosophy. If nothing else, they deserve consideration because they so often are not considered. Freedom is used more as a sloganized "buzz" word than as a carefully thought out issue of great complexity. It is sufficient that we become aware of this complexity, even if we cannot untangle it. I warn you now that the following discussion is contradictory in places and logically unsatisfying. It is intended not to settle matters but to open up, once more, an age-old discussion of our most cherished ideals. These ideals are, incidentally, strong enough to tolerate our critical probings. For all of the confusion it can generate, freedom is still a concept worth keeping.

Questions dealing with freedom and constraint are not resolved through science but through the social and political process itself. Freedom is a matter of eternal debate and negotiation and struggle. Scientific or not, any attempt to understand modern social and political movements without considering the question of freedom ignores a profound aspect of our times.

The writings of a former seminarian named Peter Berger are instructive as we struggle with these matters. Peter Berger is a present-day sociologist with theological training. His work reveals the strain between modern empirical, naturalistic, objective social science and the moralistic, spiritual, and contemplative work of the religiously oriented philosopher.[1] Berger is aware of this. He consciously brings together the conflicting views of religious beliefs and modern social science. Although this conjunction does not settle things in any final fashion, it generates awareness by the profundity of the contrasts set before us.

Berger moves directly into the question of freedom and constraint and what it means to be an individual caught up in the demands, both moral and immoral, of larger social systems. He begins by forcing us to comprehend the extent to which our individualism, our freedom, is limited. Americans proudly proclaim themselves to be members of a free nation — a nation of individualists. Still, we need to ask: How free are we? To what extent, in fact, are we individualistic?

A careful appraisal reveals that we are, in fact, free only in a limited sense. As for individualism, even a light examination quickly shows it to be more myth than reality. Let me quickly add here that calling something a myth does not mean it is necessarily bad. Whether it is a good myth or a bad myth is more difficult to assess than the fact it is a myth. I will outline what I mean by calling individualism a myth later in this chapter.

The discussion that follows is generally concerned with contrasting forces: freedom and constraint, individualism and the collective, determinism and will. Such abstracted terms cannot be pinned down precisely, and as I just said, I do not in the least pretend to offer any final statement with respect to these concepts. What I want to do in reviewing Berger's ideas is to stimulate discussion. After all, if these are terms we are willing to fight and die for or, at least, have others fight and die for, then we should give them more than a passing thought. Certainly they do not deserve the abandoned casualness that marks their use in Fourth of July political oratory and in so much journalistic editorializing.

Possibly Berger's best known work is *The Social Construction of Reality* written with Thomas Luckmann.[2] The major premise of this work is that there is an interplay between the communities we live in and the reality we experience such that major parts of that reality are shaped by the community itself. In other words, what we give substance to — the real and living world around us — is not something we experience directly. It is forever "filtered" through the lenses of our social and cultural experiences. We, for example, see dogs as pets and not as food for the table. In other cultures one can be attracted to a dog because it might make a nice roast for the evening's feast. We have a well-defined sense of the future. There are cultures in which the future does not exist in the same way it does for us. These are minor examples of the way in which a culture or society can shape reality. If society shapes reality, then the community plays a major role in shaping not only our actions but also what we come to think of as the reality we see and touch in front of us.

Another well-known work by Berger is *Invitation to Sociology*.[3] Despite the lightness of its title, this book struggles with the determinism of modern social philosophy and the contrary issue of freedom. The following discussion draws largely on this work and, to a lesser degree, *The Social Construction of Reality*.

Berger accepts the idea that we define ourselves through our community. In doing so he reflects the current view of Western social science. This view claims that the reality of personal experience is not detached from the community. For example, if we see ourselves as free and as individualists, it is because such ideas serve the interests of the society in which we live. While freedom and individualism are real qualities for us as individual men and women, they also come out of a social unit for which they operate as functional beliefs and ideas.

The myth of individualism that prevails in our own culture inhibits our ability to recognize the extent to which we are virtually completely dependent on others. Although we emphasize the self, the greater reality is that the individual is nothing without the support of social units. A simple power outage or a strike by the local garbage collector's union reveals, rather quickly, that without the assistance of hundreds of other people, on a daily basis, life quickly moves from a relatively serene routine into a miserably uncomfortable and uncontrollable mess.

As a humbling exercise, try carefully to assess the number of people you depend on, one way or another, simply to get through a typical day. If you ask this question of your friends, you are likely to find them responding in terms of less than a dozen or so. It is, of course, an astonishingly gross underestimate. Even if you spend the day doing nothing more than sitting on a couch watching football on television, the number is probably greater than your imagination will allow — we depend daily on millions of people.

Our dependency on others involves *all* of those on whom we rely for anything. In the instance where we are by ourselves, passively watching television and eating junk food, it seems we are alone — relying on no one. However, begin the count simply by thinking of the numbers of people who: designed, created, produced, and distributed the television set you are watching; built the home in which you are living; constructed the materials for those who built the home; provided the materials for and built the couch on which you are lying; prepared the food you are eating; support the game you are watching; designed and operate the electrical systems on which you depend; and on and on and on. The count gets higher and higher. Remember, as well, that the people who are doing those things are, in turn, dependent on thousands of others. The dependency network becomes huge as the multiplying effects of interdependency themselves grow in size.

Or, if you want to look at it from a slightly different angle, ask what you might be able to create for yourself working without the assistance or support of anyone — starting when you are born. In all likelihood, without powerful support from others you would not survive even a few months. Even after reaching maturity, what would you have if what was given you by others were taken away? If you start to think about it — even for the briefest time, you quickly see that you are sustained, as it were, by a sea of hands and unheard voices that puts together the things of your world. You float in a cultural world that is the creation, the end product, of innumerable, unseen men and women.

At this point the idea of cultural support and the rejection of individualism is being pushed to its *reductio ad absurdum*. However, mythologies of individualism, such as those offered by writers of the Ayn Rand genre, can blind us to how much individuality, though real, is considerably more than balanced by the powerful attainments of human beings working in concert.[4]

In sum, the more you possess and the richer your life, the more you depend on the support of nearly unimaginably large numbers of "invisible others" who grant you your privileged life. So it is that today we each depend on literally millions of people, on a day-to-day basis, to sustain each of us as individuals. We are the dependent creature *par excellence*. Few of us could manage to survive more than a few months alone and without weapons, clothing, and knowledge that were created through the efforts of others.

The paradox of the idea or myth of individualism is that in order for it to come about, there must be large collective systems capable of bringing it into being. People who live in simpler and possibly more individualistic societies are less likely to brag about individualism in the same way we do.

In America psychology prevails over all other approaches to understanding ourselves. Psychology places emphasis on the individual. The social sciences, of course, place an emphasis on the community. In our own culture, with its inclination toward individualism, there is a tendency to ignore the power of the community. Berger attempts to correct this bias by forcing us to become aware of the extensive powers of a society, through both the legitimate government and informal systems, over the individual. Only when we gain an idea of the power of the state can we begin to see the problems involved in the quest for true individualism and freedom. (As a by-product, we might also acquire a better understanding of the strengths and limits of purely psychologistic approaches to human concerns.

This chapter is based primarily on three concepts or topics that are a part of Berger's interests:

1. Social control
2. Alternation
3. Freedom

Eventually we shall want to consider how these concepts provide us with new perspectives on the nuclear arms issue.

SOCIAL CONTROL

We gain a sense of our vulnerability to control from the community by examining the varied ways any society coerces individuals into carrying out collective imperatives. A sociocultural system cannot rely on random individual responses to create the structure and the cohesiveness required for organized effort. A society cannot, in other words, rely on people simply "doing *their* thing." A society must, in effect, generate ways that ensure that what gets done is "society's thing." What we might want to do as individuals and what society seeks of us are, commonly enough, considerably different matters.

As a quick aside, let me mention that this is the basic observation underlying Freudian theory. From a Freudian perspective, individuals are inclined to be indulgent and pleasure-seeking. Societies, however, are oriented toward order and the discipline required for living communal existences. There is a built-in contradiction between the demands of social systems and our biologically established desires to gratify ourselves. From a Freudian point of view, our personal lives are a reflection of how the struggle between social and our individual biological impulses is resolved.[5]

Before we discuss social control devices, we should acknowledge that what a society "wants" is likely to prevail over what individuals might want if they were not socialized. That is to say, in simpler or so-called primitive communities the wants of people are relatively simple: food, shelter, companionship, and a few other basic gratifications. Not only have people lived in simple communities where their needs went little beyond this elemental list, but there is also evidence to suggest that as individuals they were happy enough and their lives were full. (Americans are usually astonished, if they happen to visit small, so-called primitive communities, to find that the people living within such communities are as satisfied with life as they are. We account for this by claiming they don't know any better.)

With the development of more complex social systems people change to meet the demands that come from the sociocultural order itself. As social beings we want what our society leads us to want. For example, modern-day capitalistic-commercial Western culture demands, by its very structure, people who consume. So, we consume. We consume as though it were a natural instinct. It is not. Consumption, as we indulge in it, is an acquired taste.

Modern ideology leads us to think that people, as a consequence of their inner nature, seek progress and material innovation. This is not at all as certain as we might be inclined to think. It is instructive, in thinking about individuals, societies, and culture to note that nearly every major invention in recent Western history was introduced against strong individual opposition. We commonly think inventions happen because people want them. Instead, it appears that inventions take place *and then*, after a period of adjustment, people come to want them. Societies and cultures force an eventual acceptance and then a dependency.[6]

An obvious case in point is the current arsenal of thousands of hydrogen weapons spread about the world. No sane and thoughtful person is happy with their presence, but this is beside the point. Nuclear weapons are social creations. They serve the interests of collectives not individuals. So we seemingly must make our personal adjustments to their presence. No normal individual has any particular use for such devices. They make no sense at the individual level. They make sense, to the extent they make sense, as the creations of social systems.

So far, we have lightly examined the relationship between the individual and society and argued, for the moment, that society has the upper hand in things — even in societies where individuals take pride in their freedom. Let us now take a closer look at one of the processes that must, by definition, take place in any human community — social control. In this section we shall be concerned with gaining a sense of how pervasive social control is. Only after we develop a strong case for the dominance of society over the individual will we return to the theme of individualism.

Berger identifies eight sources of social control: force, belief systems, ridicule, fraud and deception, ostracism, occupational control, the sphere of intimates, and contractual relations. We consider these control devices so that we can become aware of how extensively our lives come under the domination of the communities in which we live. The question then becomes: Is freedom possible, given the extent to which we are subjected to such pervasive and powerful forms of constraint over our individual lives? Berger replies with a strong "Yes." However, his arguments are at best controversial. Like all who have gone before into the dense thickets of this dispute, Berger does not resolve much of anything. He does, however, manage to tease us into thinking about matters that are worth our time and consideration.

Force

The use of violence, threats of physical harm or injury, or the application of physical force is the most obvious and perhaps most common form of social control. It is used in simple societies and in complex ones. A relatively small amount of applied force can achieve major effects. A commonplace example is the quick change that takes place in the driving habits of people speeding down a highway when they see, ahead of them, a state patrol car parked by the edge of the road.

However, force is capricious. It is also true that a major application of force can achieve surprisingly small effects. Force alone is not sufficient to create a human community. Air Force officers, for example, still seem to find it difficult to believe that bombing a civilian population, as was the case in London in World War II, does not cause an immediate collapse of morale. The violent bombing of North Vietnam, in a later war, was also surprisingly ineffective—considering the massive force that was applied—in terms of what it sought to achieve.

Sending people to prison is an obvious form of applied force. America has one of the larger prison populations of the world. Our prisons are crowded. Despite this, the present prison population of the United States amounts to about 1 or 2 individuals out of every 1,000 members of the civilian population. Prisons represent force, but they affect a small proportion of the society. I cannot help adding that our prisons have not accomplished much with respect to lowering crime rates; the United States has the highest violent crime rate of any industrialized nation in the world.

The police also represent force. Police officers are given the right to carry weapons and use violence, if necessary, to achieve public ends. The police represent legitimate force. The number of police and detectives, at all levels of government (federal, state, and local) amounts to about 2 or 3 people out of every 1,000 members of the civilian population.

The most extreme use of force, capital punishment, involves a very small proportion of the total population. From 1950 to the present, approximately 1,000 persons were executed for various crimes. The number in recent years has been low. A majority of the 1,000 were executed before 1960. However, if we determine the average number of executions to amount to 30 or so each year, then fewer than 1 person out of every 10 million members of the society was subjected to the extreme application of force since 1950.

These facts are instructive in several ways. First of all, as was indicated earlier, it appears that a relatively small amount of force is capable of maintaining order across large populations. We must conclude from this that either a small amount of force is sufficiently effective or that other factors are at work.

Second, we notice that force itself is rarely employed—threat is sufficient. The threat should have a "bite," however. That is to say, people should be aware the threat is not empty. This might help account for the fact so little real concern is given to prison as a reform experience or to capital punishment as a just form of punishment. Prisons, and the occasional state killing of some wretched derelict or crazed psychopath, exist as the material substantiation of threat.

Finally, these facts indicate that the use of force is so limited it could not possibly be effective unless other factors were working alongside it. After all, 3 police officers controlling 1,000 members of the general population would be badly outnumbered if they lost the good will and support of those they presumably control. (Recent extensive riots in South Korea reveal the extent to which the police are ineffective, even when used in force, against broad-based popular resentment.)

Violence and force are dramatic devices for social control; and perhaps for this reason, they attract our attention more than other devices. After all, prisons, police, executions, and the like are the stuff of which movies and television melodramas are made. We might be inclined to think force is the single, primary social control mechanism. Such thinking is much too simple. Violence and force are evidently necessary, but they are rarely sufficient to maintain an ordered human community.

For one thing, force is expensive. It costs time, money, and effort to maintain prisons, the police, military police, state troopers, armies, navies, helicopters, weapons, and all of the other agencies and mechanisms of force. For example, the United States could completely wipe out the drug problem through pure brute force. However, such an effort would be astonishingly costly. It would also be an ugly exercise—probably resulting in conditions considerably worse than the condition it was supposed to correct. Ugly or not, Americans prefer to spend their money on something else.

Another reason why force is limited as a social control mechanism is that it generates considerable antagonism. There are occasions when force is such an irritant that people throw themselves against it with astonishing courage and recklessness. History, past and recent, abounds with examples. Consider, as one case in point, the courage shown by the black men and women of the civil rights movement in the United States who, holding their children by the hand, walked into the teeth of spitting and murderous mobs.

There are others: Sir Thomas More chose to have his head lopped off rather than conform to unacceptable demands from his king; union leaders in the United States at the turn of the century were hanged, tortured with razors, and beaten, yet they continued their organizational work; early Christians allowed themselves to be fed to lions rather than surrender their faith. History is replete with examples of men and women standing against force and, in so doing, displaying the greatest courage and integrity. They become the stuff of legends.

Another problem with the unlimited or unrestricted use of compulsion is that it undermines the legitimate use of force. In order for the state to rely on legitimated force, it must have the goodwill of those who are governed. To go too far in exercising force risks losing that goodwill and the right to use systems of force that belong properly to the government or state. To abuse the right to use force is to risk civil war.

Finally, violence obtains only outward conformity. You can generally (though not always) get people to do your bidding by pointing a gun at them. However, the moment the gun is hidden from view, you can expect those you coerced to turn against you. *For force to work totally, it must be omnipresent and it must be certain.* This is difficult to manage as a logistics problem. The application of force is generally localized, and it is usually sufficiently uncertain that people feel they have a chance against it. For this reason pickpockets used to find their best opportunities to work their trade by moving through crowds drawn by the public execution of another pickpocket.

Nuclear weapons are omnipresent and certain and, in that sense, they solve the basic logistics problem with respect to the use of force as a social-control device. This is one of the great appeals of these devices. However, although they appear to solve the problem of force, the solution is flawed because once the force is applied, nothing is left. That is to say, the force is so powerful that it destroys what it is supposed to control. Destruction and control are two different things. In this we recognize yet another problem with force; it tends to destroy what it seeks to control.

If war is fought to achieve control through force, then nuclear weapons fail as a forceful technology. This feature of these weapons has, in all probability, inhibited their use up to the present. However, in conflict the subtlety of the distinction between control and destruction is sometimes lost. We should be mindful of this.

In order for social systems to work they must rely on force, but they must also rely on other, more powerful devices for getting individuals to do what is necessary. With force you get people to do what you want, but they harbor resentment and they conform grudgingly. As soon as the force is removed, they return to their own concerns. What would be much better is to have them carry out the will of the community, so to speak, but do so as though it were their own. Then, the coercive element remains constant, pervasive, and relatively effective or certain. Berger claims societies achieve this control over the individual through belief systems.

Belief Systems

We come into the world with no beliefs. A dramatic example of this appeared in a recent newspaper article about a boy who had been kept in a coffin-like box for several years by his guardians. When he was finally released he told officials he thought all children were brought up in this fashion. He did not know he was supposed to believe differently.

It is difficult to trace our memories back to the time when we had no beliefs because memory and belief come into being together. We begin to believe when we begin to remember. If we have no established beliefs at birth, then, like the boy in the box, we are vulnerable to believing whatever is set before us.

The full range of what people believe in is difficult to grasp through an act of the imagination. Significant numbers of people, at one time or another and in different places, have believed such things as: A part of the soul or spirit is found in one's urine; the future can be determined by sifting through animal intestines; a true leader will show a cleft in his teeth; men who wear dark blue suits, white shirts, and striped red ties know what they are talking about; the world was created all at once a few generations ago; Jewish people, running secret organizations, control the earth; eating beef makes you tough; love is a proper justification for marriage; if a member of your family dies, you should go out and cut off the head of the member of another family living nearby; a high-status person should not be punished for a crime against a lower-status person.

In the preceding list of beliefs, I tried to include one or two I am pretty certain the typical reader would accept and one or two that sound "wacky." Actually, what is "wacky" and what is good, solid common sense is a matter of the society in which you are brought up. A large number of societies, for example, would not accept the idea that love is the proper justification for marriage. There are places where leaders are more believable if they reveal a cleft in their teeth. In our society they are more believable when they wear dark suits and red ties. (Journalists now refer to such attire as a "power" suit.)

The important point for our purposes at the moment is not so much that belief is astonishingly varied among the people of the world but that belief comes out of a society and feeds back into the interests of the society. Belief is a sociological variable as much as it is a psychological variable.

When, for example, an economy rests upon a broad labor force that must be kept in servile circumstances, it is interesting to see how quickly beliefs supporting such a system come into being. Slavery becomes the will of God. When a human community is operating on marginal sustenance, codes of thrift and a deep-rooted belief in making everything count become a part of the community's belief system. When a community is rich in resources, codes of waste come into being and a belief in the virtues of consumerism takes over.

The analogy is awkward, but it might help if we saw ourselves like schools of fish that change direction according to the needs of the school *as a whole*. No single fish can change its direction and have the entire school also change its direction. However, when the school changes its direction, all of the separate members of the school conform. By itself, an individual fish is not able to change either its own direction or that of the school. The direction in which the school moves is, virtually by definition, the direction in which all of the individuals move.

Beliefs serve the interests of the community. Like force, belief induces the individual to conform to the demands of the group. Unlike force, belief gets the individual to conform and boast about it. Even more interesting, belief gets the individual to conform to the interests of the collective and not even know it. An example worth giving thought to is the new "punker" style affected by the more daring fashion darlings of the younger set. Although appearing totally nonconformist, the "punker" style is the epitomization of deeply ingrained Western values — one of which is that you should "express" yourself and be aggressively assertive.

In relatively simple societies, belief systems are powerful agents of social control insofar as they are not challenged. They possess the qualities of an ideal use of force as an agent of social control. That is to say, traditionalistic belief is omnipresent and virtually completely certain. These qualities, remember, were qualities that an effective form of control through force should possess.

In modern complex societies belief systems begin to break down in terms of their omnipresence and certainty. Even so, modern societies are surprisingly effective in maintaining belief systems. A great deal of energy, time, and material is consumed by any society in retaining its beliefs — modern societies are no exception. A modern person, for example, cannot get through an ordinary day without being subjected to a "sermon" from at least a dozen sources pertaining to what he or she should believe, do, or think.

Ridicule

Force and belief are two major agents of social control. Berger, however, adds several more to his list of control agents. Among these is ridicule. People, young or old, are vulnerable to ridicule. Yet, when it is examined closely, one wonders how ridicule ever manages to work. It is little more than a veiled threat to withdraw affection. The spoken portion of ridicule takes the form: "If you don't smoke a joint with us, you're a wimp." The unspoken part is: "We do not like wimps." In other words, all ridicule ever amounts to is the threat of withdrawal of affection as a form of force.

However, ridicule is especially effective because the threat of withdrawal of affection is indirect. Compare the following forms of the same threat:

Indirect: "If you don't smoke dope with us, you're a chicken."

Direct: "If you don't smoke dope with us, we won't like you."

In the indirect form the responsibility for the threat is directed toward the individual rather than the group making the threat. In the direct form the threat is still powerful, but not as effective as in the indirect form. Responsibility for the moral position being asserted rests more on the shoulders of the group. The direct form makes the choice apparent—join the group or lose *its* affections. In the indirect form if *you* do not join the group, *you* are defective. The choice now appears to be whether you want to accept the possibility you are defective or hold firm to your faith in yourself.

Whatever it is that makes ridicule work among human beings, a small amount of it seems to go a long, long way. Ridicule is powerful as a control agent. However, if it is to work, the individual must already be emotionally related to the group. Still, it is difficult to throw off ridicule, even when it comes from groups we do not want to be associated with or whose opinions we do not especially respect.

Fraud and Deception

Berger adds yet another device available for bringing about social control— fraud, deception, misdirection, and trickery. American moral codes are such that deception is considered, if not the worst of sins, certainly something improper. Yet, without deception and "trickery," human social systems probably could not be sustained for a day. Instead of approaching deception with a moralistic chip on our shoulder, it might be better to stand back and examine the extent to which it is a pervasive part of nearly any human community.

Deception is broadly defined here as actions that divert attention away from a negative evaluation of what is really going on toward a socially acceptable definition of the situation. I am, in this short discussion, ignoring the problem of intent. Deception, whether intentional or not, is neither good nor bad.[7] Deception is not a moral problem; the moral issue lies in the ends toward which it might be directed. We would all agree, for example, that it would be evil to deceive the people of the world into a final nuclear confrontation. Would it, however, be morally acceptable to deceive the people of the world into peaceful relations? Deception, as a moral issue, is not in the least a simple matter. In any event, its use as a social control device is common and can be found in any human social or cultural unit.

Deception ranges from the little white lies we tell people to make them feel better (a form of manipulation and control, but a benign one) to whole- sale propaganda campaigns. It can be carried out unconsciously or con- sciously. It can be used to serve a variety of ends ranging from the use of cosmetics to make ourselves look better to the use of deceptive advertising claims to sell commodities in mass markets. It can be simple or elaborate. It can be formal (as is the case with theatre, which—when it works well—is a magical form of deception), and it can be informal (as is the case when a husband lies to his wife about working late). It can be useful and it can be damaging. It can be subtle or blunt. Deception, when you begin to think about it, is a many-splendored thing.

What Berger makes us aware of is that any social system necessarily relies on deception and trickery, along with force, belief, and ridicule to keep us "in line."

For a nice example of an unconscious, formal, elaborate, and rather subtle use of deception, state lotteries work well. The trickery we are interested in here is practiced by newspapers and the media. It is an unwitting form, but it is still deception. To see the deception, all one need do is consider the daily stories that appear about winners while there are no stories about losers. A winner in a state lottery may be one person out of the several million who happened to play in a given month (which, of course, gives you one winner and several million losers). The fact that the winner gets a story and the losers get none slants perception so that people are more inclined to think the proportion of winners is greater than it really is. After all, if all the losers got a story, not only would the media be swamped, but the message would also be overwhelming—don't buy lottery tickets.

Even though we cannot reasonably expect the papers to write about all losers in state lotteries, they could print stories about the more interesting losers. After all, great losers are as engaging as great winners in the game of life. Losers can occasionally be newsworthy. Actually, they are generally more interesting than winners. For example, several years ago in Colorado, 20 people entered into a "combine" and paid $1,000 each for lottery tickets. They bought 20,000 tickets and eventually went broke. They wondered if such an outcome was possible and wrote a letter to a university professor of statistics asking for help with their problem. The professor, of course, informed them that the elementary laws of probability lead to the conclusion it is not only possible, it is highly probable.[8] This is an interesting story, in its way, but it never got in the papers.

Generalizing from the lottery case, we note that our culture celebrates winners. We get television programs about the life-styles of the rich and famous. Presumably everyone knows about the life-styles of the poor and ignoble. Nothing, of course, could be further from the truth. Americans, in general, are strikingly ignorant of what it means to be wretchedly, wretchedly poor.

From the media we get the impression that America is a land of winners. Like our impression of the lottery, this view is distorted. America is also, and to a far greater extent, a land of losers. I need to add here that describing America as a land in which losers occur in substantial numbers is apt to get anyone in trouble with those who like to censor political and social philosophy. However, I am not using the term *loser* as invective in this instance. I am using it instead as a casual social category—one that Americans are especially fond of using. In terms of plain and simple logic, you cannot have a land of winners without also having a land of losers.

At a more serious level we must consider the extent to which we are misled by the media in their reporting of international events, particularly those taking place in locales not in favor with the current administration. The American press is presumably a free press. At the same time, it is evident that the news can be manipulated and is manipulated. How extensively this is done knowingly or unknowingly is difficult to assess. What is easier to assess is that a great deal of selective reporting takes place. For example, in the five-year interval from 1976 to 1981 the *New York Times* mentioned the imprisonment or torture of the critics of right-wing regimes only 64 times (36 references were to Salvadoran Archbishop Oscar Romero). They mentioned the harassment of critics of Soviet programs 499 times in the same interval.[9] What the press omits is as important as what it includes, and it is obviously selective. We are controlled as much by what we do not know as we are by what we do know.

The major point is that we are deceived; we deceive ourselves, and we deceive others as a matter of social control. The example of the selective attention given to lottery winners in America is simply one of thousands of examples. The selective attention given to matters of governmental (that is, control) concerns is considerable. To the extent such attention is selective, we are manipulated. It is not necessary to be explicitly deceitful with people. It is not necessary to lie, though lying is useful as a social control device. It is sufficient, much of the time, merely to be selective in how you inform people. Keep in mind that a major portion of the information we obtain about ourselves comes from televised programs—and television is a rich study in deception.

By now the reader should have a sense of where we are headed. If a society has so many devices to control us, then how can we be "ourselves"? Are we all contained in this free-floating prison that, despite our love for it, is still a prison? Or are there other options? Berger wants to show us how strong the prison is before showing us possible ways out. To give us a deeper sense of the strength of social control, he adds a few more devices to those already discussed.

Ostracism

Ostracism is control through the threat of removing the individual from the group. Though it can involve force, ridicule, and other devices, it can be used by itself as an effective means of holding individuals in check.

We find this simple device being used by children before they enter school ("If you don't share your candy, you can't play with us any more.") It is used, in one fashion or another, in all communities. The Amish engage in "shunning" as a device to control their children's actions. An easy example is the university. Students with bad records are merely told to leave. Educational structures, generally, are set up in Western cultures in such a fashion that ostracism can be used as the major social control mechanism.

Students are not forced to stay in college; they are not subject to any great amount of ridicule, nor are they tricked into staying. They know the basic rule: Shape up, or ship out. However, the individual must already have a well-established belief system or relationship with the dominant group if ostracism is to be an effective threat.

Occupational Control

Yet another device among the various ways a society has of controlling the individual is occupational control. This is a matter of regulating the "better" forms of work—usually work that is clean, has "dramatic" qualities, and pays relatively well. This device is especially interesting because, in its more general form, it amounts to economic control. That is to say, if you do not shape up, you will be impoverished in some form or another. Impoverishment is life-threatening. Occupational control is then another, though quite indirect, form of force.

In order for occupational control to take place, there must be a moral or social order in which economic inequality is an established structural form. There must be better and poorer jobs. Those who control the better jobs or one's economic hopes are those who, themselves, have the better jobs or are in positions of economic power.

From this perspective, economic inequality is a structural demand of the social order; this is a profound barrier to any kind of true democratic expression where each individual is, in fact, equal to other individuals. Pure equality would remove from a community one of the powerful means it possesses for controlling individuals. A society would be abandoning a potent control mechanism serving its collective interests if it were to create genuine equality. There is also the implication that some jobs will be made to seem better than others, regardless of their functional utility. So long as there is the appearance of occupational hierarchy, a social system has an effective control agent at its command.[10]

Whether this speculation is entirely valid or not, the fact remains that Western culture, along with virtually all other modern nation-states, uses occupational control to hold the individual in check. We can draw on an example that achieved national attention as this chapter was in preparation —the fate of Supreme Court nominee Douglas H. Ginsburg.

Mr. Ginsburg made the mistake of experimenting with marijuana while teaching at Harvard. It was enough to cost him a high-status, lifetime position. His life will not be ruined; he will retain a good position despite his rejection. However, the message is obvious—if you want a good job, do not engage in *any* acts that might later be viewed as delinquent or improper. It is a relatively pure example of the use of occupational control to impose constraints on the broader population through example.

The American practice of letting its "losers" wander around in the streets dying in the cold and suffering from disease and assault, when seen from a social control perspective, is a matter of publicly demonstrating what happens when you "get out of line." The homeless, then, have a functional utility as social control agents—they remain on display, 24 hours a day, to remind those who are thinking of jumping the traces what the consequences well might be.

The Sphere of Intimates

The community comes at us, as it were, from various directions. Force, trickery, occupational control, belief systems, and ridicule confront us whenever we might be about to step outside the limits of propriety. Berger adds still another device to this imposing list: control coming from one's *sphere of intimates*.

This form of control is different from the others we considered. We do things not only because we are forced into them or because we believe in them, but also because those with whom we closely associate happen to be doing them. Soldiers, it was found, do not fight for lofty ideals (perhaps we give too much credit to belief systems as the control agent behind fighting). Soldiers fight for a more basic reason—their buddies are fighting.[11]

A nice example of what Berger is trying to convey with this control device can be found in the works of Albert K. Cohen.[12] Cohen noticed that juvenile delinquents engage in actions that are not only antisocial but that also commonly carry into bizarre and extreme forms. What happens in such instances is that the group in itself generates ideas and plans of action that range beyond what the individual alone would tolerate. The popular term for such a moment is "getting swept up" in the group.

To gain a sense of the control that comes from the sphere of intimates simply ask yourself how many things you do in the course of a week because your friends, relatives, and associates are doing them. Would you do the same things if they were not doing them? Why, for example, did you get started playing Trivial Pursuit? Or, how was it, actually, that you became interested in football? Automobiles? Drinking beer? Reading the current best seller?

The Contract

Finally, Berger offers one last social control device to round out his discussion of society as a kind of prison within which we are contained and controlled—the contract. The contract, basically, is a conditional proposition taking the form: If you do this, then I will do that. Once we enter into a contract, our actions are controlled by its stipulations regardless of whether we like the situation or not. One of the major contractual devices used by social systems, of course, is the marriage contract. Working relations in modern societies are predominantly a matter of contract.

It is interesting, in this regard, to reflect on how much our own society has moved toward contractual forms of social control. At the turn of the century, for example, it was unheard of that a college student would bring a lawsuit against a professor for failing to live up to the educational contract implicit in the act of matriculation. Today, several states provide malpractice insurance for professors working within the state system of higher education. Teachers are being held to contractual commitments more than was the case in the past where traditions (that is, belief systems) were accepted as the primary controlling agent.

One of the more striking indications of how prevalent this form of control is becoming in our times is the increasing reliance on the courts to resolve disputes. When Berger mentions the contract as a form of social control he refers, as well, to the power of civil law as a control agency.

SOCIAL CONTROL AND THE NUCLEAR IMPASSE

We have spent considerable time on the topic of social control without discussing our central concern—nuclear weapons and nuclear war. We need to bring our awareness of social control to a place where it can be used more concretely. Once again, let me warn you that this discussion is not offered as dogmatic truth to be "bought into." Instead, it is offered for debate and consideration. The point of the discussion is to explore the *implications* of social control as it pertains to nuclear weapons.

I have already alluded to one aspect of the relationship between control and nuclear devices. Force is a major form of social control, and nuclear devices exist as the most forceful devices for the implementation of policy ever created. However, as I noted earlier, they immediately reveal the problems that exist with force as a social control mechanism—they are too forceful. Instead of achieving control, their use leads to simple destruction and chaos—the opposite of control. As a form of social control, they are effective only as a threat. At the same time, threat is effective only if there is a material substantiation to back up the threat. The only tolerable form of material substantiation to back up the threat offered by the real use of nuclear weapons is testing.

From this vantage point, testing becomes a peculiar ritual, however. One would think the material substantiation would be most effective if the testing were highly publicized. However, it is done secretively. It is done secretively, and yet publicized.

There is a curious analogy here with the manner in which we carry out executions. If executions are the material substantiation of threat, they should be public. But they are not public. They are done secretly and yet publicized. This situation leads one to wonder if the secret-public substantiation of threat is now seen as more effective than the purely open form. This is worth thinking about. The brute display of force can rally counterforce. The secret-public display can, possibly, disarm counterforce while, at the same time, carrying out its threat function.

It is interesting to note, in this regard, that both nuclear testing and criminal executions were, in their early stages, public matters. We hanged people before large crowds, and newspapers displayed photographs of men strapped to electric chairs. Nuclear weapons, for a brief period after 1945, were set off before audiences and representatives of the media. Eventually, however, they became secret-public matters. We still learn of them through public media, but not in any great detail.

In all of this there are other things to consider — such as security and technical secrets. However, when thought of exclusively as social control devices, one must consider the fact that a too-secret testing of such weapons would defeat one of the intended functions of the weapon — the revelation of its reality as a threatening form of force. Because it is primarily a threat device, the problem of establishing its reality as an existent force is a central one. The situation might be different with a weapon one really intended to use.

Nuclear weapons, as a control mechanism, are unbelievably dangerous and awkward. They are not like any other forceful device ever employed, and it is a serious mistake to see them simply as another form of force. They prove, in the final analysis, to be a force that works only if the object of its use is to destroy and demolish rather than control and constrain. Once again they demand that we recognize how paradoxical their status is. They cannot be used as agents of control if they are detonated in any fashion other than in underground testing sites. They can be used as threat; but not otherwise. However, threat, as we noted earlier, constitutes the major portion of force as a form of social control.

Controlling Social Control

The relevance of the concept of social control with respect to nuclear weapons can possibly be made more clear by asking the question: How do we control social control? Virtually any complex society has strong inclinations toward enhancing and extending its social control. When the various elements of control listed by Berger are strong and working in concert, the result is a highly authoritarian system in which individualistic expression is muted.

Nazi Germany, at its peak, provides a lesson. Here was a society in which force, ostracism, ridicule, occupational control, belief systems, spheres of intimates, the contract, and deception were applied with great energy. The result was one of the most efficient and effectively organized large-scale social systems in history. Ultimately, the only way this organization could be checked was through the massive application of counterforce.

Now, nuclear weapons make sense only as social control mechanisms. There is no other rationale for their existence. They are too radioactively dirty to be used as explosives for removing earth to build dams and canals; they cannot, as yet, be used as a means of propulsion for spacecraft. They represent pure, simple, overwhelming brute force. It is the peculiar property of these weapons that they represent more than mere force. They are an entirely new and distinct form of social control mechanism — unusable, destructive power directed against national units in the form of threat.

Although they came out of the social imperative for control, nuclear weapons transcend the demands of control—moving into the domain of devastation. The proper goal of a control procedure is to constrain antithetical elements in such a fashion that the ends of the dominant social unit are achieved. Nuclear weapons, however, do not do this—except insofar as they are effectively threatening. Nuclear weapons, as the culmination of the evolution of social control imperatives, now bring social control itself into question. How do we control the controlling devices we have created for ourselves?

In conventional and "civilized" warfare, constraint of the policies of the enemy is achieved not through destroying but rather through weakening the opposed forces. Destruction should be sufficient to achieve the ends of control but no greater. The enemy's control devices must be subordinated to the victor's control devices. War is a matter of achieving control over the other system's control agents. Nuclear weapons, at least in their present state, devastate rather than weaken. They are, once again, paradoxical devices: They are control agents incapable of performing their task.

Let us come at nuclear devices from yet another angle. We shall assume, for the moment, that no sane person in the world is comfortable with the fact we all live beneath a nuclear sword of Damocles. Nuclear weapons are useful to social systems, not individuals. Few other implements are as capable of revealing the difference between sociological and psychological utility. Nuclear weapons are purely social devices or entities. They belong to entire societies, not single individuals or even small groups of individuals. They are the social entity *par excellence*.

This means, then, that in attempting to control nuclear weapons we are attempting to control social systems. Because the agencies of social control are already in the hands of the state, the task becomes one of controlling social control itself. In other words, those who are working to somehow constrain the production and the deployment of nuclear devices must find ways to counter the control devices used by the state to preserve these emblems of collective power.

The state is faced with two forms of control problems. On the one hand it must control its external enemies. On the other, it must control dissension, rebellion, and other forms of disruption that threaten to destroy the unity of the system from within. The same kinds of devices are used in either instance: force, deception, contracts (for example, treaties), propaganda designed to promote belief systems, and so on.

If nuclear weapons represent social control carried to pathological extremes, the question becomes how we control control. No one has any good solutions. To undermine social control endangers the comforts that the collective is capable of providing individual members of the community. Yet, if we continue in the direction we have been headed over the past several thousand years, we shall certainly destroy ourselves in the effort to control ourselves. Berger has the courage to face the problem even if the solution he offers is, at least in my opinion, more sentimental and romantic than realistic. I leave the matter to the reader's judgment.

THE INDIVIDUAL VERSUS SOCIETY

There are writers, popular and academic, who argue that in the face of state control, the individual is helpless. Berger does not offer a philosophy of helplessness. At the same time, he does not offer any great possibility for hope. He argues that if there is to be a transformation, if the problem of social control is to be solved, it must come from that which sustains the state in the first place — the individual members of the society. At this point he moves from a social science stance to the stance of a religiously trained moral philosopher.

Social control works, he suggests, because we so readily concede its power over us. We, in effect, play the kinds of control games society wants us to play. This trait is seen in the extent to which we use the phrase "have to" in our ordinary discourse. We "have to" go to class. We "have to" make money. We "have to" get better clothes. We "have to" clean our room. We "have to" take flying lessons. We "have to" learn Spanish. We absolutely "have to" watch the hometown NFL team on television. Life becomes one "have to" after another.

For Berger, this "have to" complex reflects how extensively we capitulate to letting our lives be controlled by forces outside ourselves. As long as we believe we "have to" do whatever we are doing, we are conceding that we are the pawns of external forces. We are playing the control game just as society would like us to play it.

So, we "have to" accept nuclear weapons. We "have to" fight the enemy. We "have to" put more money into arms. We "have to" hate. We "have to" kill. We "have to" do this or we "have to" do that. Of course, in other societies, the same thing is going on. Social control creates a sense of necessity that is expressed in the same language we use to express the necessities imposed on us by physical nature. That is to say, we use the same expression for "having to" wear a style of clothes that we use for "having to" eat to live. The "have to"'s in this instance are different.

Berger attacks the power of society through the spirit of the individual. The power of society is vast and overwhelming. However, the spirit of the individual remains greater — unless it is lost in the demands of the state. How does the spirit of the individual retain any kind of integrity? Berger's answer is a tough one and not too easily swallowed, but in the quest for answers to the problems posed by ultimate forms of social control we must consider all possibilities. The power of the state can be curbed only if individuals recognize that any action the state might impose on them is also one they are free to reject — if they are willing to pay the true price that freedom demands.

In effect, after painting a grim picture of society as a prison with numerous powerful control mechanisms to hold individuals in check, Berger turns right around and says the state can never control people who are truly free in spirit and who retain a profound sense of their personal responsibility for anything and everything they do.

To gain a better sense of what Berger is trying to say, try going through a single week without once using the phrase "have to." Instead, substitute "choose to." I "choose to" watch football this afternoon. I "choose to" go to work. I "choose to" eat this greasy hamburger. I "choose to" study for my calculus examination. I "choose to" be an avaricious consumer. And so on.

Notice how much those things you consider a matter of necessity become a matter of personal choice. Berger argues that we all have an inclination to hide the essential self beneath a social self that acts not out of choice but in terms of social control. When we look "deeper" we recover the essential self—that form of self capable of not capitulating to social demands. There is, however, a terrible catch in this romance of the free spirit. You might have to accept death itself as the price you will pay for your expression of freedom.

In the realm of nuclear weapons, the attempt to control social control is, so far, without any significant noticeable effect. Perhaps it is a lost cause. For Berger, that is beside the point. What is to the point is that those of us who accept the situation as it is because we "have to" have sold out. Worse yet, we have lost ourselves. We must ask, each day, do we "have to" live with this situation or, instead, have we "chosen to"?

Having said all of this, it is now time to express a major reservation. People like the romantic idealism that is contained within a philosophy of volition. It appeals to our sense of responsibility and the idea that we are granted a degree of control over our fates. It is a liberating belief. After all, how can one be liberated if one's life is determined? At the same time, it is a notion that also serves oppressive and tyrannical interests as strongly as it serves liberal ones.

After all, if we are free to choose our fates, we need to wonder why large numbers of people suffer such miserable ones. If we buy everything Berger says, then we must conclude they suffer because they choose to. If they had any real sense of their condition, they would choose death over their miserable lives. Somehow, this reasonable derivative of a philosophy of choice has the peculiar twist of making choice look more like another social control device than a form of liberation.

ALTERNATION AND LACK OF CHARACTER

The theme now swings from the authority and the massive power of the state to the individual. Berger cannot comprehend one without looking at the other. We are social beings. We do respond to the power and the might of social control mechanisms. At the same time, there is something repugnant about abandoning one's essential self—one's soul—for a mess of social pottage. Berger tries to find a way out of the binds of social control by coming back to the focus of that control—the individual.

His central argument—that we do not need to cave in to the demands of society—is based on a common observation, a phenomenon he refers to as *alternation*. Alternation refers to a radical change or transformation in the identity of an individual. President Reagan was once a liberal Democrat and then became a conservative Republican. This is an example of alternation. Others come to mind: A militant hawk goes off to war and comes back dedicated to promoting peace. A peaceful civilian is transformed into a professional killer in a military boot camp. Alternation is a relatively common experience.

Although Berger reserves the term for major shifts in character, it can occur in milder forms. In small ways we experience alternation on a daily basis. A woman, for example, might be a science student in the morning, a junior executive in the afternoon, and a jazz musician in a nightclub in the evening. In such an instance a person must alternate roles and, in the course of so doing, experience alternation.

We all have the capacity to be one thing at one time and something else at another. The fact that we can move through various alternations points to another feature of the self. Berger has a nice term for this other feature: "lack of character." Whatever the social occasion demands of us, we respond to. We change character as the occasion requires.

On the one hand, this is further evidence for the extraordinary powers of the collective over the individual. If we have little inherent character, then our character must come from the social units in which we are expected to perform. The extent to which individual character is manipulable by social setting is considerable. On the other hand, as Berger argues, it can be viewed as an avenue to freedom.

Berger, along with the other writers discussed in this book, agrees with the argument that people are surprisingly malleable with respect to character. This flexibility can be both useful and dangerous. For one thing, it permits human communities to create an astonishing variety of social types as the needs of the community require. However, if people are too flexible, they might not remain within roles that call for long-term commitments. Societies, then, find ways to fit people into various social types and then commit them to their obligations over long periods of time.

For example, a person who joins a secret intelligence or secret police organization in nearly any modern state is sworn to remain loyal to the organization throughout the remainder of his or her life. Loyalty becomes a powerful social tool for attaining the ends of the system as a whole. It is in the establishment of commitment that the state leads us to conclude we do what we do because we "must" do it. Loyalty is a moral concept directed toward the end of restricting socially dysfunctional alternations.

However, the fact that we are capable of being one social type one moment and a contrary type the next, suggests we do not have to perform given social roles. We are more flexible than that; we can perform a great variety of roles. Berger, for example, notes that the hardened and vicious concentration camp commander is the same man who also writes sentimental and gentle little letters to his family back home.

If the commander says he must be cruel and vicious, then it would seem necessary, if he is to remain consistent, that he not write sentimental and gentle little letters to his family. He does so anyway. It seems more reasonable to conclude he is capable of both qualities. Therefore, he is not vicious because he must be but, instead, because he elected to be — after all, he displayed an ability to be gentle. He can be one thing or the other. He does not have to be either.

When we say we "must" be what we are, given the fact of alternation, we give ourselves over to the social type into which we are placed. We accept the forces of social control and, in effect, state that we are little more than puppets dancing at the ends of strings manipulated by the community above us. We are acting in bad faith.

Let us now come back to the problem of nuclear weapons and consider how our discussion of alternation might be relevant to this issue. I made the point that nuclear weapons are, as it were, "desired" by social or national systems as a whole but not by particular individuals. At the same time, social systems seek to assure control over whatever is necessary for the integrity of the system.

Therefore, social control devices are set into play that are directed toward the end of making individuals believe or somehow conform to the notion that nuclear weapons are necessary or good or otherwise worth devoting one's life to. At least, such control devices work toward the end of promoting passive acceptance.

When we say, then, that there is nothing we can do, that we are helpless, that we must go along with whatever we are told to go along with, we are acting in bad faith. If nothing else, Berger suggests, we should have the strength and the understanding to accept the fact we are choosing the course of our lives. If, for example, we argue we "must" have nuclear weapons because the Russians have them, we are in effect rationalizing away the freedom we use as an argument against the Russian system. It is, after all, one thing to say we "must" destroy the Russians and another to say we "choose" to.

We come, then, to the final section of this chapter. To read Berger is to explore, in various ways, the idea of freedom. We cannot properly conclude our discussion without coming more directly to grips with this elusive, powerful, charming, and evocative human notion. Let it be understood, as we move throughout this discussion, that Berger is aware that freedom is much too important a concept to be left to politicians and ideologues. It deserves our deepest philosophical and intellectual concern.

FREEDOM

The social sciences, over a period of nearly a century and a half, did not produce one solidly deterministic proposition with respect to the interplay of *social* variables. Physical variables, within a certain range, are so deterministic as to permit earthbound scientists to control the course of small artificial satellites hundreds of millions of miles away. No one, as yet, has achieved such predictability with respect to social forces.

No matter how carefully we establish our policies, no matter how assiduously we compile evaluations, no matter how systematically we review our proposed course of action, the unanticipated event is always waiting for us. There is always a "surprise" in the outcome of social policies. We are forced to be free by the complexity of our social lives. The logic is sound: Any event is free to the extent it is less than perfectly determined. Social events are never perfectly determined; therefore, there is always an element of freedom in human social actions.

We cannot talk about freedom without considering the converse of freedom: determinism. Whether our lives are free or determined is an old debate, and people have endorsed philosophies ranging from the idea that everything we do is a matter of choice (we see this in some forms of Christian theology and existential philosophy) to the idea that everything we do is determined (a position endorsed by Sigmund Freud, Kurt Vonnegut, and others).

There are advantages and disadvantages to be obtained from either perspective. Determinism implies understanding and control. The more we can establish the determinants of an event, the closer we come to achieving control over it. Presumably, if we knew the determinants of everything, we could ultimately control everything. Though scientists rarely express such a grandiose ambition, they are not the least disinclined to leave us with the impression that science desires nothing less than to arrive at a grand theory (understanding) of the entire universe (everything). Those things for which determinants cannot be established cannot be understood and remain beyond control.

Freedom implies lack of control. Whatever is free remains beyond our understanding. For all of our love of freedom in the United States, we still do not like what we cannot understand or control. There is a major cultural contradiction in our love of science, technology, machines, and control and our love of freedom, liberty, and — by implication — that which is beyond control. People who do not conform to the constraints of social control are people with whom we generally feel uncomfortable. If they do not conform at least to a reasonable degree, we place them in confinement. Confinement, of course, is another word for control.

It is interesting, in this regard, to notice how narrowly we now evaluate those who assume positions of public office. We do not like and will not tolerate freewheeling officials. The degree of freedom they are granted is narrow — leading to the thought that the ideal politician would be the perfect and quintessential conformist, the ideal manifestation of social control forces.

We need not worry about getting such perfected leaders; politicians are another example of the fact that the social world is not a deterministic system. Our leaders are always full of surprises for us — no matter how carefully we go about examining their credentials before we vote for them. Regardless of the intensity of our desire to control our public officials, they are free enough to carry out actions we did not anticipate when they were voted into office.[13]

But what is the further relevance of such philosophical and "airy" notions as determinism and freedom? What is their pertinence to social science? Few concepts, I am certain, are more relevant. Our distrust and fear of control inclines us, on the one hand, to praise freedom and seek it in virtually all aspects of our lives. The quest for understanding and the need to control incline us, on the other hand, to become determinists. From this position, freedom is an irritant.

For example, military systems exist as determinant forces used by nations to control the actions of others. If one believes control can be established through the application of force, then this becomes a deterministic philosophy. We, along with other nations, look for devices that will control activities not to our liking. And so we turn to the ultimate in deterministic force — nuclear weapons.

Behind nuclear weapons stands a crude deterministic philosophy grounded in the belief that social actions can be understood in terms of and controlled through the application of force. There is a great deal of paradox in this statement insofar as the United States, rhetorically the bastion of freedom, offers freedom to other nations so long as they are willing to accept the American conception of freedom. The Russians, in a similar manner, offer freedom on their terms.

The Russian conception of freedom is that people are not free until they are free from material wants. People are not free when they are hungry, cold, sick, poor, ignorant, and exploited. The American conception of freedom is that people are free to compete in the marketplace and the job market at any time. If you are hungry, cold, sick, poor, ignorant, and exploited, you are still free to compete all you want. (George F. Will, in a column of his, reports that an American judge commented on the plight of a homeless woman by saying: "To the passerby seeing her lying on the street or defecating publicly, she may seem deranged . . . [but] . . . she may be a professional in her lifestyle." It is a peculiar, but nonetheless instructive comment on the American notion of freedom.)

Looking at people through the broader abstractions of philosophical terms such as determinism and freedom leads to an awareness of the astonishing paradox that now seems to exist on this tight little planet. We have two great powers — both driven by differing beliefs in freedom not only for their own people but also for all the other people of the world — relying more and more on devices that are the penultimate antithetical response to the concept of freedom.

If there was ever any mechanism that virtually guarantees all loss of freedom — indeed, was designed to control freedom — it is the exercise of armed, military might and modern nuclear weapons. Only if death is liberating, can these devices be looked on as the agents of freedom. If nothing else, a social control interpretation of military force lets us view it from a different angle. Where popular conceptions view nuclear weapons as protectors of liberty, a social control approach permits us to see the contrary side of this argument — a side different from what is popularly expressed.

We must, then, come to terms with this idea of freedom. What is it? How do we define it? Is the American conception of freedom the only way of defining the concept worth listening to? What is the American conception of freedom and how might it differ from other peoples'? What is the relationship between the lessons of modern social science and freedom? Do we really like freedom for everyone or are we more inclined to enjoy freedom for ourselves while denying it to others? Just how far can freedom be extended before it must be curbed? How far must authority go before it moves into pathological forms?

These are not new questions. In a sense, they are not logically or scientifically answerable questions. That does not make them any the less important. They are questions that become, in part, the fundamental stuff of the political process; for we can define politics — and war, which is an extension of the political process — as the process through which we negotiate freedom and constraint, lack of control and control.

This discussion, drawing principally on the work of Berger, brings us to the point where we begin to see that the existence of nuclear weapons might not represent a program for freedom but quite the contrary. Weapons exist only to free us from our fear of the constraints implied by the weapons of the other side. At the same time, their weapons exist to free them from their fear of our constraining devices. But nuclear weapons have not freed us from fear. They only enhance our worst expectations. So it comes to pass that in our desire to be free, we entrap ourselves ever deeper in the devices of constraint.

The picture seems once again a gloomy one. Nuclear weapons stand above us, now, as symbols of the almighty power of social systems and their dedication to control. There are always elements seeking to bring the social order under final control. At the same time, people resist control — consciously or unconsciously. It is in this resistance that freedom remains available. Until social order becomes absolute, freedom is not in peril.

Berger argues eloquently that, whether we like it or not, we are "condemned to freedom." We can escape the consequences of our freedom only by pretending we must engage in actions that through courage, we can deny. There is another, perhaps deeper, reason we are "condemned to freedom." It comes out of the thousands of studies of human social systems done by modern social scientists. No matter how we apply ourselves to the study of ourselves, we are left in a state of uncertainty. Freedom is an inherent element of social life. It can never be completely eradicated.

Writers like Berger provide us with a sense of the extent to which modern social science remains closely allied with broader humanistic studies, the arts, and the old, eternal questions that enliven philosophical and religious arguments. These broad philosophical and religious questions are not irrelevant to a discussion of such hard and scientific technologies as nuclear weapons. They provide us with an understanding of why such weapons exist in the first place. They also provide us with a clue as to how we might move toward their elimination.

Berger suggests nothing less than that a true understanding and comprehension of the nature of freedom, along with a willingness to endorse it for others as well as ourselves, is the best hope we have against the excessive abuse of social control. Certainly if the time comes when we are forced to witness the use of nuclear weapons in global warfare we will know that the agents of control prevailed, in a final and total manner, over those who believed in the dream of freedom.

EPILOGUE: FREEDOM AS THEORY

Throughout these chapters I have left the question of what constitutes a social theory up in the air. I use such terms as social theory, social philosophy, speculation, fantasy, and belief systems in a way that might lead people to think I do not see any differences in these notions. There are differences, of course. Modern academic social theories are directed primarily toward the end of promoting research. As such, they commonly take the form of a system of interrelated hypotheses or propositions that lead to critical expectations. I use the term "critical" to mean simply that if the expectation is sustained by facts, it sustains the theory. Speculation, fantasy, and belief systems are not as formal, but they also lead to expectations of one kind or another.

There is one form of social theory that is difficult to define, but it is also difficult to refer to it as anything other than a theory. I refer now to systems of belief that literally create social forms of one kind or another. Their task is not to arrive at some testable hypothesis but, instead, to shape people into living manifestations of the belief system itself. For example, if one believes in education, then one is impelled to get an education and, in so doing, becomes a living representation of the belief. In this instance a theory is directed toward the end of creating itself or manifesting itself through the people who endorse it. Whether it is true or false might be beside the point or, perhaps more correctly, impossible to establish by rigorous empirical testing. Ultimately it is a matter of faith in a belief.

Great myths take this form. The western European myth of romantic love, for example, is neither true nor false. It is an elaborated set of beliefs that generates actions of a particular form. A myth of this sort might have benign consequences or, as was the case with the Aryan myths endorsed by the Germans, some evil ones. However, the truth or falsity of myth is, in a sense, beside the point. It is evaluated in terms of moral consequences, not scientific tests. The task of myth is not to establish truth but to generate action among people—to give form to their lives and a sense of meaning and substance to what they do. Myths cannot, the popular media and bad science to the contrary, be sustained or invalidated by scientific means. Erroneous statements about the physical world can be checked and found in error. When myths speak of the physical world they reveal their naivete. However, when myth is restricted exclusively to human affairs, it moves beyond scientific acceptance or rejection.

Returning then to the notion of freedom we must ask ourselves: Is it a form of theory, philosophy, speculation, fantasy, belief, fiction, reverie, whimsy, invention, or what? It does not fit well into the deterministic mentality of modern social science. Berger, for example, runs into a great deal of trouble trying to jam the idea of control and freedom together. At the same time, it is difficult to abandon the notion of freedom. What is it? It is a strange notion. It does not seem to fit into modern-day academic social theory as an explanatory concept. At the same time, we might not care to think of it as a myth or fiction. If we cannot figure out what it is, then we are placed in the awkward situation, when we defend it, of defending something we have little understanding of—which takes us back to the paragraph that began this chapter.

Chapter 8

Taking the World for Granted: New Wave Thinking in Western Social Science

A BRIEF CAUTIONARY FOREWORD

We all know stories of early mariners who followed maps that marked an unknown territory with the warning: "Beware—here be monsters." Later, after ships sailed where the monsters swam and lived, people discovered the maps were wrong. There were no monsters. The arguments we are about to consider are similar. At first they seem peculiar. The theoretical territory we are about to stroll through is different from anything else in modern social theory or social research. It is new territory and, as such, it is looked on by orthodox social scientists as a place where social theory has gone slightly mad. That, certainly, was my own judgment when I first encountered it in the works of Harold Garfinkel and Alfred Schutz. As I read different books and articles dealing with phenomenology and ethnomethodology, I was convinced it amounted to little more than sputtering metaphysical nonsense. For various reasons, however, I found myself returning to Garfinkel and others of a similar persuasion; and, eventually, the power of their arguments impressed me forcefully.

The one argument I could not dismiss, no matter how I tried to get around it, was the ingenious counseling study that Garfinkel carried out at the University of California, Los Angeles. Here was a study that was simple, factual, replicable, and profound in its implications. It was science, but science such as I had not encountered before. It was social science that granted a place for the subjective rather than dismissing it. It was social science which concluded that one of the interesting things about people is their ability to generate, in effect, their own "social science." The counseling study revealed that people can get caught up in a conversation with a random event and make useful sense of it. (I had trouble believing this, but it was demonstrated beyond any shadow of a doubt.) It was social science that considered how astrology works rather than condemning it as irrational spoofery. Worse yet, the writings of Garfinkel led me to the point where I could begin to see that, in various forms, a lot of what we do on a day-to-day basis relies on "astrological" devices of one kind or another. It was, please believe me, a shattering experience for a young positivist who still dreamed of finding objectively definable mathematical structures in social systems.

I warn the reader, then, that what follows is relatively easy to understand if approached with an open mind. However, it is nearly impossible to understand if you believe human actions are merely another form of *behavior* (as opposed to more complex *actions*) to be analyzed by strictly scientific or rational means — as these are traditionally defined. With Garfinkel we move into a domain where nothing is quite what it appears to be. The world becomes a slippery place. Meanings are embedded within meanings. One can get "messages" from bubbling tea pots and other peculiar sources. It is a place where people manage to accomplish the impossible task of transcending the subjective boundaries that block them off from each other. It is a world in which people do not react to stimulus events as other creatures do but instead reinterpret the stimulus and then react to their own interpretations of the stimulus. It is a world in which each individual becomes an *infinitely* rich source of information and is, therefore, forever beyond being understood in any finite scheme of things. It is a world in which a mundane eight-word statement by a little girl, "The baby cried, the mommy picked it up" can become the basis for an extensive series of 30 or 40 lectures.

Here is social theory that is not directed toward any kind of practical application but that is totally concerned with being as honest as possible about what it means to study ourselves. It is a hardheaded philosophy — though it is generally viewed as "soft." It is philosophy that struggles to back up its claims with the best forms of evidence it can find; and in this sense it is an empirical philosophy or theory. However, it tends to conclude that we really can never understand ourselves in any total and realistic way.

So, take your time as you move through the following material. There are occasional monsters here and there, but if you stay with them long enough they become passably tame. Over time they even prove to be vigorous, though never — for the rational mind — fully lovable companions.

THE PROBLEM OF SUBJECTIVITY

A profound problem faces anyone who seeks a rigorous and truly scientific understanding (or, indeed, any other kind of understanding) of human beings and their actions. We now need to consider the problem of subjective experience.[1] A major portion of whatever takes place when we observe human actions is forever hidden from direct observation. It takes place in what we commonly call the "minds" of the actors.

Any human social interaction requires an assessment of such intangible qualities as the intent or the motive underlying the interaction. Intent and motive are, of course, perfectly subjective matters. Subjective concerns, then, are an integral part of human social life. However, what is subjective is completely and forever beyond being known in any certain way. At the same time, we cannot interact with others without having a working idea of what, in effect, is "on their minds." Because it is self-evident that we do interact with other people casually, daily, and routinely, the subjective problem is obviously easily handled by most of us.

The question becomes: How do people, on a day-to-day basis, resolve the impossible problem of the assessment of subjective states? The pursuit of this question leads into a profound understanding of the role that sociocultural forces play in creating and constructing realities where none in fact exists. As we begin to see the nature of the riddle, we begin to see that human beings are, indeed, astonishingly unique creatures. Though we are shut off from one another, each of us an island of isolated experience and awareness, we nonetheless come to have fairly "solid" notions of each other.

Any knowledge of the subjective nature of others (and to a surprising extent of ourselves — if psychoanalysis has any truth to it whatsoever) can be acquired only through indirect methods. Pain, for example, is a subjective experience. If someone is experiencing pain we must make inferences drawn from observations or we have to ask questions (that is, conduct a survey) to discover the nature of the pain. This is why the suffering of pets is so frustrating; we cannot gain access to their subjective feelings. Their moans suggest they are hurting, but we cannot penetrate their "minds" any further than that.

To make the point all the more firmly, we are not only separated from each other by the wall of subjectivity; but, in a sense, we are separated from ourselves. One form of this is exemplified in psychoanalysis where an individual may undergo "treatments" to determine what the real motives are behind his or her penchant for exhibitionism. Another form is exemplified in aging. As we age we become alienated, in a sense, from our very selves. That is to say, we cannot recapitulate with much detail or accuracy the subjective states we experienced even a few days earlier. In order to have a continuous sense of self we must constantly reconstruct ourselves.[2]

Science is now the established method of resolving questions about the objective or "outer" world. The dominance of modern science as an intellectual discipline was well established by the late 19th century. It is not surprising, then, that turn-of-the-century philosophers and intellectuals quickly began to speculate that science, so effective in its studies of the objective realm, might work as well with the "inner" or subjective realm.

In Western culture one consequence of this particular vision was the growth of that powerful and pervasive Western institution we call psychology. By the beginning of the 20th century psychology was well established as a discipline. Literally translated *psychology* means "words about the spirit." In classical Greek mythology, Psyche was a beautiful girl who represented the personification of the soul. More specifically, the root term *psycho* is derived from the Greek *psychein*, which means to breathe or blow; hence, to live, to have spirit. From its inception the history of psychology was marked by struggles over how to deal with the problem of subjective experience.

Basically two positions emerged and remain current. One side argues that scientific integrity must be protected at all costs. In effect, this position argues that method is more important than topic. To abandon methodological precision is to abandon any hope of obtaining reliable understandings. Therefore, because the subjective is beyond scientific means of study, it should be discounted, ignored, bypassed, or otherwise sloughed off as a scientifically disreputable concern.

The members of this school of thought argue that you cannot study the "mind." You can, however, objectively study *behavior* or the movements of organisms. Therefore, behavior is *all* that should be studied. As a consequence, the members of this school of thought refer to themselves simply as behaviorists and their school of psychological study is called behaviorism. They have a point. Do you dare let down the standards of evidence by which science determines what is worthwhile and what is not?

The other side argues essentially that what is important in human affairs is the complex web of sentiments, feelings, beliefs, attitudes, emotions, motives, knowledge, awareness, and other qualities that are part of the subjective realm. To ignore these matters is to ignore the most significant and unique of all human qualities. Several psychological schools of thought ranging from psychoanalysis to current attribution theory allow for subjective elements in human affairs.

In sum, with respect to subjective reality, we are wretchedly stuck between the horns of a dilemma. If we want to be objective and rely on factual evidence, we must ignore the subjective. However, if we want to deal with the human condition, we cannot ignore it. Whatever the human condition might be, it is something that cannot be contained by scientific methods. The question then becomes: If not science, then by what methods do we comprehend the subjective nature of others and ourselves?

The sociological relevance of this introduction is that any attempt to deal analytically with social action must puzzle over what to do with the problem of subjectivity. The more readily one can ignore the problem of subjectivity, the more scientific one can be. Modern social science, in its quest for scientific respectability, is willing to embrace any approach that manages to bypass subjectivity.

For example, in Western sociology the subjective problem is not a major concern in the area of population studies. Population studies are the most factual and empirical of all forms of sociological research. Pure population research, at a fundamental level, is an examination of the fertility of human populations. It is as much a biological study as a sociological one. Fertility rates can be examined without asking questions about what people are feeling or what their attitudes are. Fertility rates are purely objective data. They might be high for one population and low for another. Regardless, they can be expressed simply and by themselves without recourse to subjective concerns.

Although bare-bones population studies of this restricted nature are important, they are also obviously limited. They do not tell us much, if anything at all, about the societies, the culture, and the people in which the rates are occurring. We want to know more. For example, how do people in these populations "feel" about having babies? Obviously, as soon as we begin asking how people "feel" about having children, we move into another area of concern—one that moves from direct observation into the more tenuous and uncertain domains of indirect observation.

The point of the discussion, so far, is to make a case for the necessity of subjective judgment in *human* social affairs. I would not even argue the point were it not for the prevailing effort of academic writers to argue that the proper quest of the social sciences is to remove subjective judgment from the social science curriculum. The major thrust, for the past century, has been to move toward more objective social knowledge. Whether a science of humankind and of human societies can be developed that bypasses the subjective remains to be seen. So far such a science has yet to demonstrate its powers.

Behaviorists might take exception to this statement, pointing out that behaviorism conducted several impressive demonstrations of control over animal behavior ranging from teaching pigeons how to play Ping-Pong and mice to play "basketball" to getting chickens to tap dance on a drum when they hear a bell ring. This, without doubt, is astonishing virtuoso animal training. However, with respect to alleviating serious *human* problems and probing into the complexities of human actions, behaviorism appears to be no more successful in pinning things down than any other point of view.

While academic intellectuals fight over the place of subjective experience in the study of human affairs, ordinary people, going through ordinary day-to-day experiences, have to live and deal with subjective evaluations constantly. They make hundreds, possibly thousands, of judgments daily about what other people have "on their minds." What is a perplexing and probably impossible problem for the careful and meticulous academic mind is apparently resolved every day in a natural or casual fashion by billions of people—including children who have yet to enter school!

THE PROBLEM OF COMPLEXITY

In addition to the problem of subjectivity there is the further problem of complexity. One frustration of social science is the awareness, at least on the part of its more sensitive practitioners, of the overwhelming complexity of even brief and commonplace social encounters. For example, the story is told of Harvey Sachs, a professor who gave an entire lecture course based on an eight-word statement by a six-year-old child. The child's statement was: "The baby cried, the mommy picked it up." Sachs points out that even the simplest and trivial ordinary social "datum" is astonishingly complex and rich in its meanings, its background, and its implications.[3]

At the same time, nothing appears more obvious, more readily understandable, and more accessible than social knowledge. By the time we are eight or nine years of age we have a good grasp of what is expected of us in amazingly complicated social settings. We know when to be awed and when to be arrogant. We know which of our school chums we should taunt. We are aware of who deserves our respect. We have a sense of our personal destinies. We know what is funny and what is not. We know the difference between being mannerly and unmannerly.

In sum, we are capable of making countless subtle social distinctions. Moreover, we do so as a matter of course. Indeed, we commonly wind up taking the social world in which we live pretty much for granted. What is impossibly complicated for intellectual analysis is surprisingly easy to deal with in the course of ordinary living.

A nice case in point is the way intellectuals cope with the topic of humor. A significant variety of academics and theorists ranging from psychoanalysts to mathematicians specializing in catastrophe theory have tried to define the nature of comedy and humor. None has succeeded especially well. This failure is odd insofar as humorous exchanges do, in fact, take place on a day-to-day basis without fail. Children have no trouble "understanding" humor; that is to say, they comprehend forms of humor and respond appropriately at an early age.

Whatever humor is, then, it is readily and casually "understood" by those practicing it. The question then becomes: How does ordinary understanding of this sort take place when intellectual methods of understanding fail? Or, to put it another way, how does ordinary experience manage to define humor so readily when intellectual efforts encounter so much difficulty? By what methods do people, in day-to-day life, solve riddles that defy rational analysis?

We take so much for granted that only through an unusually conscientious effort can we "step outside" our social constructions of reality and gain a different sense of our lives. The act of stepping outside our ordinary understandings rarely occurs by an act of will. It is more likely to take place when we find ourselves forced to experience a new way of life.

For example, consider an instance where a husband who had to stay home with the children (while his wife went out to earn the family's income) thought it would be a "piece of cake." To make a droll story short, he said the experience nearly did him in. His perceptions of what his wife's life was like were radically altered by actually experiencing that life. More importantly, his understanding of his own life was altered. Though he continued taking much of his social world for granted, part of that taken-for-granted mentality was eroded.

A more intense illustration is obtained from a reading of John Howard Griffin's *Black Like Me*.[4] Griffin, a white man, darkened his skin and then posed as a black man in a southern community in the 1950s—before the civil rights marches of the 1960s altered southern life. He placed himself in a position where he could contrast his taken-for-granted understandings of the life of black people with the actual in-the-life experience of being a black person. His experience was more profound than anything he imaginatively anticipated; what he had taken for granted to be the life of the black man was nothing like what he experienced. Again, it is important to note also that what he had taken for granted as the nature of whites—his own cultural mentality—was radically altered.

This section begins, then, by underscoring what seem to be two more-or-less self-evident truths. First of all, any human social encounter, even a relatively brief one, comes close to being infinitely complex in all of its ramifications. At the same time, vast portions of its meanings are hidden in the inaccessible domain of the subjective. Second, people are not completely incapacitated by either the subjectivity or the complexity of human experience. They manage to "cut through it" somehow; in the complex and tangled world of human social interactions, people get things done. Infinite complexity is met and almost casually dispensed with. People know what to do even though a small amount of thoughtful, careful, probing examination of the situation would reveal that what should be done is never certain. Indeed, it is perfectly uncertain in terms of any kind of precise and complete logic.

A simple, ordinary action, such as getting a soft drink from a vending machine, is casually undertaken. If people gave the matter serious thought, they would stand around the machine for days trying to figure out if pouring highly sugared and badly flavored carbonated water into their bodies is the best way to spend their time and money. What, on the surface, appears to be a simple rational act is not in the least simple and is not rational in any well-defined sense. Or, to put it slightly differently, we commonly do things without thinking much about what we are doing. If we thought about our activities in any total fashion, which is what rationality seeks, we would be paralyzed, unable to act.

In Chapter 5 on Weber, we discussed the central significance of rationality as a dominant component of Western ideology. Now we are raising serious questions about what is involved in rational action. On the one hand, people do manage to get through the affairs of the day; and their conduct is, in that sense, perfectly rational. On the other hand, rationality is a form of method, and it is obvious people are not rational in strictly logical ways. There is an obvious hiatus between rationality as it is understood by analytic intellectuals—who are the high priests of rationality—and the ordinary person in the street.

This ordinary form of rationality—the ability to act in the face of abstracted complexity—is a central concern of a point of view in modern sociology known as "ethnomethodology." Ethnomethodology stands among the more novel and "strange" current social philosophies. Just as modern physics assaults commonsense understandings of the physical world (a cement block, for example, is mostly space and very little substance), ethnomethodology assaults commonsense understandings of the social world.

Ethnomethodology refers simply to the methods people use in ordinary moments to resolve problems confronting them in their social affairs and day-to-day social lives. The term *ethnomethodology* was coined by Harold Garfinkel, and this chapter draws heavily on his work. While a student at Harvard, Garfinkel became interested in Durkheim's notion of *anomie*. According to Durkheim, people who are placed in situations where social rules are ill-defined become, in effect, "lost." The appropriate response to anomic conditions is one of distress. In the extreme, the anomic person gives up on life and commits suicide.

Garfinkel attempted to reproduce anomic situations by placing people in social contexts where definitions of the situation were contrary to what they expected or what they might accept as a matter of course. What he discovered was that people are surprisingly capable of redefining the anomic situation and then continuing as though nothing were wrong. There is a method or way of dealing with social reality that is readily accessible to people and on which they rely for nearly any kind of circumstance. This everyday method for dealing with social events is evidently not the same as the methods employed by intellectuals in their analyses of social happenings. Hence the term *ethnomethodology* or "folk methods."

We can now ask the question: How do ordinary people handle problems that high-powered intellectuals, using high-powered methods and techniques, are not able to resolve in any definitive fashion? How does the ordinary person make the leap, as it were, into the subjective world of others? By what methods do we resolve the constant demands of abstracted, subjective, and extremely complex human social existence? How do we get "into" and "out of" the minds of other people as we go through a typical day? How do we slice through the unending complex social Gordian knots that threaten to bind us?

THE COUNSELING STUDY

To gain a quick appreciation of the directions taken by Garfinkel's thinking, nothing works better, in my estimation, than a summary review of a simple demonstration reported in his major work *Studies in Ethnomethodology*.[5]

The demonstration, which was repeated in various settings — including cultures other than the United States — comes up with the same general results. Note, in the description of the demonstration which follows that:

1. It is simple in its design. It is readily understandable by people untrained in the social sciences. It does not rely on complex statistical computations. It does not involve quasi-experimental procedures.[6] Nonetheless, the results are convincing.

2. It is easily replicated. Anyone wishing to verify what Garfinkel discovered can do so by repeating the demonstration.

3. It is an empirical and not a logical demonstration. What was found in this demonstration is a matter of fact and not conjecture.

4. The results of the demonstration have profound implications with respect to prevailing philosophies, theories, perspectives, and commonsense thinking about what we humans are like.[7]

Now, let us briefly summarize what took place. Garfinkel advertised, on the campus of the University of California, Los Angeles, that the sociology department was conducting studies in counseling procedures and volunteers were needed. Volunteers for these "studies" were told that the counseling technique being investigated was one in which the counselor would provide limited responses to the volunteers' questions.

Student volunteers were seated before a counselor who sat behind a screen. They were told to give the counselor background information about their problems and then ask questions that could be answered with a "Yes" or "No." Because the study was interested in problems of counseling, the students were also told they should record their reactions to the counselor's "Yes" or "No" in a tape recorder before going on with the next question.

The following account is an abbreviated imaginary description of how one such counseling session might have gone.

Volunteer (giving background information): Well, I am a married student. My husband is a pre-law student. He spends all of his time studying and has become seclusive. My question is: Do you think our marriage is headed for the rocks?

Counselor: My answer is no.

Volunteer (speaking into the tape recorder): I expected that. I am being too impatient with my husband. He is simply overburdened with work and I am not paying enough attention to his problems. I am being selfish. My next question (turning back to the counselor) is: Will things improve after we get out of school?

Counselor: My answer is no.

Volunteer (speaking into recorder): Well, that is a shock. If things are not going to get any better, then perhaps I should leave now and get on with my own work without having to put up with trying to save my marriage. My next question (turning back) is: If I leave my husband and continue my studies, will the stress of separation cause my grades to go down or will the freedom I find enable me to do better with my course work?

Counselor: My answer is yes.

Volunteer (into recorder): Well, that is understandable. The counselor is saying I should leave and start over. That certainly makes sense. But perhaps my parents will object. If they get angry they might not support me through school. I had better find out about that. My next question is: Will my parents be angry and, if they are, will they cut off my school allowance or will they continue supporting me?

Counselor: My answer is yes.

Volunteer: I wonder what I should do? It is encouraging to know that they will continue supporting me. The picture is becoming clearer. My next question . . .

It is time to bring this mock interview to a close. It summarizes many of the features of the lengthier real interviews conducted and reported by Garfinkel.[8] Several things came out of the counseling study. First of all, the volunteers reported that the counseling they received was excellent. They commented that the counselor had unusual sensitivity. Second, *few of those involved ever tested the credentials or the procedures being used.* The volunteers accepted the situation as it was defined for them—that is, as a counseling experience. Third, the "Yes" or "No" responses of the counselor elicited fairly elaborate responses on the part of the volunteers.

In sum, the volunteers liked the counseling they received and considered it to be meaningful and worthwhile. What makes the counseling study significant is that the "Yes" or "No" responses of the counselor were pure chance responses. Each volunteer received the same answer to his or her first question, the same answer to the second question, and so on. The pattern of "Yes" and "No" responses was the same for each volunteer, and the pattern was established by a purely random procedure.

In other words, in a peculiar sense, the volunteers were holding a conversation with a random event. Moreover, they found the "information" they received was unusually useful and significant. The counseling was "good" counseling. The interested reader should, of course, turn to other accounts of the study, especially the original report. Few studies in modern social science are as significant in terms of their implications for an understanding of the human condition.

Several things stand out in the counseling sessions. First of all, the volunteers accepted the counseling as counseling—even though in reality it was not. This might seem unfair insofar as they were told it was counseling. The appropriate reply is that, in effect, they were responding to what they thought was the situation rather than the underlying reality, which, in fact, was the pure chance nature of the Yes and No responses. This is significant. It raises the question of how extensively the realities we deal with on a day-to-day basis consist of what we are told is real. More interestingly, it raises the question of how extensively, in talking to ourselves, we regenerate reality and respond to our characterization of it rather than what that reality actually is.[9]

Second, the volunteers "constructed," so to speak, the character of the stimuli they then responded to. The volunteers were not responding to a simple stimulus event but were, instead, reconstructing it. Consider the instance where the volunteer asks if her grades will go up or down. The question cannot be sensibly answered with a "Yes" or "No." Yet the volunteer accepts the counselor's "Yes" and then goes on to establish its meaning. After reinterpreting the "Yes" reply of the counselor (which is, remember, not a response to her question but simply the expression of a term selected at random from two alternatives), the student then responds to her own reconstruction of the stimulus event and concludes she should leave her husband. Logic, as we commonly understand it, is not at work here. Nonetheless, the probing of the volunteer has a method or a kind of "logic" to it. The volunteer, in some manner, knows how to do whatever it is she is doing.

This simple demonstration reveals that what constitutes a stimulus and the response to it is not a mechanical stimulus-response happening, but rather a matter of what kind of subjective "background" a person brings into the situation. This observation reveals clearly the problems that a simple behavioristic approach to human actions runs hard against. The reason is clear: Behaviorism rejects subjectivity. However, subjective background evidently profoundly influences how people respond to stimuli. Behaviorists, therefore, reject any consideration of a powerful factor in how human actions are formed.

It is apparent in the counseling study that people expect to find patterns in what is before them and that they engage in a kind of search until the pattern reveals itself. The young lady in the mock session reveals this in her last comment when she says the picture is "becoming clearer." Again, keep in mind *there was no pattern in the responses of the counselor.* There was no picture. Even so, the volunteers had no trouble finding a pattern in the counseling they were receiving. Where does the nonexistent pattern come from?

This, rather obviously, provides us with a clue as to why astrology, the reading of tea leaves, Tarot cards, and other such purely random fortune-telling devices work. What Garfinkel's study does is to make more than a suggestion that we rely on similar devices much more in our social "divinations" than we probably want to think we do. The trick with ethnomethodology is to discover the various forms of "astrology" that surround us at all times and influence our lives on a daily basis, but that we do not see as "astrology."

ETHNOMETHODOLOGY, TAKEN-FOR-GRANTEDNESS, AND ACCOUNTS

At this point we shall take three ideas or concepts from ethnomethodological work as a basis for dealing with our central topical concern—the nuclear arms crisis. These are:

1. Ethnomethods
2. Taken-for-grantedness
3. Accounts

Despite all efforts to promote a rational approach to arms management, the fact remains that nuclear armaments exist within a human social context. This means people are confronted by people, and the problems of subjectivity and complexity are found here just as they are anywhere else. This further implies that people draw on ethnomethodological devices to cope with nuclear armaments just as they do with any other kind of human social issue. For this general reason, then, a good concept to begin with is the concept of ethnomethods itself.

A second concept we shall focus on is the notion of taken-for-grantedness. Nowhere in the domain of human interrelations is the problem of taking things for granted more dangerous than in the realm of nuclear weapons. At the same time, it is a domain that differs little from other arenas of human social interaction in that so much is, in fact, taken for granted. Ethnomethodology leads us to raise doubts about what is taken for granted and, in its taken-for-grantedness, is potentially dangerous.

Finally, we shall consider the matter of *accounts*. Our understanding of social events is rarely acquired through direct experience with a social event in itself but through various accountings of the event. In any specific moment we cannot deal with the social reality that confronts us except in terms of how it is accounted for by those with whom we are involved and by ourselves. We are constantly engaged in accounting for ourselves and others.

In the counseling study the volunteers created elaborate accounts of the meanings of the "Yes" and "No" responses of the counselor. In this instance we can see rather clearly that the account is more important than the stimulus that provoked the account. In the case of nuclear arms we have little to deal with other than accounts handed on to us by others. I might point out, further, that what we commonly have to deal with are accounts of accounts. It is not surprising that, after a while, our comprehension of an event is something radically different from the event in itself.

THE OPPENHEIMER STORY: HOW ETHNOMETHODS WERE USED TO DESTROY A MAN OF POWER

One of the central characters in the creation of nuclear weaponry was the lean and cerebral figure of J. Robert Oppenheimer. We need not concern ourselves with his biography here. A number of books on the life and the trials of Oppenheimer have been written, and anyone interested in the future of humankind should read them.[10] They force us to consider the fate of those who advocate mild policies regarding nuclear proliferation where entrenched power is convinced otherwise.

For our purposes, we need only consider those events in Oppenheimer's life that illustrate aspects of what concerns sociologists such as Garfinkel. Very briefly, J. Robert Oppenheimer was called on to direct the Manhattan Project in World War II. The Manhattan Project was funded by the American government after experiments by Enrico Fermi, at the University of Chicago, established the possibility of sustained nuclear chain reactions. Oppenheimer, a brilliant scholar and physicist, dedicated himself to the task of overseeing the creation of the first nuclear weapon. He was energetic, dedicated, intelligent, and wholly committed to the task. Not only was he dedicated to the task but he also communicated his enthusiasm to others. Those involved in the development of the first atomic weapon still speak of the nearly demonic fervor that drove the engineers, mathematicians, scientists, and everyone else who had a part in the project.

The shock waves of the first nuclear blast were felt on July 16, 1945.

Oppenheimer's team was successful. It is what followed that becomes especially interesting from an ethnomethodological point of view. Oppenheimer was stunned by the power of the device he had been so instrumental in producing. His words are now famous. Quoting from the Bhagavad Gita, he muttered, as the eerie glow of the bomb lit the New Mexico landscape, "I am Vishnu, the bringer of death."

He, along with his colleagues, was aware that a device of previously unimaginable destructive power was now about to be placed in the hands of the political and military leaders of a nation-state. In brief, the "bomb" would soon be the general property of the world unless something was done to check the growth of such devices. A creature who has mental problems making the shift from Standard to Daylight Saving time was about to be in charge of the most destructive force the world has ever seen. He was immediately aware of the devastating implications of his work.

Oppenheimer's fears were further heightened when nuclear devices were exploded over two Japanese cities. Hundreds of thousands of noncombatant people were killed, maimed, burned, blinded, and exposed to intense radiation—to die later and more slowly. Oppenheimer was horrified.

In one account he went to Truman to appeal that nuclear weapons not be produced. However, for Truman the bomb was a means of concluding the war quickly. He felt little remorse over its use. On the other hand, Oppenheimer was stunned. Physics, which had been a kind of intellectual game for Oppenheimer, was no longer a disembodied exercise in rationalistic problem solving. "We [natural scientists] now have blood on our hands," he is reputed to have told Truman. A nation-state, driven by the demands of national interests, has obvious uses for such weapons. Who could ask for a more potent means for implementing international diplomacy? At the same time, the men and women closest to the bomb were having second thoughts.

At this point ethnomethodological perspectives become especially interesting because Oppenheimer, after the close of World War II, argued that the Russians should be informed of the nature of nuclear weapons and invited to join the United States in banning their future production. Because his work during the war could not, in any fashion, be shown to reveal either incompetence or disloyalty and because it was such a major achievement, his advocacy of a ban on the development of nuclear weapons could not be ignored.

The outcome of this juxtaposition of policies—the government wanting more weapons and Oppenheimer and powerful colleagues in the sciences wanting fewer—is now obvious. Oppenheimer lost. What interests us is *how* he lost. What methods were used to discredit Oppenheimer and eventually strip him of his post as Chair of the General Advisory Committee of the newly formed Atomic Energy Commission? Oppenheimer had proved himself dedicated and brilliant during the war. It was not enough.

Oppenheimer was discredited when others claimed to have established what was in his "mind." It was the subjective rather than the objective character of Oppenheimer that was of paramount significance in determining whether he would be allowed to have a major voice in the future disposition of nuclear weapons. The investigation into his loyalty was an investigation into his inner being. The final conclusion was that Oppenheimer could not be trusted — he was, in effect, unstable and potentially traitorous.

Yet, the nagging problem remains: How is the subjective nature of someone's "mind" established? By what methods were people able to conclude that although Oppenheimer's objective record had been one of astonishing accomplishment, his inner nature was nonetheless one that could not be trusted? Because scientific means could not be used, some other method or set of methods had to be employed to resolve the question — an ethnomethodology, if you will. Indeed, the term takes on special significance here because the methods used to discredit Oppenheimer were methods established by and employed in the interests of highly ethnocentric political and military officials.

Let me add that this does not necessarily mean ethnocentric political and military officials do not try to be fair. The fairness of Oppenheimer's trial remains a controversial matter and cannot be debated here. Ethnomethodological perspectives lead us to conclude that no human trial can ever be fair or just in any total sense. That is to say, the "realities" we accept through ethnomethodological devices are incapable of perfectly paralleling the realities they are supposed to represent. Like maps, they are constructions. Also like maps, they are not the same thing as the territory they represent.

"Mapping" a subjective landscape is, however, a peculiar activity. We know already that it is easy to see what you want to see even when mapping a physical landscape. In this regard, Percival Lowell's detailed 1907 maps of the "canals" on Mars come to mind. Lowell was a meticulous and highly respected astronomer in his time; and it seems peculiar, from our present view, how he managed to "see" what he thought he saw. It should be fairly obvious, then, that when we go about mapping the subjective landscape, "seeing" things becomes a tricky business. If we can clearly see canals that do not exist on a visible surface, then it must be even easier to see anything we might be led to see on the invisible surfaces of subjective states.

How was it possible, then, to see into Oppenheimer's subjective character? By what kind of trial could his real character be established? Again, we should not be concerned with the fairness of the trial. The thing about trials is that they tend to accomplish their ends, fair or unfair. How is this managed? In the case of the Oppenheimer judgment three things are clear: He displayed great loyalty and dedication to his country during the war years. Second, he personally proclaimed and avowed he was loyal to his country. He fought all attempts to impugn his loyalty. Third, he was seen and then actually treated as a disloyal person.

We know, from the events of the time, that his loyalty became suspect only when he no longer found himself supporting the idea that national interests would best be served by creating nuclear arsenals. He argued, however, that national security can be enhanced through federal support of basic scientific research. Was he loyal? Was he not loyal? The question that becomes interesting from an ethnomethodological point of view is: How can you resolve such a matter? Moreover, because the matter is so significant, how can you resolve it to the extent you become convinced you have the right to strip one of the most powerful figures of his time of his influence on national defense and war policies?

At the outset we begin to see the impossible nature of the problem. For example, in order to uncover the underlying "reality" of what took place during the Oppenheimer hearings we must make assumptions about the subjective states of those who directed the hearings. Were they sincere, for example, or were they cynical? Were they honestly concerned with determining the nature of Oppenheimer's loyalty? Or were they merely staging an elaborate show whose outcome was predetermined? What methods were used to determine their loyalty or sincerity? (Who guards the guardians?)

This is no small matter. At the same time, it is apparent that we are dealing with a set of issues and problems that cannot be resolved in any incontestable fashion. Nonetheless, the matter is resolved and in ways that prove, finally, to be incontestable. So much effort goes into their resolution because it does, in fact, mean a lot to know whether the investigation into Oppenheimer's loyalty was conducted by people who were, themselves, loyal. It is essential to know whether they were led by sincere or cynical motives. In a nation that values fairness, it is essential to know if they sought to be fair. If we cannot establish this, then how can we establish Oppenheimer's loyalty?

Let us assume, for the moment, that the trial was sincere and the only subjective problem we must deal with is the one of Oppenheimer's loyalty. Given this problem, we can now examine the question of the *methods* used to resolve it.

Simply acquiring a sense of the problem forces us to comprehend why Garfinkel settled on the awkward term *ethnomethods*. An astonishing variety of devices, methods, or procedures exist within the community for resolving the problem of intersubjectivity. These methods come out of the community, its culture, and its traditions; and they are applied to day-to-day problems with sufficient success to enable people to confront impossible intellectual problems in a casual and relatively certain fashion.

So it is, then, that the investigation, in and of itself, was a folk method. We generally are so inclined to take investigations for granted that we lose sight of their ethnic nature. The fact that they are conducted by authorities seems to lift them out of their ethnic or folk base. However, what constitutes an investigation in one ethnic community does not constitute an investigation in another. We shall consider this observation further in later discussions. Determining Oppenheimer's loyalty involved a long period of time, the examination of thousands of documents, and a reliance on the testimony of witnesses. In sum, the basic method was a matter of relying on accounts of Oppenheimer's character. Actually, the trial became a series of accounts of accounts. One account, in particular, proved especially damning. The testimony of Dr. Edward Teller, a physicist sympathetic to the idea of building up nuclear arsenals, did not support Oppenheimer.

For now, it is enough that we see that what was taking place in the Oppenheimer case covered considerably more than what appeared to be taking place. The reality that was created through the hearing and what was, in fact, the subjective reality of Oppenheimer are, without much doubt, two entirely different things. This leaves us with the question, of course, of how we are to investigate the investigation. Was the investigation really concerned with Oppenheimer's loyalty or was it concerned simply with removing from power a man who disagreed with the higher political and military leadership of the nation? Depending on one's social background — that is to say, depending on the set of ethnomethods available for dealing with such an issue — different people will reach different conclusions.

The Oppenheimer case is an isolated incident, drawn on here to illustrate the concept of ethnomethodology. You cannot appreciate the sophistication of ethnomethodology until you begin to apply it across a wider range of events. We saw how a given folk method (for example, an investigation) can establish a particular understanding — but we arrive at particular understandings of all sorts of similarly complex matters. For example, what methods do we use to determine the subjective state of the enemy? (What makes the Oppenheimer case such a sad one is that it involves a person who was a national hero one moment and a suspected potential traitor, an enemy, the next.)

How, do we assess the mind of the enemy? How do we know, for example, what is on the Russian "mind"? This is again a major issue. To resolve it one way has one set of implications for military policy and national security. To resolve it another has yet a different set of implications. If, for example, the Soviets are determined to conquer the world and enslave and viciously exploit people, then we are facing one situation. If, to the contrary, they are concerned only with improving the plight of impoverished people, that is something else. Yet, as we saw in the Oppenheimer case, the determination of the subjective state of a single individual is an impossible task. Determining the subjective character of an entire nation is, so it would seem, no simpler. Nonetheless, through folk methods, we are capable of creating a constructed understanding of both individual and collective subjective states.

With respect to the mentality of the enemy, the question becomes: What methods do we rely on for assessing that "mentality"? What conclusions do we reach? If we relied on different methods, would we come to different conclusions? What different methods are available? How is it possible to know what is on the mind of an entire nation-state when the mind of a single individual is beyond any kind of certain determination?

Not only are we faced with the problem of establishing the mentality of the enemy, but we also establish understandings of the mentality of our friends. We view, in a general way, the Soviet mentality as hostile and paranoid—though it shows recent signs of warming toward us. The Japanese mentality we view as polite and competitive. As a consequence, we devote our industrial strength and economic power to the end of staring down Russia with nuclear missiles. In the meantime, the Japanese, who immediately after 1945 redefined the nature of national conflict and struggle in terms of bucks rather than bullets, are quietly dominating world markets and buying huge hunks of American real estate and industry.

One aspect of Garfinkel's approach is the observation that people believe in and are capable of creating "patterns" with respect to nearly anything that might be taking place—whether such patterns exist or not. In dealing with the enemy, for example, we presume that a pattern is behind their actions. The volunteers in the counseling study were convinced there was a pattern in the advice they were receiving—though none existed. The investigators in the Oppenheimer hearing were also convinced that there was a kind of pattern or "meaning" behind Oppenheimer's advice to curtail production of nuclear weapons. They went looking for it and they found it.

It should be emphasized, once more, that it is characteristic of ethno-methods that whatever is available is generally sufficient to provide a sense of the pattern being looked for. This was true in the counseling study and in the Oppenheimer investigation. What was available was sufficient. In a similar manner, though we have only limited access to the lives of others who are distant from us, we nonetheless seek a pattern in what they do; and we generally find it. Whatever is available, no matter how scanty or removed from the reality it points toward, is sufficient; and we find comfort in the strength of our knowledge.

TAKING THINGS FOR GRANTED IN THE NUCLEAR AGE

Once it is pointed out, the extent to which people take their worlds for granted is impressive. Before discussing ideas and theories about the origins of religion in introductory classes, I used to ask my students: "How about it? Aren't you awed by all of this—the blackboard, the fluorescent lights above us, the people sitting around you, the sunlight pouring through the solid panes of glass, the magic of it all . . . ?"

The invariable response was a blank look. There was no doubt about it—there was a "things-as-usual" attitude on the part of the class and certainly nothing to be awed by. If anything, what could be a more boring situation? Yet, when you think about it even a little bit, the world is an awesome place and nothing, absolutely nothing, about it is boring.

I shall not even try, in any serious way, to argue that the room, the students, and everything else in our brief lives, no matter how simple or ordinary it is, is overwhelmingly mysterious and awesome. People do not seem to want to believe it. Boredom, rather than awe, is the modern experience. It is a nice demonstration of the extent to which our experiences, with occasional exceptions, become taken-for-granted commonplaces.

Boredom is, in itself, an interesting topic.[11] There are aspects of the world the community does not want people to be generally interested in, and people get their cue from the community. They lose interest. However, there are certainly reasons for the taken-for-grantedness of the world other than ethnomethodological ones. For one thing, it is simply damned exhausting to go around being totally awed all the time.

For an ethnomethodologist, what is interesting about people is not that they are awed or overwhelmed by reality but, instead, the contrary observation—they are not. There is a taken-for-granted quality to the world. We take the physical world for granted—until we begin to examine it more closely, as do natural scientists. We also take the social world for granted— until we begin to examine it more closely, as do social philosophers or people who are jolted by some social event.

I should note here that there is tenuous evidence to suggest that people who have little trouble with the social world—who have little reason to question it—are less likely to take social science courses and major in the social sciences. On the other hand, people who experience social upheavals or shocks find their taken-for-granted notions of social life weakened. They begin to question. Such people are more inclined to come into the social sciences.

The relevance of this for students of the human community is that we take so much for granted about the social world that we rarely test our understandings of it. Garfinkel demonstrated this in various ways. In the counseling study, for example, the student volunteers took it for granted that the sessions were counseling sessions and the advice they received was advice. Keep in mind it definitely was not. Few students ever bothered to test the situation.

The matter of testing was examined further. In his classes Garfinkel asked students to bargain with local merchants by offering 10 or 20 percent less for any item they purchased during the semester that cost more than, let us say, $25. This was difficult for American students who are not used to bargaining and haggling under nearly any circumstances. Those who bargained made a discovery! By simply opening their mouths and offering less than the asking price for an item, they commonly saved money.

When they tested something they had taken for granted, they found out that things were not what they appeared to be. The price was not solid. The merchant was willing, on more than one occasion, to sell at a lower price. All the students did not want to test the norm. When they did, they found it was more soft than they had been inclined to believe. There are, evidently, deeply established understandings or "norms" that are removed from testing. A modest example might be the extent to which we all use the term *Doctor* when we visit our physician's office. The possibility of other forms of address is a matter we give little thought to. If we do think of it, we rarely bother to test the alternatives.

In order for a human social system to work, much must be taken for granted. Little should be questioned. Despite the fact we consider ourselves a questioning and skeptical people, we actually question an astonishingly small proportion of our experiences as we progress through an ordinary day. As was just noted, we accept the prices of commodities as fixed when we go into stores (sometimes they are fixed; and sometimes they are not). We not only question very little, but we also do not like to be questioned. We prefer the world as a taken-for-granted state of affairs.

Garfinkel, for example, had students question the phrase "How are you?" when they were greeted during the day. When someone said, "How are you?" the students replied by questioning, "What do you mean, 'How am I?'?" The common response was, "What do you mean, 'What do I mean?'?" The general reaction was one of irritation and mild anger. Yet, if you take the question seriously, what does it mean? What is it referring to? Health? Grades? Love life? Financial situation? Everything? Nothing?

Obviously, one is not supposed to take the greeting seriously. It is left to the reader's imagination to ponder all of the things that can be questioned in the course of an ordinary day. If you have trouble wondering what can be questioned or tested in the course of a typical day, it should tell you something about yourself. Given that human beings are possessed of strong, natural curiosities, we gain a different perspective on the nature of social influences by becoming aware of how extensively that curiosity is curbed or controlled.

The primary concern of ethnomethodology is the way in which this is accomplished within the human community. How is questioning closed off and a sense of the acceptable reality of the communal system established? Ethnomethodology, then, asks us to consider two facets of human social life. First: What do we take for granted? Second: What are the devices that create the taken-for-granted nature of the social world around us?

With respect to what we take for granted in a nuclear age, there is perhaps no more straightforward statement than the one offered by C. Wright Mills in his discussion of modern political and military "realism."[12] This "realism" is more than political and military realism, however. The "realistic" attitude that constrains modern attempts at resolving international tensions is pervasive throughout the country and, we must presume, is characteristic of the thinking of people in other nations. (The possibility of several significant modern exceptions will be briefly mentioned later.) I must add a little note pointing out that while military realism has a taken-for-granted quality to it, it is not as deeply ingrained as other forms. We are beginning to challenge this realism. Nonetheless, it is an ideology that can be drawn on as at least a relevant illustration for our purposes here.

The label "realism" suggests that any questioning or contrary stance is unrealistic and should, therefore, be dismissed.[13] At the same time, let me note that few serious efforts to test the realism of modern political "realism" have been made. I should point out that what is commonly referred to as political realism is not being attacked here. Certainly any number of idealistic moments in history were shot down by the cannons of war or some other form of corruption. On the other hand, realism has had its bad moments as well. All I am arguing here is that it is necessary to continue to question and test what is set before us as "realism." We must not allow authoritarian conceptions of what is "real" and what is not to become taken-for-granted aspects of our lives.

What, then, is modern political realism according to C. Wright Mills? We shall consider seven aspects of this taken-for-granted ideological component of modern international relations as Mills outlined them in *The Causes of World War III.*

One: Modern political realism argues that war rather than peace is the natural character of people and of nations. It is, therefore, only realistic to assume as warlike and as belligerent a posture as possible. Safety and security are achieved through one's ability to intimidate through a display of destructive power. The more destructive power you can display, the safer you are.

Two: It is taken for granted in national affairs that nations want to see the other side fail. Hostility, ill will, suspicion, paranoia, and fear are simply human nature. They are the way people are. Therefore, it is simply human nature to gloat when other people screw up their affairs. In turn, we can presume they are likewise amused and pleased when we mess up our affairs.

Three: It is easier, given the way people are, to prepare for war than to prepare for peace. Peace is abstract and difficult to understand. It is taken for granted that the greater masses of the world's people are basically ignorant and incapable of dealing with the problems of peace. They can, however, understand and be motivated by preparations for war. Therefore, it makes more sense to motivate people through war and through the threat of the enemy than through peaceful procedures.

Four: If we take it for granted that people are naturally paranoid and that war motivates people more easily and intensely than preparations for peace, then we can also take it for granted that the military deserves greater support than any kind of civilian agency dedicated to the promotion of peace.

Five: We take for granted that people are motivated by the desire to accumulate good "things." Modern political realism leads us to presume, further, that it is only realistic to take advantage of the prevailing military and political realities and to profit through the quest for greater destructive power.

Six: It is taken for granted that the economy is sustained more effectively by war productivity than by peace productivity. Therefore, whether the state of war we are in is "hot" or "cold," war in itself stimulates the economy and is rewarding.

Seven: The taken-for-granted nature of political-military realism in modern times is so pervasive it transcends party ideological differences and denies any opportunity for any kind of serious political test. It makes little difference whether a political figure is a Democrat or Republican with regard to this set of "realisms." The public has little choice in this particular matter. (A cursory review of the record suggests Mills has something of a point here. American reliance on nuclear diplomacy has been as great during Democratic administrations as during Republican ones.)

These seven items provide at least an introduction into the taken-for-grantedness mentality that Mills saw as a massive setting of the mind—drawing into its fixed vision people from all walks of life. Business people, intellectuals, scientists, military figures, the celebrated person-in-the-street—the entire nation is caught up in the massive hold of this "reality." Small groups that manage to challenge the taken-for-grantedness of the nuclear age are labeled "idealistic," "unrealistic," and "impractical." Business goes on as usual because few of us are willing to go beyond what is being done and test whatever we accept as "reality." Mills was infuriated by the inanity of the logic of this realism and scathingly referred to it as "crackpot" realism.

Virtually by definition, a taken-for-granted understanding of things acquires its strength through the fact it does not have its possible weaknesses revealed. They are not revealed because the understanding in itself is taken for granted. Although Mills's description of crackpot realism dominates much of what is taking place in international relations at the present time, there are a few developments that suggest it is not an entirely "realistic" or unchallengeable grasp of global dynamics.

Especially impressive among these new developments is Japan's dominance as a new force in geopolitics. In effect, the defeat of Japan in World War II stripped the Japanese of their military power. They were then forced to redefine the "reality" of global relations by drawing on the most powerful device they happen to possess for sustaining power—their industrial-commercial system. In effect, they redefined the process of making war by moving it from a military front to a purely monetary front. One can retain all of the "realities" in Mills's outline except the references to military systems or weapons and describe the situation that currently exists with respect to American-Japanese relations. It is war with a smile and soft words.

Over the coming years the intricacies and the novelty of the Japanese and, more generally, the Asian thrust will be written about and understood. Here I want to illustrate that only when a taken-for-granted understanding is tested, can its limits be found. The political realities described by Mills do not need to be manifested in terms of military confrontations.

One of the basic points of ethnomethodological studies is that only as we begin to test the social reality in which we live do we come to see the tenuous nature of its hold over us. Blacks, for example, discovered in the 1960s that white business establishments could not withstand boycotts by black citizens. They tested the rule of segregated facilities and, as they did so, an earlier taken-for-granted reality crumbled.

Women, throughout this century, tested male definitions of what it is to be a woman, and earlier realities of sexuality have crumbled. At the same time, these realities have not crumbled as completely as challenging groups would like them to have. Not only are established customs and cultural practices resistant to testing, but they also remain resistant to change even after they are tested and found lacking.

For the nuclear age, one of the questions before us is: Are the prevailing political-military taken-for-granted "realities" that I've outlined capable of withstanding any kind of serious test? What would such a test be? How could the people of the world reorganize themselves and come to new understandings about themselves in such a way that these "realities" might be transformed?

These are huge questions. However, one lesson of ethnomethodological studies is that understanding comes through testing and questioning whatever we take for granted. (There is a wicked bind here, however, because what is truly taken for granted is so secure in its taken-for-granted status that it remains beyond questioning.) Certainly nothing in modern life deserves greater and more constant questioning than the manner in which we are currently dealing with the production, the deployment, and the use of nuclear weapons to sustain national interests.

ACCOUNTS IN A NUCLEAR AGE

In the next few pages of this chapter, we will consider several contentious points of view and arguments. These arguments are also generally difficult to see. The primary argument is that ethnomethods, because they rely on the community for the efficacy of their ability to create solutions to impossible problems, are effective only within the community. The logic is simple, although its implications are, I am inclined to think, horrendous for anyone who believes social truths can be established in any final and absolute fashion.

The logic follows this pattern:

1. If the problems generated by subjectivity and complexity are impossible, then they cannot be "solved" in any demonstrable or logical fashion.

2. These impossible problems must nonetheless be dealt with and "understood."

3. Therefore, such understandings must be "created."

4. *The community provides the methods whereby these understandings are created.*

5. The efficacy of the created understanding is, then, totally relative to the communally defined method used to achieve it.

I tried to make these arguments as straightforward as possible. Even so, what follows calls for careful and thoughtful reading.

We can begin by coming back to the counseling study. The ability of the students, in the counseling study, to make sense of nonsense — to see significant and personally meaningful patterns in purely random "Yes" and "No" responses to their questions — is both instructive and disturbing.

We are forced to wonder to what extent this is going on in other areas of our lives. In other words, to what extent do we "make up" things as we go along? To what extent are we generating significant meanings — our notion of reality — out of chance happenings? Where does reality leave off and fantasy begin? To what extent do we talk ourselves into a sense of reality, while reality itself — whatever it is — remains something different?

In Garfinkel's work there is more than a suggestion that ethnomethodology is ethnomethodology is ethnomethodology. By this I mean that whatever the formal differences are with regard to the methods people use for dealing with impossible problems, the substantive nature of the methods remains basically the same. In other words, ethnomethods, wherever they are found, appear to be "solving" a problem when, in fact, they are *creating* a solution. There is a difference between a solution that comes from logical or factual forms of resolution, as is the case with scientific solutions, and those where the solution is created.

I shall try to make the above paragraph clearer and make more apparent its disturbing implications. The practice of the Navaho, when attempting to determine if a man is a witch, is to deny him food and drink and not allow him to take off his trousers until he confesses. This is a simple example of a folk method used to determine whether someone has the mentality or the spirit of a witch. (This becomes more relevant to our consideration of nuclear matters if we keep in mind that enemies are a form of witch and that witches are a form of enemy.) In New England, in the 18th century, a different folk method, directed toward the same end, was used. A woman suspected of being a witch was dunked in a lake until she confessed.

If there is a common belief, subject to little or no testing by people, that witches exist in the community, then one of the problems that immediately develops is the problem of identifying them. Ethnomethodology argues that, given this kind of situation, the means for identifying witches will be found. Whatever is available to the community will suffice. The Navaho, for example, are a water-poor culture, and dunking women in lakes is not a readily available or likely device for witch finding. In other cultures, other means will be found according to what their circumstances offer. Whatever is available is sufficient.

These crude methods for dealing with the realm of the spirit are now looked on as primitive, superstitious, barbaric, and foolish. In this day and age we have trials, investigations, hearings, and other more elaborate and rational devices for achieving essentially the same end. Are they any better?

The disturbing implications of an ethnomethodological philosophy is that they probably are not. This does not mean such devices or methods are to be abandoned. They cannot be abandoned if the community is to carry out its tasks. It means, at the very least, that we must be satisfied with means for dealing with human problems that are, in themselves, all too human.

Implicit in ethnomethodological philosophy, then, is the notion that these devices—trials, investigations, and hearings—as elaborate and as convincing as they generally prove to be, are little better than those employed by the Navaho or the stern Protestants of 18th-century New England. Once again, remember it is the function of such procedures to be convincing —to make real whatever resists any kind of ready definition or observation. We keep forgetting, perhaps, that the Navaho and the Protestants were as convinced by their methods as we are by ours.

Occasionally people are able to recognize the limits of their own ethnomethods. For example, the excesses of the McCarthy hearings in the 1950s made it obvious there was a discrepancy between the conclusions of the hearings and the reality—that is, the prevalence of communists in government—those hearings sought to establish as fact. When such methods are blatantly abused we clearly begin to recognize them as "witch hunting" devices or "astrology" or "hocus-pocus."

For the ethnomethodologist, on the other hand, *any* device or method concerned with uncovering the reality of complex subjectivity is a kind of witch-hunting procedure or a form of hocus-pocus. The logic of the reality being dealt with in this instance forces us to this conclusion. If the subjective domain is beyond knowing in any direct sense, it can only be dealt with indirectly. The indirect means used by people to deal with subjectivity are not the same as the indirect means used by natural scientists—measuring instruments, gauges, etc.—for assessing natural phenomena.

The extent to which ethnoprocedures are considered rational is not a function of what they accomplish in fact, but is instead a matter of whether they are *our* methods. The methods of a different culture or society are generally suspect—if not considered downright barbaric or foolish. The Protestant ministers of New England would have thought the Navaho were crazy. The Navaho would have wondered about the peculiar practices of the black-coated ministers.

The propriety of any folk method rests in its ethnocentric base, not in its factual accomplishments. The reason for this is not easy to see, perhaps, because ethnomethods create a sense of facticity. However, the facts that ethnomethods deal with cannot be established through observation and pure reason. In this regard, ethnomethodology provides yet another way of looking at cultural relativism. The methods employed by a community to deal with communal problems must be relative to the community.

There is the further disturbing implication in all of this that, with respect to purely human social events, there has been no real social, as opposed to material or technological, progress—nor is there much hope for such progress. We have witnessed obvious technological and material innovation and advancement over the millennia. We are astonishingly inventive with respect to machinery and technology. However, when we come to that most complex and evolved of all realities—human social systems—the fundamental substance of such systems remains much the same. Only the forms change. There can be no progress because the problem of subjectivity and complexity force us to rely on ethnomethods. Ethnomethods cannot be compared in terms of superior and inferior forms.

At this point even an unusually tolerant spirit must feel ethnomethodology and its exponents have gone too far. Surely some ethnomethods are better than others. However, if people believe in witches, then what method is the best for finding them? Solve the problem and you can challenge the arguments that come out of this newer social philosophy. Obviously, however, it is an unsolvable problem and you might as well spend your time trying to build a perpetual motion machine.

Well, you might say, it is the belief in witches that is at fault. If people would quit such nonsense, then we would not need to worry about the problem of enthnomethodological relativity. The ethnomethodologist might reply that, in some form or other, people in all cultures believe in witches. Witches are essentially individuals considered threatening or subversive to the interests of the culture or community. Among the witches we persecute, for example, are atheists, homosexuals, communists, "undesirables," subversives, amoralists, pinkos, radicals, etc.

When you begin to see that witches are actually people defined, in various ways, as potentially disruptive, you begin to see more clearly the ramifications of the ethnomethodological point of view—along with its rather dismal implications for the progress of humankind. If we add a Durkheimian twist and recognize that communities rely on criminal or disruptive elements to generate communal solidarity, then the argument becomes still tighter. The impossible problem of subjectivity makes social progression impossible. That puts the argument much too briefly, but it forces us to review more carefully what we mean when we talk about progress in general and social progress in particular.

All human societies are confronted with the problem of subjectivity. Subjective states cannot be known directly. They, nonetheless, must be described and responded to. We are forced to make sense of the complex subjective elements that play such an influential role in our lives. We can, however, make sense of these forces only in terms of methods that the sociocultural system itself provides us. In other words, the cards are, to a marked degree, stacked in favor of the community.

This is true whether a social encounter is a modest, ordinary day-to-day kind of event or a major institutional or social movement. To make this discussion more concrete, we can see in the counseling study how the volunteers made sense of nonsense. There was a way of dealing with the "counselor's" responses—a method, if you will. How this method is acquired is a study in the socialization of the individual, but the key word here is socialization. We come to learn, in the course of maturing in any culture, how to interpret whatever is going on around us. This mode of interpreting the world, our personal sense of the folk methods given us, is used for dealing with personal encounters. At a broader level, it becomes the set of culturally established devices we rely on for "seeing" other human communities and other sociocultural mentalities.

Regardless of the culture or society within which a particular set of ethnomethods is operating, the objective of such methods is an account or an accounting of what is taking place. We do not know what has taken place until an account is given. There is a difference, for example, between experiencing an adventure and giving an account of it.[14] The method whereby such accounts are constructed is a central concern of ethnomethodological studies. Because the methods whereby accounts are created are ethnically relative, the accounts themselves are subject to deep and profound distortions of one kind or another. This is the natural character of social accounts. They cannot be otherwise.

This, of course, makes ethnomethodology the *enfant terrible* of contemporary sociology insofar as the basic idea of modern sociology and anthropology is that there is an objective and at least essentially true understanding of the social order to be achieved through scientific study. Ethnomethodology looks on the social sciences as merely another form of ethnomethodology: They are procedures, given the availability of the natural sciences as a resource, for dealing with the impossible problem of subjectivity and complexity. Social science, as a form of accounting for what is going on, derives its validity not from its scientific rigor but, instead, from the fact it is *our* modern way of accounting for things.

All accounts of happenings and events, insofar as those accounts deal with social reality, are valid only within the ethnic context that sustains the methods whereby those accounts were obtained. In sum, accounts of social events are hopelessly slanted by the sociocultural milieu within which they are generated. Moreover, because it is the task of ethnomethods to make accounts acquire a taken-for-grantedness character, we come to see as "real" whatever is created for us by the community itself.

This discussion will now briefly consider two types of accounts relevant to the nuclear age. First of all, we must have a way of accounting for the mentality or the motives or the "inner nature" of entire nationalities, including our own. We must establish what is "on their minds" and what is "on our minds." It is not possible to deal with nation-states or any other social entity exclusively in terms of its material movements or acts. We must get behind actions as it were and decipher what they *mean*. Deciphering the "mind" of the enemy is, obviously, important.

Second, there is the problem of the motives or the mentality of those who build and maintain nuclear arsenals. This second issue is not as significant as the first, and only a few paragraphs will be devoted to it before we turn to the important issue of how you go about finding out what is on the mind of a nation — especially, the mind of the enemy.

Do We Need to Know Our Scientists?

What is interesting about those who build and maintain nuclear arsenals is not that we have a rich literature or accounting of their inner character but that we have so little. Not only are nuclear weapons in and of themselves relatively secret devices, kept under tight security, but those who create them and work with them are also secretive and kept secret.

While our newspapers and popular magazines (a rich source of accounts) carry countless stories about celebrities, political figures, baseball outfielders, singers, and football quarterbacks, those whose work is of far greater import for the future of all of us are rarely heard about or heard from. They are an invisible corps of technicians, engineers, and scientists. If we think of them at all, we think of them as a kind of quiet, busy, hive of nerds. (The columnist Ellen Goodman once referred to nuclear weapons as a "triumph of the nerds.") They are obviously very busy and perhaps they are quiet, but they are certainly not nerds.

Where do these people come from? What are they like? What is on their minds? What kind of person can dedicate himself or herself to the creation, development, and maintenance of weapons dedicated to the wholesale slaughter of millions of people? They appear in stories in specialized magazines, and they can be seen in pictures, on occasion, posing beside a death weapon smiling and looking pretty much like a novice fisherman pleased with a six-inch trout. They apparently are much like anyone else — football players, singers, dancers, and others who get publicity. If so, then why are we kept in the dark about them? If they are different, then in what ways are they different? Should we be concerned with what they are like? Does it make any difference what they are like "inside"?

Because so many people who work, in significant ways, with nuclear devices, are either scientists or engineers, we gain an indirect — and probably highly romanticized — accounting of what they are like. The popular account of the scientist-technician is one of the cerebral seeker after truth. The scientist is an intellectual — a bookish grind. The reality of the scientific mentality is more complex and mixed.

The question of what the keepers of nuclear devices are really like can never be answered. Yet, we have stereotypes. You should understand that a stereotype is in itself a type of account. The intriguing question becomes: How do the accounts of, let us say, nuclear scientists become established and what form do they take? What are popular sources of such accounts? Are scientists who dedicate themselves to working on destructive weapons different from those who dedicate themselves to pure research?

The question is not a trivial one. If the American scientist is motivated to work on nuclear weapons because such work offers prestige and status, then the problems we must deal with in terms of controlling the production of nuclear weapons are different than if the motives or the "spirit" behind such work is purely patriotic or is a last-ditch recourse that the scientist or engineer must rely on simply to meet domestic obligations.[15]

Doubts, for example, were raised recently about the judgment and the reasons behind why top-level scientists made several recent recommendations in both weapons research and in space exploration. For example, in one recent case scientists involved in space and weapons research protested that powerful colleagues were more interested in gaining the ear of politically powerful and influential people than they were in scientific technicalities. Scientists whose motives are primarily status-oriented are probably going to function differently from those whose motives are held to the pure resolution of curiosity or those whose motives are simply to find a secure job.

The American scientist, however, unlike movie celebrities and political figures, works in the comfort of privacy and the protection of a culturally established stereotype of the intellectual as an uninteresting individual whose personal life is not worth accounting for. Scientists, generally, are not celebrities. The term *celebrity* has its roots in a Latin word referring to the multitude. A celebrity is an individual who, through fame, represents and is sustained by the multitude or, as we say today, the public. Occasionally, however, an especially famous person's life becomes a characterization of a particular group—Beethoven characterizes our notion of classical composers; Pasteur represents the daring medical scientist; Lindbergh is the personification of the adventurous pilot, etc.

In the case of nuclear scientists, the most celebrated figure by anyone's reckoning would have to be Albert Einstein. The accounts we receive of this man lead us to conclude that he was selfless, devoted totally to pure scientific research, and gentle. We conclude, then, that the modern nuclear weapons designer is similar. However, as I suggested earlier, modern nuclear weapons designers and creators may be different in nature. Is it a difference that makes a difference?

What needs at least a little thought is the fact that, at least in the United States, there is little popular or general interest in knowing what these people are like. For an ethnomethodologist, the question of how curiosity is curbed is as worthy of consideration as the question of how it is heightened. The odd thing about accounts of nuclear scientists and weapons makers is that such accounts are so limited. Where they appear, they are doubtless subject to distortions. We are left in the dark.

Accounts of the Enemy

I will conclude the discussion of accounts by turning to accounts of the enemy. Any community or nation, to the extent it is involved with other communities and nations, must gain an understanding of those other communities. Nothing could be more simple, and yet it is obvious that nothing is more totally impossible. We constantly sustain a sense of knowing what the enemy is like. Moreover, we retain a sense of certainty about our knowledge. On occasion we are so certain that we are willing to imprison or even kill those who have the temerity to see things differently.

Nonetheless, it should be apparent that such knowledge must be biased. It is biased, first of all, by the biases intrinsic to ethnomethods. Secondly, it is biased by animosity between two communities. Just as it was argued that if witches are believed in, they will be found, then if the enemy is believed in, the wickedness of the enemy's "spirit" will be somehow established.

An anecdote will at least illustrate the direction of the argument here. I recall an account I came across, a number of years ago, of a device used by a barbaric chief to inform his people of the nature of the enemy. If an enemy soldier was captured in battle, the chief would have him placed in a cage for several weeks. The prisoner was not allowed to clean himself; he was fed badly; he was given no change of clothing; and, in addition, feces and urine were not cleaned from the cage.

After a few weeks the prisoner was "ripe." At this point the barbaric chief would have the prisoner paraded through the community as an example of what the enemy was really like — you could see it and smell it right in front of you. There could be no doubt about the "real" nature of the enemy in this instance. What conclusions do you think people drew about the character of the enemy from the sad spectacle they saw being paraded before them? This, incidentally, is a nice example of an ethnomethod.

In both the United States and Russia images of the other nation's character are obtained, in part, from dissidents. Accounts from such sources are a little like the prisoner in the cage — that is to say, they are not exactly a representative sampling. Where accounts of the enemy are concerned, it appears to be the case that people are not interested in representative samples. A limited account can carry a great deal of persuasive weight.

At the same time, it is understood that the accounts of dissidents are not especially significant in the game of geopolitics. They help maintain negative images of the enemy, but they have little further importance. What is more important is the problem of accounting for visible collective movements such as the redeployment of troops or the movement of missile bases or the transportation of weapons into, let us say, Central American countries. What do such movements mean?

At this point we can at least gain a small insight into why such important matters as obtaining treaties for the reduction of missiles or cease-fire accords is so difficult. For men and women of goodwill and the desire for peace, the slow and generally ineffective efforts of nations to stem the madness of a policy of Mutually Assured Destruction has an Alice in Wonderland quality to it. Why must nations spend fruitless years deliberating when the solutions to the problems of the world appear to be in front of everyone's nose?

The answer to this question provides at least a teasing further insight into why nations fight each other. From an ethnomethodological perspective, the elaborate truce-negotiating teams and disarmament committees and experts are faced with the primary problem of penetrating the mind of the enemy. In a sense, they have before them the task of being mind readers. What does a given movement on the part of the enemy "mean"?

Consider, for example, the consequences of actually being able to read the enemy's mind. Suppose, on the one hand, we successfully looked into the enemy's mind and found it is motivated by the desire to destroy us. We can then respond accordingly. Suppose, on the other hand, we probe the enemy's mind and find it is motivated only by the desire to liberate oppressed people and sustain security. Our response would possibly be of a different nature.

The deliberations, then, of the various representatives of treaty organizations have to do, basically, with an impossible task. No matter how much care is exercised in the proper interpretation of a movement by the enemy, one cannot be certain it is a correct interpretation. It must be reviewed and then reviewed again. Too much is at stake to make an error. But any kind of definitive interpretation can never be established. So, the meetings turn into elaborate devices not only for the "reading of minds" but also for the construction of interpretations that will have the imprimatur of official understanding. No wonder the process is slow, deliberate, elaborate, and — in its final consequences — always disappointing to those who had hoped the world might find a better way of conducting international affairs.

Traditionally the logic of reading the enemy's mind is based on the fact that good will cannot be proved — nor can ill will. However, ill will is the better assumption in terms of being prepared. The propositions that make up what C. Wright Mills called "crackpot realism" are the logical derivative of the impossible problem of subjectivity.

SUMMARY AND CONCLUSIONS

The complicated and subjective nature of human relations forces people to rely on "folk" procedures for dealing with human problems. These procedures are uncertain but, at the same time, necessary. The study of these procedures or methods is known as ethnomethodology.

Students of ethnomethodology, such as Harold Garfinkel, note that such methods are generally sufficient to provide satisfactory *created* solutions to what are inherently impossible problems. One of the consequences is a taken-for-granted attitude toward the ways in which one's own community defines situations and delimits its own conceptions of reality.

Among the consequences of this for the nuclear weapons issue is an acceptance of political realities that endorse paranoia and military solutions as "realism." Ethnomethodology offers at least a general insight into why nations are generally incapable of moving quickly with respect to such matters as establishing disarmament treaties. In a sense, though nations shift alliances and enmities, the fact they have always faced the problem of the subjective meanings of national movements and will always confront them in the future — so long as boundaries are defined in nationalistic terms — implies that no kind of effective disarmament will ever occur.

Chapter 9

The Quest for Dramatic Realization: War as Drama

DRAMATISM AS SOCIAL SCIENCE

Eric Sevareid, I believe it was, once said sociology is "slow journalism." Sevareid has a good point. At the same time, there can be little doubt that journalism is usually much too quick with its "sociology." Additionally, we could say that the study of history is belated journalism. Whatever the case, journalism shoots first and meditates later—if ever. Social science, ideally, meditates first and then, if there is any shooting to be done, debates the matter until the feeling goes away.

The theoretical perspective we are about to examine first appeared in 1956 in a small book by Erving Goffman, titled *Presentation of Self in Everyday Life*. This was the first in a series of books that established dramaturgy as a new point of view in sociological literature. It was a departure from established and orthodox forms of social science. It did not test any hypotheses; it contained no tables of statistical data; it was not concerned with controlling variables, and it did not rely on questionnaires, scales, measuring devices, or the other accoutrements of modern quantitative social science. It read as if it had been written by a philosophically inclined journalist.

Is sociology, as Sevareid contends, merely slow journalism? Is it different? I want to spend a few paragraphs arguing that social science and journalism, though similar in some ways, also differ (beyond the fact that one is fast and the other slow). There is, after all, a scientific quality to what a person such as Goffman does, though it is science that does not fit our stereotypes of lab technicians and mathematical geniuses in front of blackboards covered with esoteric formulas. Such work is not journalism nor is it like other approaches to human affairs. The distinction can be found in the fact that social scientists, whether quantitative in their approach or not, share common rational concerns.

The social scientist relies on a deeper comprehension of one or another "theory" of human actions. The theory might be conflict theory, structural-functionalism, symbolic interactionism, behaviorism, exchange theory, or something else. The main point is that a social scientist finds inspiration in a theoretically grounded point of view. Journalists, on the other hand, tend to divide along political lines and obtain their inspiration from political perspectives.

Journalists tell stories and so does Goffman. In this they are similar. However, journalism is concerned with stories that will attract readers. It tends, therefore, to move toward describing sensational events. Goffman's writing acquires its force not through *what* it describes — a housewife cleaning the living room before guests arrive or a nurse chatting with a patient — but through its analysis of everyday life. Goffman's work is concerned with revealing the depth of dramaturgic concerns, and it does this by turning not to sensational moments but to our commonplace actions. After all, if dramaturgy is to be found in what we generally think of as undramatic times, then it can obviously be understood in instances where it more openly reveals its nature.

Goffman's works have a journalistic quality about them only in the sense they do not resort to the standard statistical methodologies that now commonly define social science as science. The social sciences place a great deal of weight on statistically obtained information — across broad and representative samples. Goffman's writing contains few, if any, statistical accountings. Although journalists occasionally rely on statistical reports, journalism typically uses as its factual base incidental events of the moment. It is Goffman's reliance on incidental examples and events that gives his writing a journalistic look.

This roundabout introduction to the work of Erving Goffman has a purpose. Goffman's work was a radical departure from the sociological and social psychological writing published from roughly 1925 down to the present time.[1] Here was a writer of major influence who rarely, if ever, relied on statistical procedures. His work makes little or no use of questionnaires, tests, or scales. He openly and without apology makes use of literary examples to support an argument or point of view. Stylistically, his work is easy to read and not loaded with the usual heavy-handed jargon of social science. There is a casual quality to his writing. In sum, Goffman's work does not appear to be even close to what we commonly think of as scientific in nature.

So simple do his work and methods appear that university students commonly see them as easier approaches for completing a research paper than carrying out, let us say, a statistical study. They discover, later, that it would have been easier had they gone ahead and collected questionnaire data and done a lot of "number crunching." Goffman's work characteristically reveals an unusually imaginative naturalistic observation of human conduct. It relies on a *trained* imagination — it is not at all easy to do.

His work can be broadly classified as analytic and interpretive. It is grounded heavily in a specific theoretical orientation that is generally referred to as *dramaturgy*. I have also seen the term *dramatism* used. He wrote for professional rather than popular audiences or special interest groups. His acceptance by professional social scientists is mixed: Older, established professionals tend to reject Goffman; younger professionals and graduate students appear to be more enthusiastic.

His work is singularly nonjudgmental. Although he certainly had political interests of his own, the nature of those interests does not reveal itself clearly in his writing — his observations are of equal value or disvalue to a political conservative or a liberal. His work displays a detached quality. Whether a situation under consideration involves prostitutes or priests, it receives the same cool and dispassionate consideration. In this sense, then, he is a social scientist. Yet, as we get into his writing and his way of looking at the world, we shall see that it is not social science as it is commonly stereotyped. It is, to paraphrase the title of a book by Suzanne Langer, social science in a "new key."[2]

THE NATURE OF A DRAMATISTIC PERSPECTIVE

Goffman's work rests on an elementary, but nonetheless profound, metaphor. He turns his attention toward the implications of the apparent fact that, whatever else they might be, people are dramatic in nature. Once again, as we saw in other cases, social philosophy commonly begins with a simple, even obvious, theme. Usually, good social philosophy is attained not through the novelty or complexity of a theme but, instead, through how it is orchestrated. By *orchestration* I mean that Goffman takes a relatively simple concept and applies it to hundreds of different situations. It is in the general applicability of this point of view that we come to recognize its strength as a way of interpreting our actions.

What is meant by the assertion that people are dramatic? How does this differ from other assertions about the nature of human social life? To what extent are we dramatic? What makes us this way (assuming the dramatic perspective to have an element of truth to it)?

Because words in common use in America tend to have their meanings eroded — perhaps because of mass media superficiality — the term *dramatic* now refers to anything unusual, alarming, astonishing, bizarre, violent, extremely rapid, distinctive, etc. This is an unfortunate waste of a powerful concept. Drama, in its more careful usage, refers to the staging of human social and moral concerns. The other creatures of the world may share common qualities with human beings. However, no other creature stages its social world as elaborately and as constantly as human beings do.

Essentially the dramatic perspective notes that we are forced to perform before audiences — whether we like the idea or not. At the minimal level, we perform before ourselves. There is something peculiar about the human ability to put on a performance and, at the same time, be an audience to whatever one is enacting. We are, simultaneously, performers and audiences to our own performances. We act and then judge our own actions.

Ordinarily we perform before audiences, either real or imagined. We may perform knowingly or unwittingly; but one significant feature of our lives as social creatures is that we are viewed by audiences. Moreover, those audiences either extend or withhold their applause or acceptance. As was just mentioned, we are also audiences to ourselves, and we applaud and boo ourselves much as we might any other actor.

Incidentally, the power of an audience to influence matters should not be overlooked. An impressive example of the extent to which an audience can manipulate an actor can be observed in a common children's game. In this game somebody is designated "it." The other people, the audience, agree on something the person who is "it" should do. The person who is "it" is not told what this is. Then the audience directs the actor simply by applauding when the actor is close to doing the action and withholding applause when the actor is not going in the right direction. It is impressive to observe the extent to which complex actions can be accomplished merely by following the applause of the audience *without any other form of instruction.*

At this point we are called on to recognize an elementary but significant feature of human actions. Goffman's point of view moves us toward seeing what people do in terms of two basic units of action—the actor on the one side, the audience on the other. Any particular social action, virtually by definition, is never purely individualistic. It involves the individual *and* the audience with which the individual is involved. As a consequence, when we try to understand the actions of an individual, we should also examine the nature of whatever audiences might be relevant to those actions.

I shall elaborate further on the dramaturgic approach to human life in just a moment. First we need to deal with the question of how it differs from other philosophical views. We have time to consider only two major perspectives for contrast: Marxism and behaviorism.

Where Marxism is materialistic, dramaturgy is symbolic. Where Marxism suggests that the struggle between classes is a struggle for wealth, dramaturgy suggests it is a struggle for control over who gets to play the big scenes. Where Marxism predicts that the struggle between classes will end with the successful revolt of the proletariat, dramaturgy suggests conflict is an inherent part of social life. Conflict, in itself, is a dramatic condition, and it is engendered and augmented by our penchant for dramatizing events. In sum, dramaturgy and Marxism are different in their ways of looking at human social life.

Where behaviorism denies the subjective in favor of observing purely behavioral responses, dramatism accepts subjectivity as unavoidable. People perform not only before real audiences but before imagined ones as well. Even when performing before real audiences we are typically forced to imagine what their impression of our actions might be. Behaviorism is concerned only with what can be observed; in the strictest sense this means the motions of organisms or their behavior. Dramatism, on the other hand, is concerned with whatever affects performances and dramatic actions. The difference between *behavior* and *action* is a major one. It might be summed up by suggesting that experimental rats *behave* and people *act*. The term *action* implies a much broader scope than is implied by the concept of *behavior*. People do more than "behave." They attribute meanings to events, they construct elaborate settings, they wear costumes, they anticipate audience responses, and so forth. Action is behavior plus a lot more.

In the following discussion, I shall draw on three of Goffman's ideas as a basis for discussing the nuclear arms crisis:

1. Dramatic realization
2. Dilemmas of expression
3. Symptomatic actions

DRAMATIC REALIZATION

The dramatic task confronting us is to give a sense of reality to our actions. Goffman uses the term *dramatic realization* to make the point. In theatre, for example, it is the task of an actor to make the audience accept as "real" the artificial performance it is witnessing. Each of us, as a social being, wittingly or unwittingly impresses others by what we do. We have no choice in this. We constantly give off impressions. We can try to control the impression, and we might succeed to a greater or lesser degree. However, whether or not we try to manage our impressions, the fact remains that others observe us and interpret what they observe.

In this regard it is worth noting that as we proceed "up" the mammalian hierarchy into simian and then humanoid beings we also move more and more toward beings who consistently monitor each other visually. Where, for example, cats pay relatively little attention to each other, chimpanzees more constantly monitor each other's activities. One of the more unique features of human beings is their evidently genetically acquired inclination to watch each other constantly and intently. People seem to gain some kind of profound gratification or satisfaction out of watching other people. When you give it a little thought, you can see that it is a peculiar aspect of the human condition.

In its more bizarre extremes this inclination to look at other people takes the form of large groups of individuals paying to watch others enact artificial social moments that we refer to commonly as the "theatre." The fact that on any given evening in the United States as many as 30 or even 100 million pairs of eyes might be watching a single individual tell a joke or toss a football on television is almost eerie. Certainly, it is difficult to find any parallel to this in the rest of the animal world. We are creatures who watch each other; and, one way or another, we are creatures who are concerned about being watched.

In order to sustain a given social role, say that of a teacher in a college classroom, we must "give off" impressions within a relatively narrow band of all possible impressions. To act in a manner that destroys the impression we are making also destroys the validity of the social performance. For example, a powerful belch can be devastating with respect to the impression a lecturer wants to generate. Such an impression falls outside the band of all possible impressions available to the performer. Through such examples Goffman approaches the puzzling question of what constitutes *social* conduct as opposed to, let us say, purely physical or physiologically grounded behavior.

Social reality lies in how we perform before others. A performance is socially effective if it is accepted as such by the audience observing it. For Goffman, then, social reality is suspended on the fragile threads of impression. If the impressions fail, then the social moment collapses. If the impression is convincing, then social reality is brought into being.

Social reality is a matter of dramatic realization. The analogy with theater is a close one. The task of theatre is to create the illusion of reality. The form of the illusion might be pure fantasy, but the audience must be drawn into a sense of the "realness" of the drama unfolding before them. It is Peter Pan asking the audience to clap if they believe Tinker Bell is "real." It is a matter of experiencing a "real" concern over whether Luke Skywalker is going to be killed by Darth Vader.

If the "reality" of the illusion is not generated, then the empathetic response of the audience is flat. We do not believe what we are witnessing. We reject it as "phony" or, curiously enough, we reject it as not being realistic. Keep in mind that theatre is, in a sense, never, never, never realistic—even when it is "realistic." Theatre is always created. It is an impression of reality, but it is never real. It is just what it is and nothing more and certainly nothing less—it is, quite simply, theatre.

Social reality requires that we sustain, on a day-to-day basis, what Goffman refers to as "dramatic realization." For certain roles it is relatively easy to achieve dramatic realization. A state trooper, for example, who pulls your car to the side of the road has little difficulty convincing you that you are being apprehended by an officer of the law.

From this perspective we can begin to see why people who must enforce social regulations or carry out especially serious social performances are generally given dramatic advantages such as special costumes, the right to carry weapons, special badges, or certificates. Moreover, they are generally selected to have appropriate physical builds or to "look right" for the performances they must carry out. Where impressions must be made quickly and without dispute, the community provides special theatrical devices to enhance the problem of impression management.

Other performances lack inherent dramatic realization. A professor can be working hardest when he or she is sitting looking at the ceiling and merely thinking about a problem—the difficulty is that in this circumstance the individual does not appear to be working. In such situations people invent little devices that are not necessary for what they are doing except insofar as they enhance a sense of dramatic realization. Because their real work gives the impression of not working, they introduce dramatic devices that make it appear to any audience of the moment that they are working.

Goffman refers to this as "make-work." The simplest example of make-work is when workers on a warehouse floor exaggerate their working routines when the boss comes on the scene and then lapse back into a more relaxed and ordinary effort when she leaves.

Where the working performance is uncertain, make-work devices can become routinized in themselves. A possible example is the continuing reliance of universities on an outmoded form of conveying information known as the lecture. In a day and age when books are available, instructional TV cassettes are easily come by, and computers provide access to super-libraries of enormous scope, our predilection for lectures is difficult to understand. It is an awkward, inefficient and, all too commonly, tedious way to convey information — though in moderation it has its positive side.

If we view the lecture as a form of make-work for an occupational category that is denied nearly any other way of impressing audiences that it is doing the work it is supposed to be doing, then the lecture begins to make sense. Of course, lectures serve other purposes as well. As an educational device, however, they are relatively limited.

This is at least suggested by the innumerable gaffes and errors that professors are always chuckling over. (I recall a student referring to Mac E. Velly's great work *The Little Prince*.) It is easy to make mistakes when taking down notes from a mile-a-minute lecturer or from one who drawls out inarticulate commentaries in a hall that was designed not with acoustics in mind but rather to house as many students as possible as cheaply as possible.

The lecture system tests the stenographic skills of students as much as anything. Lectures primarily offer the lecturer an opportunity — in an otherwise undramatic occupation — to engage in moments of self-display and impression management before captive audiences. An occasional lecture might be refreshing; but time might be better spent, at least for superior students, using more efficient learning devices.

One of the simple, but still effective, insights Goffman offers is that in any interaction between two or more people there are at least two or more performers and two or more audiences. We commonly think of a performance as an event in which an actor carries out an action while the audience observes what is taking place. In fact, the actor observes the audience while, in turn, the audience also performs for the actor.

Students in a classroom, for example, are faced with the problem of how to perform before the instructor. How do you "enact" being a student? It is a tough act to dramatize. One fairly common response is to abandon the performance and simply go to sleep — though this occasionally leads to a rude awakening when the sleeping student discovers his audience (the professor) does not appreciate the performance. Students, generally thought of as "audiences," are also actors. Moreover, the acting task they must fulfill is a demanding one, if it is carried out properly.

In legitimate theatre actors comment on how some audiences are better to perform in front of than others — implying that certain audiences act better than do others. Once again, the division of a performance into a particular actor performing before a particular audience is too simple. In any performance there are at least two sets of performers and two sets of audiences.

We perform before others, then, whether we are on stage or in the audience. We have no choice in this. We are performing whether we know we are performing or not. The extent to which life as performance can be carried is recognized when we consider that during stage performances it is necessary, sometimes, to "act" the part of a corpse. This is not a difficult role to carry out, though it has dramaturgic problems attached to it. What is implicit in this observation is that in real life a real corpse is also, in an odd way, "acting." When we comprehend the implications of this observation, we begin to comprehend the extent to which acting permeates human relations.

The elemental argument on which this discussion is based is simply that others judge our performances. Throughout this process there is always an element of uncertainty over the extent to which the audience to a performance will accept the performance for what it seeks to convey. A performer on stage cannot be sure of applause. Likewise, in day-to-day life, we can never be certain how our "act" is going over.

A young man, for example, might try to convince a young lady she is his only true love. Whether she will buy his line is a matter of how convincing the young man is in making his case. The quest for dramatic realization is a constant and an uncertain one. The dramaturgic approach to human affairs assumes an element of uncertainty in performances. At the same time, people seek control over their affairs. There is, then, built into the human community a kind of "tension" between the uncertainty of performances and our desire for control.

Curiously enough, the uncertainty of dramatic devices creates tensions or communication breakdowns that are then resolved or shored up by even more dramatic responses. This is the basic dynamic of arguments. As we find ourselves being more misunderstood or denied (the equivalent of withdrawal of applause), we find ourselves resorting to more dramatic devices — pounding the table, raising our voices, making threats, gesturing, and so on. To the extent this observation is true, it suggests a profound bind with respect to the future of human conflicts. That is to say, the natural tendency of the dramatization of conflict is toward ever greater escalation of the drama — and, of course, the conflict.

When we combine this observation with the observation (discussed later) that drama relies on weapons, we have yet another way of looking at arms escalations. Human conflicts and their expressions are like nothing else on the face of the globe — they are astonishingly intense and they are capable of being sustained over long, long periods of time. Subhuman animals fight and then walk away. It is impressive how quickly dogs return to a passive state after fighting. People rarely do. A dramaturgic perspective lends further understanding to this property of human conflicts, for one of the characteristics of drama is the intensification of emotions.

DILEMMAS OF EXPRESSION

In the course of a performance an actor encounters moments when sustaining a particular impression becomes difficult. This happens on the stage; it happens in day-to-day living. Such moments reveal a great deal about moral as well as dramatic issues in our lives. Basically, a dilemma of expression occurs when actors must choose to violate a social norm in order to retain their audience or conform to the norm and consequently lose the audience.

A nice illustration occurred a few years ago during an amateur theatrical performance of *The Merchant of Venice*. One of the performers, a professor of English, forgot his lines during the opening moments of the play. Without hesitation he launched into a few minutes of highly creative monologue that sounded as though it belonged to the play, but was, in fact, just a bit of Elizabethan-sounding gibberish. He eventually recalled his lines, spoke them, and the play moved on.

He had a choice. He could have honestly indicated he had forgotten his lines and, in doing so, interrupted the performance and destroyed the illusion of reality that is so tenuous in theatre. The entire play would have been ruined. Or, he could "fake it" and simply make up his Shakespeare. Keep in mind that faking things is essentially a matter of deception and dishonesty. The absent-minded professor elected to deceive the audience and succeeded. The integrity of the play was sustained, and few who witnessed the moment were any the wiser about the deception.

Dilemmas of expression occur commonly in the course of carrying out a performance or in the effort to manage and sustain impressions. For example, doctors must be careful about their presentation of professional self before patients. If they talk openly of their uncertainties and worries, then the patient becomes uncertain and worried. If they hide or disguise their uncertainties, they engage in a kind of deception.

American political performers, indeed political performers anywhere in the world, are constantly faced with dilemmas of expression. If they are honest, for example, they can lose their audiences. If they are dishonest and discovered, they will also lose their audiences. The common response to this dilemma is to present a "front" in which deception becomes functionally necessary. If all of this has a degree of truth to it, who is to blame—the politician or the political audience?

The engaging thing about dilemmas of expression, in addition to the fact that they commonly put us into deceptive postures, is that they are concessions to the demands of our audiences. They are, still more broadly, concessions to the demands of sustaining the social moment. What sometimes appears to be a psychological characteristic—hypocrisy, for example—can just as well be seen as a response to the demands of an audience. When we see it this way, we move from a psychological to a more sociological perspective.

Goffman forces us to become more aware of the extent to which we shall share in each other's neuroses and imperfections. The hypocrites and deceivers we must deal with in our lives are, in part, our own creations. Would we deceive if we were not called on to deceive? Would we be deceived if we could learn to accept nondeception with greater serenity and decency? Goffman does not provide answers to questions such as these, but his work forces us to consider them.

THE SYMPTOMATIC RANGE OF ACTION

The dramaturgic perspective offers new ways of thinking about old human questions. For example, one peculiarity of human social life is our inclination to judge people not in terms of what they are but rather in terms of how they appear to us. A man might be sensitive and knowledgeable, but if he has a bashed-in nose and cauliflower ears, we will dismiss him as an illiterate lout—until he does a powerful job of convincing us to the contrary. A woman might be a monstrous and venomous exploiter, but if she is pretty we conclude she must be "nice."

In brief, there are two "layers" in social interactions that influence the manner whereby impressions are created and the social moment sustained. One layer consists of the content or the substance of the action. Or, as former Vice President Walter Mondale might suggest, it is the "beef" of our social lives. In the famous televised debates between candidates in the 1984 Democratic primary campaign, Mondale asked his opponent: "Where's the beef?" He was implying that his opponent's presentation of self was all style and no content. It swayed the audience. What is interesting about this is that Mondale's question was not so much substantive as it was stylistic. There was no "beef" in the question: "Where's the beef?" At the same time, it was one of the memorable lines of a particular campaign and it won the attention of the audiences Mondale was trying to impress.

Another layer consists of elaborate (but at the same time extraneous) actions, gestures, appearances, articulations, costuming, poses, glances, thrusts, movements, and other devices that package the "beef." Any social action, then, has two parts: the content of the action and the form in which that content is presented. Or, to put it still another way, any social interaction is marked by its substance on the one hand and its style on the other. There is nothing terribly new in this observation. The basic idea is common and relatively simple. Goffman, however, offers us new understandings of the power of style vis-à-vis content.

In the following discussion I shall concentrate on style, this second layer of social interactions, because it is uniquely human. Goffman called it the "symptomatic range of action." The interesting question becomes: What makes this second layer of human exchange so significant? Why can a modest loss of control over the stylistic aspects of social relations be so catastrophic? What are the implications of stylistic power? What happens when style prevails over content? Even a small amount of time spent in musing over these questions alters our conception of human communal life.

The symptomatic range of action is significant in human interactions because it establishes the right of the performer to convey the content of a particular action. Indeed, so powerful is the symptomatic range of action in this regard that if one has good control over it, the content of an action can be relatively weak and the performance nonetheless accepted.

An example of the symptomatic range of action is the variety of idealized qualities attributed to leadership roles. We might call this the Charlton Heston or, perhaps, the John Wayne complex. The stereotypical leader in American culture is generally a man of powerful physical stature, tall, somewhat heavy, broad-shouldered, Caucasian, thin-lipped, clear-eyed (unblinking), square-jawed, and clean-shaven.

Comic books hyperbolize these qualities in their heroes. What is interesting about Superman, for example, is not so much what he is as what he is not. For example, he is not black. He is not nerdish — though Clark Kent is. He is not Jewish, Catholic, nor, to my recollection, atheistic. He is not pimply. He bears no scars. He is not, in a strange way, sexual. In fact, when you think about it, he is one remarkably peculiar character. He is the dramatic model carried to its complete *reductio ad absurdum*. Even though he is a pure parody of leadership qualities, he is nonetheless instructive.

In addition, the idealized leader should symptomatize leadership by wearing the right clothes — a dark business suit (with a handkerchief coyly tucked in the chest pocket); a red striped tie; a very clean white shirt with enough cuff to display simple but expensive cuff links; freshly pressed trousers with a sharp crease; and nicely shined, not flashy, plain dark shoes. Moreover, his voice should be well modulated. He should speak in a clear and articulate manner — but his vocabulary should not be too extensive or strange.

A leader who displays command over an unusually large or strange vocabulary might be seen as either an intellectual, a homosexual, or worse yet, both. Depending on the context, these can be stylistically ruinous impressions. Another ruinous impression is that a large or eccentric vocabulary is being used to show off or is symptomatic of bombast. This might be called the Senator Claghorn syndrome.

When we lay out, even in a cursory manner, the stylistic characteristics of leadership qualities in American culture — they take on a strange quality. Why should we care whether our leaders are basso macho males who look like Charlton Heston or John Wayne? Why is it important not to look like a wimp if you possess the character of a brilliant strategist and leader? Isn't character enough? Public figures, however, obviously need to be concerned with appearance as well as character.

I am fond of a story told of General George Patton to the effect that he would suspend himself from a chinning bar while his aide held freshly pressed pants beneath him. The general would then put his pants on both legs at once. He did not sit or otherwise endanger the crease before walking out on the parade ground. He was aware of the power carefully creased trousers exert over men. The rather funny, but serious, philosophical question now is: Why should we care whether our leaders are wearing meticulously creased trousers (or the stylistic equivalent)?

From a dramaturgic perspective, social interactions are a matter of maintaining impressions. There are types of interaction in which the content of the action is clearly defined and cannot be faked. For example, it is impossible to fake being able to play par golf. Either you can do it or you cannot. Although there is a lot of stylistic ''layering'' in golf, it has relatively little effect on one's ability to play the game. Certainly this is one reason why we have an affection for sports. They are well defined. They cannot be faked upward. (It is possible, of course, for a fine athlete to pretend to have lower skills in order to ''gull'' a ''pigeon.'') Excellence in sports is true excellence.

But what about social situations that are ambiguous? The chapters on Durkheim and Mead suggested that social situations are heavy with ambiguity and uncertainty. We cannot define the moment until it is defined for us. There is, then, in the social moment, a kind of ''motive'' to define the situation as fully as possible. A leader cannot convey to those being led that he or she is a leader except through the process of creating this impression. This can be done (1) by displaying the knowledge, the skills, and the abilities of a leader — in sum, the content of leadership — and (2) by displaying the trappings of leadership — in sum those stylistic mannerisms that are symptomatic of leadership.

Full control over both content and the symptomatic range of action (style) generates a powerful effect — regardless of the action being carried out. It is the professor who looks knowledgeable and is knowledgeable. It is the doctor who has the skill *and* the style of a doctor. It is the athlete who has both ability and style.

But, in these examples, the content is fairly well defined. What about situations where the role being enacted has a loosely defined content? At this point, style tends to become increasingly significant and blurs with content itself. For example, what is the content of the performance of a clothes model? The performance is virtually entirely a matter of display of style. What is the content of the role of a hostess in a restaurant? What is the content of someone who claims she hears the voice of God speaking to her in the small hours of the morning? In these instances, performers must rely more heavily on stylistic devices to convey to an audience that they are ''really'' what they appear to be.

A role that is relatively easy to fake or put across to an audience by "winging it" is one that generally relies heavily on stylistic qualities as opposed to content. There are problems with trying to distinguish between roles in this manner, however. The general evidence suggests that social roles (in contrast to physical actions such as we find in sports) are, regardless of their nature, relatively easy to fake before common audiences. A modest control over content and a strong control over the symptomatic range of action can generally suffice to carry nearly any deception a long way.

Those who believe they are immune to social deception are being naive. Several years ago I had an opportunity to demonstrate this to a group of honors students who were convinced they were sophisticated enough to see through any kind of flamboyant deception. So, a meeting with a "Russian rocket expert" was arranged for the students. The "expert" was actually a Denver businessman. He visited with the students. In articulate Russian he asked them to wait until after their discussion to practice the "mother tongue" if they so wished. (This immediately disarmed several students who spoke to him in Russian.) He then talked about Russia, rockets, engineering, space, and history. This went on for several hours, and the deception was then dropped. The students were dumbfounded and refused to believe him when he said he was actually a public relations worker in Denver who had never been near Russia.

Indeed, the fact that social roles are easily faked is what makes the question of honesty, integrity, sincerity, loyalty, and a host of other valued qualities so significant. If social roles were not easy to fake—if deception was not a common problem in any human community—we would have little need to concern ourselves with problems such as sincerity. Certainly in modern large-scale systems where we interact with so many people, deception becomes a profound problem. One consequence is a culture in which sincerity is highly valued—after all, whatever is rare acquires a special value.

This distinction between content and style is nothing new in the discussion of human affairs. What is new in the recent development of dramaturgic perspectives is the increasing awareness of the pervasiveness, the power, and the functions of style in an interaction. Because a term such as "style" implies artful devices, early sociology and psychology in America tried to bypass any consideration of it. A review of social science texts from the turn of the century into the middle of the century shows a world of human interrelations strangely devoid of the hypocrisies and deceits of style.

Also, the dramaturgic perspective enables us to see more clearly the interplay between the two layers. For example, I already mentioned that to have power or control over both the content and the style of a performance conveys a strong sense of the reality of the performance to an audience. To use Goffman's term, it generates dramatic realization. The audience accepts as real the performance—and all it implies. Conversely, someone who lacks content and style is rejected out of hand. These two types of interaction between the layers are not especially interesting. More interesting is the moment when individuals possess one or the other but not both qualities.

Consider first the case where an individual has content but lacks style or control over the symptomatic range of action. My favorite example is the American turn-of-the-century economist Thorstein Veblen. Veblen was the foremost American social philosopher of his time. Veblen clubs sprang up around America to discuss his books and ideas. Hundreds and hundreds of students flocked to his classes at the University of Chicago. Within a few weeks, however, only a handful of students were grimly hanging on. What happened? Veblen was not a hard grader. He was certainly not lacking in knowledge and wit. His mastery of content was unexcelled. However, he lacked something. What he lacked was control over form. His classroom delivery was "flat." One student wrote about him that if the light had gone out behind his eyes as he was talking, no one would have noticed.

Playing with the idea of the discrepancy between content and style is a popular theme in fiction. My favorite story along these lines is one by James Thurber in which he tells the saga of an early flier who manages to circumnavigate the globe, solo, in a biplane while towing his fuel in a blimp-like appendage. The content of this heroic accomplishment is overwhelming. However, to the horror of insiders it is discovered he has none of the style of a real American hero. To the contrary, he is a dirty, foul-mouthed, boozing, wenching, egotistical lout. At the end of the story a secret service agent, at the president's order, pushes him from a window. He falls to his death — to be immortalized and aggrandized as the victim of an accident. Thurber hints, in this, that granting or removing stylistic properties from individuals posthumously is part of what history is about.

The other interesting discrepancy between style and content appears in the case where the individual has control over the symptomatic range of action and modest control over content. A general example can be commonly found on American campuses in the form of teachers who are just entering their field (or, for that matter, newcomers in any profession) but who "look and act the part." Students give instructors high ratings *as teachers* on the basis of such things as "the way he smoked his pipe" or "her cute hairdo" or "his deep voice" or her "pep and affection for people." (These are actual quotes taken from university student teacher evaluation questionnaires.)

What else can the students do? If they knew the material, why would they be students? If they do not know the material, then how can they evaluate an instructor on the basis of what he or she knows — other than by established reputation? However, established reputations among teachers are relatively rare. Only an extremely small proportion of teachers establish reputations of any note in their fields. Most have local reputations based on local performances in highly local classrooms.

This discussion of the symptomatic range of action can be summarized in a table. The table sums up the relationship between style and content by

	Content	Symptomatic Range of Action
Strong dramatic realization	+	+
Uncertain realization	+	−
Uncertain realization	−	+
Audience rejection	−	−

showing the four fundamental possibilities available. I have argued, though I would not push the argument too far, that style tends to be more significant in controlling moments of uncertain realization than is content. This is probably more true of brief performances than of those that need to be sustained for longer periods of time — if, for no other reason, than that a longer period affords a greater probability of revealing problems with respect to content.

The point of this discussion is to introduce an awareness of elements of larger actions that serve to sustain the total action by representing or "symptomatizing" the propriety of the action. If nothing else, becoming attuned to how extensively style is an element of human actions moves us away from a purely rationalistic and scientific approach to ourselves into one that allows greater critical freedom. We must concern ourselves not only with *what* people are doing but with *how* they are doing it as well.

The claim that a concern with stylistic problems over problems of content moves us away from scientific interests toward irrational matters is probably correct. At the same time, we cannot ignore everything that lies beyond rigorous scientific logic and measurement. Certainly, in the realm of human affairs it is disastrous to ignore matters of style or what Goffman calls the "symptomatic range of action." In the final countdown, it might be that those anxieties and fears driving us toward global annihilation come as much from our desire to sustain a "style" of living as they do from purely material interests.

DRAMATISM AND NUCLEAR QUESTIONS

I briefly sketched in several of the ideas contained in Goffman's dramaturgic approach to human affairs. We have yet to consider how they might be applied. It is obvious, at the outset, that weapons, in and of themselves, possess a kind of "dramatic" quality. It should also be obvious that weapons serve purposes other than simply dramatic ones. However, in this discussion we are coming at the issue of nuclear weaponry from a dramaturgic perspective, and we are therefore limiting ourselves to this point of view.

The dramatic nature of weapons is strongly suggested by the movie sections of our daily papers. Invariably one turns to these pages to find a celebrated actress or actor posing seriously in front of the camera while fondling a pistol, knife, bomb, bazooka, spear, machete, shotgun, hand grenade, rifle, machine gun, or some other engine of destruction. The more lethal-looking the gun, the more dramatic the effect. If nothing else, weapons evoke a sense of seriousness. They achieve a quick and cheap dramatic effect — they enhance dramatic realization.

In talking about dramatic realization I suggested that the primary objective of dramatic realization is to obtain audience acceptance. We want our audiences to believe our act. To get any audience to believe our act we must first get the audience's attention. Weapons get attention.

There is a strong temptation here to argue that weapons must be implicit within any interaction if it is to accomplish the ends of the dramatic imperative. For example, in the dramatic interplay between George and Martha in Edward Albee's *Who's Afraid of Virginia Woolf?* George points a gun at Martha, pulls the trigger, and a flag pops out of the barrel. The gun is not a real gun. There are no real weapons in this powerful drama. Where are the weapons, then, that provide the threats, the anxieties, the fears and conflicts that are inherent in human dramas? The real weapons in this drama are the acid tongues and bitter words that move the actors to attack each other. The attacks are not physical, yet the attacks are real and the audience is moved by them. Is it reasonable to think of words as weapons? From a dramaturgic point of view the answer must be yes.

Let us play with this theme a bit. We saw that social reality is created through dramatic devices. There is, then, a powerful and universal motive among people to engage in dramatic actions. It was further suggested that weapons are a quick and cheap way to achieve dramatic enhancement. We can then consider the possibility that the more significant a set of social relations is, the more likely we are to find weapons being overtly employed to enhance the dramatic character of those relationships.

Where the problem of being taken seriously is a major problem, you will find weapons of one variety or another being displayed or the threat of their use made explicit. The more serious the interaction, the more serious the weapons become. Absolute seriousness implies absolute weapons. This kind of logic forces us to conclude it is our serious people who are especially threatening. Conversely, it is threatening people who are taken seriously — not our clowns. Violence gets attention.

This is a radical statement of the implications of a dramaturgic point of view with respect to the place of weapons in human affairs. It moves beyond the simple notion that weapons are merely offensive and defensive devices employed in physical conflicts. We are forced to conclude that weapons cover a much broader realm. Weapons are inherent aspects of any kind of social interaction that is invested with dramatic qualities. Without weapons of one kind or another, social interactions cannot take place in any dramatic manner.

In order to come to this conclusion the entire concept of weapons must be extended to include any kind of device that can threaten injury of either a physical or mental nature. This means nearly anything can be a weapon—depending on the context within which it is contained and the manner in which it is displayed. Above all, the effective use of weapons relies as much on the proper display of the weapon as it does on the actual employment of the weapon.

From a dramaturgic point of view, this becomes the central problem with weapons as a dramatic device. Once a weapon is displayed or its use is implied in an interaction, the destructive power of the weapon must be revealed in some fashion. Otherwise, the threat of the weapon becomes impotent. The destructive power of the weapon can be revealed indirectly by injuring or damaging something peripheral to the action or it can be revealed directly.

In small contexts, where the "weapons" involve little more than exchanges of invective, the power of wit, if it is to be taken seriously, must be demonstrated. This means someone must be symbolically "destroyed" by the razor tongue of the wit. The wit seeks a sacrificial victim of sorts. The safest targets for wit are people who are distant and removed. Thus, common wit all too often takes the form of attacks on people who are distant from the attacks—politicians, celebrities, etc. We all practice this sort of thing in front of our friends on one occasion or another. By directing our wit against a remote celebrity, we show those around us that we can be dangerous. We make ourselves more threatening when we engage in the direct symbolic destruction of someone who is present at the party.

At higher levels, as at lower levels, the power of the weapon must be displayed. So it is, then, that the armies and navies of world powers find themselves engaged in constant exercises. These exercises have as their manifest function the maintenance of alertness and readiness for combat. The dramaturgic latent function is to display before the enemy the effectiveness of the weapons one possesses. Military exercises are sometimes done secretly, but never too secretly. Nuclear weapons are tested in secret, but the fact they are being tested is made public. It is to the advantage of those testing such devices that the destructive power of the weapon is conveyed by means of underground tremors detectable by the enemy.

It is not enough simply to display weapons during May Day parades and the Fourth of July. They must be fired. With nuclear weapons, unlike conventional weapons, there is reason to be concerned about indirect as well as direct tests. In direct tests, of course, the weapon is dropped on the enemy and the destructive power of the weapon is made manifest. In indirect tests these new weapons must now be placed deeply underground.

We are only now beginning to discover the extent to which our military and scientific experts were "innocent" in the tests of the late 1940s at Bikini and Eniwetok. The residual damage done by those tests was far greater than anticipated. The damage being done by current testing is difficult to assess. However, so far, these tests have been the safest manner by which the capacities of the weapon can be conveyed to its audience (that is, the enemy, potential enemies, and our allies). Once more it should be noted that though the manifest purpose of such tests is to determine whether the weapons work or to make them more efficient, the latent dramatic function is to display them. The enemy must be aware they exist and that they do, indeed, work.

One of the powerful appeals of the Strategic Defense Initiative, despite its costs and the expressed concern of large numbers of scientists, is that it fits well into the dramatics of international relations. Whether it ever actually comes into being or not, it remains a system that is "on stage" at all times—even during its research and development period. It is a weapons system appropriate to the era of mass communications. What could be a more impressive staging of a weapons system than hanging it in the sky where it can be seen by the leadership, along with everybody else, of all the world's nations?

If we grant that weapons are inherent to drama, then the deprivation of weapons is at the same time deprivation of dramatic control. The dramaturgic perspective implies that dramatic control is central to human social affairs. Dramatic control requires the implicit or explicit existence of weapons. Achieving dramatic control requires negating the effectiveness of the weapons being employed by the other agent in the interaction.

There can be little doubt this is indeed a pessimistic conclusion to reach. It implies nothing less than that in any interaction of a dramatic nature, even at the lowest and more common levels of relationship, at least a degree of enmity is generated. Keep in mind that the important term here is the word *dramatic*. Dramatic action is directed toward convincing audiences of the reality of the social performance being conducted by the actor.

The basic quest of a dramatic performance is to convince a potentially skeptical audience that the act is "real." The fact that any audience can reject the performance introduces an element inherently in opposition to the ends of the actor. It is in this sense, then, that enmity is integral to human social relations. It varies in degree from one set of social relations to another, but the logic of a dramaturgic perspective implies that it is never entirely absent.

In a staged theatrical performance the weapons of the actors consist of the symbols, gestures, trappings, props (which commonly include conventional weapons), and story lines used to "con" the audience into believing they are witnessing a real human drama. The weapons of the audience consist of applause or rejection. These are admittedly such ethereal devices that it verges on the absurd to claim they are weapons. Yet, anyone who has had the experience knows that rejection or the threat of rejection can, on occasion, be as effective as a gun when it comes to coercion.

It is pushing things to look on props, gestures, symbols, and applause as possible weapons in dramatic enactments. However, it makes sense. Recall that in the Iran-Contra hearings of 1987 interrogators were criticized for being threatening in their demeanor. It was argued that it is better to ask incriminating questions in a "soft" and gentle fashion. Dramaturgically speaking, this is the equivalent of hiding your gun in your pocket instead of letting it show.

I have pointed out that a dramatic performance contains within it an essential "tension" between the performers and the audiences involved. Each side in the drama must have ways of protecting itself from excesses on the part of the other. Where the tensions are relatively easy to deal with and not serious in their implications, the protective and coercive devices are in themselves of a minor nature. Whatever pain their employment evokes is of a mental or emotional nature. Where the tensions between performers and audiences are great, the performers and audience are uncertain of each other, and the relationship is loaded with significance for both sides, then weapons become more lethal in nature and are more openly displayed.

I have also suggested that acquiring dominance within an interaction is a matter of "disarming" the other party. This is virtually a tautology. However, it is an instructive point. The dramatic imperative implies that people are powerfully motivated to control dramatic situations. They are, therefore, motivated to acquire those devices—dramatic "weapons" of one kind or another—that sustain this effort. Depriving an individual or a group of its dramatic devices is the equivalent of "stripping" away those things necessary for being human.

Goffman uses the term *stripping* in much the same fashion it is used in the preceding sentence. The various ways in which people are stripped of the qualities that endow a performance with dramatic realization is a fascinating study in itself. I cannot go into this subject here, but possibly mentioning the techniques used by concentration camp officials will offer insight into what is being talked about. Cutting off hair, forcing people to wear ugly clothes, making people beg when they need to go to the toilet, making people do work that is meaningless (cleaning bathrooms with a toothbrush)—these are just a few of the ways in which stripping can take place.

Stripping is a matter of removing what I refer to broadly as the "weapons" of dramatic performances. At one level it consists of stripping away the symbols we use to manage the impressions we want to convey. To take away those devices we rely on to sustain our human performances is to take away our very humanity. Small wonder, then, that people react emotionally (and with an intensity that sometimes seems disproportionate to the circumstances) when deprived of dramatic devices. Why, for example, should a woman be shamed to the point of total despair because her hair was cut off? (This was a punishment reserved for French women in World War II who were believed to have collaborated with German troops.)

Stripping, even of insubstantial or purely symbolic elements, is threatening to the dramatic sense of self. So it is, then, that a wealthy person (and wealth, let there be no doubt about it, is a weapon) clings with great emotional intensity to the material items that symbolize his or her stature. So do we all. Whatever the device might be, if the person employing it believes it enhances his or her act, then the device will be defended with great vigor. The more significant the weapon for maintaining dramatic control, the greater the intensity with which the weapon will be protected.

I need to bring the discussion back to nuclear arms—those most dramatic of all weapons. Here are weapons that, by threatening total hell, reach the ultimate in dramatic quality. If so, then they also become dramatically symbolic. They are the measure of a nation's capacity to command center stage in international relations. They are valuable not only as purely defensive or offensive physical weapons but also as dramatic props. No nation possessing them is going to abandon them—any more than people would be inclined to abandon any other device that gained them a respectful audience from others.

In sum, the quest for freezing or reducing nuclear stockpiles is not simply a military problem—it is also a problem with respect to international dramatics, so to speak. Indeed, there is more than a suggestion here that the continuing arms race is not motivated by military logistics. From a purely military position, it is obvious that a relatively small number of these weapons should suffice for nearly any kind of killing problem. However, with respect to resolving the dramatic problem, no finite number is ever sufficient. It is one thing to seek dominance with respect to physical realizations and another to seek dominance with respect to dramatic realizations.

Nuclear Weapons and Dilemmas of Expression

There are moments in human relations when we find ourselves confronted with a damned-if-we-do-damned-if-we-don't situation. One common form of this is the situation in which we will lose our audience if we go in one direction and are also likely to lose it if we go in the other. In such circumstances, the effective dramatic alternative is the one most likely to retain our audience.

For instance, suppose that if we are honest, we lose our audience, and if we lie, and our audience discovers it, we will also lose our audience. This is a dramaturgic "no win" situation. Dramatic rationality calls for retention of the audience over nearly any other alternative—for loss of the audience is a form of ultimate loss. President Reagan, during the Iran-Contra crisis, faced a dilemma of expression. If he appeared unaware of what was happening, he presented the image of a president who was not aware of what was going on. If he knew, then he could be accused of supporting illegal activities. The threat of audience rejection existed no matter which way he went.

With a dilemma of expression the choice confronting the actor is basically between a nearly certain loss of the audience if one is honest and only the possibility of loss if deception is engaged in. The consequence is that people generally engage in a variety of deceptions. These can range from modest and polite personal deceptions all the way up to covert actions among nations that must be kept secret from the broader public.

That deception is a part of social life is not a novel insight. What dramaturgic thinking brings to the topic of deception is the role played by the audience. Where ordinary thinking lays blame for deception at the feet of the deceiver, dramaturgic thinking lays it at the feet of everybody involved in the relationship — to the extent it is concerned with blame.

At one level the forms of deception that are employed with regard to nuclear weapons are modest. They would be almost amusing were the issues not so profoundly of consequence for the future of the world. I turn now to the manner in which nuclear weapons are described in the press. At one point in recent years, for example, although this is not seen as often these days, the press referred to neutron weapons as "clean bombs." No nuclear weapon is clean. Nor, actually, is a strategic nuclear weapon a bomb. It makes about as much sense to call a strategic nuclear device a "bomb" as it would to call a two-ton conventional bomb a "firecracker."

This leaves the question open as to what these things should properly be called. I would like to propose a contest in which the American public is called on to create the most realistic term possible for describing these weapons. Imagine, then, entries such as "doomsday machines," "mass population incinerators," "indiscriminate people killers," "city burners," and so on. The emotional responses such terms evoke should make it clear that the euphemisms carefully created by those whose task it is to manage such systems are intended to mollify a public seen as incapable of accepting a more realistically descriptive terminology.

No small number of people have been struck by the mind-twisting contradictions implicit in calling our nuclear systems "peacekeepers." I am not interested, here, in condemning this practice, and I am certainly not interested in blaming militarists or "hawks" or any other particular group for this terminology. My concern is more detached. What is interesting is how such a term somehow became attached to a device which, if it is ever used, will bring an end to peace on this earth certainly for decades, if not for centuries. The name is so peculiar that it is the stuff out of which ironic satire is created.

Such terminology makes sense from a dramaturgic point of view, if few others. It is a term acceptable to large numbers of people. It is a concept that eases the conscience and makes the moment tolerable. It is one thing to be in the presence of a "peacekeeper" or "peacemaker" and something else to be in the presence of a "baby killer" or "mass civilian burner."

The point is not that the term *peacekeeper* is bad or good. The point is that in many ways the leadership of a nation must find those means that are effective with respect to controlling the hearts and minds of large audiences. The point of view of dramaturgy is that the nature of those means is defined by the audience itself. *Peacekeeper* is a term that the audience wants as much as the leadership does.

Where leadership is faced with the problem of losing its constituency (audience) by being honest, it has little choice. It can abandon its leadership position to someone with fewer scruples, or it can abandon its own scruples with respect to honesty. It is not much of a choice. However, to the extent it is a choice, it is one imposed by the audiences before which leadership must stand.

The commonplace view of lying is expressed well in a comment by Scott Turow, who writes: "They lie for the fun of it, or because that is the way they have always been. They lie about big details and small ones, about who started it, who thought of it, who did it, and who was sorry. But they lie. It is the defendant's credo. . . . Trumpet your innocence."[3] This is the ordinary view. Lying is done by bad people, or at least those in defensive situations. They do it for the fun of it or because that is the way they are. It is not an especially deep look at the problem of lying.

A dramaturgic perspective suggests it is done by everybody and it is done most intently and intensely when the audience sets up the situation so that lying is at least a rational, and possibly even a preferred, alternative to telling the truth. The locus of attention is shifted from the liar to those who strongly encourage being lied to.

Let there be no misunderstanding here. This argument is not intended to encourage lying nor is it a proposal to justify deceit. My intention is to promote argument and further thought about the nature of deception and lying in human affairs — especially with respect to serious matters. The only thing of concern here is to raise several troubling questions about human social performances.

First of all, to what extent do audiences function as a part of deception and deceit? To what extent, and under what circumstances, is a performer made to look foolish by being honest? Is lying and deception a psychological or moral quality, or is it a dramaturgic condition and found to a greater or lesser extent in all human social interactions? Is there an option other than lying and deception to those dilemmas of expression that make us face rejection if we do not lie?

The second question is more profound and more difficult to deal with. It is possible to ask the question, but its answer is probably beyond human abilities at the present time. Even though the question cannot be answered, thinking about it leads to new awareness of the nature of social relations — especially an awareness of their nature as dramaturgic creations. Our question, then, is: What is the underlying reality or true nature of a performance?

At one level it is whatever is accepted as dramaturgically realized. This is Goffman's claim. Yet this is an unsatisfactory answer. Such an answer allows the audience to determine social truth or reality. America comes dangerously close to this cop-out as a consequence of its metaphysical reliance on a concept of democracy that makes popularity the arbiter of what is real.

At another level we live with the effects of mass pollings and Nielsen ratings and media-determined decisions concerning matters whose substance lies deeper. If everybody accepts the notion that "peacekeeper" is what our nuclear weapons defensive system really is, then that is what it is. If it is not that, then what else might it possibly be? It is a question that relatively few people struggle with in any consistent fashion.

The question of how social realities are established is at the heart of social philosophy. It is the central concern of the dramaturgic perspective. Indeed, even to have a grasp of the implications of this question, regardless of how it might be answered, is to have a fair comprehension of what social theory is about generally and what, more specifically, dramaturgic theory is about.

Style and Substance in the Nuclear Age

This discussion of dramaturgy and nuclear weapons will close with a consideration of what Goffman called the "symptomatic range of action" and what we shall more lightly refer to as "style." Nothing, at least at first glance, appears to be more substantial and locked into the hard reality of physical force than nuclear weaponry. If we view the world of fashion and fads as being at one end of the substance/style continuum, then surely nuclear devices are at the other. They are unusually substantial objects.

Here is a place, so it would seem, where solid actions are called for and rhetoric is beside the point. At the same time, it is obvious that nuclear weapons are significant to the extent that they represent social and political systems. Social and political systems are, among other things, dramatic systems; that is to say, they rely on dramatic devices of the variety described by Goffman and others to influence and control the actions of their members.

Before continuing, let me add that the topic about to be addressed is amorphous. The essence of dramaturgic theory is that human affairs are ill-defined and people achieve the illusion of definition primarily through theatrics. Dramaturgic theory is, in itself, reliant on terms that are difficult to define in any precise fashion but that, at the same time, are instructive. They have critical value. In this spirit, then, the following discussion is designed to provoke discussion, not delimit it. It is intended to open up new possibilities for discussing the global terrorism that is now a taken-for-granted part of everyday life.

Let us consider, for purposes of illustration, various styles associated with nuclear discourse as well as the pertinent substance or content of such discourse. We shall consider three styles with which most of us are generally familiar: the military, the scientific, and the political. Although there are a variety of other styles relevant to the manner in which nuclear strategies and nuclear weapons are discussed and within which such weapons are embedded, we cannot deal with all of them here.

The military style   The content of military activity is to engage in war. For the normal person, the waging of war—seen up close and in its real forms—is a matter of being brutish, murderous, nasty, and cruel. We vindicate our cruelty, of course, by pointing out that the other fellow is being cruel to us, but the main point is that war is a brutal and grisly embrace between cold-blooded elements. Given the fact people are not generally kindly disposed toward those forms of brutality that are common to war, it is curious how we become so enamored of military forms of conduct.

Perhaps more than any other component of human communal systems, the military reveals the power of style. For it is through military style we come to glorify and ennoble the most despicable and disgusting of human endeavors. The appeal of the military does not lie in its basic functions and its substantive nature. Nothing in the entire spectrum of human actions is more unappealing to the normal, mentally balanced person. The appeal of the military comes out of the extent to which it acquires control over style. No other agency of human communal life is more meticulous in its adherence to stylistic forms.

Another highly stylized agency, of course, is the church. The race is close between the monastic discipline of the more rigorously ritualistic religious systems and the fierce discipline of elite military units. Certainly, when you combine these two forces you get a military-religious community that is marked by unusual zealotry and ultimately the capacity for nearly unlimited cruelty. This was characteristic of the medieval religious crusades — an early case of armies that did not hesitate to slaughter thousands of innocent people. We find it in modern times in the religious-military zealotry of the armies of the religious leaders in Middle Eastern nations.

There is the suggestion, here, that as a group activity becomes more serious (that is, more associated with the mysteries of death and dealing in death), stylistic actions become disciplined and routinized. What is there, for example, in the creased trousers, freshly pressed shirts, badges, medals, billed caps, shined shoes, goose stepping, epaulets, uniforms, parades, drumbeats, swagger stick, insignia, patches, flags, salutes, hazings, visors, boots, traditions, bugle calls, belts, helmets, stripes, plumes, and all the other various accoutrements of the military impression other than a style of presentation? Does one need such things explicitly for the act of fighting?

Evidently not — because in those moments when the military is being military (that is, fighting in combat), style gives way to the functional demands of fighting. Men do not fight in dress uniform. They fight in baggy and ungainly costumes. The parade ground and the trenches are two distinctly different worlds. There was a time, of course, when they did fight in dress costumes. The history of the stylistic shift and the reasons for it would be a worthwhile study of the interplay between style and substance in human affairs.

The greater proportion of people, including those who are in the military itself, do not directly see their military organizations in actual combat circumstances. Americans were completely stunned by the televised showing, during the Vietnam War, of a man raising his pistol to the temple of a captive (whose arms were bound) and then pulling the trigger. It was real violence and real death under pitiless circumstances. The film clip offered an insight into the discrepancy between the substance and the style of military roles. That this film is still occasionally shown today is further indication of the revulsion the incident created.

The general public does not see military organizations in combat circumstances. At best they see reenactments in popular films that somehow always seem to romanticize the subject of cruelty and blood. Reality is reality; theatre is theatre. They see military units, instead, when they are literally "paraded" before the members of those communities for which they fight. It is in the parade or dress mode version of the military that public discussions of the role and place of nuclear weapons takes place.

On occasion the military carries its stylistic pretensions into total absurdity. I am now thinking of a current Marine Corps film inducement for enlistment being shown in local movie houses. It shows a young knight on a white horse carrying a lance riding into the great hall of King Arthur's court. Lightning flashes around King Arthur as he takes his magical electric sword and touches it to the shoulders of the knight. The crowd in the castle is awed. Then, somehow, the sword turns into the dress sword of a modern Marine and we are told that the Marines are looking for a few good men. A veteran Marine, I like to think, would laugh at this or perhaps throw up in disgust. At the same time, I would not bet good money on it.

As I said earlier, the intent of this section is to initiate debate and argument, not to close it. It was argued that the context within which discussions of nuclear weapons take place is one permeated by stylistic irrationalities. In this instance, the bearing and uniforms, the slogans and insignia pertaining to loyalty and duty gloss over the deeper implications of nuclear weapons.

To make the argument all too simple, but at least to outline its general form, the military incorporation of nuclear devices brings such devices within the traditions of the military establishment. The "bomb" then becomes, and is treated as, merely another weapon to be used in the quest for military glory. If it is not on parade, the devices that deliver it — missiles and bombers, sleek and "dramatically" painted — are.

It is in this reduction of weapons to the service of the parade that we must be careful we do not come to view nuclear weapons as just another part of a communal celebration of a society's war-making forces. If we do so, we become blinded to the reality before us. We lose our sense of horror as we become caught up in what amounts, finally, to little more than military tinsel.

To diminish our continuing reliance on these weapons calls for an examination of how such weapons are sustained by the "style" of military operations as well as an examination of the extent to which such weapons are tactically feasible. In other words, we should consider how much our inclination to continue producing and deploying these weapons is a concession to the demands of military tradition and the imperatives of what I have referred to as the "military style" as well as the demands of tactical nuclear strategy itself.

Science as style Nuclear weapons are military devices, and they are also the creation of modern science. People rely not only on military experts but also on scientists for help in understanding the nature and use of nuclear weapons. The style of the scientist differs from that of the military. Where militarists seek to convey loyalty, duty, and aggressiveness as an impression, the scientist seeks to convey certainty, understanding, and dedication to pure science. The strange thing about facts, even physical facts, is that they acquire different qualities depending on the contexts within which they are presented.

There is a sense in which a purely scientific description of the destructive and lethal powers of a major tactical nuclear device appeals more to our intellectual curiosity than to our sense of horror. It is one thing to be given information about nuclear weapons by someone wearing a lab smock and carrying a clipboard and something else to be told the same thing by someone wearing a clerical collar and carrying a Bible. It is yet something different when told by someone who survived a nuclear attack.

So it is that when we are told by scientists that a single nuclear weapon can destroy a city the size of Los Angeles and kill, maim, and blind several million people within a matter of seconds, we listen. But we listen in much the same fashion we might listen to a lecture on eccentricities in the orbit of Pluto. The style of the presentation moves nuclear weaponry into a realm of scientific detachment and rationality. The bomb exists, but scientists, *as scientists*, wash their hands of any moralizing or sense of horror over their creation.

I once experienced a chance meeting with a physicist who left his teaching position for a high-paying military research program. I registered my disappointment over his decision and chided him for joining with those who had already placed the world in enough peril. His reply was unforgettable and informative from a dramaturgic point of view. "Oh," he replied, "you are not talking about me. You are talking about those technicians." In other words, the blame was on the shoulders of mere technicians. His preferred reference group, with respect to style, was that of the pure scientist — detached, factual, and dedicated to understanding the mysteries of nature.

There are, of course, scientists who give their energies and time to the cause of informing the world about the perils of nuclear confrontations. The more effective forms of this occur in instances where the scientist steps outside his or her role as a scientist and accepts the fact that here is a problem that cannot be effectively described, for purposes of social reform, in purely scientific terminology.

Though there are "good" scientists, it is, nonetheless, in the style of science to disparage and "pooh-pooh" any kind of attempt to suggest through literary devices that nuclear weapons are doomsday devices. The work of Jonathan Schell, for example, was referred to as "laughable" by one scientist because it toyed with the theme of extinction of all life as a possible consequence of a devastating unleashing of the world's nuclear forces.

The style of science is "cool." Emotionality and irrationality are anathema to the scientific code. Science is a powerful, though not dominant, institutional complex within Western culture. Consequently, the cool mentality prevails in decisions of importance. And so we are encouraged to remain cool about the missiles and the weapons ranged around the world. Science will handle whatever science creates. It is merely a matter of amassing more facts and technology—there is little need to get emotional about anything.

It is, at times, an exasperating stance for those of us who are aware that the picture is sufficiently well defined to call not for more facts but rather for moral action grounded in strong emotions and a sense of commitment to the survival of humankind.

Modern political style   Finally, in discussing style and the nuclear problem, we turn to politics. Politics, within Western culture, is becoming increasingly dramatized. Much has been made of the "imaging" of presidential candidates and the use of Madison Avenue advertising agencies as "packagers" of political personae. So powerful are the dictates of style that political leaders of both liberal and conservative persuasion rely on basically the same persuasive techniques. That is to say, during a typical campaign it is difficult to tell Republicans and Democrats from one another by how they look, how they are dressed, and the perpetual smiles on their faces.

Above all, in American politics particularly, the smile is now symptomatic of nearly everything good. It informs a political audience that the candidate is in control, is at ease, is not tired, has nothing to hide, is not worried, is likeable, cares for people, and is optimistic about things—the economy is in good hands and will grow. American audiences do not like scowlers or people who are willing to concede that the times might be ambiguous. The leader should define things clearly. It is not as important that things be defined correctly as that they be defined.

The consequence has been a legion of smiling candidates grinning in front of television cameras with a "What, me worry?" look intended to captivate the hearts and minds of millions. I know of few, if any, candidates who ever appeared before any large American political audience and, with an intensely worried look, said something to the effect that nuclear weapons are dangerous and possibly out of control. (I recall, a few years ago, a speech by a member of the United Nations in which he told his audience it was no longer a problem of who would push the button that would unleash nuclear weapons on the world. The problem, he said, is whether the button will eventually push itself.)

American political style is upbeat. People want to hear good news, and good news is what politicians bring to their constituents. One consequence of this is that very little ever appears in the conventional American press concerning the day-to-day status of nuclear weapons and the nuclear threat. The matter is kept from the public, and the question arises as to why.

The answer, from a dramaturgic perspective, is that it is simply good political theatre. That is to say, the American public does not want to hear, on a day-in-and-day-out basis, that nuclear missiles threaten their existence. Politicians exist to accommodate the wishes of the public.

Political style says as much about the American public as it does about the politicians who appear before that public. Americans want their politicians looking like good salesmen — wearing a shoe shine and a smile as they cover the territory. A politician who cries in public, no matter how justified his or her rage, grief, or pure frustration might be — no matter how authentic the inner sentiment — is dead in the water.

What, then, can the public expect with respect to political statements concerning nuclear crisis? The answer would seem to be that we can expect the same thing we have been getting: bland and evasive commentary, a bit of joking, banalities, and little provocative content — style and no substance. The ghost of John Wayne permeates the American ethos and its public personification, while political realities go their way in secret war rooms, the brief-laden and complex tangles of corporate executive offices, and the intricacies of higher administration.

On this note it is time to conclude this introduction to dramaturgic theory. Our consideration of this perspective and its application to the issue of nuclear weapons was on the acerbic side of things. The dramaturgic approach is not always a flattering one. And, like every other social theory or perspective currently popular in academic circles, dramaturgy certainly does not possess all of the answers. Even so, it is in the search to uncover its strengths and weaknesses that we find out more about ourselves and become better informed about why we do the things we do. If this introduction encourages such a search, then it has served its purpose.

Chapter 10

Symbols and Sacrifice:
The Place of Language
in Human Conflicts

THE DRAMATURGY OF KENNETH BURKE

As with Chapter 8, which discussed the work of Harold Garfinkel, I once again need to warn you that the following material, based on the writing of Kenneth Burke, is different from nearly anything else commonly associated with Western social science theory. Because it is different and because it runs against popularly established points of view, it does not always make for easy reading. In addition, it suffers from an even more serious problem: Burke is not generally recognized as a sociologist. However, because dramatism is a sociological point of view now enjoying considerable acceptance, I elected to introduce Burke along with the other theorists discussed in this book. My reason for doing so is, I am convinced, a solid one. Burke is the most subtle and ingenious of those who can be listed as dramatistic philosophers. Though Goffman popularized dramaturgic theory, Burke gave it its fullest and deepest expression. Small wonder that one sociologist referred to him as "the master."[1]

The perspective we are now going to examine is, then, similar in some ways to the material covered in Chapter 9 on Goffman's approach to dramaturgy. It considers the extent to which drama gives form to our social lives. Unlike Goffman's treatment of drama, however, Burke deals not only with what drama is (an exasperatingly difficult issue, by the way), but also with the question of *why* drama is a uniquely human indulgence. If we accept the argument that we are driven by a kind of dramatic imperative, then we should ask why this is so. What makes us vulnerable to the dramatic moment? We also need to think about the consequences of being "hooked" on drama.

The finest examination of these matters can be found in the writings of an American literary critic–philosopher named Kenneth Burke.[2] Burke is an unusually wide-ranging and penetrating interpreter of human affairs. Without doubt, he is one of America's greatest contemporary thinkers in the realm of the humanities and in social philosophy.

Let me take a paragraph or two to distinguish between the perspectives presented in the last three chapters. Garfinkel is concerned primarily with the problem of the subjective in human relations and what the subjective problem forces us to do. Ultimately the subjective problem leads us to a state where we must contend with appearances rather than reality. Goffman is concerned with the problem of how the social moment is created. He, like Garfinkel, accepts the argument that life, for human beings, is largely a matter of appearances. However, his work differs from Garfinkel's by its emphasis on the devices we use to sustain appearances. Burke is concerned with the problem of language. What does language force us to do?

The three writers come to similar conclusions. People, they argue, must live in a world where the appearance of knowing is as much a part of human affairs as is true awareness. However, they reach this conclusion by quite different routes. Garfinkel places people in peculiar situations and watches as they wiggle their way out. They generally manage to find a way. For Garfinkel, the individual human being is capable of endowing reality with extra qualities by virtue of possessing a rich, but hidden, subjective ability. The primary focus in Garfinkel's work is on the subjective aspect of being human. Goffman observed people in their natural day-to-day lives and saw that they use various "deceptive" devices to maintain images or control the impressions they want to convey to others. His work is largely a cataloguing of the techniques people use to carry off a social act. Burke turns to language as a problem. His conclusions are based on observations of the literary forms people draw on to persuade each other about how they should conduct themselves. Burke's question is: What are the consequences of being a language-using being? *What does language force us to do*? It forces us, he argues, into irrational postures; and there is no way out. One major difference between Burke and the other two writers is worth mentioning here. Burke sees language as forcing us into severely conflicting relationships. This aspect of the human condition is lightly touched on or ignored in the writings of Garfinkel and Goffman.

Reading Burke is not easy. (Several of my colleagues tried and eventually gave up in despair.) As he said himself in a recent lecture at the University of Colorado, "I still read my own stuff, but I can only take a little bit of it at a time." Those in the audience familiar with his books knew what he was talking about. His philosophical works are especially intellectually demanding, but they are worth the effort. With trepidation, then, the following discussion attempts to generate further sociological interest in the writings of Kenneth Burke.

Burke cannot strictly be labeled a social scientist. He is a hybrid, partly a student and critic of literature and partly an astute theorist of communication and the place of literature, *as a form of institution*, in society. His early training was in the humanities. However, it was largely an informal training;

he left Ohio State University after only one year of college. As a freshman at Ohio State he wanted to take advanced courses in literature. The faculty, however, insisted that he take required undergraduate courses. Burke rebelled. He begged his father to let him live in New York and study on his own while working for a literary magazine. His father agreed.

To help pass the time during his brief year as a college student, he translated into English Thomas Mann's *Der Zauberberg — The Magic Mountain*. The translation was published shortly after he left the university — earning him early recognition as a brilliant and precocious student of literature. (In effect, he achieved recognition at a time when, had he remained in college, he would still have been a junior or a senior.)

Although Burke spent the first years of his career as a literary and music critic, he later became interested in the relationship between literature and day-to-day life. The ideas he developed as a result of this interest led to his recognition as a major figure in the fields of philosophy and communications. Burke's writing also influenced such contemporary social theorists as Erving Goffman and Hugh Dalziel Duncan.[3]

Those familiar with even a few pages from Burke's major works know it is impossible, within the confines of a short essay, to capture the depth, richness, and variety of his approach to human cultures and human actions. It will be sufficient here to offer a general sense of his vision and perhaps stimulate a few readers to begin a more serious examination of his ideas.

THE SOCIOLOGICAL QUEST FOR RELIABLE AXIOMS

To get started, we can turn to a general observation concerning the natural sciences. Characteristically, natural science moves from exceedingly simple into exceedingly complex arguments. The beginning points of science are almost idiotically simple, and there is a reason why. The idea is to produce axioms so straightforward that they cannot be readily disputed. Science begins with consensus.

The quest for simplicity in science comes out of the desire to establish arguments so elementary that they must be accepted by anyone who hears them. Once such understanding is created, it becomes the basis for more elaborate arguments that, given such solid support, are in themselves substantial and difficult to refute. New knowledge that threatens the integrity of the fundamental principles in natural science is revolutionary. Any finding in natural science that challenges its basic foundations is important. The Einsteinian revolution in physics was significant because, in part, it challenged the self-evident notion that energy and matter are somehow fundamentally different. Einstein demonstrated they are not — they are equivalent.

However, we are not interested in the natural sciences except insofar as they inform us about the social sciences. Our primary interest, as social scientists, is in working toward a naturalistic, coherent understanding of human communal life — the same interest the natural scientist brings to the workings of physical and organic nature. We would like to reach a set of understandings capable of winning the same degree of general acceptance as those developed in the natural sciences. One way to begin, then, might be to establish a basic argument for the social sciences so simple in its claim that it would have to be accepted by virtually any reasonable person. Once such a foundation is established, further arguments might be built upon it.

Now, we must move on to the tough part. It is apparently impossible to establish a simple axiomatic argument regarding the *social life* of human beings. Though it sounds like an easy enough assignment, it definitely is not. (I occasionally offer my students an A+ for the course if they can come up with a pure, noncircular, sociological proposition that is incontrovertible.) In fact, no one I know of has ever managed to solve the problem. Any statement, no matter how simple or apparently incontrovertible, that we might make about *social* actions can be contradicted about as reasonably as it can be asserted.

Here are several examples of simple statements that seem obvious and beyond contradiction.

1. All human sociocultural systems have religious institutions.
2. People gain their primary emotional gratification from intimate associates.
3. Human characteristics can be acquired only through maturation within a human community.

As simple and reasonable as these statements are, they do not have the argumentative power of basic propositions in mathematics and natural science. Each one can be debated.

There are two primary reasons why statements such as these cannot serve the same function as primary axiomatic statements in the sciences or in mathematics. First of all, they permit exceptions. Second, and this is where we begin our introduction to Burke's thinking, it is difficult to define the terms being used in the propositions in any precisely definitive manner. This second weakness leads us into Burke's view of human affairs and human institutions.

Consider the limitations of these simple propositions. The first proposition invites a debate concerning the "true" meaning of religion. If, by religion, we mean the establishment of a church, then any number of societies have existed over long periods of time without religion. If we mean something else, we come to a different conclusion. The truthfulness of the proposition obviously hinges on the meaning or the definition we give to the term *religion* — a concept that defies precise definition.

The second proposition also invites a debate concerning the meaning of its terms. What, for example, constitutes "gratification" or "intimacy"? I recall, in this regard, reports to the effect that prostitution flourished in

Victorian England because, presumably, men could not find certain gratifications in the home — supposedly an intimate environment.

The third invites a discussion of what we mean by a "human" being. There are any number of people who grant human qualities to the newly conceived fetus — an organism that has not as yet experienced life in a human community.

No matter how simple a social proposition might be, we can always wrangle over its concepts. Indeed, in real life this is precisely what we do all the time. Young lovers struggle to determine the meaning of true love; scholars struggle over what defines wisdom; everyone struggles with the meaning of terms such as success, femininity-masculinity, morality, violence, superiority, or sanity.

A nice example of an artistic struggle with the meaning of sanity is the film *The King of Hearts* in which the gentle folk inhabiting an asylum for the mentally ill in Europe during World War II are contrasted with the men who are screaming, shooting, and killing each other outside the asylum's walls. Who, the film asks, is mad and who is sane?

SEMANTICS REVISITED

The response to all of this is likely to be: "Well, so what? It sounds like nothing more than playing around with semantics." True enough, it is playing around with semantics. However, we delude ourselves if we think semantics is a trivial part of day-to-day life. Burke suggests that much of our social world and the way we do things is a consequence of problems that are inherent in making language itself work.

The problems of semantics are always with us, and they are always profound. At the same time, we somehow manage to get on with things. We define terms that defy any kind of precise definition. Sometimes we define them with apparent sharpness and certainty. How does this happen?

In the quest for an answer, we begin to discover the ways we manage to dodge and otherwise cope with the semantics of daily life. We also begin to see how societies, in themselves, generate systems at least partly dedicated to making social concepts take on the appearance of well-defined terms.

We can begin to see the radical nature of Burke's thinking by considering the extent to which it turns ordinary conceptions of social life upside down. Consider a particular institution — for example, politics. Traditional thinking about politics assumes politicians come under the influence of a set of ideas (symbolic fantasies, we might say) and they then act in the name of those ideas.

Burke does not deny this. However, he adds a novel twist. The politician must constantly re-create and give a sense of concreteness to the symbolic fantasies that describe human political realities. Political institutions not only come out of older symbolically established traditions but they also exist to give political symbols the appearance of well-defined concepts.

Another way of trying to make this difficult point is to observe that social language is inherently, eternally, essentially, and necessarily confusing. However, as language-using beings we cannot tolerate confusion and ambiguities in language. We attempt to rid language of its confusions as much as possible. One task of large-scale human social institutions is to create the appearance of order and meaning where none inherently exists. Social institutions, from this point of view, stand as grand *rhetorical machines*. (This term is mine, not Burke's.) Institutions, among their other functions, serve the major function of sustaining social language by drawing on a variety of devices ranging from force to trickery.

To make the point all too simply: The church exists to define God — an undefinable essence. The university exists to define wisdom, or, more properly in this modern day and age, expertise. (Wisdom is passé — an archaic term, at best.) Business exists to define economic relations. Politics exists to define government. The courts exist to define justice. The military exists to define security. The social sciences exist to define social language. And so on.

If we are to appreciate Burke, we need to examine the implications of so-called semantic problems. Where the American reaction commonly is to get past or ignore semantic problems as much as possible, they nonetheless are a universal and constant feature of human social relations. We cannot wish them away by ignoring them. After we begin to understand Burke, we come to see that they have implications for everything ranging from individual sanity to international acts of destruction. The confusions of social language merit our serious consideration.

ACTION, RHETORIC, AND OPPOSITION

With this introduction behind us, we can now turn back to the ideas of Kenneth Burke. First of all, his ideas spring from a simple argument: Human actions *always* involve symbols. It is about as simple a proposition as we might turn to as a springboard for understanding human affairs. Although this proposition can be argued and debated, like any of the others we discussed, it is nonetheless simple and reasonable. It is not a wild-eyed notion. It is not complicated. It fits with our commonsense understanding of the world. It does little more than note the fact that people are unique insofar as they possess the ability to manipulate experience through symbols.

He also assumes that the most unassailable simple argument upon which a philosophy of human affairs can be built is that it is impossible to establish an incontrovertible social proposition. Once again, a lot of people would disagree, but it is a fairly strong assumption.

A second major element in Burke's thinking is that *symbols that deal with social reality are different from those that deal with physical reality or purely logical constructions*. Out of this distinction — symbols used for social discourse are not like other symbols — comes an elaborate and radically novel approach to human life.

We have time to consider only three of Burke's primary concerns:

1. The concept of action
2. The concept of rhetoric
3. The idea of opposition

First, we shall consider the concept of social *action* from Burke's point of view. This concept is significant insofar as it stands as a correction to the errors we unconsciously make when we use the more popular term *behavior*. Later in this chapter, I will try to show the strength of the distinction between social *action* and the idea of *behavior* by examining peace and disarmament initiatives from an action perspective.

A second concept central to Burke's writing is the ancient, even slightly archaic, concept of rhetoric. The term *rhetoric* refers simply to the effective use of language. In common thought we think of rhetoric as flowery and seductive oratory. In real life, rhetoric is a day-to-day kind of thing. We use rhetoric any time we are involved with other human beings. We use rhetoric any time we use a social concept. We use rhetoric on ourselves when we are alone! We even try to make inanimate objects bend to our will by rhetorically exhorting them. Swearing at a car that will not start is a good example.

We are rhetorical beings. Rhetoric is part of our nature. The fundamental distinction that exists between human beings and other creatures of this earth is that people are rhetorical and they, so far as I can tell, are not. To anticipate where we are headed, let me add here that Burke takes rhetoric seriously. Where Americans think rhetoric is "empty," Burke sees it as the *fons et origo* of all of human social life. Without rhetoric, we have no human society — either small-scale or large-scale.

Finally, we will consider as a third basic concept from Burke's writings the idea of *opposition*. Once again, the notion being considered is not new. We are all familiar with opposites: Hot is the opposite of cold; hate is the opposite of love; poverty is the opposite of wealth; and high is the opposite of low.

In Western culture we endorse the notion that qualities can be "opposed." *Keep in mind that such qualities as hot and cold are actually not "opposed."* They simply are conditions of temperature, nothing more, nothing less. If oppositional qualities can be ascribed to nonoppositional conditions in the physical world, what happens when we do the same thing with social qualities?

For example, what are the implications of saying white is *the opposite* of black when dealing with racial issues? Or that masculinity is *the opposite* of femininity in dealing with sexist issues? Or that capitalism is *the opposite* of socialism in dealing with world issues? The notion of linguistic opposition opens up a troubled can of worms for human relations.

THE STRUGGLE BETWEEN RATIONAL AND DRAMATIC FORMS

To make Burke salient and to relate his writing to the central problems of our time, I shall use a few of his ideas to focus on the nuclear arms crisis. It is fairly evident that military confrontations and the rattling of weapons are dramatic actions. We had one look at the "drama" of military actions when we drew upon Goffman for interpretive inspiration in the last chapter.

In this chapter we want to probe further. We want to know not only *how* the drama is being enacted but also *why* we have this penchant for dramatic confrontations and dramatic resolutions of human affairs. There is more than a hint in Burke's philosophy that drama exists because it is the only way in which we can resolve what are otherwise impossible semantic problems.

If this is true, consider the overall implications. We rely on dramatic devices to resolve the inherent semantic problems we live with on a day-to-day basis. However, drama is partly an emotionalization of life. Drama also tends toward excess. As we dramatize our lives and our fates we move toward those excesses that are part of the dramatic imperative. In an earlier age, such excesses were tolerable. In this nuclear and highly mechanized age they have a fierce potential.

We must also consider the fact that this is a day and age of communications. We live more completely within symbolic worlds than was the case even a few centuries ago. There is, then, the further implication in Burke's writing that people will continue to move toward an ever more intense dramatization of life — of which nuclear conflict would be the ultimate and final form. I do not mean to imply that nuclear war is a necessary consequence of the dramatization of life (whatever we might mean by this term). However, it is reasonable to observe that nuclear weapons are now contained within a sociocultural matrix that gives great significance to the dramatization of life.

Burke's ideas provide an interesting counterpoint to the arguments of Max Weber. Where, for example, Weber saw Western culture caught up in rationalism and the quest for efficiency, Burke sees a culture involved with the dramatization of life. Where Weber's institutional emphasis was on grand bureaucracies, organized in terms of productivity and the efficient fulfillment of official duties, Burke's emphasis is on the arts, particularly literature and theatre. After gaining an understanding of Burke, one comes away with a more serious respect for what the arts are about as institutional elements of any human culture. They are not merely entertainment or casual, impractical amusements. They are essential to social organization. Most intriguing of all is the extent to which Burke leads us once more to a consideration of the irrational element that permeates the rational forms Weber describes. There is a rational thrust in modern societies, and Weber makes us aware of it. However, Burke argues with great effectiveness that there are limits on reason. Language itself stands as the barrier to any kind of ultimately or totally rationalized human community. No wonder that modern social scientists, dedicated to rational systems of thought, turn away from Burke. (One of my colleagues dismissed Burke with the phrase: "He's a radical obscurantist.")

We gain a sense of the limits of reason when we consider the extent to which our own so-called rational lives are permeated by the arts. We like dramatic politicians and leaders, dramatic performers on the stage, dramatic consumer items, dramatic journalism, dramatic jobs, dramatic play and games (consider the evolution of a once-elitist collegiate sport played on various campuses before small but highly partisan crowds into modern professional football). We prefer dramatic teachers teaching dramatic material. We dramatize our sex lives and feel deprived if sex is only "ordinary." We like our food served in dramatically accoutred restaurants to which we drive in cars sold to us through dramatic images and the rhetoric of power. (Although economists might lead us to think otherwise, the truth of the matter is that we sell commodities in this culture dramatically, not rationally.)

We like dramatic clothing (the punk style is especially amusing in this regard). Our popular musicians play what might be called "dramatic" music (contrast a Gregorian chant — a dramatic form in its own right — with acid rock). Moreover they play their music in what are certainly dramatic costumes under staging that becomes a total parody of the dramatic setting. The dramatic motif, whatever we might mean by such a notion, is solidly interwoven into nearly every aspect of our individual and collective lives.

I mentioned before that drama is difficult, if not impossible, to define. (It is, after all, a social concept.) At the same time, we are all aware of its significance. We must struggle, then, to gain a better comprehension of this aspect of our lives. In this chapter we shall note that whatever drama is, it is directed toward achieving *action*. It does this through various dramatic devices, of which *rhetoric* is possibly the principal form. Finally, it involves *opposition* — either implicit or explicit — as part of the dramatic accomplishment.

THE CONCEPT OF ACTION

In the following discussion we shall hold rather closely to Burke's notion of action. We gain a sense of what is implied by the term *action* by comparing it with the concept of *behavior*. When an organism makes an adaptive adjustment or response to its milieu and/or its own internal organic state, it is behaving. A rat moving through a maze in a psychology laboratory is behaving; a dog barking at a cat is behaving; or a cow munching hay is behaving.

Basically, such behavior is a matter of motions. When a creature engages in motions, we say it is behaving. When it is not making any discernible motions, it is not behaving. Psychology, the field that studies the *behavior* of organisms, is concerned primarily with physical motions — organic physics, if you will.

Now let us consider nearly any motion engaged in by a human being: a woman running through a maze in a psychology laboratory; a man barking at a cat; a teenager munching hay. The motions are exactly the same as those described in the preceding paragraph, but the simple fact that a human being is doing them somehow changes things.

Most significantly, we find the motions, in and of themselves, singularly unsatisfying as a *total* description of what is taking place. The concept of behavior is too limiting. Suppose we discover that the woman running the maze is a graduate student and that if she does not get through the maze her instructor will say she is stupid. The man barking at a cat is convinced the cat is a reincarnation of the devil whose evil presence can be removed only by barking. The teenager munching hay is caught up in a fraternity hazing rite. It should be evident that simply examining the motions people go through in their daily rounds is not going to satisfy us with respect to comprehending what they "really" are doing. The question of what else we want to know about besides pure behavior or motions moves us closer to a sense of what Burke means by human social actions.

Burke argues that there are five elements contained in any social action. We must know or presume something about each of these elements if we are to comprehend the nature of the act in its fullest sense. The fact that five elements of action appear to be the lowest fundamental reduction we can make leaves us with an awareness that actions are more complex than behaviors. The five things required in any action are:

1. *Someone doing the action.* This is as obvious as you can get. However, the character of an *action* changes as the person performing it changes. For example, I watched a sailplane landing at a local glider port a few weeks before I began this chapter on Burke. The sailplane came smartly to a stop within a foot of its bay. The canopy opened and the solo pilot stepped out — a young, attractive wisp of a girl. It altered my notion of the *action* of flying sailplanes.

   This is a simple yet powerful insight for it suggests that we have stereotyped notions of what constitutes a proper action. (I shall confess here that I had stereotyped the act of flying a sailplane as a semisuicidal practice intended for macho males. I was, of course, all wet.) The point is that *we stereotype not only individuals and groups, but social forms as well.* Stereotypical forms are to be carried out by the proper people in the proper manner in the proper place.

   Violations of our stereotyped conceptions of an *action* are disturbing, and we reject the action as a whole because it was not carried out properly. Such stereotyping might ultimately be far more serious in its social implications than the stereotyping of individuals and groups. Indeed, there is the suggestion here that the stereotyping of individuals and groups is a consequence of the stereotyping of action forms.

2. *What is done.* What is being done can be simple behaviors of one kind or another — running, eating, belching, jumping, pounding with a hammer, sitting, climbing, and so forth. It can also be symbolic action — talking, persuading, singing, posing, gesturing, and so on. If the other four features of action are held constant, then an action varies according to whatever is being done.

3. *The context.* Context refers to the setting or the staging within which an action takes place. The same behaviors or acts carried out by the same individuals can be given different values or qualities simply by changing the context in which the actions occur. Taking off your clothes to change into swimming briefs on a hot crowded beach, while possibly creating trouble for you, will not create as much trouble as if you were to do the same thing in the main study hall of the campus library at noon. As we continue, note that Burke is trying to convey a sense of the richness of human actions and bring us back to an awareness that behavior is only one component of human action.

   Setting or context is important, of course, in establishing the propriety of action — that is, in bringing it into conformity with our stereotypical conceptions of its proper enactment. A young man inviting a woman into his quarters with amorous intent "sets the mood." That is to say, he creates a context for action. This context is so stereotyped in our culture that it is not necessary to describe it.

   In theatre the power of setting is revealed in moments when the scenery literally acts along with the performers. Gothic mystery films, for example, heighten the moment when the murder occurs with a flash of lightning and the rumble of thunder. The scenery "acts" along with everybody else. It is an artistic concession to the power of setting as an element of action. In real life great wealth is expended to create appropriate settings for desired social effects — richly paneled boardrooms, grand ballrooms, royal gardens, palaces, and so on.

4. *The agency.* By the agency of an action Burke refers to the means or the devices whereby an action is carried out. In the name of what agency do we do the things we do? When an actor can draw on an institutional affiliation as the agency of the act, the action is different from those carried out in the name of or by means of individual efforts.

   For example, if a robber kills a man during a robbery, the individual is the agency. If the same act is carried out, but the person engaging in the action is doing so in the name of national defense, the agency becomes the government. The government is the means whereby or through which the action is performed. Precisely the same act, the killing of a human being, acquires a different character according to the agency in whose name the act is performed.

In literature and the theatre, playing with the theme of "hidden agencies" is common. The primordial form of this is the story in which the heroine discovers she is not a lowly kitchen maid but a princess. Her actions are transformed as her audience comprehends that she is a different person who represents different interests or agencies.

5. *The purpose underlying the action*. In discussing purpose, Burke considers an issue that is also of significance to social scientists such as Garfinkel (Chapter 8). I want to emphasize this aspect of human social action because it is important. An action engaged in by any human being cannot be completely defined, as an action, until the purpose underlying the action is established.

Occasionally one encounters the argument that you do not need language to know a hostile dog is going to bite you in the leg and you do not need to worry about the dog's intent or purpose. Again, we need to call on the distinction between behavior and action to deal with this confusion. The dog is behaving and behavior does not, by definition, require the ascription of purpose. However, if a human being acts as though he or she is going to bite you in the leg, you might need to think about whether the intent was to initiate a love scene or a battle.

American criminal law makes much of the intent behind an action. After all, it is one thing to injure a person accidentally and another to do so because you wanted her job. The establishment of intent cannot be done through direct observation. We must always infer intent or come at it indirectly. We cannot directly "see" or "sense" another person's purpose.

Human actions, then, involve an actor, an action, an agency, a setting, and a purpose. A change in any single element changes the nature of the action as a whole. This fivefold approach to social action offers a deeper sense of how complex human actions are in contrast to simple behavior. As we deal with this complexity we again become aware of the problems confronting us when we deal with the nuclear arms issue. Actions taken by any nation-state or representatives of those states are not simply behaviors that can be managed in terms of stimulus and response mechanisms. Nuclear matters are embedded in social actions, and we gain further insight into their nature by remaining aware of this fact.

Peace Initiatives from an Action Perspective

This section is devoted to showing how a particular kind of event — peace and disarmament talks — displays internal incongruities when we look at it as a form of social action. We begin with the effect on such actions that results from the character of the person engaged in the action. For example, politicians are generally aware that two different people can initiate precisely the same policy and that in one instance it will be rejected and in the other accepted.

A case in point is President Nixon's announcement in July, 1971 of his intention to visit Red China. His record as an enemy of communism in any form made it possible for him to visit China without being accused of being soft on communism. The same conciliatory gesture, at that time, from someone less noted as an anticommunist in the United States would likely have been greeted differently.

If this is so, we can perceive constraints on the peace process. Effective overtures to peace cannot be initiated by anyone at any time and have the same consequences. The question then becomes: Who has the power to bring peace to the world? Are our world leaders really in a position where they can accomplish this generally desired end? What kinds of constraints are placed on individuals who seek to gain peace through making peaceful rather than warlike gestures?

If this interpretation of the Nixon visit to China has any merit at all, it suggests that, paradoxically, the people best capable of engaging in potentially effective peace overtures are those who have the strongest records as bellicose leaders. Those whose reputations establish them as conciliatory figures are not so likely to be considered "strong" leaders when they try to establish peaceful relations. We are led into the implicit oxymoron that the best people for creating peace are those who are not peaceful. For this reason even conciliatory leaders must maintain a bellicose posture. In the 1988 campaign for the presidential nomination, for example, the Democrats, as well as the Republicans, felt obligated to maintain a strong belligerent posture toward those nations defined as enemies.

Continuing with Burke's concept of action, we need to consider next the context or setting in which peace talks are carried out. We can presume that peace initiatives would be particularly enhanced in settings that convey a sense of peace — one imagines a remote, neutral, serene, and quiet monastery as the appropriate setting. Nations, however, commonly conduct peace negotiations in halls of power. The setting itself conveys a sense not of peace but of a challenge for status dominance. At times, concern over the appropriate setting and its arrangement can become an index of the extent to which any kind of accord is likely to be achieved. Attempts to achieve peace during the Korean War were interrupted for extensive periods of time as the negotiating parties wrangled over seating arrangements at the peace table.

In my opinion, the finest recommendation for an appropriate setting for peace negotiations on a global scale was made by Jacob Bronowski, who was among the first to see what was left of Hiroshima after it was wiped out by a nuclear blast. At the time, discussions were under way with respect to locating the building to house the newly organized United Nations. Bronowski suggested that the United Nations building be placed at the epicenter, the point where the atomic weapon exploded, in Hiroshima.[4] The ruins would have been left intact. Bronowski envisioned a building designed so that any room would have at least one window looking out on the desolation. United Nations delegates would, every instant of the day, be reminded by the setting of what their deliberations were about.

The idea was turned down as impractical (truly practical ideas are commonly rejected as impractical) and, as we all know, the United Nations building was erected in one of the more hectic cities of the world—New York. Bronowski's recommendation showed great sensitivity to the power of setting as an element of effective and affective action. The rejection of his idea showed little sensitivity on the part of those who rejected it. Then putting the building in New York, of all places, showed still further lack of sensitivity.

However, there are cases where the quest for peace leads to reasonable considerations of what constitutes an appropriate setting. This occurs when the primary concern is to find a neutral territory in order to avoid the distortions created by settings established on the other side. The use of Geneva as a setting for numerous peace talks in recent years, along with the partial successes of the Camp David talks, suggest that people are generally aware of the significance of setting in working toward peace.

When we move into the question of the "agency" in peace initiatives, we are faced with a difficult problem. Peace must be established between nation-states with conflicting interests. Any peace initiative that attempts to bypass the nation-state as agency amounts to much the same sort of thing as a declaration of war in which the agency is a small town in Nebraska—it makes little sense. At the same time, it is the nation-state, through its leadership, that defines conflicting interests with enemy states. To expect the leadership of nations to be the overseers of peace is not too different, perhaps, from expecting the fox to be the overseer of pleasantries in the henhouse.

More importantly, we need to consider the question of whether effective peace agencies exist—we know effective war agencies exist. There are a variety of popular peace movements, ranging from people who quilt for peace to organizations whose members sit on railroad tracks in front of trains carrying nuclear weapons. We should applaud such work, and I am open in my admiration of those involved in it. However, in no instance are overt populist peace actions operating through the device of a truly powerful agency.

The outstanding possible exception I know of is the Peace Corps, a federally supported program of volunteer assistance to participating countries. The Peace Corps is a fine idea. It is recommended for those who are adventurous and idealistic. However, in terms of the attainment of global peace, it has a major failing. Peace Corps programs operate within countries where peaceful relations already exist. In a way, the Peace Corps program offers a sense of doing something toward peaceful relations while not actually achieving any great effect where it is desperately needed.

The most powerful agency through which an individual or group can act is that agency which represents the collective as a whole — in effect, the government. However, the government does not support peace programs with the same vigor it supports military programs. In sum, the government leaves the issue of peace primarily in the hands of the military, an agency sanctioned to use destructive weapons.

Until governments can recognize the value of peace studies, there is little likelihood the situation will change. The only way such recognition can be brought about is through civil unrest and popular protest. There is evidence that this is taking place, particularly in Europe and Japan, where modest efforts have been made to recognize the concerns of protesters. However, the United States and the Soviet Union, two nations particularly in need of such efforts, remain passive toward supporting peace programs in any serious fashion. Meanwhile, the arsenals continue to develop in sophistication and lethal ability.

We have examined, in a general way, peace actions in terms of those involved in the actions, the settings in which the actions take place, and the agencies through which such actions occur. We are left with the issue of purpose.

This element of human action, as it bears on the nuclear issue, was considered at length in the discussion on ethnomethodology in Chapter 8. There we talked about the problems of arms negotiations and the problem of what is going on in the "mind" of the enemy. Peace talks and disarmament negotiations involve us in the same impossible problem — what is the enemy *really* up to? Because this cannot be established by any known means, we are forced to rely on what we imagine the enemy is up to. The realm of the imagination is also the realm of literature; and, in the final analysis, we create literary images of the enemy that become our political realities. Politics and literature, from Burke's point of view, are never far apart.

The ostensible purpose of peace talks, obviously, is to achieve peace. This catches us up in what eventually proves to be a series of impossible problems. However, peace talks have a variety of other purposes. Although they never — if one interprets the historical record accurately — lead to any certain peace, they nonetheless accomplish other ends.

For example, American presidents certainly use such talks for political "imaging" purposes — a dramaturgic function. Peace talks can serve the purpose of calming a jittery stock market. They make the greater public aware that our leaders are out there struggling to achieve peace in our time. They provide a diversion from the fact that weapons parities are being jealously looked after even as the peace talks are under way.

They may also serve the purpose of lulling those who are naive into a sense of false security. An especially notorious example in current history was Neville Chamberlain's return from a meeting in Berlin just before the outbreak of total war, World War II, in Europe. Upon his return he told his constituents that he actually had achieved "peace in our time." Chamberlain's experience has been used by world leaders ever since as an example of the duplicity of peace talks. We shall probably never again hear another national leader say we "achieved peace in our time" after coming back from peace talks. It is something to think about.

We are concerned, then, with the purpose or motive underlying social action. Within any human social action there lurks the question of the purpose behind it. How do we ascertain purpose? How does it become defined for us? Usually we take the purpose underlying an action for granted. But there are times when purpose suddenly becomes suspect. When do we take purpose for granted? What makes us become suspicious and uncertain of the purpose of an action?

In peace talks the nature of the action itself arouses suspicion. That is, if peace talks are necessary, then it is obvious there are hostile relations between the parties involved. A peace talk confirms the existence of the condition it is designed to overcome. One cannot be against peace talks because they are at least an attempt to correct a bad situation. Such talks, however, are burdened with heavy problems. I keep thinking of that haunting moment when Chamberlain appeared before news cameras proclaiming that peace had been established in Europe and, in so doing, became the 20th century's biggest sucker. No world leader today wants to take Chamberlain's place in holding this dubious distinction.

Peace talks today have no way of establishing goodwill on either side except through extreme measures. So it is that we now read about "verification." Verification is a matter of proving the intent or purpose of the parties involved in the peace accord. Small wonder it is a major sticking point.

At an individual level, imagine that a young man tells his parents he can be trusted not to get in trouble on a date. The parents seek proof. In this act they impugn the son's assertion that he can be trusted. The son, however, seeking to demonstrate he can be trusted permits his parents to engage in verification acts. They elect to go along with him on his date. (As it turns out, during a moment when the parents are not looking, the son cheats.)

Peace talks presume suspicion and mistrust of the purposes of the talk itself. That is to say, neither party is completely willing to accept the idea that the other party is seeking peace. If they were, problems of verification would not be problems. The peace accord would be enacted on the basis of trust. The fact that verification is required to establish the true purpose of the peace action in itself impugns the purpose of the act. It is itself an overt act that makes trust pointless. If both parties trusted each other to begin with, peace talks would not be necessary.

From a Burkean point of view, peace talks appear as dramas staged for the world to demonstrate that "our" side can be trusted, even if the other side cannot. What is difficult to see is how social devices come to deal with issues that arise out of psychologistic matters such as individual subjectivity. For Burke, one of the functions of drama is to generate pseudo-solutions to irresolvable problems — such as the problem of motive or purpose. Peace talks obviously do not solve the problem of trust, but they make "us" seem more trustworthy than "them." At least they give the sense we are trying — though you simply cannot be certain what "they" are up to.

In other words, the avowed purpose underlying peace accords is, in a sense, beside the point. It makes no difference whether the parties involved are sincerely dedicated to the attainment of peace or cynical about the whole thing. The drama can retain the same form in either event and have the same consequences. Because the sincerity of the parties cannot be established and, indeed, the historical precedents for presuming goodwill are not at all heart-warming, peace accords boil down eventually to maintaining power parities already in place.

I have briefly examined, from the perspectives offered by Burke's definition of human *action*, the issue of peace talks as a form of action. We found that such talks are vulnerable to who is conducting them; the agencies through which they are conducted; the settings in which they are conducted; and, finally, the purposes behind the action.

This discussion is intended as an exploratory example of what Burke means by an *action*. More to the point, it is intended to show how a particular theoretical notion can highlight aspects of what is going on around us. It is not intended as any kind of final or definitive commentary on peace talks — the topic is far, far too big for that. Readers interested in this issue should think the matter through on their own and bring their own perspectives and sentiments to bear on the matter. It is one well worth discussing and debating. As is the case throughout this book, my intent is to open debate, not close it.

THE PECULIAR RHETORIC OF THE NUCLEAR AGE

We move into the heart of Burke's ideas with the rather ancient concept of rhetoric. The American people, it appears, are confused about rhetoric. There is the common notion in our culture that "Actions speak louder than words." On the other hand, we are probably the wordiest culture that ever lived — words pour from our journalistic factories, our radios and television sets, magazines, novels, lectures, sermons, churches, schools, books, and dozens of other sources. We carry radios into the wilderness to hear the voices. We listen while we drive, work, play, and — on occasion — sleep. We live in a veritable tropical rain forest of words and symbols. As words and symbols prevail we seem to become less active — the image of the couch potato, listening to and watching a sitcom on television, while idly reading a magazine, looms larger as one stereotype of the American character.

It is Burke's contention that anything so central, so common, so pervasive, and so continuous in our lives is not to be ignored. We survive through language, and languages survive through us. People can be defined as rhetorical creatures. Unfortunately, there are always people who claim their dog or cat or pet gerbil is also rhetorical because it begs for its dinner, bays at the moon, or knows how to scratch at the door to be let out at night. I do not want to argue the matter. If you are willing to accept this as rhetoric, then you should find it easy to accept the argument that people are unusually rhetorical in nature — even if they don't generally scratch at the door to be let out at night.

So much is language a part of our life that we apply it, naturally, to situations where language is inappropriate. Think about sophisticated lab technicians shouting "Go, go, go" as a rocket lifts off, trying, with words, to encourage the missile to fly. The missile, so far as anyone can tell, is deaf to their appeal. This, basically, is Burke's definition of magic — the inappropriate application of symbolic controls. So natural is language to us and so effective in its general utility that we apply it willy-nilly to all kinds of circumstances where it is actually without effect.

Rhetoric is primarily a matter of appeal, and we use rhetoric constantly to get things done. Through rhetoric we are inspired to act, and *through rhetoric our language is simplified for us.* We could not readily use a language that offered itself in its full complexity. Consider the difference, for example, between a philosophical consideration of a concept — let us say, freedom — and the manner in which it is used in political speeches or propaganda designed to inflame people and lead them into action. Those who seek action do not want people thinking too deeply about the meaning of freedom or other complex concepts. Slogans are effective because they shortcut meanings, not because they elaborate them.

Rhetoric, the persuasive use of language, has several functions. It is used to achieve control — to make things happen, to generate action. It is also used to close off endless discussions of what is meant by one social term or another. At some point social descriptions must be closed. Otherwise, we are led into endless regressions in the attempt to close the meaning of even a single simple concept!

Consider the concept *peace* in terms of its rhetorical implications. Rhetorically two problems have to be attended to. First of all, rhetoric is used to create simple definitions or understandings of peaceful states. People do not question the concept — despite the fact that it is a difficult term to define. Second, it is fairly evident that peace is effective as a kind of rhetorical "buzz" word. It is a term that generates action. It is used, ironically enough, as the symbolic agent for actions ranging from killing large populations to sit-ins on nuclear test sites.

One of the tasks of rhetoric is to close off endless questioning. Most of us do not want to be troubled with the matter of examining, thoughtfully and intensely, all of the implications of the concept of peace. We have simple understandings, and they are generally good enough. It seems characteristic of people, in this day and age, to view peace in a negative fashion — it is the nonuse of military devices or armed force to attain social ends. We are at peace if we are not at war.

Such a conception of peace, in and of itself, is a constraint on the attainment of peace because peace is more complex than we are willing to grant. The fact we are "blinded," as it were, to the complexities of peace, can be attributed to how we talk about peace. Peace is a rhetorical term — much like freedom or justice or success. (Success, for example, is viewed in America primarily in materialistic terms — to have money is to be successful. This limited perception exists because the rhetoric of success in America sidesteps the messy issue of the myriad ways in which success can actually be seen. In fact, if you think about it at all, the American success ideal is a rotten notion of success.) In a similar fashion, the rhetoric of peace in our time limits it to military peace.

Peace, seemingly so simple, is nonetheless, like other social concepts, extremely deceptive. For example, I stood at the center of a peaceful scene a few years ago. It was quiet. The air was warm. People were not up in arms. The place was a South American barrio in which people live short, foul, horrible lives in filthy squalor. Children died of malnutrition and dehydration and were buried in shoe boxes. Mothers kept little, faded, cheap photographs of the shrunken corpses lying open-eyed in their tiny cardboard coffins. Was it a peaceful place or not? Is peace different from war simply in terms of the length of time it takes to kill people — slow death is peaceful; violent death is not?

Once again, it is possible only to raise a few questions. We cannot probe far into the vagaries of a concept such as peace. It is a term worthy of an entire library. It is sufficient, here, simply to note that a social term such as *peace* is not easy to define. Social terms are "shaky." At the same time, we have little doubt about their meaning. People do not need to be told what a peaceful society is; nor, on the other hand, do they need to be told what war is. Somehow, social terminology remains well enough defined for us to use. We have a sense of certainty about it, regardless of whether that sense of certainty is justified.

How do we come to know these terms with a strong sense of their specificity? In effect, Burke argues, we acquire a sense of certainty through the artful devices of rhetorical appeal. One of the functions of rhetoric is to close off thinking about what is endlessly thinkable. Our especially powerful rhetorical devices lie within literature. For this reason, Burke looks on literature as something much more profound than merely the fantasies and entertainments provided by storytellers. Stories are energetic forces within any human culture — from the most simple to the most complex. The story-teller is as powerful today as at any other time in history. Literature conveys to us a sense of the meanings of social concepts by drawing on dramatic enactments of their consequences.

Burke forces us to return to a consideration of literature as a functional element within our own society. Keep in mind that, until recently, textbooks in sociology completely ignored literature and the arts as significant elements of society. Where they were not ignored, they were considered primarily to be little more than entertainment or distractions. Puritan rhetoric, Burke might argue, must have been at work to bring about such a major oversight and distortion of reality.

Without doubt the major source of our social knowledge is the story. We derive our stereotypes, our idea of who is an enemy and who is not, how to love and how to hate, what is funny, what is wicked, what to buy, and what to aspire to from stories rather than from experts in the social sciences. We might then ask the question: How do our stories inform us about peace? The question itself reveals the depth of rhetorical force as an element in our own society insofar as a quick answer seems to be that they inform us very little. We, as a society, do not indulge in stories of peace.

There is, of course, religious literature, which is perhaps unique in its dedication to the theme of peace. Even here the concept of peace is tempered. Christian religious practice, though inspired by the "Prince of Peace," has a long history of being bellicose and intolerant and delivering sermons that beseech congregations to smite the enemy hip and thigh. Such literature cannot be said to be entirely pacifistic in its rhetoric. Certainly some of the most bellicose rhetoric I have ever encountered in my half century of listening to people has come from television evangelists. They are not exactly peaceful people. It is not simply that they want to demolish the forces of Satan but that they see so many people as belonging to the legions of wickedness. You get the impression, at times, that they would be willing to annihilate a fair portion of the world's human population—at least that is the direction their rhetoric takes.

Our stories, our literature, our fetish for dramatic action inclines us toward stories of conflict, violence, and opposition. A film that consisted of two hours of unmitigated peaceful activities by peaceful people in peaceful settings enjoying full and serenely peaceful lives would bore American audiences to tears. (A variant form of this observation is the common complaint that newspapers print only stories about violence or disruption. The reply to that is: People don't buy newspapers to read about peaceful things.) One is almost forced to ask: Do we really want peace, or are we just kidding ourselves? What are the real demands of true peace? If we cannot be peaceful in small ways, can we hope to avoid the cataclysm implied in not being able to find peace in large ways?

I have briefly considered peace as a social concept whose problems and complexity are rarely carefully examined. What happens is that we simplify the term, and it is simplified for us in the tales and stories in which it appears as a theme or concept.

Peace, of course, has rhetorical value as an agent for action. It is used like other powerful rhetorical terms—freedom, equality, happiness, progress, triumph, and others—to inspire people to act. Peace becomes a rhetorical agent. We act in the name of peace. If nothing else, Burke makes us aware that any specific act can, at least in theory, be carried out in the name of any purpose. One manifestation of this is found in national rhetoric that, in effect, fulfills the prophecies of George Orwell's *1984* by suggesting that the purpose of war is to achieve peace. Our deadliest weapons are viewed as agents of peace.

There is a mystifying rhetoric in war and the preparation for war that serves the purpose not of enlightening or rationally accounting for things (although it gives this appearance), but rather of making people act. It is one thing to use language to describe and account for things. It is another to use language to generate action among people.

We must conclude then, that when seen from a dramatistic perspective, peace is more a rhetorical than an analytical or descriptive term. It is an aspiration or a dream—a fantasy rather than a reality. When young people are asked what they would want if they could have one wish, they generally say "world peace." I rather like that. It implies that the rhetoric of peace has led to a desire for peace. However, at the same time, has it generated any understanding of the real problems of peace? Would those who say they want peace find a totally peaceful world interesting or, like a pure-peace movie, a tedious bore? Do they really know what they are asking for?

The task of rhetoric is to get people to act by making things look simple and easy. As Burke likes to point out, social language is never as simple as it looks. Through the artful devices of rhetoric, however, what is impossibly complex is transformed into what is simple enough to inspire action.

OPPOSITION

Burke's philosophy begins and ends with the enormous hold upon us of language (or, more correctly, symbols). We must have language to survive as social beings. Where commonsense views of language see it merely as a device for transmitting information, Burke views it as another "environment" within which we live—an environment with properties and demands of its own.

Like physical environments, the symbolic environment has both life-sustaining qualities and those that have lethal implications. To put it yet another way, in addition to the biosphere, we humans also move within what might be termed a symbo-sphere—the cloud of language and symbols that surrounds us all. This symbo-sphere (this term is mine, not Burke's) has its own unique properties and demands to which we, who live within it, must somehow adjust.

Consider, as a starting point, an elemental aspect of language. Any representative symbol (one supposed to represent a quality, condition, event, or action) always implies its opposite. Love implies hate; tall implies short; good implies bad; fast implies slow; "we" implies "them." Keep in mind that, in the real world, conditions, events, actions, and qualities are not opposed — they simply are. Cold, for example, is not "opposed" to hot; these conditions are simply different degrees of molecular or atomic movement. *Opposition, then, is a property of symbols rather than of the world referred to by those symbols.*

The ability of symbols to stand in opposition has implications for those who are forced to rely on those symbols. Symbols refer to events in the real world, and so the real world becomes interpreted through symbols. Because symbols imply opposition, the real world becomes constructed in terms of oppositions. As a consequence, conflict becomes integral to human affairs through the language used to define our affairs.

Marxists — correctly, I happen to think — see human conflict arising out of a struggle for scarce physical resources. Burke sees it coming out of the inherent characteristics of language structures. Immediately we want to know which of the two is correct. (In so doing we reflect the extent to which we think oppositionally.) The correct position, from a Burkean stance, is that both are right. Conflict arises out of several sources. In addition to the struggle for limited economic resources, we have human conflict being further enhanced by the language upon which we depend for survival.

Stories, in their basic structure, provide us with insight into Burke's concerns. The primary nature of dramatic stories is one of opposition. One of the characteristics of dramatic tales is the definition of a social concept (or several concepts) through an enactment in which those who personify the concepts encounter opposition. For example, in a love story we are informed of the meaning or nature of love, a social concept. Love is enacted. The nature of love is revealed in its encounters with forces that would destroy it. The greatest love story in Western culture is the story of Christ's love for the world. The nature of ultimate love, in this instance, is revealed as it stands in contrast to the hate and vileness that culminate in the torture and then the bloody hanging of Christ from a cross.

We can now begin to see the general drift of the argument. Social concepts are defined, so to speak, in stories in which the concepts are "acted out" against opposed concepts. The forces of justice go up against the forces of lawlessness; the lover struggles against being disliked; Luke Skywalker enacts goodness, and Darth Vader enacts the forces of evil.

The more concerned the story becomes with the power of the concept whose meaning it is trying to convey, the more hyperbolized the enactments of the opposed conditions become. For example, a story of a profound and perfect love requires a confrontation with an equally profound and perfected hate. So it is, then, that tales of great heroism call for encounters with hyperbolized evil. Or, to put it another way, you cannot have a super, albeit melodramatic, hero such as James Bond without a super and equally melo-dramatic villain such as Goldfinger.

It is, perhaps, for this reason that we are not interested in stories of peaceful serenity. It is not that we might not like peaceful serenity, but rather that such tales do not inform us of anything. They do not tell us about what we need to know in order to live as social beings. They do not tell us about love, hate, heroism, evil, good and bad, and the myriad abstracted issues that can only be revealed within the context of the story and, equally significantly, can only be resolved there.

The structure of the common stories that shape our lives is basically an oppositional structure. Dramatic action involves opposition. At the same time, dramatic action informs us of the meaning and worth of abstracted social concepts. A limited sense of the validity of this view of common stories can be established by noting how moralistic they are. The ordinary entertainments of television and the mass media are loaded with "sermons" about the nature of good and evil, what is proper and what is not. In a sense, the television screen is a pulpit from which secular sermons pour forth daily in the charming guise of sitcoms, western dramas, soap operas, adventures, and a variety of other forms.

A common theme in stories is the matter of how "we" should conduct ourselves in the presence of "them." In order for the lesson of the story to work, there must be an oppositional relationship between the two categories *we* and *them*. Stories are characteristically the working out of conflicts. When we add the further idea that we want to look good in the story, the logical consequence is that they will have to look bad.

The relevance of this for the study of conflict and issues such as nuclear war in our time is fairly evident. One of the ways in which nations establish their identity is through their national cultures. A major element of any national culture is its literature. Nationalistic literature extols the people within which it is created. (There are, of course, always exceptions. There is, in any modern nation-state, a body of literature highly critical of its leadership. This literature is generally condemned as "subversive." Subversive literature is a fascinating subject, but I cannot pursue it here.)

We now have a kind of literary dynamic in which it becomes inevitable that *they* will be presented negatively in folktales, novels, dramas, and journalistic reporting. Moreover, literature is free to employ any rhetorical devices that might make for a more effective drama or tale. Within a story, the reasons behind the negative qualities of a bad character do not need to be listed in detail. In fact, accounting for why a bad person is bad in any rational fashion weakens the depiction of a character whose nature is designed to elicit our hate or contempt. For this reason, the "bad guys" in melodramas are commonly simply presented as the "bad guys." How they got the way they are is not only beside the point but threatening to the general intent of the dramatic enactment as well.

We see this in typical "shoot 'em up" movies in which the hero beats up the villains who enact current ideas of evil. The reasons behind the villainy are rarely examined in detail. It is sufficient that the villains are villainous and the good guys are good. Indeed, in staged dramatic enactments, any serious probing of how the antagonists, good or bad, acquired their qualities is generally ignored. The play moves along with the characterizations already established. The important thing is the conflict itself, the conflict between the antagonistic principles the characters represent—the forces of good and evil.

If we really understood the underlying forces that led the bad guys to become bad guys, we could not be as emotionally antagonistic to their actions. One of the ends of dramatic enactments is to commit us emotionally to a particular moral position—to close off further argument. However, to portray the evil forces understandably would open up argument. This, by the logic of drama, is not reasonable. It is, after all, the task of drama to close off argument. So, when we watch Dirty Harry blast evil with his oversized pistol, we are given no opportunity to examine further possibilities. We delight in the victory of the forces of good over the forces of evil.

We cannot go very far into the matter here, but it is worth mentioning that dramatization leaves the issue of good and bad essentially to choice. The audience is generally left with the view that the evil forces simply chose their fate and the hero or heroine chose the path of righteousness. Burke makes several astute observations on the concept of choice and volition—viewing choice as a dramatistic necessity. You cannot have drama if the hero was forced to do good and the villain forced to do evil. Unfortunately, I cannot go further into this issue except to point out that as an explanatory principle choice is a pretty lousy concept. As a rhetorical principle it is astonishingly powerful.

The argument, so far, suggests that you cannot have your cake and eat it too. If you follow the dictates of the dramatic imperative, then the world is simplified and emotionalized. It also becomes, in a pathological way, a hell of a lot of fun. If you follow the dictates of reason and wisdom, then you must deal with the world as infinitely complex and endorse a cerebral over a visceral attitude. Explanation becomes a greater concern than does dramatic conflict with its reliance on volition.

A love for wisdom is not as easily acquired as the childish love we all have for drama. However, if the dramatic imperative is driving us toward greater levels of emotionality and conflict, then, to the extent we recognize this as a problem, the solution would seem to be to cool it. However, drama is powerfully addicting and for good reason—it is rooted directly in the language we are all forced to use.

Although the dramatic approach to the problems of good and evil generates engaging drama, it makes for deadly international relations. When stories of "we" versus "them" are told in which we are the people of the United States and they become the people of the Soviet Union, morality is simplified to a dangerous degree. The "logic" of opposition in literature and drama places the other side in a position where it must represent a morality contrary to our own. The reasons underlying this opposition do not need to be examined in any great detail; the story is sustained by virtue of the fact that opposition is a property of the language itself.

As a consequence, we rarely examine the vast and grinding forces lying behind the industrialization of nearly any major modern state. The industrialization of western Europe took place at the cost of great and massive suffering. The United States went through a period where differences between labor and slavery were minimal. We still "trash" great numbers of men and women who are unfortunate enough to be in the wrong job at the wrong time. The Soviet Union fares little better in its attempts to industrialize its people. However, given the nature of opposition, the suffering we went through is rhetorically sanctified while the suffering they experience is cause for condemnation. Such is the "magic" of social language.

There are other examples, of course. Few people outside of Germany today have any real comprehension of why Germany became the nasty and astonishingly well-organized military state of the Nazi era. Part of the reasons was the impossible set of circumstances Germany was forced into as a result of the demeaning surrender terms that followed World War I. However, such is our natural affection for dramatics that we much prefer a dramatic presentation of the Nazis as pure evil over a more reasoned examination of what happened and what might be learned from the lessons of history. The German people, we like to think, "chose" their fate. It is a dramatic rather than a rational way of looking at human affairs.

The Love of Sacrifice

In morality tales and plays, opposition takes the form of good triumphing over evil. The most dramatic form of triumph, of course, requires killing those who represent the forces of evil. The representatives of evil concepts must be destroyed. Those who are witless enough to endorse the wrong social categories are sacrificed.

This chapter concludes, then, with a brief commentary on the practice of sacrifice in literature, its endless appeal as a literary theme, its presence in real life, and its dangerous implications in a day and age when people can be sacrificed by the millions in vast atomic bonfires merely by pressing a button.

The common view of sacrifice is that it is a relatively extinct ritual practiced among older and more superstitious societies, that it is no longer a part of modern civilized living. If we think of sacrifice in terms of images of ancient priests tearing the living hearts out of ritualistic victims, then the common view is correct. Such activities, as public rituals, would not be tolerated in the most backward of modern nations. Of course, in hidden rooms in country villages and remote gray-walled prisons, something not all that different takes place in the most sophisticated of societies.

If we think of societies as systems within which the forces of symbolic opposition are at work, we begin to see the presence of sacrifice in more elaborate and more subtle terms. We sacrifice people today in the name of secular social concepts rather than in the name of gods. Our stories are stories of heroes "trashing" the unworthy. We accept the idea, in our common literature, that those who accept ways that are wrong are those who deserve to die. In common stories this theme appears over and over and over.

Perhaps the difficulty with the idea of sacrifice is that we tend to see it in terms of older primitive rituals—the masked priest plunging a stone-age knife into the breast of a sacrificial virgin tied to a pagan altar. But sacrifice, like any other social idea, has many forms. Sacrifice can be slow and indirect and can involve millions of people. It can be carried out by clean-cut bureaucrats wearing white lab coats. It can be unwitting. The outcome, however, is always the same—social principles are paid for with human life and suffering.

My own favorite and modest little example of a mild form of "sacrifice" is the habit of American educational systems—particularly higher education systems—to set up courses so that a given proportion of people are forced to experience failure. (I have encountered several deans who formally demanded, in threatening terms, that I fail students—even if they were good!) Those who succeed in the American university do so by means of a system that forces failure on those who do not conform immediately. We call our sacrificial victims "losers." They do not, of course, always die quick deaths.

I am attempting here to raise the question of what constitutes the nature of sacrifice along with the question of the extent to which people still practice, in different ways and less formally, the ancient rituals of imposing pain on the undeserving. More importantly, I am interested here in examining what lies behind our eagerness to destroy others who do not conform to our principles—our eagerness to destroy them symbolically or physically. If we can come to a deeper understanding of this matter, perhaps we can also understand why we engage in war—for war is a form of sacrifice.

Among other things, Burke offers us a thoughtful speculation on the practice of sacrifice. Pared down to its barest form, Burke's argument consists of the following basic steps. (1) We are contained within languages. (2) The inherent structure of language is such that social terms are not the same as logical or physically descriptive terms. (3) Social terms are created primarily through stories. (4) Stories present social concepts in terms of opposition. (5) Out of opposition comes the dramatic enactment of social values. (6) One element of drama is sacrifice. (Keep in mind that this distillation of Burke's views encompasses a dozen or so major books. It is hardly definitive.)

We saw that stories attempt to define social concepts through enactments in which fictional or real people act out the implications of different kinds of social identities or concepts: the fool, the hero, the villain, the innocent, the exploiter, the ruthless tyrant, the scholar, and so on. Stories, however, do more than simply define social terms. They also are designed to promote action with respect to these terms. We are expected to fight crime, not simply recognize it. We are expected to be brave and heroic, not simply observe these qualities in others.

We begin to see the nature of rhetoric when we observe the problems social scientists have with respect to creating "objective" social knowledge. (The idea of objective *social* data is actually a contradiction in terms.) for example, if a social scientist discovers that the typical adult American loves TV football, the implication is that if you do not love TV football you are not a typical American. Being atypical has social implications. There is a rhetorical appeal in the social scientist's fact that says: You should love TV football if you want to be normal — and you do want to be normal, don't you? In other words, *any fact placed within an action context acquires action implications.*

Stories are designed, by their very nature, to have action implications. This commonly occurs through the device of having the hero or heroine triumph over villainy. American films and stories rarely present a case in which true villainy triumphs over primary social values. Because the form of the story is oppositional, the superhero requires a supervillain and the story ends in the "super-triumph" of the hero. The person playing the role of the bad guy is sacrificed.

I can only briefly touch on the implications of this for international relations. International relations, at least as they are commonly presented to the American public (and this holds for other countries as well), take on the character of melodramatic confrontations. The American public is not interested in global dynamics in which economic, cultural, political, religious, linguistic, and ethical differences are interwoven in complex ways. Instead, it is drawn to depictions of confrontations between superpowers that take the form of globally staged dramatic entertainments.

As a consequence, we move toward a form of leadership that offers itself as the embodiment of stereotypical forms of heroic action. We are enamored of the John Wayne approach to dealing with problems of evil and alien forms. John Wayne, however, is a purely literary concoction. He is a theatrical form. John Wayne's task was to enact dramas in which he served as a representative of American values. How he carried out this task is instructive — he destroyed whatever he found intolerable. He was a popular priest of vicarious sacrifice.

Obviously, it should not be argued that American foreign policy is decided on the basis of old John Wayne or Sylvester Stallone movies (though strange stories circulated that Mr. Reagan enjoyed *Rambo* movies). However, the resolution of opposition, whether in literature or in human relations, tends to move in the direction of sacrifice. Indeed, from Burke's point of view, it is probably impossible to have a human community, grounded in language as we know it, that does not practice one or another form of sacrifice.

Thus we conclude this discussion of Burke's vision. It is, in the final analysis, the gloomiest of those we have reviewed. It suggests nothing less than that sacrifice and destruction are built into the language systems we must rely on to survive. Peace is an illusion. We must struggle because the words and symbols that are so important, so indispensable, to our lives entangle us and turn us against each other. In the course of the struggle we become dramatic beings seeking heroic moments and looking for the enemy who, in the name of a higher agency, must be killed.

The dramatic imperative forces us on. In earlier times it periodically erupted in the form of collective dramas to which we give such names as the Civil War, World War I, World War II, the Korean War, and the Vietnam War. Today, as we seek still greater dramatic highs, we must wonder—will the final drama see the heroes and the villains mutually destroyed in a final mad scene of mass sacrifice that closes beneath the curtain of a planetary nuclear winter? (In keeping with our discussion of Burke, I should mention that I am using the term *winter* in its morbidly, but *perfectly valid*, rhetorical sense.)

Chapter 11

The Uses of Social and Political Imagination: "Solutions" to the Nuclear Arms Crisis

INTRODUCTION

We now need to bring this consideration of social theory and its relevance to the nuclear arms issue to a close. Each of the perspectives or theories examined in the previous chapters offers lessons to ponder. In most instances, such speculations, at least as I see them, give little initial reason for optimism. Durkheim reveals the binds created by collective representations and the extent to which they intensify human animosities. Weber awakens us to the peculiarities and the potential lethality of the pursuit of rationality in modern social life. Marx presents a picture of human history in which conflict over the means of production and wealth is unceasing.

Mead uncovers a sense of the extent to which our self-identity is threatened by some forms of peaceful overtures. Garfinkel makes us more aware of why national disarmament delegations accomplish so little and do it so slowly — in a period when time is growing ever shorter. After reading Goffman and Burke we begin to comprehend the extent to which the irrationalities of the quest for drama might force us to continue the mad movement toward ever greater and greater weapons systems.

At the same time, positive structural changes are taking place in the world, and we can begin to see these as we gain a better grasp of the theories of Merton and Parsons. These structures, developing largely through modern technologies and the rise of international corporations, are not Utopian structures in any form or fashion. I considered them exclusively in terms of the effect they might have on "welding" nation-states in such a fashion as to diminish the threat of nuclear war. The fact that these corporations are exploitive, unsentimental, brutally competitive, and a serious danger to the environmental resources of the planet is another issue.

A consideration of modern social thought should not incline us toward either pessimism or optimism. As thinking men and women we should be more guarded in our conclusions. Instead of locking into one mood or another, we must keep in mind that theory is speculation — a form of fantasy, if you will. We are not absolutely held to the demands of theory. After all, until just recently, physicists were convinced by their theories that superconductors could not function at temperatures much above zero degrees Kelvin. Their theories were wrong. If physical theories can be wrong, certainly social theories are even more vulnerable to the possibility of error. In the realm of social theory and interpretation nearly anything can happen.

I am not saying that theory should be ignored. The ideas covered in this book are among the best to come out of modern Western social philosophy. They deserve serious consideration. At the same time, the scribblings of social philosophers all too often become museum pieces — enshrined and then accepted as dogma by those who seek belief and security over the risks that are always part of the imaginative and creative mind. These theories provide understandings we could not otherwise reach. Such understandings should never be viewed as the final word on what we are and how our social and institutional systems work. Instead, as I have argued throughout this book, social theory is intended to open up imaginative possibilities — not close them off. Social theory should stimulate the imagination, not stifle it.

This chapter, then, takes up the problem of considering the various ways in which we might put what we have learned to a final imaginative effort. What does all of our study tell us with regard to the one nagging question that now hovers above the human habitations of the world: Is there a "solution" or set of solutions to the nuclear arms crisis?

The nuclear arms crisis is complex — with physical, technological, biological, psychological, cultural, economic, and sociological factors involved. Any kind of solution will obviously be complex. Indeed, the common question "Is there a solution to the nuclear arms crisis?" is in itself misleading. It suggests a singular solution where there is no single solution. Whatever way we find to get out of the mess we are now in will have to involve a major act of the imagination and of human intellectual and emotional commitment. It will have to involve the acceptance of a variety of solutions — all directed toward the common concern.

In this spirit we can now turn to a brief consideration of as many imaginative — some fantastic and some official — solutions to the nuclear weapons crisis as one might reasonably think of and that, at the same time, have a degree of plausibility. Each solution is considered in terms of the extent to which it derives from and is supported, or not supported, by the sociological perspectives that make up the major substance of this book.

It should go without saying these solutions are controversial. A short overview such as this can hardly do any one of them justice. The solutions are offered to generate discussion and further thought. Of course, it would be nice to think that such discussion might, one way or another, help bring the world a few inches closer to the point where future generations would find such weapons less threatening to global survival.

THE DO-NOTHING APPROACH

Because we need to consider all possible ways of dealing with the nuclear arms crisis we must include doing nothing as a form of solution. A character in a *Peanuts* cartoon once said that no problem is so big or so difficult that it cannot be run away from. There is a degree of truth in the observation. The nuclear arms issue is so big that the only way to deal with it seems to be to hide from it. Yet, there is something about running from problems, *Peanuts* notwithstanding, that is unattractive.

Certainly many of us believe there is nothing we can do, so why do anything? (As an aside, I would like to mention that a good sociologist is interested in where such attitudes come from. What kind of communal system creates feelings of helplessness and why might it do so? Which groups in our own society are particularly likely to feel helpless about their future? Who might benefit from having other people believe they are helpless?) This attitude of helplessness is, of course, closely associated with Karl Marx's idea of alienation. To the extent we feel helpless about having any sense of control, we are alienated from our own affairs. Marx considered alienation to be unnatural. Men and women cannot fulfill themselves through their communities if they are alienated from them.

It is tempting to account for a do-nothing attitude by relying simply on sociological theories such as those set forth by Marx or by Durkheim. After all, the social deterministic theories of Durkheim reduce the individual to little more than a helpless atom in the larger social structure. This view of the individual vis-à-vis the community is characteristic of anthropological and sociological thinking.

For example the American anthropologist, Leslie White, a follower of Durkheim, described the individual as merely the conduit or "lightning rod" of cultural forces. The individual, he argued, is helpless against the massive powers of culture. If things are going wrong, he went on, the best thing one can do is try to hide and hope for the best.[1]

Sociologists can find other reasons why the individual acquires a sense of helplessness. Structural-functionalism subordinates the individual to the structural demands of the greater community. Ethnomethodology, from a different angle, comes to the same conclusion — it is characteristic of any society that its members come to take their worlds for granted and not test or question anything ordained as proper by the greater community. Taken-for-grantedness is not the same feeling as helplessness, but its policy consequences are exactly the same.

There are, however, factors other than the ones just mentioned that promote a do-nothing attitude. For one thing, nearly half a century has gone by and, other than the two weapons dropped on Japan in 1945, not one nuclear device has been detonated directly against an enemy by any nation. Keep in mind the fact that 50 years, for the people of the United States, is a long, long time. The nation itself is only a few hundred years old.

Nuclear threat remains constant, but the threats have not, as yet, been backed up with any kind of overt atomic destruction. Throughout the world, this has led to a greater optimism with respect to the future. There may be a growing sentiment that little needs to be done because earlier fears were unjustified. If we were successful in preventing nuclear war for 50 years, then there is little need for further worry. We will manage the next 50, and the 50 that come after that.

The general alarm played on by Stanley Kubrick in the film *Dr. Strangelove: Or, How I Stopped Worrying and Learned to Love the Bomb* (1964) belongs to the past. Doomsday machines, people evidently want to believe, are science fiction, with emphasis on the word *fiction*. The greater the number of years we manage to get by without a nuclear device going off over some unfortunate city, the safer we are. (The truth probably comes closer to being exactly the opposite.) In any event, the fact we managed this long reduces the need to worry. Although people have not come to love the bomb, Kubrick may have put his finger on something—they definitely have become tolerant of it.

This view is supported by polls revealing that between 1981 and 1985 the percent of those believing nuclear war was likely within 10 years dropped from 47 to 29.[2] Lack of concern is also reflected in the fact that out of 30,000 doctorates awarded in the social and behavioral sciences in the United States between 1979 and 1984, only 155 (or about one in every 200) dealt in any fashion with international peace and security.[3] It seems, from the general drift of things, that people not only are not doing much about the problem but that they also feel little needs to be done.

Doing nothing about nuclear weapons means the problem remains with us. The probability of nuclear war remains with us as a real, though indeterminant, probability. We somehow tolerate living in a world in which nuclear roulette is considered a practical way of life. At the same time, modern social and political systems are so complex and varied it becomes absurd to expect people to be involved in all aspects of a community's activities.[4] Alienation, though it has its unnatural qualities, is nonetheless now functionally necessary.

People cannot take a full, active part in all aspects of the community—and this becomes increasingly the case as societies become more complex. What is possible in a simple society is simply impossible in a complex one. Academics are inclined to chastise people for not knowing academic information such as the historical meaning of the year 1066 or the name of the town where John Brown fired up things at the beginning of the American Civil War. However, academic knowledge grows ever more elaborate. Individuals have relatively fixed capacities for knowing things, and knowledge is capable of growing exponentially. Something has to give.

So it is that while academics know one thing, other people know something else—and they generally know a great deal about whatever the something else might be. For example, how many academics know and are capable of controlling the gear system of a semi-tractor, let alone the mechanics of a Boeing 747? How many have specific information on the level of carcinogenic compounds in their tap water? How many can list the names of the popular celebrities their children, almost unanimously, endorse as vitally significant in their lives? Which information, the year 1066 or the gear boxes and carcinogens, is most important in terms of getting the affairs of the community accomplished? (Once again, one should not jump to quick conclusions here—the question is a toughie.)

I do not want to join the raging discussions over cultural ignorance that have become popular in the past few years. I am trying to make a different point—that the elaborate division of labor, resulting in and combined with the fragmentation of modern societies into ever smaller special interest groups, has produced a situation in which massive, popular responses to major social issues are increasingly attenuated.

We might be confronted with what amounts to a dismal paradox in this regard. In the first place, in order for massive responses to develop, the community, in its present form as disparate but well-ordered smaller special interest groups, must be broken up and returned to a more primitive form of cohesion—a form of cohesion Durkheim referred to as a state of mechanical solidarity. Societies held together by mechanical solidarity are those in which common interests prevail—a kind of "birds of a feather stick together" solidarity.

America is held together organically, by large numbers of uniquely different units all functioning in close interdependence—like the organs in a body. To gain any kind of massive protest or action against nuclear weapons, the fragmentation process that comes with interdependency would have to be halted and people turned away from their more narrow special-interest concerns to those of the larger collective.

This suggests that in order to save the system you would have to change it radically—in a general sense, you would have to halt a form of social development that evolved over thousands of years and enter into a kind of regression. That is to say, in order to save the United States from nuclear holocaust, we must quit being the way we are now and become more "communal" in our awareness of our common peril. We must abandon the modern American practice of letting everyone do his or her thing because that fragments and isolates us.

However, because this is obviously not about to happen, we must let nuclear matters remain in the hands of specialists who, like the rest of us, become alienated from greater communal concerns as they pursue their specialized professional interests. There is no way out. Because there is no way out, we might as well go on doing what we are doing, which—for the ordinary person in the street—is not much of anything. What a miserable argument this is. Miserable or not, it is not totally illogical and, such being the case, it must be considered along with other pertinent arguments involving nuclear weapons and the problems they pose.

This dismal "paradox" proposes nothing less than that if people were to begin pouring their energies into finding out about nuclear issues, studying the problems, becoming concerned, organizing and so forth, they would have little time for the other demands that a highly interdependent system makes on people. A do-nothing approach, as morally repugnant as it sounds, is functionally imposed on us.

Whatever the theoretical arguments might be, a do-nothing approach to the problems of peace is reflected in polls which show that, even at little more than an attitudinal level, only a small proportion of the general public is prepared for any kind of active involvement in organized peace movements. For example, while 40 percent of West Germans indicated in a 1986 poll that they had a positive attitude toward the movement, only 9 percent said they were prepared for active involvement in such movements.[5] The proportion who consistently contribute their time and effort in any actual or effective manner is, surely, considerably less.

If we may presume a kind of "do-nothing" attitude is generally prevalent — a passive attitude characterizes the people of the world — then what are we to make of this? Should people become more actively involved? If so, what promotes resistance to involvement and how can such resistance be overcome?

Should we, on the other hand, accept this presumed passivity? There has, after all, been surprisingly little protest raised over the proliferation of nuclear weapons throughout the world. To the contrary, the morbid progression of nuclear weaponry is accepted pretty much as a necessity of modern life; there have been revolts against nuclear proliferation, but none has been particularly effective.

It is my impression that the various philosophies, theories, and ideas we considered in the earlier sections of this book tend to justify, in one fashion or another, a kind of do-nothing approach to the nuclear arms crisis. Sociology, along with anthropology, is inclined to emphasize the power of social and cultural systems over the individual. Given the power of collective systems over individuals, what is surprising is not that so few people are involved in the quest for peaceful solutions to the nuclear crisis, but that as much awareness and concern is being expressed as we now find.

I do not myself endorse a do-nothing policy. If nothing else, one can at least worry about the problem and discuss it with friends, write one's congressperson, and not let too many weeks go by in the luxury of pure passivity. At the same time, there is truth in the observation that social systems stand above the individual — even in nations where individualism is believed to prevail over the power of the state. Perhaps, then, the best we can hope to do is to encourage, as individuals, those trends within our own and other societies that give promise of bringing an end to the threat implied in a policy of Mutually Assured Destruction.

Foremost among those trends in recent times is the rise of international corporations. Such structures, dedicated to the development of markets and the exploitation of profitable ventures over all other concerns, show a considerable lack of concern for nationalistic sentimentalities. Although the United States, for example, is fearful of losing its land and its economic prerogative to Russian encroachment, it is oddly willing to sell vast chunks of its real estate (that is, its material "self") to foreign investors from around the world. On another level, American businesspeople are not in the least disinclined to do business with their Russian counterparts — given a chance. Indeed, they are not unwilling to engage in illegal trade with the Soviet Union if there is the possibility of profit. Where money is concerned, nationalism takes a back seat.

Whether such trends should be encouraged or discouraged is a matter of debate. At present they do seem to offer hope for alleviating the bitter animosities that arise between nations. Surely they are trends worth thinking about. If international corporations hold any promise of integrating the diverse and bellicose nations of the globe, then, whatever their faults, such corporations would appear to be the lesser of two evils. In other words, I would rather see the world organized in terms of multinational corporatism than destroyed through a nationalistic nuclear war. However, one should hope we can do better than settle for this.

Given such a state of affairs, we are led to the possibly ironic conclusion that one can be working toward the development of internationalism and the easing of world tensions in simply attending to business at the office and, after work, having dinner at a sushi bar or perhaps in relaxing by buying goods now being produced within an international system of commodities production and distribution.

THE STRATEGIC DEFENSE INITIATIVE (SDI)

The Strategic Defense Initiative is basically a technological counter weapon solution to the threat of nuclear attack. It entails weapons, driven by nuclear fusion devices, that shoot down incoming enemy missiles. The publicity given to this "defensive" system suggests that it is incapable of shooting at and destroying anything but enemy missiles. Of course, the question remains whether it might be used to blast something else. Be this as it may, SDI is touted as a purely defensive system. (It is difficult to think of a weapons system that is powerful, extensive, massive, and, above all, *mobile*, yet can only be used defensively. Somehow, though, the American people appear to have bought the idea. If so, it is testimonial to the powers of Madison Avenue, the persuasive rhetoric of defense, and the appeal of "umbrellas" as a metaphor for national policy.)

Purely defensive or not (and it stretches credulity to the limit to think it is simply defensive), it is definitely a military solution. It is a solution in which a *new* weapons technology, that of the United States, is intended to negate the powers of an *old* weapons technology, that of the Soviet Union. In the final analysis, it amounts to little more than an attempt to control the weapons systems of the enemy through a superior weapons system of our own. That is to say, it is a variant form of escalation and the arms race. It is based on the belief that by creating more rationalized weapons we will solve the problems our rationalized weapons got us into in the first place. It is the same old heady wine being poured into new bottles.

The controversy surrounding SDI is well publicized. We cannot go over the pros and cons of such a complex technology here. Even its strongest proponents admit that no device can be 100 percent effective against an all-out nuclear attack. Given the destructive power of nuclear weapons, anything less than 100 percent effectiveness is reason to worry.[6]

The reader should be reminded, once more, of the dismal general statistics. Just 30 large strategic weapons, striking 30 major population centers in the United States, would kill more people than were killed in all wars throughout the world in the entire 20th century. If the enemy unleashed an attack force of, let us say, only 1,000 weapons with their covering decoys and deception systems, SDI would need to be better than 97 percent accurate just to keep casualties down around 100 million immediate deaths. It makes one wonder if the real justification for SDI is its defensive capability or, instead, its threat capabilities. As a defensive system it sounds like a bad game of nuclear roulette.

The major limitation of SDI is not in its cost effectiveness — though this problem should not be ignored. A trillion-dollar defense system, barring corruption and cost overruns, is not a minor budget item. Nor is the major limitation the problem of making it work with 100 percent effectiveness — even though few people imagine it will ever, even at its finest and most perfected state of development, achieve such efficiency. Its major problem is that it is a technological approach to a problem that is not, at its roots, technological in nature.

To see what I mean, consider two possibilities. In the first we have several mythical nations armed with nuclear weapons but not hostile. In the other, we have the same nations conventionally armed, but in a state of extreme hostility. Which is the more dangerous condition? Or course, at present we have the worst of all possible worlds — nations armed with nuclear weapons and in a state of perpetual hostility.

Keep in mind that since the beginning of the century, nuclear weapons have killed, at most, between 120,000 and 240,000 people — with others being affected by long-term catastrophic illness.[7] During the same span of time over 100 million people were killed in over 100 wars.[8] The ratio of people killed by conventional weapons versus nuclear weapons, since the turn of the century, is roughly 500 to 1. I mention this only to point out that the capacity of conventional devices to kill is also impressive.

To concentrate exclusively on technological devices while ignoring the desperate need for social and institutional reforms that might lessen international tensions is one-sided and, ultimately, probably doomed to failure. The picture is not a good one. On the one hand, the people of the United States are more tolerant of nuclear weapons, while on the other they are institutionally and culturally more bellicose. The weapons become more dangerous as those who possess them become more dangerous.

Nuclear weapons are less frightening, though still dangerous, where international relations are amicable. If we escalate both enmity and weapons, we are creating the worst of all possible worlds. Until the very recent popularity of Gorbachev, there is evidence to suggest that this is what is taking place. Fitch, for example, notes that in State of the Union messages between 1946 and 1950 about 19 percent of the references to threats and crises had to do with external as opposed to domestic threats. Between 1977 and 1982 over 85 percent of the references to threats had to do with foreign entities. Fitch also points out that in polls in the United States the proportion of respondents indicating "unfavorable" attitudes toward foreign elements dropped from a high of 91 percent in 1954 to 30 percent in 1973. However, by the early 1980s the percentage rose to over 60 percent.[9]

The birth of the SDI is, from a purely intellectual stance, a fascinating moment in human history. It amounts to nothing less than a technological effort to solve the problem of major human conflicts by generating a machine that can be *trusted* to be purely defensive. It is the problem of trust that, once again, lies at the bottom of things. We saw, in the chapter on Garfinkel's work, that trust, certainly at the international level, becomes an impossible problem. If the SDI could be trusted to be purely defensive, there might be less cause for concern. The technology of SDI is supposedly of such a nature that it can function only as a purely protective "umbrella" or technological shield over America. It is difficult, however, to trust a system that could, as Lowell Morgan, a Livermore scientist, put it, turn its lasers at cities and cause enough fires to "turn a town into hamburger."

To make the thing worse, however, even if we go ahead and presume the SDI can be trusted to be purely defensive, we still have problems. The Russians will counter with the argument that if we had a purely protective umbrella, we could attack them with impunity and then retreat, when the counterattack occurred, under the safety of our defensive shield.

Once more we are led to the wretched conclusion that trust, in a situation of conflict, is beside the point. One must act always as if trust does not exist. This, however, is an intolerable idea. It suggests nothing less than the belief that the human social condition is grounded in eternal paranoia. There must be a way out. About all one can say here, with any certainty, is that SDI does not seem to offer much promise with respect to solving this depressing aspect of the human condition.

The United States has, then, committed itself to perhaps the greatest effort ever expended in human history to create a machine that can be trusted to do no harm unless it is attacked — and, even then, it is supposed to direct its powers against the central weaponry of the attack. What a marvelous concept! The impossible problem generated by subjectivity and complexity is supposedly resolved, once and for all, by military technology. Such faith in technology calls for a greater suspension of disbelief than any sophisticated person is capable of managing.

Obviously the problems of intersubjectivity and complexity cannot be resolved by technology—unless we reach the day when someone invents a machine that can "read" what is on the mind of the enemy. Meanwhile, to make the situation more clear, though certainly overly simplified, consider two gunshooters of the Old West confronting each other. One is equipped with an older model .45 and the other with the latest Strategic Defense pistol. The new pistol fires powerful bullets capable of shooting any bullet fired from the older model .45. Put yourself in the position of the gunshooter equipped with the older model pistol. If you try to shoot the other guy, he will deflect all of your bullets—and still have a few bullets left! How might you react to this situation? What would the other guy have to do to get you to trust him? Does his Strategic Defense pistol inspire your trust? Would you try to get hold of the newer model for yourself? Would you sneak up on him and shoot him while he was sleeping?

FORMAL CULTURAL EXCHANGES

The cause of international peace is promoted by "cultural exchanges" between nations. In this regard it might come as a slight surprise to note that, according to at least one source, the French regard Germany more highly than they do any other nation. In part this regard is reflected by the fact that approximately 1,200 French towns and villages share cultural, educational, and sports exchanges with Germany.[10]

Certainly such exchanges are better than doing nothing at all, but they have serious limitations. First of all, they generally take the form of exchanges between elite elements on both sides—celebrated entertainers or artists, scientists and technologists, best-selling authors, leading politicians, world-class athletes, "art" films, etc.

Second, they commonly become devices employed by either side to propagandize its case. American films sent abroad in World War II were the product of carefully censored efforts designed to create films that had propaganda as well as artistic value.[11] The desire to establish propaganda coups makes such exchanges vulnerable. The United States, for example, is delighted when, in the course of a visit from a Russian group, one or several of its members defects. This is immediately and highly publicized; and the positive accomplishments of the exchange, in terms of promoting amicable relations, is balanced, if not negated, by the bitterness generated through the exploitation of defections.

Third, formal exchanges are relatively segmented and isolated forms of cultural diffusion. By this I mean simply that a ballet troupe from Russia touring the United States is kept isolated. Its impact on the American public, to the extent there is an impact, is segmented insofar as it consists mostly of public performances. The exchange takes place and then is over with. Another takes place and is finished. Each is a kind of complete or segmented offering before relatively segmented audiences. A ballet performance, for example, appeals to those who love the ballet but has little impact on those who are not interested.

Fourth, and finally, there is reason to suspect that such exchanges do not ease tensions but are, instead, a product of more amicable periods in international relations. Formal exchanges cease when international tensions are strong. Such exchanges are most needed when they are least likely to take place. Obviously, cultural exchanges are at the mercy of the governments controlling them. Certainly the governments are not at the mercy of the artists, politicians, and others involved in the exchanges.

In sum, no harm comes from cultural exchanges, and they generate much good. However, as a device for dealing with international tensions they suffer from serious defects. They are not something on which the people of the world can pin their hopes for peace. Nonetheless, as I argued throughout this book, the solution to the nuclear crisis does not lie within a singular approach but must involve diverse approaches. Within this broader context, everything must be done to continue cultural exchanges and increase their number and their variety.

UNILATERAL DISARMAMENT

Unilateral disarmament is a policy in which any particular nation, say the United States, elects to disarm itself. Nuclear disarmament, of course, would consist of getting rid of our nuclear weapons regardless of what the Russians, French, Chinese, or anyone else might do. This proposed solution to the nuclear crisis is included only because there are people who seriously endorse it as a solution to the possibility of nuclear war.

Unilateral disarmament, whether one endorses it or not, is an instructive concept. Within the various nations of the world we find that individuals are, to a considerable extent, disarmed. We do not go about like the men of the Old West, toting six-guns on our hips — armed and ready for the slightest grievance.[12] Although individuals, in the United States specifically, can own just about any sort of weapon they desire (machine guns, for example, are common), they are generally disarmed for public appearances.[13] Presumably, this lessens the occurrence of lethal battles among individuals.[14] Why not, then, disarm at the national level?

The answer returns us immediately to the impossible problem of subjectivity and complexity. There is absolutely no device whereby we can be assured that if we disarm, other nations will not take advantage of the fact. In order to achieve even the slight advantages — if they are advantages — that come from the public disarming of individuals, there must be a higher authority that enforces the disarmament *and that also can be trusted not to exploit the disarmament.*

To the extent, then, that we can trust our police and military — men and women who are permitted to carry weapons in public and use them if necessary — to that extent we lose little by being disarmed ourselves. If we cannot trust them, we begin to see a society in which individuals are forced to find their own protection in their own fashion. When put this way, the analogy between private abandonment of weapons and unilateral disarmament becomes much weaker. The open display of weapons is discouraged; we are all aware of that. However, make no doubt about it, the United States is an armed camp. The private citizen is guaranteed the right to keep arms, and American citizens are active, vociferous, and dedicated members of a gun-owning culture.

The arguments of those who are thoughtful about private arms and who have developed rationalizations for keeping weapons, beyond the ordinary Freudian justifications, are worth thinking about. Whether you accept or reject them is your free decision. However, listen to the arguments before you reach that decision. Their argument basically is: One cannot trust higher authority. Though it might be benign today, it could turn bad tomorrow. If it should ever turn bad, one needs weapons to fight the new tyranny. Where citizens are unarmed, tyranny is unopposed.

If a modern, democratic citizenry lacks trust in its sovereign authority, one of the more liberal authorities in the world, how can we expect nation-states to trust a higher authority above them? The question then becomes: What ultimate and trusted authority stands above the authority of national units? So far we do not have such an authority and, as a consequence, extreme forms of voluntary disarmament, unilateral or otherwise, cannot achieve the ends of peaceful coexistence. The United Nations comes to mind, of course, as a possible ultimate and trusted authority. However, powerful nation-states do not consider themselves subordinate to the powers of the United Nations.

The instabilities generated by even a slight arms advantage on the part of one nation over another leads immediately to compensatory arms production. What makes the problem more vexing is that the slight arms advantage just referred to does not need to be real. It is enough that nations perceive such advantages or disadvantages to exist — and nations are forever ready to make note of arms discrepancies among their kind. Even where such discrepancies might not exist, nations create them.

The counterargument to all of this is: But would not a unilateral disarmament program reveal to the world that we can be trusted? Once we were seen as trustworthy, the other nations would reveal their trustworthiness, their longing to lay down their arms, and the world could finally live in peace.

There is a kind of haunting appeal in this argument. A sensible person should not turn away from it in contempt. It touches at the most idealistic understandings we have. We are reminded, once again, of Berger's arguments on freedom. We are free to lay down our arms. We can make the hard choice. If we lay down our arms and the world follows in our path, then it was a magnificent act. If we lay down our arms and are taken advantage of, then the moral onus lies on the shoulders of those who still lack the courage to give up the old ways. At least we dared to be free.

As appealing as this argument is, drawing on courage and freedom, it still ignores the basic fact that serious, major social arguments are always resolved through the application of force. To give up weapons is, in effect, to become enslaved to the way others resolve issues. It is, from a Goffmanian perspective, to have stripped one's self of one of the primary devices guaranteeing dignity and a degree of autonomy.

Unilateral disarmament, as a policy with respect to weapons, is worth thinking about. There is little doubt that no nation is going to practice it in any serious fashion. A consideration of why this is so is sociologically instructive. Nations retain their weapons for much the same reasons individuals do. (Remember, in the discussion on Goffman, that in social interactions we rely on a great variety of dramatic devices that function, in a sense, as weapons.) Without weapons we lose control of what might be called action initiatives. In effect, we lose those devices that are especially important to our existences as human beings.

In its ridiculously and completely *reductio ad absurdum* form and pressed to the individual level, complete unilateral disarmament would ask every single person living to abandon all forms of weaponry — wit, money, power, private arms, privilege, etc. No one wants to do that. It would mean, in a way, giving up everything that enhances human life. Why, then, think nations are any more disposed to giving up those devices — armies, weapons, bombs, navies, wealth, power, technological knowledge, etc. — that establish their very nature as nations?

ARMS NEGOTIATIONS

Probably the foremost officially recognized device for any kind of solution to the nuclear arms crisis is through a negotiated reduction in arms. Disarmament negotiations were examined in the essay on Garfinkel's ideas and in the discussion of Burke's theories , and we concluded that such negotiations are, generally, doomed to failure.

Certainly, the historical record gives one little cause for optimism. From the dawn of military organizations, human communities have tried to negotiate reasonable constraints on military power. The end product of this long historical effort is, of course, the present moment. From the vantage point of the present moment there is little sign that earlier efforts accomplished anything worth writing home about. Since the beginning of the 20th century, over 100 wars have been fought around the globe and possibly more money has been put into armaments among the military powers of the world than was ever the case in the past.

In other words, if, at some point in history, arms negotiations had been set in place that were truly effective, we would have arms control today. We do not have arms control today, in any serious meaning of the term; therefore, there have never been any rigorously effective arms negotiations. The historical truth is irrefutable: Arms races prevail. Arms negotiations do not.

If disarmament negotiations were an effective device, we would at least expect to see a curtailing of world expenditures on arms. According to Rita Tullberg, the real value of the resources we devote each year to arms is 10 times larger today, in the 1980s, than it was in the period 1925–1938.[15]

Continuing international arms negotiations, as Samuel Johnson once said in a different context, are a triumph of hope over experience.[16] They accomplish little at a slow pace and at great expense. (One is inclined to think that the latent functions of such negotiations are probably more significant than the manifest ones. I touched on a few of these in Chapter 10. It is left to the more interested and imaginative reader to think up what some other latent functions might be.)

it is easy to become impatient with international disarmament negotiations. Their "track record," to use the current phrase, is not impressive in the least. At the same time, so fragile is world peace that one is disinclined to recommend that such negotiations be abandoned. No matter how slow or how costly, such negotiations are better than the holocaust they are intended to circumvent.

Perhaps the worst thing about arms negotiations is that they tend to shove other possibilities out of the way. People become focused on negotiations. Arms talks get a lot of press coverage. They have official sanction. They are an effort "from the top." They involve thousands of State Department employees, experts, military personnel, and other significant officials. In effect, they lead to the sentiment that everything is being done to solve the problem. The fact, of course, is that while a number of things are being done, the one thing not being accomplished is any real or serious solution to the problem of war.

Negotiations certainly should not be discouraged. At the same time, they should not be allowed to override the fact that other alternatives must be given equal if not greater consideration. It should be self-evident the nuclear issue is too great to be resolved in any singular fashion. It calls for an all-out, holistic, total, highly varied, imaginative, and creative set of solutions.

LIMITED NUCLEAR EXCHANGES

This hardly sounds like a solution to the problem of nuclear weapons and yet, in a fashion, it is. As I pointed out in the first chapter in this book, the problem is not really nuclear weapons. It is the *probability* that the nuclear powers of the world will engage in an all-out effort to demolish each other through the unrestrained deployment of their full nuclear arsenals. A nuclear exchange in which, let us say, only 20 or 30 million people were killed would be preferred to one in which 400–500 million people were killed.

The moral choices, here, are not nice. The ideal would be to have no one killed. Still, the option of limited nuclear war has been examined seriously by military and political strategists as perhaps a more tolerable alternative to the possibility of an all-out conflict.[17] Limited nuclear war is in effect a variant form of the idea that having conventional wars would be a better solution than having nuclear wars. Although the whole notion is repugnant to those who recognize war itself as the problem, it is still an option that sides with the lesser of two evils.

We do not need to enter here into a discussion of the basic question of whether limited nuclear exchanges are possible, given the hair-trigger responses of modern defensive and offensive high-technology military systems. We are interested only in the social dynamics underlying the playing of such an intense international "game." Given the fact that even minor incidents, comparably speaking, generate powerful collective sentiments of an immediate nature, this solution appears sociologically implausible. In World War II, for example, the American public was told the Japanese were sending balloons across the Pacific with incendiary devices attached. The public response was immediately one of increased solidarity against the wily enemy. The national hysteria and defensive response created by a few silly balloons floating across the Pacific with magnesium incendiary devices was astonishing. The balloons were more valuable to American leadership in terms of morale than to the Japanese in terms of damage. (There is the possibility that this was a rumor spread by American authorities to promote morale. It is difficult to believe that the Japanese would have done anything so stupid.)

Where a collective representation such as the Statue of Liberty is a positive icon, an enemy attack is also a powerful icon of a negative nature, achieving strong collective sentiments through commonly shared antagonisms. A nuclear device fired by a hostile nation, even if it landed in an arid region of the Southwest and detonated harmlessly on the desert sands, would arouse intense national sentiments. It would be a sociological situation difficult to control. How would Americans respond to a nuclear bomb being dropped into even the most desolate part of the country by an aggressor nation? Who can say? But there is something about being attacked that enrages people to the point where they are willing to endure nearly any deprivation in the quest for revenge. A limited exchange, at best, is terrifyingly risky.

The only way in which a limited exchange of nuclear weapons might have any feasible practicality would be under circumstances where parity was lacking in the nuclear forces of the nations involved. For example, the United States might be able to bully a third-world nation by dropping a nuclear weapon on an uninhabited area. While the victim of this affront would respond with immediate and strong collective sentiments, it could not back them up with an equally provocative response.[18] Trying a similar tactic against a nuclear power of equivalent strength would probably end in an escalation of exchanges. But to use such force against a weak country would, by definition, be unnecessary.

The idea of limited nuclear exchange is morally reprehensible as a "lesser of two evils" type of solution. It has serious practical insufficiencies as well. In the international arena when morality and practicality clash, practicality seems to have a way of prevailing.

If limited nuclear response is an extremely weak solution, the parallel idea of simply restraining war by not using nuclear devices is also weak. What if we signed a pact with all powers that we would not use our atomic weapons but would, instead, resolve our differences with them on the playing fields of conventional war?

This solution has a few attractions. It would result in fewer casualties; the planet would suffer less irradiation; cities would be demolished but not made totally uninhabitable; and so on. The question once more comes back to the central problem that we find ourselves pinned against time after time — the problem of trust. Who, under such turbulent circumstances, in a moment of unendurable rage and frustration, could be trusted not to turn to the deadliest devices they had in their arsenal — their strategic nuclear weapons?

Of all possible solutions to the nuclear impasse, the idea of limited nuclear exchange and/or reliance solely on conventional armies and navies makes the least sense. In theory it has a little justification, though not much. In practice it would, in all probability, lead to pure catastrophe.

PASSIVE RESISTANCE AND COLLECTIVE SENTIMENT APPROACHES

Since the 1960s, when the so-called flower children of America were putting long-stemmed roses down the barrels of National Guardsmen's rifles, to the present time, a small, but significant portion of the people of Western nations have subscribed to popular antiwar movements based on various notions of "spiritual" resistance. Such movements derive either from conventional religious ideas or from our deep-rooted cultural sentiment that society is little more than a broader manifestation of individual wills.

If we change our individual wills and "think peace," then we will have peace. Implicit within this kind of thinking, of course, is the converse argument that we are constantly on the brink of war because people are thinking war. The truth of the matter probably is that people generally are not "thinking peace" or "thinking war." If they are anything like what they are generally described as being, they are probably more commonly concerned about what they are going to have for dinner or whether their home team will win the pennant this year.

Now, I intend to neither discourage nor disparage such efforts. However, they probably serve most effectively as an index of the extent to which people have become frightened rather than as a deterrent to war. Popular resistance to governmental policies is not without effect, but such resistance is effective when it is militant, well-organized and massive and can generate an effective threat against the established order. Curiously enough, there is evidence supporting the conclusion that under such circumstances a government such as the more autocratic Soviet system is more likely to grant concessions than is the case with a democratic system.[19]

Each of the perspectives presented in this book is informative with respect to passive movements such as the recent New Age Consciousness or attempts made during the Vietnam crisis to "levitate" the Pentagon into outer space by "thinking" it away. Passive movements are psychologistic in orientation. They attempt to transform the individual as an individual. However, the major point being made by Durkheim, Weber, Marx, Merton, and other sociologists and anthropologists is that social dynamics and the psychology of the individual are not the same thing.

This is a difficult lesson to grasp and, at bottom, is the primary justification for the study of sociology and anthropology. We cannot change societies simply by changing individual genetics or psychologies. It takes more than that — if, indeed, societies can be changed in any Utopian manner at all.[20]

Perhaps that is the worst feature of "consciousness alteration" approaches to the problems of world peace — they are simply too simpleminded. They provide us with a sense of doing something when, in fact, we are gaining little more than personal comfort and a sense of false security while the social dynamics underlying war continue to operate on their own. We can "image" a world without weapons as much as we like, but the weapons remain. As with the Pentagon, you cannot levitate them into outer space by thinking good things. I am reminded of the bumper stickers around Colorado that read "THINK SNOW." One can "think snow" all one wants, but if the meteorological conditions are not right, it simply is not going to snow. Or, to rely on a more pertinent analogue, the starving people of the drought-ridden lands of Africa most certainly think of food constantly. Little good it does them.

Effective countermeasures in the form of civil demonstrations call for a careful assessment of what any protest movement is up against. What kinds of protest work? What kinds do not work? When and under what circumstances do they work? Although civil protest does have effects, they are slow in coming and call for supreme dedication. The most powerful civil protest in America occurred during the 1960s as American black people effectively protested their conditions. Now, nearly 20 years later, the black people find themselves, in many ways, as put upon as they were before the protests.

The black protests were regional and had constitutional support. They were also protests that could be answered by the white community in "bits and pieces" designed to mollify the protesters. Blacks could, for example, finally sit at the lunch counter in a village five-and-dime store and play high-stakes baseball along with white athletes, but gaining entry into the halls of real power remains even now as much of a problem as it was before the protests.

A similar situation confronts those protesting the much more difficult problem of state control of weapons of ultimate destruction. For reasons examined throughout this book, the state is not about to abandon the one prerogative that establishes its statehood, so to speak. The only effective protest would have to be of such widespread involvement and commitment and of such intensity as to constitute a nearly total civil insurrection — in sum, civil war.

Even though civil protest is not likely to have serious effects with respect to bringing about a significant reduction in nuclear arms, it retains a valuable purpose. It remains, constantly, a sign to authority of the real fear that exists among the people and of the responsibility that is on the shoulders of those whose aides stand nearby with the red telephone. For these reasons civil protest must never be abandoned, and for these reasons the world owes much to those who give their time in such profoundly moral and altruistic service.

WORKING "WITHIN THE SYSTEM"

Another form of antinuclear activity, in my opinion, holds greater promise of achieving positive effects. Organizations that direct their efforts toward altering the political and legislative system can fight legislation and policies that might further augment the risks of nuclear confrontation.

The work, for example, of Helen and William Caldicott is especially noteworthy in this regard. Helen Caldicott is the founder of Physicians for Social Responsibility, a highly respected antinuclear organization, and she is also the founder of another organization known as Women's Action for Nuclear Disarmament. These groups do not approach the problem in terms of passive resistance. Instead, they direct their concerns toward those elements within the social structure that are powerfully effective in themselves —the leadership, legislative bodies, political parties, business and industrial organizations, and so forth. They approach the problem by working within the system. As is the case with the civil rights movement, progress is slow and frustrating, but one is left wondering how much worse things might be if such people such as the Caldicotts did not exist.

GLOBAL INTERDEPENDENCY SYSTEMS AND SOCIOCULTURAL DIFFUSION

I have already devoted a space in the chapter on structural-functionalism and in this present chapter to the development of global interdependency systems. We shall only touch on the subject here. We can begin by noting that there is now a well-established global postal system, a global (and English-speaking, by the way) commercial airlines system, and thousands of large and small corporations that operate across national boundaries. The size and power of the larger corporate systems rivals the size and the power of major nation-states. The fleets of the biggest oil companies of the world, for example, are larger than the largest national navies of the world.

We now have corporations whose wealth readily rivals that of smaller nations. The lines between large corporate structures and national structures are becoming less well defined. The Japanese find it profitable to draw on facilities and labor available in a variety of countries other than Japan. Likewise, American corporations draw on facilities and labor from countries around the globe. (Some idea of the clash between corporate interests and nationalism appears at a local and personal level when we are asked to "Buy American." Evidently people are willing to do this — if the American product is cheaper and as well made and as effectively marketed as its foreign competitor.)

Corporate structures are still, at least in formal theory, subordinate to the authority of the state. However, it becomes less clear, as time goes by, just how subordinate they can be kept. Never before in history has there been such a systematic impetus given to the demands of secular cultural diffusion. Where just a century or two ago, the cultural traits of one community "diffused" through casual contacts or wars of religious domination, there is now a powerful economic thrust to establish markets in other nations. This means that, as we noted earlier, Pepsi-Cola, like ancient Christianity, seeks converts. Once it has them, it also seeks to protect and retain them.

This observation is not all that new. By the middle of the 19th century, astute observers such as Marx were well aware of the power of the market-place in international affairs. Money and wealth have long been the fuel for war. Today money and wealth are created through much more complex systems. In this new age total war no longer means a resolution of the problems created by wealth; war is no longer a means whereby a nation can increase its wealth. Instead, war is a losing game in terms of capital exchanges — a disruption of the process that creates wealth. Within all of this we note another factor. We can no longer simply talk of the wealth of nations. We must now talk of the wealth of corporations. It is a major shift in power relations.

It is something of a shock, if you are in your later years, to see how profoundly American culture is now infused by other nationalities. Older Americans recall and speak nostalgically of a time when foreign automobiles were rarely seen and, just as importantly, were of little interest. It is different today. How does one respond to all of this? On the one hand, old nationalistic sentiments come to the fore and one is resentful of the intrusions. (I recall my stunned reaction to discovering, while on a tour of Oregon, that an old Air Force base had been bought by Japan Airlines and was being used as a training center for Japanese pilots.) On the other hand, one can work toward promoting this interdependency and encouraging it. There should, however, be a balance. If they are to join us in owning our lands and living among our people, we should have the equal privilege of owning their lands and living among their people. Openness should be true openness if it is to work at all.

We have praised the Russians, recently, for endorsing a policy of openness — being concerned only that they might not be really honest about it. However, we should consider the extent to which other nations with which we are allied espouse or reject openness. Japan, for example, is a nearly totally closed social system. Even in its American plants the higher administration of the plants is kept in Japanese hands.

Openness will work only if all nations endorse it. If we alone stand as the most open nation among all the nations of the world, then we expose ourselves to the loss of our national identity while they retain theirs. The thing we especially fear about the Soviets, the closed and total nature of their culture, is not without its appeal in other nations as well.

Though it is only a hunch, based on current social theories, it appears that openness is being forced on the nations of the world. The old national boundaries are cracking. Marshall McLuhan put it nicely when he suggested the world is becoming a global village — and a small village at that. This must be one of the more exciting and profound of all modern social developments and the only one I can think of at the moment that holds any serious hope for alleviating the problems that intense national conflicts arouse.

All I can suggest, in an overview as brief as this one, is that any examination of global movements toward peace must examine the structural consequences — at a global level — of this rapidly developing major transformation in the social organization of human populations. It is something of a race. Will the global village take its place soon enough to acquire sufficient power to prevent nuclear weapons from ever being used to settle nationalistically inspired human disputes?

MASSIVE POPULATION EXCHANGES

Where the operation of major structural changes — such as the rise of the multinational corporation — is incremental and a response to global economic movements, the idea of actively promoting massive population exchanges is one that would call for governmental recognition and acceptance on the part of participating countries. It would require a conscious effort.

This solution would call for exchanges different in nature from elitist cultural, educational, scientific, and athletic exchanges. It would draw on encouraging "visitations" across national borders of as broad and extensive a variety as might be practical and feasible. Ranchers, bankers, housewives, cab drivers, students, older people, children — a cross-section of any national population — would be encouraged to visit other nations. The visits could have a variety of forms ranging from a short-term tourist venture to a working stay of longer duration.

Such visits would probably not radically alter already-established social conceptions. However, they might temper nationalistically sustained propaganda that heightens fears and hatreds of distant people. More pointedly, they would also serve the functional purpose of locating in "enemy" territory native populations large enough to make either side, in the case of growing hostilities, think twice about destroying its own people.

Such a program might lessen tensions only if participating countries do not try to exploit the situation by promoting defections from visiting populations. Because neither the Soviet Union nor the United States appears, at least under present circumstances, inclined to agree to such restraint, the program is not realistic. Furthermore, given any kind of tension and international paranoia, large-scale visits would be viewed as a threat to national security. National governments exploit international travel for purposes of intelligence-gathering. Once more we run into the problem of trust. Large-scale exchanges of populations could serve the interests of peace or international amity. At the same time, it is doubtful such exchanges could occur as a result of formal exchange programs.

It might come to pass, however, that global structural transformations —particularly in the area of major corporate activities — might increasingly promote the exchange of larger numbers of workers across national boundaries to facilitate corporate interests. If this should occur, it would be another way in which the social dynamics underlying international conflicts and hostilities would be altered in the direction of lessening tensions.

Sociological literature generally supports the view that living within another culture and having firsthand contact with its people provides greater awareness and, ultimately, greater sympathy for the way that culture faces its problems and develops its responses. Though such a formal massive exchange program is not feasible at present, there may come a time when it is more practical.

LEADERSHIP EXCHANGES

This is a slight modification of the idea of having major population exchanges. Kenneth Boulding, in a speech given at Northern Arizona University in 1983, suggested that the children of all commissioned military personnel in the United States be educated in the Soviet Union. Conversely, the children of their higher ranking military personnel should be educated here. Or, the children of higher ranking political officials might serve the same purpose. The purely fantastic nature of the solution was understood by Boulding and his audience. Yet there is some sense to it. We might presume that world leaders would be less inclined to attack each other if their children's lives were the consequence of any such attack.

Somewhere among these last two solutions there are possibly other, less extreme alternatives that might work toward the same end. Surely they deserve more thought than they have been given. The only kind of social solution to the problem under discussion appears to be one in which trust is somehow "cinched." The difficulty in achieving this trust is that it can be attained only through the establishment of a kind of vulnerability—such as Boulding's solution. The thing national states are not ready for, at the moment, is self-induced vulnerability. Meanwhile, in the effort to avoid vulnerability, we become vulnerable to the constant threat implied in policies of Mutually Assured Destruction.

INCREMENTAL VULNERABILITY

There is a moment in the film *Treasure of the Sierra Madre* when the three central characters get involved in a discussion over who will keep the gold they find if they are successful in their prospecting venture. The old man tells the two young men he is the best choice. They immediately become suspicious and ask why they should trust him. He replies, wisely, that there is no reason in the world for them to trust him. He is no more trustworthy than they are. Trust is beside the point. The reason they should let him control the gold is because they are younger and faster than he is. If he tries to steal it, they will hunt him down and kill him. Therefore, he is the best choice. He is the best choice because he is vulnerable if he reneges on his responsibilities.

This little scene is instructive insofar as it deals with the impossible problem of trust and resolves it. It takes trust out of the picture and replaces it with logistically established pragmatics. In previous chapters we encountered, time and again, the impossible problems of reading the enemy's mind, trust, sincerity, and so on. Policies based on trust are based on quicksand in this modern day and age. In fact, that is probably the way it has always been. We can go back to Machiavelli for some lessons on the limitations of trust.

Rather than having to be trusted or having to trust the other side to be good, it would be better if, like the old prospector, both sides had to be good. This position could be reached through a policy directed toward the attainment of mutual vulnerabilities. This statement perhaps sounds peculiar. However, it is essentially the basis for the policy of Mutually Assured Destruction that now prevails. The only thing wrong with Mutually Assured Destruction is that both sides seek to force the other into a vulnerable position. With a policy of incremental vulnerability, both sides would voluntarily make themselves vulnerable to attack through a series of reductions in defensive postures that were reciprocal. As one side made itself a little more vulnerable, the other side would reply in kind.

After all, it is our present-day defensive systems that we now have to defend ourselves against. They are the most threatening defenses ever designed by human agents. What kinds of thinking might enable us to put them behind us and get on with the more interesting things to be done in the world? If we can reduce our defensive postures, make ourselves more vulnerable and—at the same time—have our antagonists make themselves more vulnerable, then the problem of trust is pushed into the background. Everyone has to get along with everyone else or suffer the consequences that vulnerability itself implies.

This is a nice little dream, but probably little more than a dream. It is more reasonable than unilateral disarmament insofar as it suggests an incremental approach to vulnerability. However, standing hard against the dream are the arguments that the dramatists such as Burke and Goffman give us. People do not like to be vulnerable. It would be extremely touchy to negotiate reciprocal forms of vulnerability among great powers. However, it is not a completely impossible vision, and it is introduced here as another possibility for thought.

EDUCATION

The people of the United States accept education as a panacea for nearly every social problem, ranging from delinquency (where it is more of a cause than a cure) to drug addiction to protection from AIDS to world peace. Now, I happen to be a member of the educational establishment. I do not want to give the impression education does not promote social good. Once again, however, we are warned by the lessons of the structural-functionalists not to place all of our eggs, as it were, in a single institutional basket.

Indeed, the situation confronting modern education is a precarious one with respect to teaching the lessons of international amity and world peace. For one thing, such lessons are viewed by a number of jingoistic groups as anti-American propaganda. Whether it is propaganda or not, the question still remains whether such teachings might weaken American resolve with regard to the protection of national interests.

Efforts to introduce courses designed to show that we are more and more becoming a global community were fiercely attacked in the Denver, Colorado, school system as recently as several years ago; and the attacks continue. Despite the fact that nearly every social and economic indicator available reveals growing global interdependency between nations, national sentiment remains a powerful traditional block to the establishment of any kind of global community. We are reminded again of Durkheim's notion of the sacred — national icons are sacred and, regardless of world trends, not to be tampered with by educational eggheads. It is, at the sociological level, the same kind of fight against ignorance that biologists must confront with the issue of evolution.

American educational institutions, as is the case with educational systems in nearly any country, are fragile. Schools are dependent on the state and have limited autonomy. Any educational program viewed as contrary to the interests of the state has little chance of success. Once again, then, we find that educational systems, like "spiritual" or "consciousness raising" programs, reflect world tensions more than they block them.

The fragility of the school system is illustrated by an incident in Colorado recently where a local school system gave in to a small, but unusually vociferous, group that demanded an end to the celebration of Halloween at the grade school level. What is worth noting is how quickly the school caved in. At a more serious level, consider how quickly German universities caved in to Hitler in the 1930s—much more quickly, evidently, than did the church.

Still, educational systems, when supported by the other institutions of a community, are an influential force with respect to making people aware of social issues and the variety of policies that might be adopted for addressing those issues. The primary problem with American education, of course, is that it is not strongly supported. For example, Japanese parents are extremely careful about the education their children receive—attending to details few American families would bother with.

Education, in the Soviet Union, is acknowledged by the government as an important institution not only for providing knowledge but also for identifying talent among young people. The Russian educational structure is more careful than is the American system to train its people in the ways of foreign cultures. As someone noted, the Soviets have as many *teachers* of English in their schools as Americans have *students* of Russian language and culture in theirs.

Whatever education might accomplish in the United States is, to a great extent, hamstrung by federal and local policies that view education as something to be provided to as many people as possible, as cheaply as possible, as pragmatically as possible, and as quickly as possible. It is also hamstrung by cultural traditions that look on education primarily as a device for promoting social mobility—a way to move from blue-collar status to white-collar status or from a lower white-collar status to a higher one.

So it is, then, that American schools have become extraordinarily provincial in a time when provincialism is a dangerous state of mind. American students, supported by cultural and familial traditions, are little interested in and know little about the affairs of the world. Perhaps it might be asking too much of schools to teach people the complicated lessons of peace. On the other hand, it seems reasonable to settle for education that gives the American people a better sense of the world in which they live. A young person today can go all the way through high school and then complete a college degree without having to know anything about any culture other than western Europe, its traditions and history—if even that.

Is it unreasonable, then, to contend that if we are prepared to blast Russia from the face of the earth, we should at least know something, indeed a fair amount, about those whom we intend to kill? Why are they paranoid, if they are? What is their history? What was behind the Revolution of 1917? Why did American military forces invade Russian territory? When did they do it? What was the reaction of the people of the USSR? What is the basic structure of Soviet socialistic government? Was Russian industrial development any more or any less destructive of human lives and freedom than Western industrial development? And so on.

When I think back to my own time and World War II, I can now see how little we were told about Germany at the time. We were not told about the exasperatingly repressive nature of the Versailles Treaty at the close of World War I and its impact on Germany's economy and sociopolitical structure. We had no sense of the extreme frustration experienced by the German people as they experienced severe economic depressions combined with monetary inflation that made currency practically worthless.

We saw the rise of Nazi influence as a kind of perverted response to a love for authority on the part of the German people. Our learning went little beyond the pejorative belief that the Germans were psychologically screwed up. They were authority-mad. They had perverted personalities. (It seemed reasonable at the time; now it seems embarrassingly naive.) There was, perhaps, too much misguided emphasis on the German psyche and too little on the political, economic, and international dynamics that went into the creation of World War II. Certainly little mention was made of our own share in the madness — the blame was all on the other side.

What is interesting about American education, as an institutional complex, is not what it teaches but, instead, what it does not teach. Perhaps no major nation in the world today spends so little time preparing its youth for life in a global community. We are international in our military affairs and in our commercial and industrial activities while remaining isolationists in our educational programs.

We have abandoned, more and more with each passing year, the teaching of foreign languages as a wearisome and impractical effort. (Given the way colleges teach languages, there is some truth to the claim.) Why study Russia, or Japan, or Southeast Asia, or China, or India, or any other foreign culture when there is money to be made and jobs to be had through studying double-entry accounting techniques? Why become caught up in the confusions and frustrations of international cultures when one can find personal serenity by taking pop courses in self-awareness or becoming successful through increasing one's self-esteem?

It is easy to criticize American education and nearly anyone who writes a book on American political and cultural trends tends to take at least a little jab at it.[21] The truth of the matter is that American education has a great deal to be said for it. If we do not appreciate it, for example, other nations do. Graduate education is one of America's hotter export items.

I do not think the fault, with respect to international and cultural training, lies, at bottom, with education. Educational institutions are more responsive and reflective than directive. Given the form that other elements of the American social system have taken, educational systems function more as whipping boys — shouldering the blame for lacks that originate elsewhere in the system. The provincialism of the frontier and the romance of the agrarian, isolated life, grounded in simple local village virtues, is a wonderful part of American history. It has also led to educational policies that are surprisingly provincial and even anti-intellectual. Those local village virtues made for a romantic historical past. As a platform for educational policy in a complex modern world, they are totally ruinous.

NUCLEAR FREEZE

One popular and strongly supported approach to dealing with nuclear crisis is the notion of a nuclear "freeze." In effect, this means abandoning the further development of weapons. Even the simplest rational consideration of the state of world nuclear arms suggests that the great powers have more destructive capability than is reasonably necessary for achieving military and political ends.

It makes sense, then, to stop producing such weapons. The problem with this solution, of course, is that even if it were put into effect today, with estimates ranging as high as 50,000 nuclear devices now available, we would have accomplished no lessening of the terror. We must have not only a freeze, but also a reduction in nuclear arms. Despite current arms negotiations directed toward such an end, there appears little likelihood of any reduction in arms to the point where nuclear weapons would no longer pose a threat to the survival of humanity.

The difficulty here is that nuclear arms are an alternative to conventional weapons. Conversely, conventional weapons are an alternative to nuclear weapons. If we freeze the production of nuclear weapons, are we thereby encouraged to heighten the production of conventional weapons? European nations recently indicated a considerable mistrust of the effort to reduce missile strength in Europe, arguing that a reduction in nuclear arms will leave them vulnerable to the greater superiority of conventional weapons possessed by Russia.

IN CONCLUSION

The preceding discussion of solutions to the nuclear arms crisis is, obviously, in no way definitive. It is intended to accomplish two major ends. First of all, it is intended to direct attention toward the need to give full and serious consideration to social theory as a way of approaching a more complete critical evaluation of social policy. Second, it is intended to provoke discussion and argument—not close it. If it achieves these ends, the effort was a successful one. Finally, it argues that many approaches must be considered rather than any singular approach. The issue deserves our widest ranging application of social and political imagination.[22]

I did not exhaust the full range of possible alternatives. For example, the instigation of violent rebellion against established authority was not discussed here. I touched on the issue, however, in the chapter on Marxist thought. The problem with rebellion against authority is that any kind of effective revolution or violent overthrow of dangerous military programs would require an international coalition of revolutionaries; and, so far at least, revolutionaries seem to be singularly devoted to the promotion of particular national, rather than universal, global interests.

I did not consider civilian-based defense systems partly because I do not know much about this subject and partly because what little I know leads me to think the structural problems with respect to installing such a system are overwhelming for both the United States and the other great powers. Returning the military to greater civilian control is an appealing idea. It inspired C. Wright Mills and other social critics of the 1950s and 1960s. We have, in recent years, come perilously close to having American policy being formed and executed by shadow governments in which unknown Marine colonels and Navy admirals have had inordinate amounts of power. It is a matter that deserves more discussion and debate than it has received in the general press and than I was able to give it here.

I did not consider the role of the mass media. As is the case with education, Americans are inclined to think "media blitzes" of one kind or another can solve social problems. Why not try a "media peace blitz"? One can only presume that until peace draws large audiences and is capable of stimulating advertising revenues, we are not likely to see it.

Another possibility I did not mention at any length (though it is alluded to in the chapter on Weber) is that of encouraging bringing nuclear weapons under more democratic control. Nuclear issues are not openly discussed and are not, to any great extent, a matter of democratic debate or constraint. We do not get to vote on such issues as halting nuclear testing or stopping the further production of such weapons. If we are, as our political rhetoric would have us believe, a free and democratic people, to what extent are our freedom and our democracy overridden by those who control our nuclear arsenals?

If the problems of democratizing nuclear weapons at a national level are difficult ones, it seems reasonable to conclude there is little hope for any movement toward a "global democracy" in which the people of the world might be given a greater voice in the disposal of these devices. Nonetheless, as an ideal it is something to think about. If nothing else, it provides an opportunity to review the limits of democracy as a political system.

Chapter 12

Epilogue

The institutional and international problems facing humankind today are now so massive that the common response is to view them as impossible. Can we check the "greenhouse effect"? Can we rid the world of nuclear terror? Must we go to the edge of total disaster before we are capable of learning greater wisdom in our affairs?

We need to think further about what is meant by political and economic impossibilities. Why are they so impossible? Are we beyond the ability to control ourselves? Must we perish, if not from nuclear holocaust, then from the suffocating heat and fumes of our industrial wastes? Surely humankind is possessed of better stuff. We have overcome one impossibility after another in the realm of physics and in the realm of biological technology. What does it take to overcome the "impossibilities" that lie within our own social, political, and economic natures?

It is difficult to review problems as serious as the nuclear crisis and not become disillusioned, desperate, and despondent. I do not want to leave the discussion at that level. The search must continue for ways out of the impasses that appear to grow ever larger as we approach the end of this century. There is reason for hope. The situation is surely not totally an impossible one.

If nothing else, we must continue to discuss, to debate, and argue, to be involved, and to seek deeper levels of understanding. Our social imaginations must be exercised to the fullest. We must be open to new possibilities, and we must have the means for evaluating those possibilities as fully as possible. To fall back on archaic understanding, to hide ourselves in the comforting closets of religious, political, intellectual, or ideological dogma is no longer acceptable. To continue to base social policies on beliefs now outmoded is more than dangerous to the health of civilization — it is suicidal. We must move on. We have little choice.

In this spirit, then, I offer this book to the young men and women of the future. I myself am interested in avoiding nuclear catastrophe not because it can have any great effect on me — I am in the early winter of my life. This book was written in the hope that it will help those who are enjoying the springtime of youth to find the world as wonderful a place to live as I found it and continue to find it. Stay with the problems of your age — tenacity is among the finest of human qualities. Don't quit. Good luck.

Appendix: Notes

CHAPTER 1

1. Dozens of good sociological theory sourcebooks are readily available. Among them I can mention: Lewis Coser, *Masters of Sociological Thought* (New York: Harcourt Brace Jovanovich, 1971); Don Martindale, *The Nature and Types of Sociological Theory* (Boston: Houghton Mifflin, 1960); Randall Collins and Michael Makowsky, *The Discovery of Society*, 4th ed. (New York: Random House, 1988); Talcott Parsons et al., *Theories of Society* (New York: The Free Press, 1965); and William D. Perdue, *Sociological Theory* (Mountain View, Calif.: Mayfield, 1986).

2. It is worth noting that most of the influential social scientists who have reached broad publics have been good writers. In this regard such writers as David Riesman, C. Wright Mills, Margaret Mead, Ruth Benedict, Kenneth Boulding, Thorstein Veblen, Randall Collins, and others come to mind.

3. The relative versus absolute position with respect to moral systems has some parallels with the problem of individual ecological correlations in sociological and demographic research. Communities, as total units, are adaptive systems and, in that sense, serve absolute values such as survival or maximization of collective utility. At the individual level, how this is achieved varies tremendously. Relativism, itself, is relative to the level of abstraction involved in one's theoretical concerns. Any kind of moral absolutism must be generalized to a high level of abstraction. There is, of course, nothing wrong with this. For a lot of work, however, it is necessary to move into more specific concerns and, at that point, relativism becomes unavoidable. In other words, a lot of the confusion in the relativistic versus absolutistic debate is a confusion over levels of abstraction.

4. It is not necessary to deal with this subject in detail here. Suffice it to say that romantic love is an emotion. However, it is an emotion with a remarkable history. It appears in its modern form in Western culture in Provençal France in the 12th century A.D. At first it was a mannerism permitted to those of noble birth and was known as "courtly love." Eventually it became a popular sentiment. Even so, the idea of black people engaging in true romantic sentiment was

not generally acceptable as late as the 1920s in the United States. For an interesting, though highly controversial, presentation of romantic love I can think of no more fascinating work than Denis de Rougement's *Love in the Western World* (New York: Pantheon Books Inc., 1940).

5. Lewis F. Richardson, *The Statistics of Deadly Quarrels* (Pittsburgh: Boxwood Press, 1960).

6. If the probability of nuclear war in any year is .005, then the nonprobability of this event is .995. The likelihood of the event not occurring in 150 consecutive years is, then, .995 raised to the 150th power. This gives us a value of .47. This is the probability nuclear war would *not* take place in a 150-year interval if its probability, in any given year, is .005. The probability it would take place is .53 or slightly better than 50/50. The problem with this kind of thinking is that no one can establish what the probability of nuclear war is in any given year. During the Cuban missile crisis of 1962 it was terrifyingly high. At the moment it is anyone's guess. One thing is certain; it is greater than zero. The probability used here sets it at 5 out of 1,000 — a seemingly low probability, but evidently not low enough for comfort.

CHAPTER 2

1. My favorite among Durkheim's works is *The Elementary Forms of the Religious Life*, trans. J. W. Swain (New York: Free Press, 1954). Taking into consideration when it was written, it is a brilliant piece of social speculation. Other works, all published by Free Press, are: *The Division of Labor in Society*, trans. George Simpson (1960); *Education and Sociology*, trans. S. D. Fox (1956); *Moral Education: A Study in the Theory and Application of the Sociology of Education*, trans. E. K. Wilson and H. Schnurer (1961); *The Rules of Sociological Method*, trans. S. A. Solovay and J. H. Mueller (1950); and *Suicide: A Study in Sociology*, trans. J. A. Spaulding and G. Simpson (1951).

2. *Suicide: A Study in Sociology.*

3. Quoted by George Simpson in *Emile Durkheim* (New York: Crowell, 1963), p. 62.

4. Guy Swanson, *The Birth of the Gods: The Origins of Primitive Belief* (Ann Arbor: University of Michigan Press, 1960).

5. Colin Turnbull, *The Mountain People* (New York: Simon and Schuster, 1972).

6. The data in Table 2.1 are from Louise I. Shelley, American Crime: An International Anomaly, *Comparative Social Research*, vol. 8, 1985, pp. 81–95. These data suggest that the United States exceeds na-

tions similar in development in its incidence of violent crimes. Durkheim turns our attention toward the question of whether a particular incidence of crime is normal or typical for a society in a given stage of development.

7. See, for example, the bragging commentary of the Assyrian King Ashurnasirpal II, who describes one of his victories in the following manner: "I cut off their heads; I burned them with fire; a pile of living men and of heads over against the city gate I set up; men I impaled on stakes; the city I destroyed . . . I turned it into mounds and ruin heaps; the young men and maidens . . . I burned." From *National Geographic*, Vol. 154, No. 6, December 1978, p. 741.

8. Some of the problems that strategists have with this question are described in a work by Michio Kaku and Daniel Axelrod, *To Win a Nuclear War: The Pentagon's Secret War Plans* (Boston: South End Press, 1987). Perhaps, at this point in the struggle between the great powers, the only thing holding them back from a major military engagement is just this question.

9. Jonathan Schell, *The Fate of the Earth* (New York: Knopf, 1982).

10. Kaku and Axelrod, *To Win A Nuclear War*.

CHAPTER 3

1. The major works of Marx include: *The German Ideology*, parts 1 and 3, with Friedrich Engels; introduction by R. Pascal (New York: International Library, 1939; originally written between 1845 and 1846); *The Poverty of Philosophy*, with an introduction by Engels (New York: International Library, 1963; originally written in 1847); *The Communist Manifesto*, with Engels (New York: Washington Square Press, 1964; originally written in 1848); *The Eighteenth Brumaire of Louis Bonaparte* (New York: International Library, 1964; originally written in 1852); *A Contribution to the Critique of Political Economy*, trans. N. I. Stone (Chicago: Kerr, 1906; originally written in 1859); and, of course, his best-known work, *Capital: A Critique of Political Economy* (Chicago: Kerr, 1906; originally written 1867–1879).

2. One of the better known economists concerned with the extent to which capitalism has been transformed in recent years is Harvard University's John Kenneth Galbraith. Among his numerous books I recommend *American Capitalism: The Concept of Countervailing Power* (Boston: Houghton Mifflin, 1952); *Economic Development in Perspective* (Cambridge: Harvard University Press, 1962); *Economics and Public Purpose* (Boston: Houghton Mifflin, 1973); and *The Affluent Society* (New York: New American Library, 1958).

3. From Karl Marx, *A Contribution to the Critique of Political Economy*,

trans. N. I. Stone, from the 2d German ed. (New York: International Library, 1904) as reprinted in *Theories of Society: Foundations of Modern Sociological Theory*, by Parsons, Shils, Naegele, and Pitts (New York: Free Press, 1961), p. 136.

4. See William Greider, "Give Meese a Chance," *Rolling Stone*, June 6, 1985, pp. 44–47.

5. A great variety of historical works deal with the topic of Manifest Destiny during the period of territorial expansion. See, for example, Charles M. Segal, *Puritans, Indians, and Manifest Destiny* (New York: Putnam, 1977); Allen D. Kownslar, *Manifest Destiny and Expansionism in the 1840's* (Lexington, Mass.: D. C. Heath, 1964); A. K. Weinberg, *Manifest Destiny: A Study of Nationalist Expansionism in American History* (Chicago: Quadrangle Books, 1935); and E. D. Adams, *The Power of Ideals in American History* (New Haven: Yale University Press, 1913).

6. For a review of the controversy that the neutron bomb created, see S. L. Wasserman, *The Neutron Bomb Controversy: A Study in Alliance Politics* (New York: Praeger, 1983) and S. T. Cohen, *The Truth About the Neutron Bomb: The Inventor of the Bomb Speaks Out* (New York: Morrow, 1983).

7. Thorstein Veblen, *Theory of the Leisure Class* (New York: New American Library, 1953).

8. For an interesting review of this debate, expressed in nontechnical terms, see "Has Cosmology Become Metaphysical?" in *Astronomy*, February 1987, pp. 6–22. I most certainly do not want to be thought of as denigrating my colleagues in cosmology — it is an important and an exciting field of intellectual endeavor. What is important is not the finding so much as the varieties of argument underlying the impasse. The arguments are worth trying to resolve because the arguments themselves broaden our vision. It is the same with the social sciences. Perhaps we cannot determine whether class structures are getting more rigid or less rigid or staying the same. But the arguments are important in themselves — to the extent we believe in trying to comprehend what is taking place around us.

9. This is not an especially novel observation. References to workers as "prostitutes" selling themselves for a buck are fairly common today and probably were common a century ago. For an interesting treatment of intellectual workers as people who sell their brains or, to use Koestler's phrase, perform like intellectual "call girls," see Arthur Koestler, *The Call Girls: A Tragi-Comedy* (New York: Random House, 1973).

10. Cited in William D. Perdue, *Sociological Theory* (Mountain View, Calif.: Mayfield, 1986), p. 324.

11. This nice term appears in C. Wright Mills, *White Collar: The American*

Middle Classes (New York: Oxford University Press, 1951). Mills was strongly influenced by Marx.

CHAPTER 4

1. The major writings of George Herbert Mead are *The Philosophy of the Present* (La Salle, Ill,: Open Court, 1932); *Mind, Self and Society* (Chicago: University of Chicago Press, 1934); and *Philosophy of the Act* (Chicago: University of Chicago Press, 1938). His major work, *Mind, Self and Society*, was published by his students and is based on his lectures when he taught at the University of Chicago. His lectures generated intense interest. The fact that his students went to the trouble to publish them as a book attests to this.

2. Literature often anticipates themes developed in social philosophy and social theory. For example, Cervantes' pathetic hero Don Quixote is a man who sees the world through a mist of romantic symbols and finds himself, as a consequence, tilting against windmills. Don Quixote is not alone in this—one way or another we all distort the world as a result of the fact that we must view it through the prism of symbols. The novel *Don Quixote*, incidentally, is not a bad introduction to some of the basic observations of symbolic interactionism. It is a big work, worth savoring. See Miguel de Cervantes, *Don Quixote*, the revised Ormsby translation, ed. Joseph R. Jones and Kenneth Douglas (New York: Norton Press, 1981).

3. The literature on this subject is lengthy. Overviews can be obtained from such works as: *Nature Versus Nurture: Gettysburg College Senior Scholar's Seminar, 1983–84*, ed. R. D. Barnes and J. D. Pickering (Lanham, Md.: University Press of America, 1985); Lewotin, Rose, and Kamin, *Not in Our Genes: Biology, Ideology and Human Nature* (New York: Pantheon, 1984); C. J. Lumsden and E. O. Wilson, *Genes, Mind, and Culture* (Cambridge: Harvard University Press, 1981); and *Sociobiology, Beyond Nature/Nurture?: Reports, Definitions, and Debate*, ed. G. W. Barlow and J. Silverberg (Boulder, Colo.: Westview Press for the American Association for the Advancement of Science, 1980).

4. Anthropologists have found great diversity in sexual patterns among the cultures of the world. See, for example, Elvin Hatch, *Culture and Morality: The Relativity of Values in Anthropology* (New York: Columbia University Press, 1983); Walter Williams, *The Spirit and the Flesh: Sexual Diversity in American Indian Culture* (Boston: Beacon Press, 1986); and Suzanne G. Frayser, *Varieties of Sexual Experience: An Anthropological Perspective on Human Sexuality* (New Haven: HRAF Press, 1985). Within our own culture we have moved from a time when self-castration was reputedly practiced by sexual extremists to the more hedonistic philosophies of people such as Hugh Hefner.

The literature on this topic is vast, and only a few illustrative references can be cited here.

5. The famous Turing test of artificial intelligence consists of seating a person in a room with a typewriter. The person communicates, through the typewriter, with "someone" in another room. If the person cannot tell whether that someone is a computer or another human, then the computer they interacted with passes the test of artificial intelligence. Of course, the way to find out if you are interacting with a machine would be to challenge its emotions rather than its intelligence. Therefore, the computer would have to have an artificial emotionality as well as an artificial intelligence.

It would be interesting to know how often people might conclude they are interacting with a computer when, in fact, they are interacting with another human being. If errors were made in this form of the Turing test, then, curiously enough, a machine that was quite "human" might fail to qualify as an artificial intelligence. This is an amusing intellectual problem. Nonetheless, the modern pursuit of the mechanization of human subjectivity is an interesting and not especially flattering commentary on the mentality of our times.

6. One of the best known early critiques of the symbolic interactionist position appeared in a short essay by Dennis Wrong entitled "The Oversocialized Conception of Man in Modern Sociology." The article appeared in *The American Sociological Review*, Vol. 26 (April 1961), pp. 183–193.

7. There is an entire branch of the study of communications that concentrates on the nature of signs. It has been used to enhance our understanding of such diverse matters as the architecture of towns and cities and why you generally see the hero on the left side of a movie screen when he talks to the villain or someone inferior. This study is referred to as *semiotics*. Literally hundreds of books were devoted to this subject in the late 1970s.

8. Kenneth Burke makes much of this aspect of symbols. Symbols not only convey what is present, but they also have the ability to convey what is not present. The negative is a strange symbol insofar as it is not represented by anything in nature. It is a purely human creation. The moral implications of the negative are pursued in depth and with considerable charm (especially in the last section where God and Satan engage in a dialogue on the nature of the negative in human affairs) in Kenneth Burke's *The Rhetoric of Religion* (Boston: Beacon Press, 1961). I do not recommend this book as light reading, however. It is tough going in places; but for those with hardy intellects, it is a rewarding effort.

9. Older readers will recognize the allusion to a set of essays by David Riesman. While my treatment of the topic is different from his, I

still recommend Riesman as a good reading experience for those interested in uncovering further aspects of the American experience. See *Individualism Reconsidered and Other Essays* (Glencoe, Ill.: Free Press, 1954).

10. See Muzafer Sherif, *The Psychology of Social Norms* (New York: Harper and Row, 1966) and Solomon Asch, *Social Psychology* (New York: Prentice-Hall, 1952). Asch achieved considerable notoriety in the 1950s as a result of demonstrations in which he showed convincingly that people "see" what their groups tell them to see even, to a considerable degree, in structured situations.

11. Keep in mind that Mead is concerned with people as *social* creatures and is concerned with the social nature of our definitions of ourselves. For Mead the concept of self is important because it marks the point where the individual and the community are conjoined. For other approaches that reveal the broader mysteries and paradoxes of the self, see the essays in Douglas Hofstadter's *The Mind's I* (New York: Basic Books, 1981). This work is a brain-twisting foray into the philosophical and metaphysical problems that self-reflexivity imply.

12. See, for example, *Reconstruction Following Disaster*, ed. J. E. Haas, R. W. Kates, and M. J. Bowden (Cambridge: MIT Press, 1977).

13. One of the first truly modern antiwar novels was Erich Maria Remarque's *All's Quiet on the Western Front* (Greenwich, Conn.: Fawcett, 1958). Nuclear war, we all believe, will be total hell on earth. There have been earlier, though less total, forms of hell. Remarque's novel describes the hell that was World War I and offers insight into earlier global rehearsals of Armageddon.

CHAPTER 5

1. Max Weber was prolific despite his bouts with an incapacitating nervous disorder. Among his major works are *The Protestant Ethic and the Spirit of Capitalism*, trans. Talcott Parsons (New York: Scribners, 1930); *Ancient Judaism*, trans. and ed. Hans H. Gerth and Don Martindale (New York: Free Press, 1952); *Basic Concepts in Sociology*, trans. H. P. Secher (New York: Citadel, 1964); *The City*, trans. and ed. Don Martindale and Gertrude Neuwirth (New York: Macmillan, Collier Books, 1962); *From Max Weber: Essays in Sociology*, trans. and ed. H. H. Gerth and C. Wright Mills (New York: Oxford University Press, 1946); *Max Weber on the Methodology of the Social Sciences*, trans. and ed. Edward A. Shils and Henry A. Finch (New York: Free Press, 1949); *The Rational and Social Foundations of Music*, trans. and ed. Don Martindale, Johannes Reidel, and Gertrude Neuwirth (Carbondale, Ill.:

Southern Illinois University Press, 1958); *The Religion of China*, trans. and ed. Hans H. Gerth (New York: Free Press, 1959); *The Religion of India*, trans. and ed. Hans H. Gerth and Don Martindale (New York: Free Press, 1958); *The Sociology of Religion*, trans. Ephraim Fischoff (Boston: Beacon Press, 1963); and *The Theory of Social and Economic Organization*, trans. A. M. Henderson and Talcott Parsons (New York: Free Press, 1964).

2. A fast food enterprise, such as McDonald's, is an astonishingly well-put-together bureaucracy. For an engaging look at this system (it even has a school for executives—a kind of "hamburger university"—to deal with its complexity), see Max Boas and Steve Chain, *Big Mac: The Unauthorized Story of McDonald's* (New York: Dutton, 1976). A more recent work on the subject is John F. Love's *McDonald's: Behind the Arches* (New York: Bantam, 1986).

3. This form of traditional war, as opposed to modern rationalized war, is displayed in an interesting manner in the anthropological semi-documentary film *Dead Birds*, produced by the Harvard-Peabody New Guinea expedition. See also Robert Gardner, *Gardens of War: Life and Death in the New Guinea Stone Age* (New York: Random House, 1969).

4. William H. Masters and Virginia E. Johnson, *Human Sexual Response* (Boston: Little, Brown, 1966).

5. See Herman Kahn, *Thinking About the Unthinkable in the 1980's* (New York: Simon and Schuster, 1984).

6. Carl Sagan is the best known of the exponents of the totally catastrophic nuclear winter. For a recent discussion of the issue, see Mark A. Howell, *Nuclear Winter: The Human and Environmental Consequences* (New York: Springer-Verlag, 1984).

7. See Herbert Marcuse, *One Dimensional Man: Studies in the Ideology of Advanced Industrial Society* (Boston: Beacon Press, 1964). An illustration of the one-dimensionality of modern experts appeared in a local paper recently when a Martin-Marietta engineer was quoted, with reference to a Strategic Defense Initiative nuclear blast in space during an all-out nuclear war: "As far as people on the ground are concerned, it's *just another bomb* going off in space" (italics mine). From the *Boulder Camera*, September 14, 1987, p. 2C. If this attitude is characteristic of defense engineers, we are doomed.

8. This phrase appears in C. W. Mills's *The Causes of World War III* (New York: Simon and Schuster, 1958).

9. My source is the *1985 Yearbook of American and Canadian Churches*.

10. This phrase, "worldly philosophers," a rather honest way of referring to economists, comes from the pen of Robert L. Heilbroner, *The Worldly Philosophers* (New York: Simon and Schuster, 1953).

11. The Laird Wilcox collection of radical literature, housed at the University of Kansas Library in Lawrence, Kansas, offers thousands of examples of American extremist writings from both the left and the right. It is a rich source of material for anyone interested in extremist literature and the extremist mentality. It is my understanding that this collection of extremist literature is one of the two or three finest such collections in the country.

CHAPTER 6

1. A major weakness of this theory is that what is being exchanged in a social interaction, as opposed to a purely economic interaction, is extremely difficult to define. For example, what is it that married couples *socially* exchange in their relationship? George and Martha, in Albee's *Who's Afraid of Virginia Woolf?*, are apparently engaged in "exchanges." But exactly what they are exchanging is a matter of considerable interpretation and dispute. In brief, the most significant sociological question about the relationship is assumed to be already answered in exchange theory. It isn't.

2. Here I am echoing Everett Cherrington Hughes of the University of Chicago, who coined the term "master status" to refer to statuses that dominate other statuses we might have. For example, if you serve time in prison your status as an ex-con tends to become a master status, dominating all other social qualities you might have.

3. A bibliography that included all of the works of Parsons and Merton would swamp this appendix. The following list is, consequently, highly selective. Among Parsons's works we should include: *Action Theory and the Human Condition* (New York: Free Press, 1978); *Essays in Sociological Theory: Pure and Applied* (Glencoe, Ill.: Free Press, 1949); *Family, Socialization and Interaction Process*, with Robert F. Bales and others (Glencoe, Ill.: Free Press, 1955); *Politics and Social Structure* (New York: Free Press, 1969); *Social Structure and Personality* (New York: Free Press of Glencoe, 1964); *Social Systems and the Evolution of Action Theory* (New York: Free Press, 1977); *Structure and Process in Modern Societies* (Glencoe, Ill.: Free Press, 1960); *The American University*, with Gerald M. Platt and Neil J. Smelser (Cambridge: Harvard University Press, 1973); *The Social System* (Glencoe, Ill.: Free Press, 1951); *The Structure of Social Action* (New York: Free Press, 1968); *Toward a General Theory of Action*, with Edward Shils and others (Cambridge: Harvard University Press, 1951); and *Working Papers in the Theory of Action* (New York: Free Press, 1953).

   Among Merton's major writings we can list: *Contemporary Social Problems: An Introduction to the Sociology of Deviant Behavior and Social Disorganization*, ed. Merton and R. A. Nisbet (New York: Harcourt

Brace, 1961); *Continuities in Social Research: Studies in the Scope and Method of "The American Soldier,"* ed. Merton and Paul F. Lazarsfeld (New York: Free Press, 1950); *The Focused Interview: A Manual of Problems and Procedures,* with Marjorie Fiske and Patricia L. Kendall (New York: Free Press, 1956); *Mass Persuasion: The Social Psychology of a War Bond Drive,* with the assistance of M. Fiske and Alberta Curtis (New York: Harper and Row, 1946); *On the Shoulders of Giants: A Shandean Postscript* (New York: Free Press, 1965); *Social Theory and Social Structure,* revised and enlarged edition (New York: Free Press, 1957); *The Student-Physician: Introductory Studies in the Sociology of Medical Education,* ed. Merton, George G. Reader, and Patricia Kendall (Cambridge: Harvard University Press, 1957); *Sociological Ambivalence and Other Essays* (New York: Free Press, 1976); *Science, Technology and Society in Seventeenth Century England* (New York: H. Fertig, 1970); *The Sociology of Science: The Theoretical and Empirical Investigations* (Chicago: University of Chicago Press, 1973); and *Sociological Traditions from Generation to Generation: Glimpses of the American Experience,* ed. with Matilda White Riley (Norwood, N.J.: Ablex, 1980).

4. Kingsley Davis argues that structural-functional theory is so broad in its nature that it embraces virtually all aspects of social speculation. He argues, in effect, that any sociology or anthropology is structural-functional whenever it deals with the problem of the interrelations between institutions and agencies within human communities. See Kingsley Davis, "The Myth of Functional Analysis as a Special Method in Sociology and Anthropology," *American Sociological Review* 24 (1959), 757–772.

5. U.S. National Science Foundation, *An Analysis of Federal R & D Funding by Function, 1969–77.*

6. *The Statistical Abstract of the United States,* prepared by the Bureau of the Census and the Department of Commerce, for example, provides no information with regard to numbers of individuals receiving training through military programs.

CHAPTER 7

1. Peter Berger's major works include: *Invitation to Sociology: A Humanistic Perspective* (Garden City, N.Y.: Doubleday, 1963); *The Noise of Solemn Assemblies: Christian Commitment and the Religious Establishment in America* (Garden City, N.Y.: Doubleday, 1961); *The Precarious Vision: A Sociologist Looks at Social Fictions and the Christian Faith* (Garden City, N.Y.: Doubleday, 1961); *The Sacred Canopy: Elements of a Sociological Theory of Religion* (Garden City, N.Y.: Doubleday, 1966); *Sociology: A Biographical Approach,* with Brigitte Berger (New York: Basic Books,

1972); *Facing Up to Modernity: Excursions in Society, Politics and Religion* (New York: Basic Books, 1977); *Capitalism and Equality in America*, an edited work (Lanham, Md.: Hamilton Press, 1987); *Movement and Revolution* with Richard J. Neuhaus (Garden City, N.Y.: Doubleday, 1970); *The Capitalist Revolution: Fifty Propositions about Prosperity, Equality, and Liberty* (New York: Basic Books, 1986); *The Homeless Mind: Modernization and Consciousness*, with Brigitte Berger and Hansfried Kellner (New York: Random House, 1973); *To Empower People: The Role of Mediating Structures in Public Policy*, with Richard Neuhaus (Washington: American Enterprise Institute for Public Policy Research, 1977); and *The Social Construction of Reality: A Treatise in the Sociology of Knowledge*, with Thomas Luckmann (Garden City, N.Y.: Doubleday, 1966).

2. Berger and Luckmann, *The Social Construction of Reality*, op. cit.

3. Berger, *Invitation to Sociology*, op. cit.

4. Ayn Rand's novels and writings in the 1960s radically advocated an individualistic philosophy. Her heroes and heroines prevail against the base constraints of the masses. Among her novels I can recommend *The Fountainhead* (New York: New American Library, 1971) and *Atlas Shrugged* (New York: Random House, 1957). The titles of a few of her philosophical writings quickly indicate where she is "coming from." See, for example, *The Virtue of Selfishness: A New Concept of Egoism* (New York: New American Library, 1964) or *Capitalism: The Unknown Ideal* (New York: New American Library, 1966).

5. Sigmund Freud, *Civilization and its Discontents*, trans. James Strachey (New York: Norton, 1961). We can disagree with much of Freud's theories and yet appreciate his perceptiveness with respect to problems that are central to our time. This is a modern work still worth reading. The question it addresses, of course, is: Why hasn't progress brought happiness?

6. No better case for this appears anywhere in social literature than in the works of William Fielding Ogburn and Leslie White. Especially recommended is the discussion in Leslie White's *The Science of Culture* (New York: Farrar, Straus and Giroux, 1949). Though beginning to show the ravages of time, this book is still a lively work. White had a way of provoking people into thinking about things. This book displays that talent nicely.

7. Erving Goffman, whose work is discussed in Chapter 9, virtually makes deception the basis of social life.

8. If we assume that there are eight million tickets one of which is the big winning number, then purchasing 20,000 tickets gives you a probability of 20,000/8,000,000, or 1 chance out of 400 of winning. Your probability of losing would be 399 out of 400. In other words, you are about 400 times as likely to lose as to win—not good odds,

even if you did invest in $20,000 worth of tickets. If you wanted to boost your odds to a simple 50/50 bet you would have to invest $4,000,000 in tickets. Even then you would have no more than a 50 percent chance of winning (this assumes the lottery itself does not take a cut.)

9. From Edward S. Herman, *The Real Terror Network* (Boston: South End Press, 1982), p. 197, as cited in Michael Parenti, *Inventing Reality: The Politics of the Mass Media* (New York: St. Martin's Press, 1986). This book offers the reader a great number of specifically documented accounts of media bias.

10. As noted elsewhere in this book, being a doctor in the United States and being one in the Soviet Union confers quite different prestige and income. If functional utility were the criterion by which prestige is conferred, then farmers and servants would stand above Madison Avenue advertising executives and football quarterbacks. What is important, in order for occupation to work as a control device, is a prestige hierarchy, however that is achieved. In different cultures it is achieved in different ways. The fact that it is a social universal, with the possible exception of extremely small and simple systems, suggests that occupational equality is a Utopian ideal.

11. This conclusion was drawn from an excellent piece of social research at the close of World War II. See Samuel Stouffer et al., *The American Soldier* (Princeton: Princeton University Press, 1949).

12. Albert K. Cohen, *Delinquent Boys: The Culture of the Gang* (Glencoe, Ill.: Free Press, 1953).

13. There is an interesting question of diminishing returns implied in this discussion. The current practice of spending outrageous sums to obtain a leader, whether it be a national president or a college dean, has moved to ridiculous extremes. If there is an irreducible element of nondeterminism in any selection, then spending an infinite amount of money and energy can still leave you with a lemon on your hands. We seem to have lost a tradition in which we realistically accepted the fact that in dealing with people you must always and forever engage in a serious form of gambling. Because it is fairly obvious that elaborate selection procedures cannot take the chance element out of things, then the selection procedures are probably serving other functions in addition to the manifest function of leadership selection.

CHAPTER 8

1. For a probing description of the subjective plight that constrains us all, see Michael J. Reddy's essay, "The Conduit Metaphor: A Case of

Frame Conflict in Our Language about Language," in A. Ortony (ed.), *Metaphor and Thought* (Cambridge: Cambridge University Press, 1979).

2. A popular recent work dealing with the nature of social "constructions" is Peter Berger and Thomas Luckmann, *The Social Construction of Reality: A Treatise in the Sociology of Knowledge* (Garden City, N.Y.: Doubleday, 1966).

3. See Howard Schwartz and Jerry Jacobs, *Qualitative Sociology: A Method to the Madness* (New York: Free Press, 1979).

4. John Howard Griffin, *Black Like Me* (New York: New American Library, 1961).

5. For a writer of such significance, Garfinkel's major work is restricted to the single book *Studies in Ethnomethodology* (Englewood Cliffs, N.J.: Prentice-Hall, 1967). Moreover, it is a book that consists, in large part, of material originally published elsewhere. It is an awkwardly written and ponderous work filled, at the same time, with unusual insights into the problems facing anyone struggling to understand what it is to be a human being among other human beings. Garfinkel also edited a brief work with the title *Ethnomethodological Studies of Work* (New York: Routledge and Kegan Paul, 1986).

6. For an excellent review of the limitations and devastatingly serious logical weaknesses of so-called quasi-experimental studies in the social sciences, see Stanley Lieberson, *Making It Count* (Berkeley: University of California Press, 1987).

7. I cannot go into the matter in this short chapter, but I should mention that among its several accomplishments, Garfinkel's work is a major critique of simple empirical science and especially psychologistic behaviorism as an approach to understanding human affairs.

8. *Studies in Ethnomethodology*, op. cit.

9. Ethnomethodology is strongly influenced by a school of philosophy called phenomenology. Phenomenology deals with the difference between reality and what we perceive as reality. Immanuel Kant is commonly considered the central figure in phenomenological thought. Kant made the distinction in terms of noumena and phenomena. The term *noumena* refers to things as they truly are. The term *phenomenon* refers to things as they appear to us. This distinction forces us to consider the nature of reality itself and the extent to which our perceptions of it are "removed," as it were, from that reality.

10. J. Alvin Kugelmass, *J. Robert Oppenheimer and the Atomic Story* (New York: Julian Messner, 1953); John Major, *The Oppenheimer Hearing* (New York: Stein and Day, 1971); Peter Michelmore, *The Swift Years:*

The Robert Oppenheimer Story (New York: Dodd, Mead, 1969); Denise Royal, *The Story of J. Robert Oppenheimer* (New York: St. Martin's Press, 1969); Philip M. Stern, *The Oppenheimer Case: Security on Trial* (New York: Harper and Row, 1969); and Thomas W. Wilson, *The Great Weapons Heresy* (Boston: Houghton Mifflin, 1970).

11. Edward Rose of the University of Colorado had his students examine boredom as an academic exercise. It is a good one. I might add that Rose was a close colleague of Garfinkel and among those promoting ethnomethodological studies.

12. C. Wright Mills, *The Causes of World War III* (New York: Simon and Schuster, 1958), pp. 81–89. A different and more extensive treatment of Mills's work, relevant to the above discussion, can be found in R. P. Cuzzort, *Humanity and Modern Sociological Thought* (New York: Holt, Rinehart and Winston, 1969).

13. Without judging Lieutenant Colonel Oliver North, it is instructive to note how effective his defense was during the Congressional "Iran-scam" hearings insofar as it played on taken-for-granted definitions of situations—a number of them similar in nature to Mills's description of modern political-military realism.

14. The question of form and substance is one of the most difficult of sociological and anthropological issues. An early discussion of the problem appears in the writings of Georg Simmel. A recent interesting treatment of the problem appears in Jules Wanderer, "Simmel's Forms of Experiencing: The Adventure as Symbolic Work," *Symbolic Interaction*, Vol. 10, No. 1, pp. 21–28.

15. See Robin J. Crews, *The Crocodile Years: The Traditional Image of Science and Physical Scientists' Participation in Weapons Research*, Ph.D. dissertation, University of Colorado, 1985.

CHAPTER 9

1. Goffman's most significant work was probably *The Presentation of Self in Everyday Life*, which was first published as a monograph at the Social Sciences Research Centre at the University of Edinburgh in 1956. This monograph was later published as a book by Anchor Books (Garden City, N.Y.: Doubleday, 1959). Goffman's other works include: *Encounters* (Indianapolis: Bobbs-Merrill, 1961); *Asylums* (Garden City, N.Y.: Doubleday, 1961); *Behavior in Public Places* (New York: Free Press, 1963); *Stigma: Notes on the Management of Spoiled Identity* (Englewood Cliffs, N.J.: Prentice-Hall, 1963); *Interaction Ritual: Essays on Face-to-Face Behavior* (Chicago: Aldine, 1967); *Frame Analysis* (New York: Colophon Books, 1974); *Gender Advertisements* (Cambridge: Harvard University Press, 1979); *Strategic Interaction*

(Philadelphia: University of Pennsylvania Press, 1969); and *Forms of Talk* (Philadelphia: University of Pennsylvania Press, 1981).

2. Suzanne Langer, *Philosophy in a New Key: A Study in the Symbolism of Reason, Rite and Art*. For anyone interested in Goffman's writings, Langer's work on the symbolic nature of human beings is a worthwhile addition to their readings. Even if you are not interested in Goffman, this book is a fine introduction to the extent to which symbols permeate human lives.

3. Scott Turow, *Presumed Innocent* (New York: Farrar, Straus and Giroux, 1987).

CHAPTER 10

1. The term *master* is used repeatedly by Hugh Dalziel Duncan. Duncan tried to "translate" Burke into terms more comprehensible to the American social scientist. Evidently, he did not succeed in this effort. Still, Duncan's writing (several references appear below) is one of the better direct introductions to Burke. Unfortunately, though it is obviously derivative — it is little more than an attempt to clarify Burke — it is ponderous. There is a considerable need for someone with a social science background to reveal the power of Burke's arguments.

2. In addition to writing on the functional qualities of literature, Burke also wrote several volumes of poems and other essays. This selection includes works I consider particularly relevant to an understanding of his theories: *A Grammar of Motives* (New York: Prentice-Hall, 1945); *A Rhetoric of Motives* (New York: Prentice-Hall, 1950); *Die Rhetorik in Hitler's Mein Kampf und Andere Essays zur Strategie der Uberredung* (Frankfurt am Main: Suhrkamp Verlag, 1967); *Dramatism and Development* (Barre, Mass.: Clark University Press, 1972); *Language as Symbolic Action: Essays on Life, Literature and Method* (Berkeley: University of California Press, 1966); *Perspectives by Incongruity*, ed. S. E. Hyman with the assistance of Barbara Karmiller (Bloomington: Indiana University Press, 1964); *The Philosophy of Literary Form: Studies in Symbolic Action* (New York: Vintage Books, 1957); and *The Rhetoric of Religion* (Boston: Beacon Press, 1961). For those who are interested, this last work contains the best resolution of the free-will versus determinism controversy I have encountered in all of my studies.

3. The following books by Hugh Dalziel Duncan are those that deal with Burke's theories: *Symbols in Society* (New York: Oxford University Press, 1968) — about as succinct an introduction to Burke as I know of; *Communication and Social Order* (New York: Bedminster Press, 1962); *Language and Literature in Society: A Sociological Essay on*

Theory and Method in the Interpretation of Linguistic Symbols (New York: Bedminster Press, 1961); and *Symbols and Social Theory* (New York: Oxford University Press, 1969).

4. See Jacob Bronowski, *Science and Human Values* (New York: J. Messner, 1956).

CHAPTER 11

1. Followers of Durkheim such as the American anthropologist Leslie White argue that the individual is simply a conductor of sociocultural forces. The individual is powerless when cultural forces clash and can do little more than hope to find a safe hiding place. See Leslie White, *The Science of Culture* (New York: Grove Press, 1949). In a similar manner, Jules Henry, in a book titled *Culture Against Man* (New York: Vintage Books, 1963), argued that culture has turned against the individual. While perhaps less pessimistic than White's, Henry's book provides another example of the extent to which Western social science, sociology and anthropology in particular, tends to diminish the role of the individual in collective affairs.

2. Barbara Farah, "Poll Finds Fears of War Fade," *New York Times*, February 1, 1985.

3. Kenneth Pruitt, "Security, Peace and Social Science," *Society*, Vol. 23, No. 1, Nov.–Dec. 1985, pp. 31–45.

4. It is for this reason that we are all embarrassed to find we do not know information that, in earlier times, perhaps, would have been generally known. In an age of specialization, we are obligated to know only our specialty. The recent furor over A. B. Hirsch's book *Cultural Illiteracy: What Every American Needs to Know* (Burlington, Mass.: Houghton-Mifflin, 1987) comes out of a romanticized notion of what modern people should know.

5. Kim Salomon, "The Peace Movement—An Anti-Establishment Movement," *Journal of Peace Research*, Vol. 23, No. 2, June 1986, p. 123.

6. Certainly there is strongly expressed opinion within the scientific community concerning the possible effectiveness of SDI. See, for example, Bob Guldin, "Scientists Reject SDI," *Guardian*, Vol. 39, No. 8, Nov. 19, 1986. According to Guldin, nearly 80 percent of the National Academy of Science members polled in October 1986 thought the chances were poor that a survivable, cost-effective missile defense system could be built in the next 25 years. Approximately 7,000 scientists have indicated a willingness to boycott SDI research in the United States—including 15 Nobel laureates.

7. Adam Meyerson, *Policy Review Summary*, 1985, pp. 46–47.

8. Arthur Westing, et al., "Warfare in a Fragile World: Conventional, Nuclear and Environmental Weapons," *Bulletin of Peace Proposals*, Vol. 17, No. 3–4, 1986, pp. 347–365. Absolute figures such as 100 million dead have a way of horrifying us—and horrifying these numbers are, indeed. At the same time, they should not blind us to the fact that the world's average population ranged between 2 and 3 billion souls during the same period. This means that roughly 1 person or less, out of every 20 people who lived in the 20th century, was a mortal victim of war. Of course, in other ways, we are all victims.

9. Samuel J. Fitch, "The Garrison State in America," *Journal of Peace Research*, Vol. 22, No. 1, 1985, pp. 31–45.

10. See William Echikson, *Christian Science Monitor*, May 3, 1985, p. 14.

11. James Parker found that American films sent abroad during the early period of World War II were considered by U.S. officials as presenting America in a bad light. They did not support America's propaganda concerns. The film industry was then subjected to government censorship directed toward the end of creating a more favorable image of the United States abroad. See James Parker, *Box Office Madness: Institution/Industry/Audience and the Formulating of Delinquency, Crime and Mental Problems in American Films*, 1930–1950, a doctoral dissertation completed in 1983 and on file in the Department of Sociology, the University of Colorado, Boulder, Colorado.

12. Florida recently passed a law that, for a while, was thought to allow individuals to carry guns publicly so long as they were openly displayed. The loophole leading to this interpretation was immediately closed.

13. The private ownership of fully automatic weapons, so-called machine guns, is illegal in all states. Any kind of accurate estimate of how many such weapons are owned by private citizens is not available. The Federal Bureau of Alcohol, Tobacco, and Firearms seized 539 unregistered machine guns in 1984. There is probably no town in America with a population of 10,000 or more that does not have several private citizens armed with fully automatic weapons.

14. This contention is certainly controversial. Large numbers of people now carry guns either legally or illegally as "protection" against crime. See "The Armed Citizen" section of the *American Rifleman*, the monthly magazine distributed by the National Rifle Association.

15. Rita Tullberg, "World Military Expenditure," *Bulletin of Peace Proposals*, Vol. 17, 1986, pp. 229–233.

16. James Boswell, Johnson's biographer, described a gentleman who had been extremely unhappy in his first marriage. Yet, when his

wife died, the man remarried immediately. It was, Johnson said, a triumph of hope over experience.

17. Morton H. Halperin, *Limited War in the Nuclear Age* (New York: Wiley, 1963); Ian Clark, *Limited Nuclear War: Political Theory and War Conventions* (Princeton, N.J.: Princeton University Press, 1982).

18. Military strategists appear to have difficulty learning this simple sociological observation. Hitler, in World War II, thought that bombing London would devastate civilian morale. It achieved precisely the opposite effect. The stupidity of this military tactic may well have cost Hitler the war against England. A similar error was made by the United States in supporting the policy that massive bombings of the North Vietnamese would weaken their resolve. It had the opposite effect.

19. For an interesting discussion of the effectiveness of resistance movements, see David Kowalewski, "Protest Militancy in the USSR: When Does It Work?" *Social Science Journal*, Vol. 24, No. 2, 1987, pp. 170–179.

20. This is the major fallacy of racist arguments. The belief that inferior people produce inferior societies is much too simple. For example, what an ordinary person can accomplish in modern social systems is far beyond the capabilities of even the most extraordinary mental genius of a century ago. Do we attribute the productivity and competitiveness of the present-day Japanese economy to superior racial qualities or to an extremely effectively organized and developed sociocultural system? Your response to this question determines, in part, the extent to which you might be responsive to the idea that you can "think" peace into existence.

21. A notable recent example is Allan David Bloom's *The Closing of the American Mind* (New York: Simon and Schuster, 1987). It is difficult to believe that only a decade ago American schools were being severely criticized for being what Bloom now claims they are not.

22. I have only had an opportunity to read reviews of a book that was published just as this work went into production. It is a collection of articles dealing with the problem of solving the impasses created by nuclear weapons. See *Fateful Visions: Avoiding Nuclear Catastrophe*, ed. Joseph S. Nye, Jr., Graham T. Allison, and Albert Carnesale (Cambridge: Ballinger, 1988). Another book worth mentioning is Marc Ian Barasch's *The Little Black Book of Atomic War* (New York: Dell Publishing Co., Inc., 1983). This brief work reveals, as well as any, the fact that our defensive systems are possibly as dangerous as what they are supposed to protect us from.

Index

SAINT LEO COLLEGE LIBRARY

3 2213 00009 6561

DATE DUE

U 263 .C89 1989
Cuzzort, Raymond Paul, 1926-

Using social thought